Success in Book-keeping and Accounts

Success Studybooks

Success in

BOOK-KEEPING
& ACCOUNTS

David Cox, F.C.C.A., F.C.I.B.
Senior Lecturer in Accountancy and Banking,
Worcester College of Technology

JOHN MURRAY

© David Cox 1985, 1987

First published 1985
by John Murray (Publishers) Ltd
50 Albemarle Street
London W1X 4BD

Reprinted 1987 (with additional units), 1989, 1990 (with revisions),
1991 (with revisions), 1992 (with revisions), 1994, 1995, 1997

Typeset by Fakenham Photosetting Ltd, Fakenham, Norfolk
Printed and bound in Great Britain by
Biddles Ltd, Guildford and King's Lynn

A CIP catalogue record for this book is available from the British Library

ISBN 0–7195–4194–8

Foreword

An efficient system of book-keeping is essential in businesses of all sizes. Consequently a knowledge of book-keeping and accounts will prove beneficial to anyone considering a career in business. A study of book-keeping may be an end in itself or it may provide the first step towards a career in accountancy. This book is designed to provide a comprehensive, up-to-date course in book-keeping and accounts, presented in a form which takes particular note of the needs of students working or revising on their own.

Success in Book-keeping and Accounts deals thoroughly with all the basic operations of book-keeping, from the double-entry system to the preparation of year-end accounts and balance sheets, and describes the use of computers in present-day accounting. Many worked examples are included in the text so that the student can see the principles put into practice. A selection of examination questions is given at the end of Units. Those to which outline answers are provided are marked with an asterisk. In addition, sets of multiple-choice questions are included at intervals throughout the book. Some examination boards include questions with source documents which require candidates to process the documents through the book-keeping system, and a selection of such questions is included at the end of the book (page 394).

The book covers requirements of syllabuses such as:

- the London Chamber of Commerce and Industry 'Book-keeping' (First level)
- Pitman Examinations Institute 'Book-keeping and Accounts' (Levels 1 and 2)
- RSA Examinations Board 'Book-keeping' (Stage I)
- GCSE 'Accounting'

The book is also appropriate for pre-vocational courses and is recommended to anyone who, whether for business or personal reasons, wants to understand the fundamentals of book-keeping.

D.C.

Acknowledgments

In writing this book I have been helped by many people, especially those teachers, lecturers and professional accountants who appraised and criticized it at different stages. In this respect I should particularly like to thank Lionel Millmore, Peggy Rossiter and Alan Wood. I am also grateful to Jean Macqueen for editing the text so meticulously, to Jean Cox for typing the manuscript and to Anne Webster of John Murray.

The assistance of the following organizations is gratefully acknowledged: *Accountancy* magazine for permission to reproduce cartoons, Kalamazoo plc for supplying sample business documents, Barclays Bank PLC and Lloyds Bank Plc for permission to reproduce specimen bank documents, the Solicitors' Law Stationery Society for permission to reproduce a specimen bill of exchange form.

Questions from past examination papers are reproduced by kind permission of the following: Associated Lancashire Schools Examining Board, East Anglian Examinations Board, East Midland Regional Examinations Board, the London Chamber of Commerce and Industry, London Regional Examining Board, Pitman Examinations Institute, the RSA Examinations Board (formerly the Royal Society of Arts), the South-East Regional Examinations Board, South Western Examinations Board, the West Midlands Examinations Board. Questions are taken from LCCI First level, PEI Levels 1 and 2, and RSA Stage I examination papers, except for two RSA Stage II questions included as being of an appropriate level for Unit 41. Where answers are given, these are the responsibility of the author, not the examining body.

D.C.

Contents

Unit One

The Role of Book-keeping and Accounts in Business

1.1 Introduction

You often see headlines like these in the newspapers, and the same news may be featured and discussed on television. Frequently the firms mentioned are household names, with profits (or losses) running into many millions of pounds. Far-reaching decisions are taken on the basis of the results reported here so briefly: decisions such as whether a company will raise the prices of goods that all of us buy regularly, or whether it will build a new factory or close down an old one, while an investor uses these figures to help him or her decide whether to put money into, say, a construction company, an insurance firm or a brewery.

It is obviously crucial to these decisions that the profits and losses of the companies concerned, as well as other financial information, are reported accurately. The figures for profits and losses are calculated from book-keeping and accounting records that detail every single business transaction undertaken by the organization during the year. Clearly, such records are designed to fit the needs of the business: when Woolworth's sold you a bar of chocolate last week the transaction was recorded somewhat differently from, say, the sale to a refinery of a tanker's load of crude oil! Nevertheless, the principle is the same—both transactions are listed in the firm's book-keeping and accounting records, and both contribute to its profit (or loss) for the year.

1.2   What is the Difference between Book-keeping and Accounts?

Book-keeping and accounts are both concerned with the same thing, but at different levels.

Book-keeping is the recording of business transactions in books of account; we shall be concerned principally with the system known as *double-entry book-keeping*. Using this system, each business transaction is entered twice into the books of account; if this is done correctly, it will be possible to show that the books 'balance'. *Accounting* is concerned with taking the basic information from the books of account and using it to explain the financial position of the business. This, among other things, involves producing accounts at the end of each financial year to show the profit or loss of the business.

The words 'book-keeping' and 'accounts' tend to be used rather loosely; we often talk about 'books', 'accounts', 'books of account' and 'accounting', all meaning the same thing. Nevertheless you should bear in mind the distinction that book-keeping is the preparation of the basic accounting records, while accounting is the putting of these records to further use.

1.3   What Can a Book-keeping or Accounting System Tell Us?

Much information can be obtained from the book-keeping or accounting system of a business. For instance, we can find out:

(a)   the sales to date;
(b)   the purchases to date;
(c)   the expenses, such as wages, heating and telephone costs;
(d)   the gross and net profits or losses for the year;
(e)   the total of money owed *to* the business;
(f)   the total of money owed *by* the business;
(g)   the amount of cash held by the business, together with the amount of its bank balance or bank overdraft;
(h)   the premises, motor vehicles, machinery and so forth that it owns;
(i)   the amount invested in the business—its capital;
(j)   the amount of money drawn out of the business by the owner.

1.4   Business Transactions

In book-keeping and accounts we are recording the transactions of a particular business, and not those of the owner of that business acting in a personal capacity. This means that assets owned by him or her personally, such as a house, television set or car, do not appear in the books of the business; nor do liabilities (debts) owed personally, such as a bank overdraft or a mortgage. When dealing with the accounts of a small business run by one person, however, it is all too easy to confuse the owner's assets and liabilities with those of the business. This we must not do, and it will help our book-keeping and accounting if we remember that such items must always be kept separate. This idea—that our accounts record only the transactions of the business, and not those of the owner carried out in a personal capacity—is known as the *business entity* or *separate entity* concept. It means that when a person decides to set up in business and puts in some of his or her personal money, we have to record this in the business books. The owner's stake in the business is known as *capital*.

Another important thing to remember *is* that we must use *money* as the unit of measurement for all business transactions. This is because it is only possible to add together machinery and motor vehicles if both are measured in terms of money values: this idea is known as the *money measurement* concept.

1.5 Modern Methods of Book-keeping

Nowadays many businesses, even small ones, use computers to help with their book-keeping, while many others rely on handwritten systems. Several quite elaborate handwritten book-keeping systems are available, using specially printed stationery. During your studies, you will find it useful to arrange an opportunity of seeing more modern methods of book-keeping in operation. Such methods are discussed in Unit 19.

As a student of book-keeping you will often be asked to practise your new-found skills. Much of this practice will be acquired from the use of handwritten accounts. But whether handwritten accounts are produced or the aid of a computer is enlisted, the basic book-keeping procedures are the same: it is just that, in preparing the former, you yourself are providing the computer power!

1.6 Some Accounting Terms

In this first Unit you have met some accounting terms with which you will soon be familiar. Here, as a reminder, is a summary.

(*a*) *Books of account* record the business transactions, often using a system called double-entry book-keeping.

(*b*) *Book-keeping* is concerned with the keeping of books of account.

(*c*) *Accounting* puts the basic book-keeping information to further use in order to explain the financial position of the business.

(*d*) *Assets* are things *owned*.

(*e*) *Liabilities* are amounts *owed*.

(*f*) *Capital* is the amount invested in a business by the owner.

(*g*) *Business entity concept*—we record the transactions of a business, and not the *personal* transactions of the owner.

(*h*) *Money measurement concept*—money amounts are used to measure business transactions.

1.7 Questions

1. What is the difference between book-keeping and accounts?

2. State six items that can be found from a book-keeping or accounting system.

3. Explain what is meant by (*a*) the 'business entity' concept, (*b*) the 'money measurement' concept.

4. Explain the following terms: (*a*) assets, (*b*) liabilities, (*c*) capital.

Unit Two

First Steps in Double-entry Book-keeping

2.1 Introduction

Business transactions always consist of two aspects:

(i) a gain;
(ii) a loss.

It is easy to see these two aspects if we consider a few transactions that you yourself might make. For example, if you go into a shop and buy a newspaper, you have gained a newspaper, but there is a loss of cash. Furthermore, if you sell your camera to a friend, you will lose your camera, but will gain cash. If you swap your guitar for your friend's camera, then you have gained a camera, but lost a guitar.

While each of these transactions has two aspects, we would not record them formally in books of account because they are personal transactions. A business does need to keep accurate records of all business transactions, however, and to show both the gain and the loss caused by each.

As a book-keeper, you are concerned with recording the transactions of a particular business *from the viewpoint of that business*. Imagine that you have just been appointed book-keeper to a newly formed business. The first few transactions are listed below—cover up the answers and see if you can work out the gain and the loss in each, from the business's point of view.

Date 19–1	Transaction	Gain	Loss
1 Jan.	Started business with £1 500 in cash.	Cash	Capital
2 Jan.	Bought a machine for £500, paying in cash.	Machine	Cash
3 Jan.	Put £750 cash into a bank account.	Bank	Cash
4 Jan.	Bought a secondhand van for £650, paying by cheque.	Van	Bank
5 Jan.	Bought a typewriter for £150, paying in cash.	Typewriter	Cash
6 Jan.	Sold the machine as being unsuitable for £500, a cheque being received.	Bank	Machine

Perhaps the first transaction is the most difficult because it concerns the owner's capital. Here the owner is putting some money into the business. As book-keepers, we are looking at the transaction from the point of view of the business: we can see that its gain is £1 500 in cash, and the loss is that it owes this amount of money to the owner. (The capital is unlikely to be repaid to the owner because, if it were, the business would cease to exist.)

2.2   Using Books of Account

A book-keeping system consists of a number of separate *accounts* which, when put together in a book, stored in a metal tray or held on a computer disc, are known as a *ledger* or a *ledger section*. Thus, to use the filing cabinet idea, each separate card or paper file represents an individual *account*, each drawer of the filing cabinet a *ledger section*, and the entire filing cabinet the *ledger*.

The book-keeper's task is to enter the transactions of the business into accounts. The two aspects of each transaction—gain and loss—are entered into two different accounts, this is why we use the term *double-entry book-keeping*.

Dr.   **(Name of Account)**   *Cr.*

Date	Details	Folio	£	p	Date	Details	Folio	£	p

Fig. 2.1 An account

Fig. 2.1 shows a ruling for an account, together with headings. Paper preprinted with such ruling may be purchased from a stationer's—ask for ledger paper.

Points to notice:

(*a*) The name of the account is written at the top.

(*b*) The page is divided into two halves by the central vertical line—the left-hand half is known as the *debit side* (abbreviated to *Dr.* from the word 'debtor'), while the right-hand half is the *credit* (or *Cr.*) *side*.

(*c*) Both halves have identical vertical lines which give space for the date, details and amount of each transaction.

(*d*) The folio column is used as a cross-referencing device, and we shall consider it fully in Unit 15.6.

Each business transaction must be entered into two accounts: on the debit side of one, and on the credit side of another. The debit side of an account is used to record gains made by the business and amounts owing *to* the business, while the credit side records losses and amounts owing *by* the business.

We will now look again at the business transactions we considered in Unit 2.1 and see how these would be entered into the accounts. The first transaction is:

1 Jan.   *Started business with £1 500 in cash.*

We have already seen that the two sides of this transaction are that the business gains £1 500 in cash and, in effect, owes this amount back to the owner. Therefore the transaction will be entered on the debit side of Cash Account, and on the credit side of Capital Account, as follows:

Cash

19–1	£	
1 Jan. Capital	1 500	

Capital

	19–1	£
	1 Jan. Cash	1 500

Points to notice:

(*a*) In the 'details' column of each account is written the name of the other account concerned in the transaction; this acts as a method of cross-referencing.

(*b*) In practice each account would be opened on a new page but in exercises, to economize, several accounts can be shown on one page.

(*c*) In order to make this example easier to understand, we have not shown all the vertical lines on the paper (and in subsequent Units we shall omit them altogether); Fig. 2.1 shows the full ruling for an account.

'I'm worried, Doc . . . I get these uncontrollable urges to train as an accountant'

The second transaction is:

2 Jan.   Bought a machine for £500, paying in cash.

Here the business gains a machine, but loses cash. Therefore the transaction is entered on the debit side of Machinery Account and on the credit side of Cash Account, as follows:

Machinery

19–1	£		£
2 Jan. Cash	500		

Cash

19–1	£	19–1	£
1 Jan. Capital	1 500	2 Jan. Machinery	500

For this transaction, we have opened a new account for machinery but, as we had already opened a Cash Account in the first transaction, there is no need to open another one.

The full set of accounts from all the business transactions given in Unit 2.1 is as follows:

Capital

		19–1	£
		1 Jan. Cash	1 500

Cash

19–1	£	19–1	£
1 Jan. Capital	1 500	2 Jan. Machinery	500
		3 Jan. Bank	750
		5 Jan. Typewriter	150

Machinery

19–1	£	19–1	£
2 Jan. Cash	500	6 Jan. Bank	500

Bank

19–1	£	19–1	£
3 Jan. Cash	750	4 Jan. Van	650
6 Jan. Machinery	500		

Van

19–1	£		
4 Jan. Bank	650		

Typewriter

19–1	£		
5 Jan. Cash	150		

As you see, new accounts have been opened as required. It is very important to note that *money in the form of cash* has been distinguished from *money in a bank account*, and an account has been opened for each. The Bank Account shown above is the business's *own record* of how much money it has put into or taken out of its bank account; the bank, however, will have recorded these transactions *from its own point of view*. In this example, on 3 January the bank has gained cash (debit Cash Account) but owes the customer this amount of money back (credit customer's account). Thus, in our accounts, we record the transaction on the debit side because we have gained an amount in our Bank Account, but the bank will show the transaction as a credit entry, because it owes us back the money. In double-entry book-keeping *debits are always gains*, while *credits are always losses* from the point of view of the business whose accounts you are considering.

2.3   Questions

An asterisk (*) against a question number means that a summary answer to that question is given at the end of the book.

* 1.   State the gain and loss to the business in each of the following transactions:

		Gain	Loss
19–2			
1 Nov.	Started business with £500 cash.	Cash	Capital
2 Nov.	Paid £400 cash into the bank.	Bank	Cash
6 Nov.	Bought a photocopier for £200, paying by cheque.	Photo.	Cheque Bank
10 Nov.	Bought office fittings for £75, paying in cash.	Fittings	Cash
15 Nov.	Bought a typewriter for £200, paying by cheque.	Typewriter	Bank
17 Nov.	Sold photocopier (unsuitable) for £200, cash received.	Cash	Photo.

*2.   Enter the transactions from Question 1 into the double-entry book-keeping accounts of Stephen Yates.

*3.   State the gain and loss to the business in each of the following transactions:

		Gain	Loss
19–3			
1 Jan.	Started business with £1 500 in cash.	Cash	Capital
2 Jan.	Paid £1 200 cash into the bank.	Bank	Cash
4 Jan.	Bought a secondhand van for £500, paying by cheque.	Van	Bank
6 Jan.	Bought shop fittings for £150, paying in cash.	Fittings	Cash
10 Jan.	Bought a cash register for £250, paying by cheque.	Cash Reg.	Bank
11 Jan.	Bought more shop fittings for £50, paying by cheque.	Fittings	Bank
14 Jan.	Sold some of the shop fittings (unsuitable) for £25, a cheque being received.	Bank	Fittings
20 Jan.	Put £500 more into the business by cheque.	Bank	Capital
22 Jan.	Transferred £100 from bank to cash.	Cash	Bank

4.   Enter the transactions from Question 3 into double-entry book-keeping accounts.

5. Enter the following transactions into the double-entry book-keeping accounts of Harry Watkins:

19–7

1 May	Started business with £1 000 in cash.
3 May	Bought a machine for £350, paying in cash.
7 May	Put £500 cash into a business bank account.
10 May	Bought a typewriter for £100, paying by cheque.
15 May	Bought office fitting for £75, paying in cash.
20 May	Sold the machine (unsuitable) for £350, a cheque being received.
27 May	Bought a secondhand van for £500, paying by cheque.

6. Enter the following transactions into the double-entry book-keeping accounts of George Mackay:

19–5

2 Feb.	Started business with £250 in cash.
4 Feb.	Bought office fittings for £50 in cash.
5 Feb.	Paid £150 cash into the bank.
7 Feb.	Put £300 more into the business by cheque.
8 Feb.	Bought a typewriter for £250, paying by cheque.
9 Feb.	Bought more office fittings for £100, paying by cheque.
12 Feb.	Sold some of the office fittings (unsuitable) for £30, cash being received.
14 Feb.	Paid £50 cash into the bank.
16 Feb.	Bought a duplicator for £100, paying by cheque.

Unit Three

Credit Transactions

3.1 Introduction

In Unit 2, when we bought or sold items such as machines, typewriters or vans, we either paid or received cash or a cheque immediately. For example:

14 Feb. 19–5   Bought a van for £1 000, paying by cheque.

This is correctly entered into the accounts as:

Van

19–5	£
14 Feb. Bank	1 000

Bank

		19–5	£
		14 Feb. Van	1 000

Here the business has gained a van costing £1 000 and its bank balance has fallen by the same amount.

Most businesses buy or sell items *on credit*, however—that is, payment is made some time after the item has been supplied. The book-keeping logic remains the same: there has been a gain and a loss. Suppose that the transaction reads as follows:

14 Feb. 19–5   Bought a van for £1 000, on credit from Bridge Street Garage.

While the business whose accounts we are preparing has gained a van, its bank balance remains unaltered; instead, the business owes £1 000 to Bridge Street Garage. The accounts will appear as:

Van

19–5	£
14 Feb. Bridge Street Garage	1 000

Bridge Street Garage

		19–5	£
		14 Feb. Van	1 000

The second of these accounts records that 'our' business owes £1 000 to Bridge Street Garage; as the account has a credit balance we say that the garage is a *creditor* of our firm. *Thus a creditor is someone to whom we, or the firm whose accounts we are preparing, owes money.*

Let us assume that, a few days later, the van is paid for by cheque:

27 Feb. 19–5   Paid Bridge Street Garage £1 000 by cheque.

Here the business Bank Account falls by £1 000, while the gain to the business is that it no longer owes a creditor. The accounts will appear as:

Bank

		£
	19–5	
	27 Feb. Bridge Street Garage	1 000

Bridge Street Garage

19–5	£	19–5	£
27 Feb. Bank	1 000	14 Feb. Van	1 000

Clearly, 'our' business no longer owes Bridge Street Garage any money: their account with us has a nil balance.

3.2   A Further Transaction

Here is another transaction:

15 Apr. 19–6   Sold a typewriter, which was unsuitable for the business, on credit to Harrison for £75 (the typewriter had been purchased on 2 April 19–6 for the same amount—paid for by cheque).

Here the business loses a typewriter but gains a *debtor*, that is, Harrison will pay it £75 at some time in the future. *Thus a debtor is someone who owes money to us, or to the firm whose accounts we are preparing.*
    The accounts will appear as:

Typewriter

19–6	£	19–6	£
2 Apr. Bank	75	15 Apr. Harrison	75

Harrison

19–6	£
15 Apr. Typewriter	75

Some time later Harrison will pay the amount; our business will gain £75 and will lose a debtor, as follows:

28 Apr. 19–6   Harrison pays £75 by cheque.

Harrison

19–6	£	19–6	£
15 Apr. Typewriter	75	28 Apr. Bank	75

Bank

19–6	£
28 Apr. Harrison	75

3.3   Some Worked Examples

Study the following transactions and you will soon be able to enter credit transactions into the accounts.

19–2
3 May	Bought a machine for £250, on credit from Wilson & Sons.
7 May	Bought a typewriter for £150, on credit from Office Supplies Ltd[1].
15 May	Paid Wilson & Sons the amount owing to them, by cheque.
22 May	The machine proved to be unsuitable and was sold for £250 on credit to Jones.
24 May	Paid Office Supplies Ltd the amount owing to them by cheque.
27 May	Jones pays £250 by cheque.

([1] 'Ltd' is an abbreviation of 'Limited' and is used to denote a *private limited company*. Unit 41 deals with the year-end accounts of limited companies.)

The accounts appear as follows:

Machinery
19–2	£	19–2	£
3 May Wilson & Sons	250	22 May Jones	250

Wilson & Sons
19–2	£	19–2	£
15 May Bank	250	3 May Machinery	250

Typewriter
19–2	£
7 May Office Supplies Ltd	150

Office Supplies Ltd
19–2	£	19–2	£
24 May Bank	150	7 May Typewriter	150

Bank
19–2	£	19–2	£
27 May Jones	250	15 May Wilson & Sons	250
		24 May Office Supplies Ltd	150

Jones
19–2	£	19–2	£
22 May Machinery	250	27 May Bank	250

3.4   Understanding What Accounts Tell Us

It is important that, as you prepare accounts, you think about what each transaction means. In this way, besides being able to produce correct accounts mechanically, you are able to explain what individual entries mean. For example, consider the following account in the books of C. Dyer:

Machinery
19–1	£
10 Mar. Bank	350

By looking at this account, the book-keeper can understand that Dyer bought a machine on 10 March 19–1 for £350, and that payment was made by cheque.

Here is another of Dyer's accounts:

Van

19–3	£
14 Aug. Ever Ready Motors Ltd	1 500

This account shows that on 14 August 19–3, Dyer bought a van at a cost of £1 500 on credit from Ever Ready Motors Ltd.

A third account:

A–Z Supplies Ltd

19–6	£
10 Oct. Typewriter	175

Here Dyer has bought a typewriter on 10 October 19–6 on credit from A–Z Supplies Ltd for £175, and still owes this amount to A–Z.

Naturally, for each of these three transactions, there is an opposite entry in another account which completes double-entry book-keeping. Being able to explain transactions such as these will help you in your understanding of book-keeping.

3.5   Questions

*1.   State the gain and loss in each of the following business transactions:

19–6		*Gain*	*Loss*
1 Apr.	Started business with £2 000 in cash.		
2 Apr.	Paid £1 750 cash into the bank.		
4 Apr.	Bought a secondhand van for £1 000, paying by cheque.		
6 Apr.	Bought a typewriter for £250 on credit from Business Equipment Ltd.		

	Gain	Loss

11 Apr.   Bought a photocopier for £350 on credit
          from Johnson Brothers Ltd.
12 Apr.   Paid the amount owing to Business
          Equipment Ltd by cheque.
17 Apr.   Paid the amount owing to Johnson Brothers
          Ltd by cheque.
24 Apr.   Withdrew for business use £50 in cash from
          the bank.

*2. Enter the transactions from Question 1 into double-entry book-keeping accounts.

*3. Enter the following transactions for the month into the accounts of James Barr:

19–1
 1 Apr.   Started in business with £1 000 in cash.
 5 Apr.   Paid £750 of the cash into a bank account.
 8 Apr.   Bought a machine for £250, on credit from Machinery (Rowcester) Ltd.
10 Apr.   Bought a typewriter for £100, on credit from Office Supplies Ltd.
14 Apr.   Bought a secondhand van for £400, paying by cheque.
17 Apr.   Bought another machine for £100, paying in cash.
19 Apr.   Paid Machinery (Rowcester) Ltd the amount owing by cheque.
24 Apr.   Sold the van because it was unsuitable for £400, a cheque being received.
27 Apr.   Paid Office Supplies Ltd the amount owing in cash.

4. Explain each transaction appearing on the following accounts (the accounts are not connected):

(a)   **Machinery**

19–1	£		
10 Jan. Bank	175		
25 Jan. ABC (Machinery) Ltd	500		

(b)   **Office equipment**

19–4	£	19–4	£
11 Aug. Cash	110	30 Aug. Bank	110
15 Aug. Office Supplies (Rowcester) Ltd	200		

(c)   **Bank**

19–2	£	19–2	£
1 Jun. Capital	2 000	4 Jun. Office equipment	150
18 Jun. Cash	250	16 Jun. Northern Garages Ltd	1 500
		28 Jun. Machinery Supplies (Brimmingham) Ltd	450

5. Enter the following transactions into the accounts of Andrew East:

19–2

1 Aug.	Started in business with £100 in cash and £1 500 in a bank account.
5 Aug.	Bought office equipment for £250, paying by cheque.
7 Aug.	Bought a machine for £300, on credit from Matthews Ltd.
12 Aug.	Withdrew for business use £100 in cash from the bank.
17 Aug.	Bought a secondhand van for £750, on credit from Western Garage.
20 Aug.	Introduced £500 more capital into the business by cheque.
24 Aug.	Bought more office equipment for £150, paying in cash.
26 Aug.	Paid Matthews Ltd the amount owing by cheque.
27 Aug.	Paid Western Garage the amount owing by cheque.
30 Aug.	Sold some of the office equipment (unsuitable) for £75, cash being received.

Unit Four

Purchases, Sales and Returns

4.1 Introduction

The business transactions we have considered so far have frequently concerned the buying, and occasionally the selling, of such things as machinery, typewriters, vans and cars. In our double-entry book-keeping, to record the purchase of, say, a typewriter, we have debited an account in the name of typewriters, and credited bank, cash or a creditor's account. When the firm has sold it we have credited the typewriters account and debited bank, cash or a debtor's account. This is the correct procedure to follow when a business buys items with the intention of keeping them for a reasonable length of time, using them in the business, and then selling them when it can make no further use of them. Thus a van will be purchased by a business, used to make deliveries, and then sold at the end of its working life: there was never any intention of buying it solely with the view of selling it again quickly at a profit. *The goods in which a business trades* are bought for the sole purpose of resale at a higher price; however, two special accounts are needed to record such activities.

4.2 The Use of Purchases Account and Sales Account

These accounts are used only to record the purchase and sales of the *goods in which a business trades*. This expression covers those goods which a business buys at one price with the intention of selling at a higher price in the very near future. For example, a fashion shop buys clothes from a manufacturer, holds them in stock, and hopes to sell them to the public as soon as possible at a profit; a greengrocer buys fruit and vegetables from the wholesale market and displays them in the shop for sale at higher prices than he paid to the wholesaler.

When a business buys goods for resale, in the accounting records they are entered into *Purchases Account*; when such goods are sold, they are entered into *Sales Account*. Use these two accounts for 'bought goods' and 'sold goods' respectively. (Do *not* use a Stock Account or a Stock of Goods Account at this stage—this account is used only at the end of a financial year, and we shall discuss it in Unit 10.)

4.3 Purchases for Cash or Cheque

The rules we have already learned for entering business transactions into the double-entry book-keeping accounts still apply. For example:

2 Oct. 19–1   *Bought goods for resale costing £150, paying in cash.*

Here the business has gained some goods to resell and, at the same time, the amount of cash given is £150. The two accounts concerned are purchases and cash, and the transaction will appear as follows:

Purchases

19–1	£
2 Oct. Cash	150

Cash

	19–1	£
	2 Oct. Purchases	150

4.4   Purchases on Credit

Businesses frequently buy (and sell) the goods in which they trade *on credit*, that is, payment is not made for some time after delivery. For example:

14 Nov. 19–1   *Bought goods for resale costing £250 on credit from Smith.*

The business gains goods for resale and, at the same time, owes £250 to Smith. The accounts will appear as:

Purchases

19–1	£
14 Nov. Smith	250

Smith

	19–1	£
	14 Nov. Purchases	250

Smith's account shows that our business owes him £250, that is, Smith is a creditor. When the business makes payment to Smith, the accounting entries will be:

Dr. (debit)	Smith	£250
Cr. (credit)	Cash or Bank	£250

4.5   Sales for Cash or Cheque

We continue to follow the same book-keeping rules. For example:

16 April. 19–4   *Sold goods for £45, a cheque being received.*

The business has gained a cheque for £45, but sells goods for this amount.

Bank

19–4	£
16 Apr. Sales	45

Sales

	19–4	£
	16 Apr. Bank	45

4.6   Sales on Credit

Again, the usual book-keeping rules apply. For example:

24 May 19–5   Sold goods for £115 on credit to Green.

Here the business gains a debtor, that is, Green owes £115, and goods are sold for this amount.

Green

19–5	£
24 May Sales	115

Sales

		19–5	£
		24 May Green	115

When Green pays for the goods, the entries in the accounts will be:

Dr.	Cash or Bank	£115
Cr.	Green	£115

4.7   More About Sales and Purchases Accounts

You have seen in Units 4.3 to 4.6 that the price paid for goods purchased is entered on the debit side of Purchases Account, and the amount received from goods sold is entered on the credit side of Sales Account. It follows, therefore, that *there should not be any transactions on the credit side of Purchases Account, nor on the debit side of Sales Account* (except the entries to balance the accounts, which we shall discuss in Unit 5.2). You can use this rule to check that your accounts are correct as you make the book-keeping entries: to remind yourself, you could rule a line through the credit side of Purchases Account and the debit side of Sales Account. Remember too that, at present, we are not concerned with calculating the profit a business makes on the goods it sells—this is dealt with in Unit 8.

We said in Unit 4.2 that Purchases and Sales Accounts are used to record transactions of the goods in which a business trades. Therefore, as we saw, a fashion shop enters the cost of clothes bought for resale from a manufacturer into Purchases Account; when these items are sold, the money amount will be entered into Sales Account. If the same shop bought a typewriter for use in the business, then the amount would be entered on to the debit side of a Type-writer Account instead of Purchases Account (because the fashion shop does not trade in typewriters). If we were preparing the accounts of an office equipment firm, however, into which account would we enter the purchase of a typewriter? The answer is that, if it was bought for resale, it would be entered in Purchases Account, because it is the goods in which the business trades; but if it was purchased for use in the firm's own office it would be debited to Typewriter Account, because it is not intended for immediate resale. In the same way, when this firm sells typewriters—the goods in which it trades—the money amount is credited to Sales Account, but when it sells its own office typewriter after a period of use, the Typewriter Account will be used. Similarly, a car dealer buying vans for resale debits Purchases Account; but if a van was purchased to make deliveries of spares, the purchase cost would be debited to a Van Account.

4.8   Returns Accounts

At some time or another we have all bought something that has been unsatisfactory—perhaps the item was damaged, or of poor quality, or did not work—and we usually return such a purchase to the shop that sold it. A business, too, may have cause to return goods which it has purchased. Such returns are known as *returns outwards* or *purchases returns*, because the goods are being sent out, or back, to the original supplier. Also, a business may have goods that it has sold returned by a customer: these returns are known as *returns inwards*, or *sales returns*, because the goods are being received back in. A business needs to record the movements of returned goods by means of two separate returns accounts: *Returns Outwards Account*, and *Returns Inwards Account*.

4.9   Returns Outwards Account

28 Oct. 19–1   Goods for £50 previously bought on credit from Higgins are returned to him.

From the point of view of our business, the goods for resale fall, because unsatisfactory or unsuitable goods are sent back; at the same time we owe £50 less to Higgins. The transaction will be entered as follows:

Returns outwards		
	19–1	£
	28 Oct. Higgins	50

Higgins		
19–1	£	
28 Oct. Returns outwards	50	

Point to notice:
    Returns Outwards Account always has transactions entered *on the credit side*.

4.10   Returns Inwards Account

10 Dec. 19–4   Hughes returns goods to us which had previously been sold to him on credit for £75.

The business gains the goods returned to it, while the loss is that a debtor's account is reduced, that is, the business is owed less.

Returns inwards

19–4	£
10 Dec. Hughes	75

Hughes

	19–4	£
	10 Dec. Returns inwards	75

Point to notice:
Returns Inwards Account always has transactions entered *on the debit side*.

4.11   Purchases, Sales and Returns Accounts

The following worked example shows the use of Purchases, Sales and Returns Accounts; study it carefully.

Transactions:
19–1

1 Feb.	Bought goods £130 on credit from Williams.
3 Feb.	Sold goods £55 on credit to Wilson.
5 Feb.	Bought goods £210 on credit from Adams.
10 Feb.	Sold goods £100, cash being received.
12 Feb.	Returned goods which had cost £60 to Williams.
15 Feb.	Sold goods £35 on credit to Doyle.
18 Feb.	Paid the amount owing to Williams in cash.
22 Feb.	Doyle returns unsatisfactory goods which had cost £20.
24 Feb.	Bought goods £100 on credit from Adams.
26 Feb.	Wilson pays the amount owing by him in cash.

Accounts:

Purchases

19–1	£
1 Feb. Williams	130
5 Feb. Adams	210
24 Feb. Adams	100

Sales

	19–1	£
	3 Feb. Wilson	55
	10 Feb. Cash	100
	15 Feb. Doyle	35

Returns outwards

	19–1	£
	12 Feb. Williams	60

Returns inwards

19–1	£
22 Feb. Doyle	20

Williams

19–1	£	19–1	£
12 Feb. Returns outwards	60	1 Feb. Purchases	130
18 Feb. Cash	70		

Adams

		19–1	£
		5 Feb. Purchases	210
		24 Feb. Purchases	100

Wilson

19–1	£	19–1	£
3 Feb. Sales	55	26 Feb. Cash	55

Doyle

19–1	£	19–1	£
15 Feb. Sales	35	22 Feb. Returns inwards	20

Cash

19–1	£	19–1	£
10 Feb. Sales	100	18 Feb. Williams	70
26 Feb. Wilson	55		

4.12   Questions

*1.   State the gain and loss in each of the following business transactions:

19–3		*Gain*	*Loss*
1 Jun.	Started in business with £2 000 in a bank account.		
3 Jun.	Bought goods £200, paying by cheque.		
5 Jun.	Bought goods £150 on credit from D. Smith.		
6 Jun.	Sold goods £95, a cheque being received.		
7 Jun.	Some of the goods (value £50) bought from D. Smith are found to be faulty, and are returned.		
10 Jun.	Sold goods £105 credit to I. Wain.		
12 Jun.	Bought a machine for use in the business £500 on credit from Rowcester Machinery Co.		
14 Jun.	Paid D. Smith the amount owing by cheque.		
17 Jun.	I. Wain returns goods to the value of £25.		
20 Jun.	Sold goods £55, a cheque being received.		
22 Jun.	I. Wain pays the amount owing to us by cheque.		
24 Jun.	The purchaser of the goods on 20 June returns them—a refund is made by cheque.		
27 Jun.	Paid Rowcester Machinery Co by cheque.		

*2.   Enter the transactions from Question 1 into the double-entry book-keeping accounts of Ian Hall.

*3.   Enter the following transactions for the month into the accounts of Debbie Thomas:

19–4

1 Feb.   Started in business with £1 000 in a business bank account and machinery worth £750.

3 Feb.	Bought goods £250 on credit from Trade Suppliers Ltd.
5 Feb.	Bought goods £100, paying by cheque.
7 Feb.	Sold goods £110 on credit to T. Smith.
11 Feb.	Returned goods to the value of £75 to Trade Suppliers Ltd.
13 Feb.	Withdrew £200 in cash from the bank account for business use.
15 Feb.	Paid Trade Suppliers Ltd the amount owing by cheque.
17 Feb.	Sold goods £55, cash being received.
20 Feb.	Bought machinery £200 for use in the business, paying by cheque.
23 Feb.	T. Smith settles his account by cheque.
25 Feb.	Sold goods £95 on credit to M. Jones.
27 Feb.	Bought goods £85, paying in cash.
28 Feb.	M. Jones returns goods to the value of £25.

4. Explain each transaction appearing on the following accounts (the accounts are not connected):

(a)

Bank

19–1	£	19–1	£
1 Feb. Capital	1 000	3 Feb. Purchases	125
5 Feb. Sales	80	7 Feb. Typewriter	275
12 Feb. M. Kershaw	75	10 Feb. J. Smith	210
		14 Feb. Returns inwards	20

(b)

H. Lewis

19–4	£	19–4	£
14 Mar. Sales	110	20 Mar. Returns inwards	20
		27 Mar. Bank	90

(c)

E. Williams

19–7	£	19–7	£
17 Sep. Returns outwards	24	10 Sep. Purchases	254
30 Sep. Bank	230		

5. Enter the following transactions for the month into the accounts of David Hay:

19–2

1 Dec.	Started in business with £850 in cash and a car worth £1 500.
3 Dec.	Transferred £500 of cash into a business bank account.
4 Dec.	Bought goods £250 on credit from C. Long.
6 Dec.	Sold goods £100 on credit to K. Taylor.
8 Dec.	Returned unsuitable goods £50 to C. Long.
10 Dec.	Cash sales £60.
12 Dec.	Bought goods £150 on credit from T. Link.
14 Dec.	Bought machine £500 for use in the business on credit from Western Machinery Ltd.
17 Dec.	Paid the amount owing to C. Long by cheque.
18 Dec.	Obtained a loan for £1 000 from S. Scott, a cheque being received.
19 Dec.	Paid Western Machinery Ltd the amount owing by cheque.
20 Dec.	Sold goods £100 on credit to A. Hall.
22 Dec.	K. Taylor settles her account by cheque.
23 Dec.	A. Hall returns goods £25.
29 Dec.	Cash sales £55 paid direct into the bank.
31 Dec.	A. Hall settles his account by cheque.

Multiple-choice Questions—1

Read each question carefully. Choose the *one* answer you think is correct. Answers are given on page 411.

1. From the point of view of your business, which of the following is an asset?

    A bank overdraft   **C** machinery
    B mortgage on house   **D** hire purchase on car

2. From the point of view of your business, which of the following is a liability?

    A car   **C** cash
    B house   **D** bank overdraft

3. The purchase of a machine for your business, paid for by cheque, should be recorded in the double-entry accounts by:

	Debit	*Credit*
A	Cash Account	Machinery Account
B	Machinery Account	Cash Account
C	Bank Account	Machinery Account
D	Machinery Account	Bank Account

4. Some office equipment bought for use in your business is found to be unsuitable. It is returned to the supplier and a refund by cheque is made. This should be recorded in your double-entry accounts by:

	Debit	*Credit*
A	Bank Account	Office Equipment Account
B	Cash Account	Office Equipment Account
C	Cash Account	Capital Account
D	Office Equipment Account	Cash Account

5. You are given a typewriter, which you decide to use in your business. This should be recorded in your accounts by:

	Debit	*Credit*
A	Capital Account	Typewriter Account
B	Bank Account	Capital Account
C	Typewriter Account	Capital Account
D	Typewriter Account	Cash Account

6. Mr Smith buys a van on credit from City Garage for use in his business. This should be recorded by Mr Smith as:

	Debit	*Credit*
A	Bank Account	Motor Vehicles Account
B	Motor Vehicles Account	Bank Account
C	City Garage's account	Motor Vehicles Account
D	Motor Vehicles Account	City Garage's account

7. A payment by cheque to Rowcester Office Equipment in settlement of the amount owing to them for a new typewriter supplied a few weeks ago should be recorded by:

	Debit	Credit
A	Rowcester Office Equipment's account	Bank Account
B	Rowcester Office Equipment's account	Typewriter Account
C	Typewriter Account	Rowcester Office Equipment's account
D	Bank Account	Rowcester Office Equipment's account

8. Johnson buys goods for resale on credit from Adams. This should be recorded in the accounts of Johnson by:

	Debit	Credit
A	Johnson's account	Purchases Account
B	Purchases Account	Adams' account
C	Purchases Account	Johnson's account
D	Adams' account	Purchases Account

9. The purchase of a car by a garage on credit from Leyhall for resale should be recorded by:

	Debit	Credit
A	Car Account	Leyhall's account
B	Purchases Account	Bank Account
C	Purchases Account	Leyhall's account
D	Car Account	Bank Account

10. Hughes sells goods to Lewis, a cheque being received immediately. This should be recorded in the accounts of Lewis by:

	Debit	Credit
A	Lewis' account	Sales Account
B	Purchases Account	Bank Account
C	Bank Account	Sales Account
D	Purchases Account	Hughes' account

11. Smith has bought goods on credit from Robinson. Smith returns some of the goods to Robinson. This should be recorded in the accounts of Smith by:

	Debit	Credit
A	Smith's account	Returns Inwards Account
B	Returns Outwards Account	Smith's account
C	Returns Inwards Account	Robinson's account
D	Robinson's account	Returns Outwards Account

12. Scott has sold goods on credit to Fairfield. Fairfield returns some of the goods to Scott. This should be recorded in the accounts of Scott by:

	Debit	Credit
A	Returns Inwards Account	Fairfield's account
B	Scott's account	Returns Outwards Account
C	Fairfield's account	Returns Outwards Account
D	Returns Inwards Account	Scott's account

Unit Five

Balancing-off Accounts

5.1 Why Do Accounts Need Balancing?

We know that, when accounts are prepared, transactions are either on the debit (left-hand) side or on the credit (right-hand) side. Look at the following account:

Bank			
19–3	£	19–3	£
1 Mar. Capital	1 000	3 Mar. Typewriter	250
		7 Mar. Machinery	550

This account tells us that the business was started on 1 March with £1 000 in a bank account. On 3 March a typewriter was bought for £250, being paid for by cheque, and on 7 March a machine was bought for £550, also being paid for by cheque. The thing that the bank account does *not* tell us is the amount of money left in the bank after these transactions have taken place, that is, we do not know the *balance* of the account. Clearly, it is easy to work out:

Amount debited		£1 000
Amounts credited	£250	
	£550+	
		£ 800–
Balance		£ 200

Double-entry book-keeping accounts like those we have been preparing are generally balanced at regular intervals—certainly at the end of each month. Balancing-off accounts involves calculating the balance and entering it in the accounts.

5.2 How to Balance-off Accounts

The Bank Account shown in Unit 5.1 is balanced at the end of March (assuming that no further transactions take place) as follows:

Bank			
19–3	£	19–3	£
1 Mar. Capital	1 000	3 Mar. Typewriter	250
		7 Mar. Machinery	550
		31 Mar. Balance c/d	200
	1 000		1 000
1 Apr. Balance b/d	200		

The procedure for balancing accounts (which is harder to explain in words than it is to put into practice) is as follows:

(*a*) Each side of the account is added up and, if necessary, the total for each is noted in pencil.

(*b*) The smaller amount is taken away from the larger amount, and the difference is written *on the side of the smaller amount* on the next available line.

(*c*) Both sides are now added up and the total for each is entered in a 'totals box' on the same line on both debit and credit sides. Always ensure that two lines are drawn underneath the 'totals box', thus indicating a total.

(*d*) Against the balance on the smaller side is written the date at which the account is being balanced (usually the month-end); in the details column are written the words 'balance c/d' to indicate that the balance has been *carried down* to the next month.

(*e*) To complete double-entry book-keeping, an entry for the same money amount must be made on the *opposite side* of the account to 'balance c/d', but on the *next line below the 'totals box'*. In the details column it is described as 'balance b/d' (balance *'brought down'*); the date of this entry, when accounts are being balanced at the month-end, will be the first day of the next month. It is important to note that this 'balance b/d' is *not* underlined.

(*f*) Finally, when using a handwritten book-keeping system it is good practice at first to rule through any blank spaces remaining in the money columns of the account. This prevents any further entries—whether intentional or not—from being made in a section of the account that has already been balanced.

5.3   Examples of Account Balancing

Some students find it difficult to balance accounts correctly. Study the following examples; this will make the task easier, and after some practice you should find you have mastered it.

Capital

19–6	£	19–6	£
31 Jul. Balance c/d	1 000	1 Jul. Cash	1 000
		1 Aug. Balance b/d	1 000

Cash

19–6	£	19–6	£
1 Jul. Capital	1 000	3 Jul. Machinery	250
10 Jul. Machinery	250	5 Jul. Purchases	150
11 Jul. Sales	100	12 Jul. Purchases	175
		31 Jul. Balance c/d	775
	1 350		1 350
1 Aug. Balance b/d	775		

Machinery

19–6	£	19–6	£
3 Jul. Cash	250	10 Jul. Cash	250

Purchases

19–6		£	19–6		£
5 Jul.	Cash	150			
12 Jul.	Cash	175	31 Jul.	Balance c/d	325
		325			325
1 Aug.	Balance b/d	325			

Sales

19–6		£	19–6		£
			11 Jul.	Cash	100
31 Jul.	Balance c/d	265	17 Jul.	J. Smith	165
		265			265
			1 Aug.	Balance b/d	265

J. Smith

19–6		£	19–6		£
17 Jul.	Sales	165	31 Jul.	Balance c/d	165
1 Aug.	Balance b/d	165			

Points to notice:

(*a*) Every account is balanced, even those with only one transaction, such as Capital Account. You may perhaps consider this to be unnecessary: you might say that an account with only one item on it is already balanced, and nothing needs to be done. Nevertheless, it is good practice to go through and balance each account—this shows that all accounts have been looked at and brought up to date at the same time.

(*b*) Accounts that have only one transaction on them may be balanced either in the 'short form', as shown, or in the form used for all other accounts, thus:

Capital

19–6	£	19–6		£
31 Jul. Balance c/d	1 000	1 Jul.	Cash	1 000
	1 000			1 000
		1 Aug.	Balance b/d	1 000

As you see, the end result is exactly the same.

(*c*) When accounts are balanced at a month-end, the expression 'balance c/d' is always written against the last day of the month, above the totals boxes; 'balance b/d' is always written below the totals boxes, and is written against the first day of the new month. (At the end of a financial year, however, accounts are often balanced with the 'balance b/d' on the *last* day of the financial year—see Units 8.2 and 8.3.)

(*d*) The expressions 'carried forward' and 'brought forward' (often abbreviated to 'c/f' and 'b/f') are used when an account has so many transactions that it reaches the end of the page, at the bottom of that page and the top of the next respectively. It is necessary to total the debit and credit sides and 'carry forward' the totals to a new page, where the totals are 'brought forward'. These expressions are not used when balancing accounts.

5.4   Three-column Accounts

The type of accounts we have used so far have a distinctive debit side and credit side. Some accounts, particularly those produced by accounting machines and computers, have three money columns. One column represents the debit side, a second column the credit side and the third column the balance. You can see this type of account in use if you look at a bank statement or a building society passbook. With a three-column account a balance is worked out after every transaction, the calculation being done automatically where accounting machines and computers are used.

Here is an example of the kind of account we have been preparing so far:

Cash

19–9	£	19–9	£
1 May Capital	2 000	10 May Purchases	250
20 May Sales	200	12 May Bank	1 250
		15 May Typewriter	125
		25 May Purchases	125
		31 May Balance c/d	450
	2 200		2 200
1 Jun. Balance b/d	450		

Using a three-column format, this account will be presented as follows:

Cash

Date	Details	Debit	Credit	Balance	Dr. or Cr.
19–9					
1 May	Capital	2 000		2 000	Dr.
10 May	Purchases		250	1 750	Dr.
12 May	Bank		1 250	500	Dr.
15 May	Typewriter		125	375	Dr.
20 May	Sales	200		575	Dr.
25 May	Purchases		125	450	Dr.

With this type of account it is necessary to state after each balance whether it is debit or credit.

Preparing three-column accounts without a computer or an accounting machine is slow and laborious, because of the need to calculate the balance after entering each transaction; besides, the calculations are a possible source of error. In this book, therefore, we shall continue using mainly two-sided accounts; some examination questions may require you to prepare three-column accounts, however.

5.5   Questions

*1.   Enter the following transactions for the month into the accounts of Helen Thompson, and balance each account at the month-end:

19–7

1 May	Started in business with £40 000 in a business bank account.
2 May	Bought premises £30 000, paying by cheque.
3 May	Bought shop fittings £2 500 from A–Z Ltd, paying by cheque.
4 May	Bought goods £3 000, paying by cheque.
6 May	Bought more shop fittings £1000 on credit from Shopfitters Ltd.
8 May	Sold goods £340, a cheque being received.
10 May	Shop fittings to the value of £200 are found to be unsuitable and are returned to Shopfitters Ltd.
12 May	Bought goods £1 275 on credit from N. Johnson.
14 May	Sold goods £530 on credit to A. Paul.
16 May	Returned to N. Johnson goods to the value of £125.
18 May	Paid Shopfitters Ltd the amount owing to them by cheque.
19 May	Cash sales £125.
21 May	A. Paul returns goods £35.
23 May	Paid the amount owing to N. Johnson by cheque.
25 May	Bought goods £285, paying by cheque.
27 May	Additional capital brought in to the business, £2 500 by cheque.
29 May	Sold goods £145, a cheque being received.

2.   Rewrite the following, using a three-column account (the accounts are not connected):

(a)   **Machinery**

19–3	£	19–3	£
10 Jun. Cash	125	25 Jun. Bank	125
18 Jun. Bank	350		
22 Jun. Malvern Machines Ltd	150		

(b)   **Sales**

		19–2	£
		2 Jan. Cash	105
		4 Jan. A. Peters	215
		7 Jan. M. Wilson	85
		10 Jan. Bank	62
		17 Jan. G. Young	135
		20 Jan. Cash	87
		23 Jan. A. Peters	75

(c)   **Bank**

19–5	£	19–5	£
1 Sep. Capital	1 000	3 Sep. Machinery	250
25 Sep. Sales	250	7 Sep. Purchases	700
28 Sep. H. Lake	105	15 Sep. M. Johnson	150
		20 Sep. Purchases	100

Explain what has happened on this account between 15 September and 25 September.

3. Enter the following transactions for the month into the accounts of Andrew Lawson, and balance each account at the month-end:

19–6

1 Apr.	Started in business with £1 000 in the bank.
3 Apr.	Bought goods on credit from A. Hill £127; T. Lewis £85.
5 Apr.	Cash sales £45.
7 Apr.	Sold goods on credit to R. Palmer £44; K. Taylor £50.
9 Apr.	Withdrew £150 in cash from bank account for business use.
11 Apr.	Bought goods £115, payment in cash.
13 Apr.	Bought office equipment £125 on credit from F. Adcock.
15 Apr.	Returned goods £20 from those bought on 11 April: cash refund received.
17 Apr.	Paid the amount owing to A. Hill by cheque.
18 Apr.	Received a cheque from R. Palmer for the balance of his account.
20 Apr.	Bought goods on credit from T. Lewis, £114.
21 Apr.	Cash sales £75.
23 Apr.	Paid the amount owing to F. Adcock by cheque.
24 Apr.	Sold goods £65 on credit to K. Taylor.
26 Apr.	Paid the amount owing to T. Lewis by cheque.
27 Apr.	K. Taylor returns goods £40.

4. Enter the following transactions for the month into the accounts of William Rees, using three-column accounts:

19–2

1 Jan.	Started in business with £2 500 in the bank.
4 Jan.	Bought a machine for £1 000 on credit from T. Jones.
6 Jan.	Bought goods £250 on credit from H. Hughes.
7 Jan.	Sold goods £100 on credit to B. Lancaster.
9 Jan.	Bought goods £150, paying by cheque.
10 Jan.	Lancaster returns goods £20.
12 Jan.	Paid T. Jones the amount owing by cheque.
14 Jan.	Sold goods £95 to D. Morrison, a cheque being received.
17 Jan.	Paid half the amount owing to H. Hughes by cheque.
19 Jan.	Bought goods £100 on credit from K. Malcolm.
23 Jan.	B. Lancaster settles his account by cheque.
25 Jan.	Returned goods £20 to K. Malcolm.
27 Jan.	Sold goods £110, a cheque being received.

The Trial Balance

6.1 What is a Trial Balance?

A *trial balance* is a list of the balances of accounts contained in the double-entry book-keeping system. It is used to prove the arithmetical accuracy of the accounts. The list of balances is divided between (*a*) those accounts with balances brought down on the debit (left-hand) side of the ledger and (*b*) those with balances brought down on the credit (right-hand) side. A trial balance is often prepared immediately after the accounts have been balanced. It is set out as follows:

Trial balance of (name of business) as at (date)

Account:	Dr.	Cr.
	£	£
Capital		2 500
Bank	550	
Cash	150	
Machinery	350	
Purchases	500	
Sales		650
⋮		
etc		
Total		

6.2 How a Trial Balance is Extracted

First, all the accounts contained in the book-keeping system are balanced. The balances are then listed under the heading of *Dr.* (debit) or *Cr.* (credit), using the 'balance b/d' on each account. The debit and credit sides of the trial balance are totalled and, if the book-keeping is arithmetically correct, it should balance—that is, the two figures should be equal.

The following example shows the accounts of Smith after they have been balanced at the end of January:

Ledger of Smith

Capital

19–2	£	19–2	£
31 Jan. Balance c/d	1 000	1 Jan. Cash	1 000
		1 Feb. Balance b/d	1 000

Cash

19–2	£	19–2	£
1 Jan. Capital	1 000	4 Jan. Bank	750
12 Jan. Sales	55	22 Jan. Purchases	100
		31 Jan. Balance c/d	205
	1 055		1 055
1 Feb. Balance b/d	205		

Bank

19–2	£	19–2	£
4 Jan. Cash	750	7 Jan. Typewriter	150
26 Jan. J. Hughes	100	8 Jan. Purchases	200
		31 Jan. Balance c/d	500
	850		850
1 Feb. Balance b/d	500		

Purchases

19–2	£	19–2	£
3 Jan. P. Sanderson	150		
8 Jan. Bank	200		
22 Jan. Cash	100	31 Jan. Balance c/d	450
	450		450
1 Feb. Balance b/d	450		

Sales

19–2	£	19–2	£
		12 Jan. Cash	55
31 Jan. Balance c/d	155	17 Jan. J. Hughes	100
	155		155
		1 Feb. Balance b/d	155

Returns outwards

19–2	£	19–2	£
31 Jan. Balance	20	10 Jan. P. Sanderson	20
		1 Feb. Balance b/d	20

P. Sanderson

19–2	£	19–2	£
10 Jan. Returns outwards	20	3 Jan. Purchases	150
31 Jan. Balance c/d	130		
	150		150
		1 Feb. Balance b/d	130

Typewriter

19–2	£	19–2	£
7 Jan. Bank	150	31 Jan. Balance c/d	150
1 Feb. Balance b/d	150		

J. Hughes

19–2	£	19–2	£
17 Jan. Sales	100	26 Jan. Bank	100

The trial balance is prepared as follows:

Trial balance of Smith as at 31 January 19–2

Account:	Dr.	Cr.
	£	£
Capital		1 000
Cash	205	
Bank	500	
Purchases	450	
Sales		155
Returns outwards		20
P. Sanderson		130
Typewriter	150	
J. Hughes	—	—
	1 305	1 305

Points to notice:

(*a*) Where accounts are balanced at the month-end, the balances used are those recorded on each account at the *first day of the new month* (that is, the balances brought down).

(*b*) The trial balance is headed with the date of the last day of the month.

(*c*) The balance of every account must be included, even those which have a nil balance: for these a 'dash' is entered in both money columns.

A trial balance is not part of the double-entry book-keeping system: it is simply a list of balances which can be used to check the arithmetical accuracy of the book-keeping records. It is usually drawn up on a separate sheet of paper ruled with two money columns on the right-hand side. In business accounting systems, trial balances are often extracted more frequently than once a month, and are retained as proof that the accounts balanced as at the date of the trial balance.

6.3   How to Find Errors Shown by a Trial Balance

If the trial balance fails to agree, the error(s) must be found and corrected. Generally any errors will have been made since the previous trial balance was extracted, perhaps one month ago. The following procedure can be used:

(*a*) Check the addition of the trial balance.

(*b*) Check that the balances have been entered correctly from the accounts.

(*c*) In the accounts, check the calculation of each balance.

(*d*) Count the number of accounts in the book-keeping system and compare the result with the number of accounts listed in the trial balance (a good reason for including accounts with nil balances).

(*e*) Look through the accounts for an amount the same as the trial balance difference. If one is found, check to ensure that the double-entry book-keeping has been carried out correctly.

(*f*) Divide the trial balance difference by 2 and look for a transaction for this amount; if found, check the book-keeping has been carried out correctly.

(*g*) If all else fails, it will be necessary to check the book-keeping transactions from source documents. This will have to be carried out from the date of the previous trial balance by 'ticking back' each entry in the accounts.

When a trial balance agrees it proves the *arithmetical* accuracy of a set of accounts. Other errors may still be present, however; for instance, a transaction could have been entered on the correct side, but in the wrong-named account—a payment in cash, say, could have been credited to Bank Account. The procedures for dealing with errors are discussed fully in Units 28 and 29.

6.4   Preparing a Trial Balance from a List of Balances

It is relatively easy to prepare a set of accounts, and then to extract a trial balance. Sometimes students find it harder to prepare a trial balance from a list of balances such as the following:

	£
Capital	1 000
Machinery	700
Typewriter	310
Sales	850
Purchases	680
Returns inwards	55
Returns outwards	40
Bank overdraft	135
Cash	70
Johnson—a debtor	285
Wilson—a creditor	75

Here we must classify the balances according to whether they are debit or credit. Capital Account always has a credit balance because, as we saw earlier, the business in effect owes this amount back to the owner of the business. Machinery Account, Typewriter Account and other similar accounts always have debit balances, because they record items gained or owned by the business. Cash Account always has a debit balance, too—if it does have a credit balance this means a minus cash figure, which needs urgent investigation! Bank Account could have either a debit or a credit balance: when the account (in our records) shows a debit balance, the business has money in the bank; a credit balance indicates an overdraft. Purchases Account always has a debit balance because the business gains when it buys goods for resale; Returns Outwards (or Purchases Returns) Account always has a credit balance because the business loses goods. Sales Account always has a credit balance—the business loses goods when they are sold; on the contrary, Returns Inwards (or Sales Returns) Account always has a debit balance. The personal accounts of debtors and creditors should cause no problems when preparing a trial balance.

We can put the balances in this example in the form of a trial balance:

Trial balance of . . . as at . . .

Account:	Dr. £	Cr. £
Capital		1 000
Machinery	700	
Typewriter	310	
Sales		850
Purchases	680	
Returns inwards	55	
Returns outwards		40
Bank overdraft		135
Cash	70	
Johnson	285	
Wilson		75
	2 100	2 100

'I do so wish sometimes you'd taken up some profession other than accountancy'

6.5   Questions

*1.   Enter the following transactions for the month into the accounts of Henry Rich, balance each account at the month-end, and extract a trial balance at 31 March 19–8:

19–8

1 Mar.	Started in business with £2 000 in the bank and £100 in cash.
3 Mar.	Bought goods £500 on credit from A. Hands.
4 Mar.	Bought machinery £750 on credit from Southern Machines Ltd.
6 Mar.	Credit sales: B. Brittan £108; P. Newbury £74.
7 Mar.	Bought goods on credit from: M. Keegan £275; H. Lewis £350.
10 Mar.	Returned goods to H. Lewis £75.
12 Mar.	Paid Southern Machines Ltd the amount owing by cheque.
15 Mar.	Withdrew £100 cash from the bank for business use.
17 Mar.	B. Brittan paid the amount owing by cheque.
18 Mar.	Cash sales £125.
20 Mar.	Sold goods on credit £150 to B. Brittan.
21 Mar.	Paid A. Hands the amount owing by cheque.
23 Mar.	B. Brittan returns goods £68.
25 Mar.	Paid M. Keegan the amount owing by cheque.
30 Mar.	Paid H. Lewis the amount owing by cheque.

*2.   Prepare a trial balance for A. Mills from the following list of balances at 31 January 19–4:

	£
Cash	65
Sales	485
Bank	98
Van	1 250
Machinery	750
Capital	2 500
Purchases	610
H. Jones—a debtor	46
Returns outwards	84
T. Cook—a creditor	127
Office equipment	312
Returns inwards	65

3. Enter the following transactions for the month into the accounts of Adele Kaye, balance each account at the month-end, and extract a trial balance at 30 April 19–3:

19–3

1 Apr.	Started in business with £2 500 in the bank and a car valued at £1 500.
2 Apr.	Bought goods on credit from: J. Rayer £210; W. Mulligan £150; M. Thacker £350.
3 Apr.	Bought machinery £1 000 on credit from Machinery Ltd.
5 Apr.	Sold goods on credit to J. Duke £95; K. Hartley £54; D. Stephens £65.
6 Apr.	Returned goods to M. Thacker £45.
8 Apr.	Cash sales £68.
12 Apr.	Withdrew £200 cash from the bank for business use.
14 Apr.	Paid Machinery Ltd the amount owing by cheque.
16 Apr.	Sold goods on credit to K. Hartley £35; D. Stephens £100.
17 Apr.	Paid the amount owing by cheque to J. Rayer and M. Thacker.
19 Apr.	D. Stephens returned goods £40.
21 Apr.	Cash sales £125 paid direct into the bank.
23 Apr.	Received the amount owing by cheque from J. Duke and K. Hartley.
25 Apr.	Bought goods £150, paying by cheque.
28 Apr.	Bought goods £175 on credit from J. Rayer.
30 Apr.	Paid all cash, except for £25, into the bank.

4. Prepare a trial balance for P. Dawson from the following list of balances at 30 June 19–9:

	£
Bank overdraft	625
Purchases	425
Cash	24
Sales	365
Returns outwards	72
J. Ross—a creditor	221
Machinery	1 825
Car	1 600
Returns inwards	45
E. Clarke—a debtor	87
Office equipment	750
Capital	?

Expenses and Income; Drawings

7.1 Introduction

So far in this book we have dealt with accounts for the following types of business transaction:

introduction of capital into the business;
the purchase and sale of assets for use in the business, such as machinery, vans or typewriters;
the purchase and sale of goods in which the business trades;
returns inwards and returns outwards;
cash and bank receipts and payments.

However, we have not yet paid any of the expenses of running a business such as rent and rates, wages and salaries, the costs of heating, lighting and the telephone, and vehicle running expenses. Such expenses are recorded *in separate accounts*, rather than one account being opened in the name of 'expenses'.

Besides its expenses, a business may have certain items of income (sometimes called *revenue*), such as rent or commission received. These, too, should be recorded in separate accounts.

7.2 Accounts for Expenses

Consider a simple example:

17 Aug. 19–1   Paid rent £125 by cheque.

Like any other double-entry book-keeping transactions, there is a gain to the business, and also a loss. The gain is that the business has had the use of premises for an agreed time; the loss is that the bank account is reduced by £125. This transaction will be entered into the accounts as:

	Rent paid		
19–1	£		
17 Aug. Bank	125		

		Bank	
		19–1	£
		17 Aug. Rent paid	125

And another example:

14 Oct. 19–4   Paid telephone bill £58 in cash.

The gain to the business is the use of a telephone for a certain period of time; the loss is that the amount of cash has been reduced.

Telephone

19–4	£
14 Oct. Cash	58

Cash

		19–4	£
		14 Oct. Telephone	58

Point to notice:
Expenses accounts always have the transactions entered on the *debit* side.

7.3   Accounts for Income

12 Jul. 19–6   Rent received £30 in cash.

Here the business has gained cash, but has lost the use of a part of its premises for an agreed time.

Rent received

		19–6	£
		12 Jul. Cash	30

Cash

19–6	£
12 Jul. Rent received	30

(Sometimes an item appears both as expense and as income in the firm's accounts; rent, for instance, has been both paid and received. When this happens, separate accounts are opened for each.)

10 May 19–7   Commission received £100 by cheque.

The Bank Account has gained £100; the 'loss' is the time taken to earn the commission.

Bank

19–7	£
10 May Commission received	100

Commission received

		19–7	£
		10 May Bank	100

Point to notice:
Income accounts always have transactions entered on the *credit* side.

7.4   The Use of Drawings Account

From time to time the owner of a business will need to draw money from the business in order to meet his or her living expenses. Such amounts are entered in a *Drawings Account*.

21 Apr. 19–1   Owner withdrew £125 by cheque for own use.

The book-keeping entries are:

Bank

19–1		£
	21 Apr. Drawings	125

Drawings

19–1	£
21 Apr. Bank	125

Drawings Account is used to store up the total of owner's drawings for a year and, at the end of the year, that total is transferred to the Capital Account to reduce the amount the business 'owes' back to the owner. In terms of gains and losses, drawings reduce the firm's Bank or Cash Account, while the gain to the business is that a lesser amount is owed back to the owner.

Drawings Account is also used when the owner takes goods from the business for his or her own use. The appropriate book-keeping entries are to debit Drawings Account and to credit Purchases Account with the selling price of the goods taken.

10 Jan. 19–4   Goods taken for own use by owner of business £10.

Drawings

19–4	£
10 Jan. Purchases	10

Purchases

19–4		£
	10 Jan. Drawings	10

Note that this transaction breaks the rule that there should be no entries on the credit side of the Purchases Account.

7.5 Questions

*1. For each of the following transactions, name the account to be debited and the account to be credited:
   (*a*) sold goods on credit to Mrs Harris;
   (*b*) bought goods for cash;
   (*c*) sold goods for cash;
   (*d*) paid rent by cheque;
   (*e*) paid electricity bill by cheque;
   (*f*) goods withdrawn from stock for owner's personal use.

*2. Enter the following transactions for the month into the accounts of Karen Chandler, balance each account at the month-end, and extract a trial balance at 31 July 19–4:

19–4
   1 Jul.   Started in business with £4 000 in the bank and premises worth £40 000.
   2 Jul.   Bought goods on credit from: K. Ross £250; G. Harrison £175; D. Brown £550.

3 Jul.	Bought a delivery van £2 500 on credit from Central Garages.
5 Jul.	Withdrew £250 in cash from the bank for business use.
6 Jul.	Paid wages and salaries £150 in cash; cash drawings £75.
8 Jul.	Paid motor expenses £55 by cheque.
10 Jul.	Returned goods to K. Ross £75.
12 Jul.	Cash sales £145.
13 Jul.	Sold goods on credit to: P. Hughes £100; D. Bragg £85; M. Fardon £62.
14 Jul.	Rent received £250 by cheque; paid postages in cash £50.
16 Jul.	M. Fardon returns goods £12.
18 Jul.	Paid wages and salaries by cheque £175.
19 Jul.	Paid the amount owing to Central Garages by cheque.
20 Jul.	Cash sales £225.
23 Jul.	Cash drawings £100.
24 Jul.	Paid motor expenses £35 in cash.
25 Jul.	Paid postages in cash £25.
26 Jul.	Paid the amounts owing by cheque to K. Ross and D. Brown.
27 Jul.	M. Fardon and D. Bragg pay the amounts owing by cheque.
28 Jul.	Rent received £250 in cash.
30 Jul.	Paid all cash, except for £50, into the bank.

*3.   (a) Open the necessary accounts (including a bank account) and enter the following transactions in the books of T. Seaton:

1 Apr.	Seaton commenced business by transferring £6 000 to a bank account.
2 Apr.	Bought fixtures for the shop, £400, paying by cheque.
3 Apr.	Purchased goods on credit from Teal Ltd to the value of £840.
5 Apr.	Paid £420 by cheque for the first quarter's rent on the premises.
8 Apr.	Cash sales £400.
8 Apr.	Paid an insurance premium by cheque £74.
9 Apr.	Paid wages in cash £45.
10 Apr.	Bought goods for cash £200.
11 Apr.	Purchased further goods from Teal Ltd on credit £600.
12 Apr.	Paid Teal Ltd by cheque the balance on their account.
15 Apr.	Cash sales £210.
15 Apr.	Sold goods on credit to P. Swan £440.
16 Apr.	Paid wages in cash £45.
17 Apr.	Withdrew £60 in cash for private use.
18 Apr.	P. Swan settled his account by cheque.

(b) Balance the accounts (except for those with only one entry) and extract a trial balance to check the basic accuracy of your work.

[Royal Society of Arts]

4.   W. Flower commenced business on 1 March 19–8 paying £200 into a business bank account. During the next two months the following transactions took place. All payments are made by cheque.

		£
1 Mar.	Paid one month's rent	100
4 Mar.	Purchased goods for resale	500
18 Mar.	Paid vehicle insurance premium	50
24 Mar.	Banked shop takings for month	800

28 Mar.	Paid heating bill	40
30 Mar.	Cash drawn for self	100
1 Apr.	Paid one month's rent	100
4 Apr.	Purchased goods for resale	800
7 Apr.	Paid for repairs to motor vehicle	60
27 Apr.	Banked shop takings for month	950
28 Apr.	Paid heating bill	50
29 Apr.	Purchased new suit for self	100

You are required to:

(a) Write up the bank account, balancing at the end of each month.

(b) Write up all the other accounts (use one account only for all motor vehicle expenses), total and balance the accounts at the end of the two month period.

(c) Extract a trial balance as at 30 April 19–8.

[RSA Examinations Board]

Multiple-choice Questions—2

Read each question carefully. Choose the *one* answer you think is correct. Answers are given on page 411.

1. The bank account in a firm's double-entry book-keeping system appears as:

Bank

19–1	£	19–1	£
1 May Capital	2 000	10 May Purchases	250
20 May Sales	200	12 May Typewriter	125
		25 May Purchases	125

The balance of this account is:

A a debit balance of £1 700
B a credit balance of £1 700
C a debit balance of £2 200
D a credit balance of £500

2. A debit balance of £425 on P. Ross's account in the books of B. Harris means that:

A P. Ross owes B. Harris £425
B B. Harris owes P. Ross £425
C P. Ross has paid B. Harris £425
D B. Harris has paid P. Ross £425

3. A debit balance of £1 000 on Machinery Account in the books of Smith means that:

A Smith owes £1 000 for machinery purchased
B Smith has sold machinery for £1 000
C Smith owns machinery which cost £1 000
D Smith's Capital Account has a credit balance of £1 000

4. Which one of the following accounts normally has a debit balance?

A Capital Account
B Returns Outwards Account
C Sales Account
D Purchases Account

5. Which one of the following accounts normally has a credit balance?

A Returns Inwards Account
B Sales Account
C Machinery Account
D Cash Account

6. The correct heading for a trial balance is:

    A trial balance of ... as at ...
    B trial balance for the period ended ...
    C trial balance as at ...
    D trial balance of ... for the period ended ...

7. When preparing a trial balance, which one of the following is recorded on the credit side?

A	cash	**C**	returns inwards
B	capital	**D**	office equipment

8. When preparing a trial balance, which one of the following is recorded on the debit side?

A	bank overdraft	**C**	capital
B	returns outwards	**D**	purchases

9. Rent paid in cash should be recorded in the double-entry accounts by:

	Debit	*Credit*
A	Rent Paid Account	Bank Account
B	Cash Account	Rent Paid Account
C	Capital Account	Cash Account
D	Rent Paid Account	Cash Account

10. Commission received by cheque should be recorded in the double-entry accounts by:

	Debit	*Credit*
A	Capital Account	Commission Received Account
B	Bank Account	Commission Received Account
C	Commission Received Account	Bank Account
D	Cash Account	Commission Received Account

11. The withdrawal of cash from the business by the owner for his or her own use should be recorded by:

	Debit	*Credit*
A	Drawings Account	Capital Account
B	Drawings Account	Cash Account
C	Capital Account	Drawings Account
D	Cash Account	Drawings Account

12. The withdrawal of goods from the business by the owner for his or her own use should be recorded by:

	Debit	*Credit*
A	Purchases Account	Drawings Account
B	Drawings Account	Purchases Account
C	Drawings Account	Cash Account
D	Capital Account	Drawings Account

Trading Account; Profit and Loss Account

8.1 Introduction

One of the things we can find out from the book-keeping system is the profit or loss made by a business. The profit or loss is normally calculated once a year, at the end of a firm's financial year (which is not necessarily the same as a calendar year). To calculate the profit or loss for a financial year we take some of the information that has been accumulating during the course of the year, and present it in a certain way.

There are two different accounts to be prepared:

(*a*) a *Trading Account*, which shows the gross profit (or gross loss) for the year;

(*b*) a *Profit and Loss Account*, which shows the net profit (or net loss) for the year.

As the word *account* indicates, both the Trading Account and the Profit and Loss Account are part of the double-entry book-keeping system. Thus, any entry made in these two accounts must have an opposite entry for the same amount elsewhere in the accounts.

8.2 The Trading Account

The Trading Account shows the *gross profit* of a business for a financial year. In simple terms, gross profit is the difference between *the price a business pays* for goods for resale and *the price at which it sells them*. Look, for example, at some of the transactions of a photographic shop:

Camera bought from manufacturer for	£25
Sold to customer for	£50
Gross profit	£25

While it is perfectly possible to calculate the gross profit each time an item—such as a camera—is sold, it would be a tedious and time-consuming task. Instead, gross profit is formally calculated once a year, though many firms do so more frequently—perhaps monthly—to check that the business is operating profitably.

To find the gross profit for a year, we need to know the total of purchases and sales during the year. This information will have been stored up during the course of the year in Purchases Account and Sales Account. At the year-end, therefore, these two accounts have to be 'emptied' of the information they contain, which is then transferred to a Trading Account.

Here is an example of a Purchases and a Sales Account for B. Clifford which have been balanced at the financial year-end of 31 December.

Purchases

19–3	£
31 Dec. Balance b/d	33 500

Sales

		19–3	£
		31 Dec. Balance b/d	54 250

Since the financial year-end is 31 December, these two accounts will have started with nil balances on 1 January and, during the year, will have stored up the money amounts of purchases and sales. (You will have noticed that when these two accounts were balanced at the end of December, the balances were *brought down* on 31 December, rather than on 1 January.) The amounts contained in each account are now transferred to a Trading Account, as follows:

Purchases

19–3	£	19–3	£
31 Dec. Balance b/d	33 500	31 Dec. Trading Account	33 500

Sales

19–3	£	19–3	£
31 Dec. Trading Account	54 250	31 Dec. Balance b/d	54 250

These transactions leave Purchases and Sales Accounts with nil balances, and the corresponding double-entry book-keeping entries appear in the Trading Account:

Trading Account of B. Clifford for the year ended 31 December 19–3

	£		£
Purchases	33 500	Sales	54 250

As the gross profit is, broadly, the difference between purchases and sales, the amount of gross profit can now be calculated and entered on the Trading Account:

Trading Account of B. Clifford for the year ended 31 December 19–3

	£		£
Purchases	33 500	Sales	54 250
Gross profit c/d	20 750		
	54 250		54 250

Points to notice:

(*a*) The Trading Account has a different sort of heading from those of the accounts we have prepared so far. While it is still part of the double-entry book-keeping system—because it shows the total of Purchases Account and Sales Account for the year—it is headed 'for the year ended...'

(*b*) The gross profit is described as being 'c/d'; as we shall see in Unit 8.3, this profit is carried down to the Profit and Loss Account.

We shall look at Trading Accounts in more detail in Unit 10.

8.3   The Profit and Loss Account

We saw in Unit 8.2 that gross profit is the difference between buying and selling prices. Gross profit is calculated before deducting the running expenses of the business. Profit and Loss Account starts with gross profit and deducts from it the running expenses of the business for the accounting period, to give the *net profit* (or net loss). The net profit or loss belongs to the owner or owners of the business.

We have already seen how the money amounts for expenses are 'stored up' in various expenses accounts during the course of the financial year, in exactly the same way that the money amounts for purchases and sales are stored up in their respective accounts. At the end of the firm's financial year, the amounts contained in expenses accounts (and income accounts) are transferred to Profit and Loss Account, just as the amounts for purchases and sales are transferred.

Here are the expenses accounts of B. Clifford, whose business has a financial year-end of 31 December; the accounts have been balanced on the last day of the year and show the following balances:

Rent paid

19–3	£
31 Dec. Balance b/d	1 550

Salaries

19–3	£
31 Dec. Balance b/d	7 385

Heating and lighting

19–3	£
31 Dec. Balance b/d	683

Telephone

19–3	£
31 Dec. Balance b/d	429

Each account is now closed off by transfer to Profit and Loss Account:

Rent paid

19–3	£	19–3	£
31 Dec. Balance b/d	1 550	31 Dec. Profit and Loss Account	1 550

Salaries

19–3	£	19–3	£
31 Dec. Balance b/d	7 385	31 Dec. Profit and Loss Account	7 385

Heating and lighting

19–3	£	19–3	£
31 Dec. Balance b/d	683	31 Dec. Profit and Loss Account	683

Telephone

19–3	£	19–3	£
31 Dec. Balance b/d	429	31 Dec. Profit and Loss Account	429

Using the gross profit from the Trading Account in Unit 8.2, the Profit and Loss Account is completed as follows:

Profit and Loss Account of B. Clifford for the year ended 31 December 19–3

	£		£
Rent	1 550	Gross profit b/d	20 750
Salaries	7 385		
Heating and lighting	683		
Telephone	429		
Net profit	10 703		
	20 750		20 750

Points to notice:

(*a*) The heading, like that for the Trading Account, shows the time period for which it has been prepared— '... for the year ended...'

(*b*) To complete double-entry book-keeping, gross profit is brought down from the Trading Account on the credit side of the Profit and Loss Account.

(*c*) The balances of income accounts, such as rent received, are credited to Profit and Loss Account.

(*d*) Net profit is calculated by totalling all the expenses (write in the subtotal if you wish), and then deducting total expenses from gross profit (including any items of income). For a business that has made a net profit, expenses are *less than* gross profit; where expenses are *greater than* gross profit, the business has made a net loss.

(*e*) A net profit is entered on the debit side of the Profit and Loss Account, while a net loss would be shown on the credit side. For example:

Profit and Loss Account of ... for the year ended ...

	£		£
Various expenses (detailed)	11 600	Gross profit b/d	10 450
		Net loss	1 150
	11 600		11 600

A net profit (or net loss) is transferred to the Capital Account of the owner by completing the double-entry book-keeping. A net profit increases the owner's capital; for example:

Capital

19–3	£	19–3	£
31 Dec. Balance c/d	50 703	31 Dec. Balance b/d (say)	40 000
		31 Dec. Net profit from Profit and Loss Account	10 703
	50 703		50 703
		19–4	
		1 Jan. Balance b/d	50 703

On the other hand, a net loss reduces the owner's capital:

Capital

19–1	£	19–1	£
31 Dec. Net loss from Profit		31 Dec. Balance b/d (say)	15 000
and Loss Account	1 150		
31 Dec. Balance c/d	13 850		
	15 000		15 000
		19–2	
		1 Jan. Balance b/d	13 850

8.4   Questions

*1. Open the following accounts of J. Wood at 31 December 19–1, recording 'total for year' in the details column:

	£
Purchases	10 850
Sales	23 960
Salaries	6 210
Heating and lighting	870
Motor expenses	540
Postages	310
Rent paid	1 250

Prepare Wood's Trading and Profit and Loss Accounts for the year ended 31 December 19–1, showing appropriate transfers in the accounts. Show also the entry you would make on his Capital Account, which has a 'balance b/d' of £20 000 before the Trading and Profit and Loss Accounts are prepared.

*2. Enter the following transactions for the month into the accounts of Matthew, balance each account at the month-end, extract a trial balance, and prepare Trading and Profit and Loss Accounts for the month (showing appropriate transfers):

19–1

1 Aug.	Started in business with £1 000 in the bank.
2 Aug.	Bought goods on credit from A. Smith £200; C. Clarke £175; P. Martin £102.
3 Aug.	Withdrew £200 in cash from the bank for business use.
4 Aug.	Paid salaries in cash £125.
5 Aug.	Cash sales £85.
6 Aug.	Sold goods on credit to D. Jinks £54; C. Hill £102; A. Winter £76.
8 Aug.	Paid rent £50 by cheque.
10 Aug.	Cash sales £155 paid direct into the bank.
12 Aug.	Paid salaries in cash £100.
14 Aug.	Sold goods on credit to C. Hill £37.
16 Aug.	Paid the amounts owing by cheque to A. Smith and C. Clarke.
17 Aug.	D. Jinks pays the amount owing by cheque.
20 Aug.	Cash sales £102.
23 Aug.	Paid rent £50 in cash.

24 Aug.   Cash sales £154.
26 Aug.   Paid sundry expenses £25 in cash.
27 Aug.   Sold goods on credit to D. Jinks £205.
28 Aug.   Paid salaries in cash £78.
30 Aug.   C. Hill pays the amount owing by cheque.

3. Open the following accounts of M. Kershaw at 30 June 19–2, recording 'total for year' in the details column:

	£
Purchases	11 850
Sales	17 210
Salaries	5 360
Rent received	650
Rates	690
Heating and lighting	420
Postages	250
Sundry expenses	125

Prepare Kershaw's Trading and Profit and Loss Accounts for the year ended 30 June 19–2, showing appropriate transfers in the accounts. Show also the entry you would make on his Capital Account, which has a 'balance b/d' of £15 000 before the Trading and Profit and Loss Accounts are prepared.

4. Enter the following transactions for the month into the accounts of Marie Lyle, balance each account at the month-end, extract a trial balance, and prepare Trading and Profit and Loss Accounts for the month (showing appropriate transfers):

19–3
1 Sep.   Started in business with £1 000 in the bank and £500 in cash.
2 Sep.   Bought goods on credit from: A. Lawson £350; J. Kennedy £245; R. Carson £127.
3 Sep.   Paid rent £150 by cheque.
4 Sep.   Cash sales £75.
6 Sep.   Paid salaries in cash £162.
8 Sep.   Sold goods on credit to D. Worthington £154; N. North £98.
10 Sep.   Paid postages in cash £75.
12 Sep.   Cash sales £104.
14 Sep.   Paid the amounts owing to A. Lawson and R. Carson by cheque.
15 Sep.   Paid salaries in cash £150.
17 Sep.   Cash sales £84.
18 Sep.   Sold goods on credit to N. North £164; T. Jones £102.
20 Sep.   Bought goods £85, paying by cheque.
21 Sep.   Paid rent £150 by cheque.
23 Sep.   D. Worthington pays the amount owing by cheque.
24 Sep.   Cash sales £135.
25 Sep.   Paid postages in cash £105.
27 Sep.   Sold goods on credit to T. Jones £156.
29 Sep.   Cash sales £127.
30 Sep.   Paid all cash, except for £25, into the bank.

The Balance Sheet

9.1 What is a Balance Sheet?

A balance sheet is a statement of the assets and liabilities of a business at a particular time. It has three main sections:

(*a*) assets;
(*b*) liabilities;
(*c*) capital.

Assets are things *owned* by the business, such as motor vehicles, machinery, the money owed to it by debtors, or its balance at the bank. Liabilities are amounts *owed*, such as money owed to creditors or its bank overdraft. Capital is also a liability, but is different from the rest because it represents a liability to the owner of tne business, rather than a liability to 'outsiders' such as creditors or the bank. One method of calculating capital is:

$$Assets - Liabilities \ (to \ outsiders) = Capital$$

It follows that, if we know the money amount for any two of the three sections of a balance sheet, we can calculate the other:

$$Capital + Liabilities = Assets$$

$$Assets - Capital = Liabilities$$

A balance sheet has been likened to a 'snapshot' of a business: it shows the assets and liabilities at a particular moment in time—things could be different next day. This is why the balance sheet has the heading 'Balance sheet of . . . as at . . .', contrasting with the headings of Trading and Profit and Loss Accounts, which usually cover a year of business activity. Unlike Trading and Profit and Loss Accounts, a balance sheet is *not* part of the double-entry book-keeping system.

Here is an example of a balance sheet:

Balance sheet of . . . as at 31 December 19–6

Assets:	£	Liabilities:	£
Premises	30 000	Capital	45 000
Machinery	8 000	Creditors	5 250
Stock	7 250	Bank overdraft	1 100
Debtors	5 650		
Cash	450		
	51 350		51 350

9.2   A Personal Balance Sheet

You can easily prepare a personal balance sheet for yourself. Start by listing the things you own, such as clothes, books, radio, bicycle and so on, and put a money value on each. Don't forget to include the balance of any bank or building society account you may have, together with money you are holding in the form of cash. Then list the amounts of any liabilities, such as money you owe to anyone, perhaps a bank overdraft. Take liabilities away from assets (always assuming you own items to a greater value than you owe!) and the difference represents your capital, that is, how much you are worth, financially speaking.

Notice that your capital is not represented entirely by your cash. It consists of all your assets, some of which are *real* (or *tangible*) assets, such as your books and radio, less the liabilities. The same is true of a business—the capital is represented by real assets, such as premises, machinery and debtors, less the liabilities. Capital is likely to equal cash only for a new business's first transaction which might be, say, 'started in business with £1 000 in cash'.

9.3   Effect of Transactions on a Balance Sheet

It would be possible to prepare a new balance sheet after each business transaction has taken place. It *would* be possible, but it would be extremely impractical—a large business simply has not the time to do so. Instead we use the book-keeping system to record transactions and, at regular intervals, prepare a Trading Account, a Profit and Loss Account and a balance sheet. Nevertheless, you should be able to understand how transactions affect a balance sheet. We will work through a few transactions, and see how the balance sheet appears after each.

Day 1   Started in business with cash of £5 000.

The balance sheet shows an asset of cash £5 000 with a liability of capital for the same amount:

Balance sheet as at end of Day 1

Assets:	£	Liabilities:	£
Cash	5 000	Capital	5 000

Day 2   Bought a machine for £2 000, paying in cash.

Cash falls by £2 000, but a machine is gained.

Balance sheet as at end of Day 2

Assets:	£	Liabilities:	£
Machine	2 000	Capital	5 000
Cash	3 000		
	5 000		5 000

Day 3   A stock of goods, £1 000, is bought for resale, on credit from A. Smith.

The business has purchased some goods and, until they are sold, will have an asset of stock; at the same time, as the goods have not yet been paid for, the business owes the amount to A. Smith.

Balance sheet as at end of Day 3

Assets:	£	Liabilities:	£
Machine	2 000	Capital	5 000
Stock	1 000	Creditor: A. Smith	1 000
Cash	3 000		
	6 000		6 000

Day 4   Goods which had cost £200 are sold for £400, cash being received.

Here the stock of goods falls by the cost price, the amount of cash increases by £400, and a profit of £200 is made and added to capital.

Balance sheet as at end of Day 4

Assets:	£	Liabilities:	£
Machine	2 000	Capital	5 000
Stock	800	*Add* Net profit	200
Cash	3 400		5 200
		Creditor: A. Smith	1 000
	6 200		6 200

Day 5   Goods which had cost £100 are sold for £175 on credit to T. Brown.

The stock falls by £100, a profit of £75 is made, and T. Brown owes us £175.

Balance sheet as at end of Day 5

Assets:	£	Liabilities:	£
Machine	2 000	Capital	5 000
Stock	700	*Add* Net profit	275
Debtor: T. Brown	175		5 275
Cash	3 400	Creditor: A. Smith	1 000
	6 275		6 275

Day 6   Paid A. Smith the amount owing in cash.

Cash falls by £1 000 and A. Smith is no longer a liability.

Balance sheet as at end of Day 6

Assets:	£	Liabilities:	£
Machine	2 000	Capital	5 000
Stock	700	*Add* Net profit	275
Debtor: T. Brown	175		
Cash	2 400		
	5 275		5 275

When you are required to prepare a balance sheet, you will usually be expected to start from a trial balance or other accounting information. Nevertheless, once you have studied these examples you will be able to understand how a balance sheet is affected by an individual transaction.

9.4   A Business Balance Sheet

A business prepares its balance sheet by taking the figures for assets and liabilities from *the accounts which remain with balances on them* after the Trading and Profit and Loss Accounts have been prepared.

For example, the following accounts for John Doe remain at 31 December 19–9, after preparation of the Trading and Profit and Loss Accounts (note that net profit from the Profit and Loss Account has been credited to, and is included in, the balance shown on Capital Account):

Capital

| | 19–9 | £ |
| | 31 Dec. Balance b/d | 20 250 |

Motor vehicles

| 19–9 | £ |
| 31 Dec. Balance b/d | 5 000 |

Premises

| 19–9 | £ |
| 31 Dec. Balance b/d | 16 000 |

Bank

| | 19–9 | £ |
| | 31 Dec. Balance b/d | 1 315 |

Cash

| 19–9 | £ |
| 31 Dec. Balance b/d | 55 |

Smith

| 19–9 | £ |
| 31 Dec. Balance b/d | 1 110 |

Jones

| | 19–9 | £ |
| | 31 Dec. Balance b/d | 600 |

The balance sheet is presented as follows:

Balance sheet of John Doe as at 31 December 19–9

Assets:	£	Liabilities:	£
Premises	16 000	Capital	20 250
Motor vehicles	5 000	Creditor (Jones)	600
Debtor (Smith)	1 110	Bank overdraft	1 315
Cash	55		
	22 165		22 165

You can see that, to prepare the balance sheet, all the balances remaining on the accounts after completion of the Trading and Profit and Loss Accounts are listed, rather as in a trial balance. In fact a balance sheet can be likened to a special type of trial balance and, as we have said, like a trial balance it is not part of the double-entry book-keeping system.

9.5   More About Balance Sheets

(a) Layout

The balance sheets used in this book show assets on the left and liabilities on the right. You will find that many balance sheets are presented the other way round, that is, with liabilities on the left and assets on the right; you may find that some examining boards use this method of presentation. Nevertheless, both formats are perfectly acceptable in answers to examination questions, *unless you are instructed otherwise*. Another format is also in use, known as a 'vertical presentation'; an example of this is given in Unit 9.8.

Don't let these different presentations confuse you; just remember that the same information goes into each. One layout, rather than another, may better suit the preparer of the balance sheet.

(b) Listing the Assets

On a balance sheet, the assets are usually listed in 'increasing order of liquidity' (by *liquidity* is meant the ease with which things can be turned into cash). Thus the list of assets begins with the one that would take the longest to turn into cash. This is usually premises, followed by fixtures and fittings, machinery and plant, and motor vehicles, although the order for these other items is not so precise (we may guess, but we cannot be certain, that machinery is more difficult to turn into cash than motor vehicles). All these assets are known as *fixed assets*, because the firm needs them on a semi-permanent basis in order to remain in business—for example, without any premises, it would certainly find it difficult to trade.

The remaining assets are listed under the heading of *current assets*, and are those items whose nature is continually changing. They too are listed in 'increasing order of liquidity', and usually start with stock of goods for resale (discussed fully in Unit 10), then debtors, followed by balance at bank and, finally, cash. Current assets are also known as *circulating assets*—this term indicates the way in which the make-up of these assets changes as a business trades.

To summarize, the assets side of a balance sheet is usually set out as follows:

Fixed assets:
   Premises
   Fixtures and fittings
   Plant and machinery
   Motor vehicles

Current assets:
  Stock
  Debtors
  Bank
  Cash

This order, besides being known as an 'increasing order of liquidity', can also be called a 'decreasing order of permanence'.

(c) Listing the Liabilities

The liabilities side of a balance sheet is also customarily set out in an 'increasing order of liquidity'. It starts with the permanent *capital* of the business, followed by *long-term liabilities*, such as loans or a mortgage, and finishes with *current liabilities*. (A long-term liability is normally considered to be any amount repayable in *more than* twelve months from the balance-sheet date, while a current liability is any amount repayable in *less than* twelve months.)

To summarize, the liabilities side of the balance is set out as:

Capital
Long-term liabilities:
  e.g. Loans, mortgage

Current liabilities:
  Creditors
  Bank overdraft

9.6   Goodwill

As a business establishes itself, it builds up a reputation and a following of regular customers who come to rely on its services. This reputation and the connection with established customers is valuable to a business, and is known as *goodwill*. It is reasonable to expect that, should the business ever be sold, the purchaser would pay an amount for the goodwill as well as for the machinery, buildings and so forth which it acquires.

Example

A business is bought at a price of £150 000. The assets acquired are premises £80 000, machinery £30 000 and stock £20 000. Thus total assets acquired are £130 000, and the difference between this amount and the price paid of £150 000 represents the goodwill, that is, £20 000.

Goodwill is generally recorded in the balance sheet either as the first fixed asset or under a separate heading called *intangible assets*—'intangible' means that you cannot see or touch them, unlike tangible assets that can be seen and touched, such as machinery. Goodwill is only entered into the accounts *when it has been paid for*—in our example it would be recorded in the purchasing firm's balance sheet at £20 000 and listed before premises.

9.7   Final Accounts—a Worked Example

In Unit 8 we dealt with the preparation of a Trading Account and a Profit and Loss Account; this Unit has been concerned with balance sheets. Collectively, these three statements are often referred to as a firm's *final accounts*, because they are the summaries produced at the end of a financial year; together they show the gross and net profit for the year, with a statement of assets and liabilities at the year-end.

The following worked example brings together the material covered in Units 8 and 9. Study it carefully.

Example

The following trial balance was extracted from the accounts of Hodson at 31 December 19–4:

	Dr. £	Cr. £
Purchases	25 140	
Sales		43 557
Rent	1 825	
Wages	6 219	
Heating and lighting	848	
Postages	476	
Capital		22 385
Premises	20 000	
Machinery	3 280	
Vehicles	4 790	
Debtors: Andrews	235	
Hill	814	
Creditors: Johnson		543
King		677
Bank	1 310	
Cash	25	
Drawings	2 200	
	67 162	67 162

Each account is to be shown as it would appear in the ledgers of Hodson. Trading and Profit and Loss Accounts are to be prepared for the financial year ended 31 December 19–4, including appropriate transfers. A balance sheet is required as at 31 December 19–4.

Answer

Purchases

19–4	£	19–4	£
31 Dec. Balance b/d	25 140	31 Dec. Trading Account	25 140

Sales

19–4	£	19–4	£
31 Dec. Trading Account	43 557	31 Dec. Balance b/d	43 557

Rent

19–4	£	19–4	£
31 Dec. Balance b/d	1 825	31 Dec. Profit and Loss Account	1 825

Wages

19–4	£	19–4	£
31 Dec. Balance b/d	6 219	31 Dec. Profit and Loss Account	6 219

Heating and lighting

19–4	£	19–4	£
31 Dec. Balance b/d	848	31 Dec. Profit and Loss Account	848

Postages

19–4	£	19–4	£
31 Dec. Balance b/d	476	31 Dec. Profit and Loss Account	476

Capital

19–4	£	19–4	£
31 Dec. Drawings	2 200	31 Dec. Balance b/d	22 385
31 Dec. Balance c/d	29 234	31 Dec. Net profit	9 049
	31 434		31 434
		19–5	
		1 Jan. Balance b/d	29 234

Premises

19–4	£	19–4	£
31 Dec. Balance b/d	20 000	31 Dec. Balance c/d	20 000
19–5			
1 Jan. Balance b/d	20 000		

Machinery

19–4	£	19–4	£
31 Dec. Balance b/d	3 280	31 Dec. Balance c/d	3 280
19–5			
1 Jan. Balance b/d	3 280		

Vehicles

19–4	£	19–4	£
31 Dec. Balance b/d	4 790	31 Dec. Balance c/d	4 790
19–5			
1 Jan. Balance b/d	4 790		

Andrews

19–4	£	19–4	£
31 Dec. Balance b/d	235	31 Dec. Balance c/d	235
19–5			
1 Jan. Balance b/d	235		

Hill

19–4	£	19–4	£
31 Dec. Balance b/d	814	31 Dec. Balance c/d	814
19–5			
1 Jan. Balance b/d	814		

Johnson

19–4	£	19–4	£
31 Dec. Balance c/d	543	31 Dec. Balance b/d	543
		19–5	
		1 Jan. Balance b/d	543

King

19–4	£	19–4	£
31 Dec. Balance c/d	677	31 Dec. Balance b/d	677
		19–5	
		1 Jan. Balance b/d	677

Bank

19–4	£	19–4	£
31 Dec. Balance b/d	1 310	31 Dec. Balance c/d	1 310
19–5			
1 Jan. Balance b/d	1 310		

Cash

19–4	£	19–4	£
31 Dec. Balance b/d	25	31 Dec. Balance c/d	25
19–5			
1 Jan. Balance b/d	25		

Drawings

19–4	£	19–4	£
31 Dec. Balance b/d	2 200	31 Dec. Capital	2 200

Trading Account of Hodson for the year ended 31 December 19–4

	£		£
Purchases	25 140	Sales	43 557
Gross profit c/d	18 417		
	43 557		43 557

Profit and Loss Account of Hodson for the year ended 31 December 19–4

	£		£
Rent	1 825	Gross profit b/d	18 417
Wages	6 219		
Heating and lighting	848		
Postages	476		
Net profit	9 049		
	18 417		18 417

Balance sheet of Hodson as at 31 December 19–4

	£		£
Fixed assets:		Capital	22 385
Premises	20 000	*Add* Net profit	9 049
Machinery	3 280		31 434
Vehicles	4 790	*Less* Drawings	2 200
	28 070		29 234
Current assets:		Current liabilities:	
Debtors	1 049	Creditors	1 220
Bank	1 310		
Cash	25		
	30 454		30 454

Point to notice:

The balance of Drawings Account at the year-end has been transferred to the debit of Capital Account, while net profit has been credited to Capital Account. On the balance sheet, however, it is usual to show the owner's capital at the start of the year and then to add net profit (or deduct net loss), and deduct drawings. This is preferable to showing only the closing balance of Capital Account, because the balance sheet then sets out clearly the net profit made by the business and the amount of owner's drawings.

9.8   Vertical Presentation of Year-end Accounts

So far in this book we have presented the year-end accounts—Trading Account, Profit and Loss Account and balance sheet—in a horizontal form, each shown with two sides. As we said in Unit 9.5(*a*), the *vertical presentation* can also be used. Using this method, also known as a *narrative* or *columnar* method, the columns of figures are set out with no division into left- and right-hand sides. In vertical form the final accounts from Unit 9.7 will appear as:

Trading and Profit and Loss Account of Hodson for the year ended 31 December 19–4

	£	£
Sales		43 557
Less Purchases		25 140
Gross profit		18 417
Less Expenses:		
Rent	1 825	
Wages	6 219	
Heating and lighting	848	
Postages	476	
		9 368
Net profit		9 049

Balance sheet of Hodson as at 31 December 19–4

	£	£
Fixed assets:		
Premises		20 000
Machinery		3 280
Vehicles		4 790
		28 070
Current assets:		
Debtors	1 049	
Bank	1 310	
Cash	25	
	2 384	
Less Current liabilities:		
Creditors	1 220	
Working capital[1]		1 164
		29 234
Financed by:		
Capital		22 385
Add Net profit		9 049
		31 434
Less Drawings		2 200
		29 234

[1] This vertical presentation balance sheet has the virtue that it shows the figure for *working capital* (£1 164 in this example), that is, current assets minus current liabilities. We shall discuss working capital more fully in Unit 40.4(*a*).

9.9   Questions

*1.   From the following list of assets and liabilities at 31 December 19–1, you are required to draw up a balance sheet which should show clearly fixed assets, current assets, long-term liabilities and current liabilities.

	£
Capital	20 000
Motor vehicles	5 000
Net profit for year	3 127
Stock	2 350
Premises	20 750
Creditors	3 020
Debtors	4 110
Cash	85
Bank overdraft	3 938
Loan (repayable in ten years' time)	6 000
Fixtures and fittings	1 250
Drawings	2 540

*2.   From the following list of assets and liabilities as at 31 March 19–3, draw up a balance sheet as at that date, paying particular attention to its layout.

Harold Skimpole
Assets and liabilities

	£
Goodwill	3 000
Capital	40 000
Motor vehicles	8 000
Premises	20 000
Investments	10 000
Debtors	5 000
Creditors	8 000
Stock	6 000
Net profit for year	5 000
Fixtures and fittings	4 000
Bank overdraft	3 000

[*London Regional Examining Board*]

3.   Complete the following table:

	Liabilities £	Capital £	Assets £
(a)	360		890
(b)		3 670	6 500
(c)	5 289	2 345	
(d)		1 788	6 555
(e)	4 380		4 380
Totals			

[*Pitman Examinations Institute*]

4. From the information given below, prepare the balance sheet of the business owned by F. Boots for the end of its accounting year, 31 March 19–1.

	£
Freehold property	12 700
Mortgage	8 200
Cash in hand	60
Loan (repayable in six months)	1 050
Leasehold property	5 300
Debtors	135
Creditors	825
Delivery van	1 710
Office equipment	1 340
Capital	12 810
Stock of wrapping materials	80
Furniture and fittings	1 560

The closing balance of capital is made up from the following items: balance from last year £14 530; loss for year £630; and drawings £1 090.

[*Pitman Examinations Institute*]

5. (*a*) What is meant by 'drawings' from a business?

(*b*) During the first quarter of 19–0 Julie Wilkinson, a hairdresser, draws out £240 in cash for her own use at the end of each month.

   (i) Prepare the accounts in her books necessary to record each one of these transactions.

   (ii) Show how the Drawings Account is balanced at the end of the quarter and the transfer to the Capital Account. Then complete and balance off the Capital Account.

Balance on Julie Wilkinson's Capital Account at January 1 19–0 £18 100. Net profit (for first quarter) £1 280.

[*Royal Society of Arts*]

6. Complete the following table.

Business	Capital at 1 Jan. £	Profit for year £	Drawings £	Capital at 31 Dec. £
W	2 170		620	1 775
X		920	170	2 175
Y	2 195	630	320	
Z	6 270	1 340		7 250

[*Pitman Examinations Institute*]

The Asset of Stock

10.1 Introduction

In book-keeping and accounts, the term *stock* refers to the goods in which a business trades. We have already seen (in Unit 4) that Purchases Account is used to record the money amount of goods bought by the business for resale; Sales Account is used to record the money amount of goods sold. Most businesses maintain throughout the year stocks of the goods in which they trade: thus the shoe shop, for instance, always has a stock of shoes, and the record shop a stock of records. At regular intervals, and certainly at the end of a financial year, a business must place a value on the stock it holds. You may have seen notices in shop windows saying 'closed for stocktaking'—this means that the stock is being listed and valued.

10.2 Stock Valuation

Generally stock is valued at the amount it cost the business, but if it can only be sold at a price below its cost, then this lower price is considered to be its value. In accounting this valuation method is summarized as being *at the lower of cost and net realizable value.*

Look at an example. Consider a fashion shop that, in the autumn, buys in a stock of winter coats for £60 each. By spring, a few of these coats are still hanging on the rails, and the owner of the shop considers they can only be sold at a sale price of £30 each. Therefore, at this time, the coats have a cost to the business of £60 but a net realizable value of £30. They will therefore be valued at the lower of the two figures—£30.

It is important for a business to keep accurate stock records; we shall consider this in Unit 31.

10.3 Closing Stock and the Trading Account

Stock is always valued at the end of a financial year, and the valuation must be brought into that year's Trading Account. (Stock may well be valued more frequently than once a year, but it is the year-end valuation with which we are concerned at present.)

Let us consider the business of Mrs Smith, who started selling teenage fashion clothes on 1 January 19–1. On that date, of course, she had no stock of goods for resale, but her accounting records show that during the course of the year to 31 December 19–1 she bought goods for resale totalling £40 000. At the same time her Sales Account shows total sales for the year of £60 000. On 31 December, Mrs Smith values the stock in the shop at £5 000. This means that, of the purchases for £40 000 during the year, goods valued at £5 000 remain unsold at the year-end. When preparing her Trading Account we must deduct £5 000 from the purchases figure as follows:

Trading Account of Mrs Smith for the year ended 31 December 19–1

	£		£
Purchases	40 000	Sales	60 000
Less Closing stock	5 000		
	35 000		
Gross profit c/d	25 000		
	60 000		60 000

We already know that, as the Trading Account is part of double-entry book-keeping, opposite entries must be entered in Purchases Account and Sales Account. An opposite entry in the accounts is also needed for the closing stock, and for this purpose a *Stock Account* is used. As the closing stock of the business at 31 December 19–1 is an asset of the business, the entry in Stock Account is made as follows:

Stock

19–1	£
31 Dec. Trading Account	5 000

At first glance you might think that the entry in Stock Account has been made on the wrong side—we appear to have made *two* debit entries in our accounts. Look again at the Trading Account, however: we put '*less* Closing stock' on the *debit* side, which is exactly the same as if we had *added* the amount on the *credit* side:

Trading Account of Mrs Smith for the year ended 31 December 19–1

	£		£
Purchases	40 000	Sales	60 000
Gross profit c/d	25 000	Closing stock	5 000
	65 000		65 000

As you can see, the gross profit is the same, and we now have a clear debit and credit entry in the accounts—debit to Stock Account, credit to Trading Account. In the Trading Account, however, it is usual to *deduct* closing stock from purchases to show the figure for *cost of goods sold* (sometimes called *cost of stock sold*), thus:

	£
Purchases	40 000
Less Closing stock	5 000
Cost of goods sold	35 000

The cost of goods sold figure tells us the cost price of the goods which Mrs Smith sold during the year for £60 000. We shall use the cost of goods sold figure later in this book (Unit 40.2(*b*)) to enable us to interpret aspects of the Trading Account.

10.4   Opening Stock and Closing Stock

In the example in Unit 10.3, Mrs Smith had a closing stock valuation of £5 000 at 31 December 19–1 after her first year of trading. This *closing stock* for the first year will form the *opening stock* for her second year of trading in 19–2. During the second year Mrs Smith will record the money amounts of purchases and sales of her fashions in the accounts. (Remember that Purchases Account and Sales Account were 'emptied' at 31 December 19–1 of the information stored in them, so that they started 19–2 with nil balances.) At 31 December 19–2 she again values her stock. Suppose that the figures for the year are:

Opening stock at 1 January 19–2	£5 000
Purchases	£50 000
Sales	£75 000
Closing stock at 31 December 19–2	£8 000

For this—the second—year and for all following years, we must take into account the *opening stock*, as well as the closing stock, when preparing the Trading Account, as follows:

Trading Account of Mrs Smith for the year ended 31 December 19–2

	£		£
Opening stock (1 Jan.)	5 000	Sales	75 000
Add Purchases	50 000		
	55 000		
Less Closing stock (31 Dec.)	8 000		
Cost of goods sold	47 000		
Gross profit c/d	28 000		
	75 000		75 000

What we are saying in the Trading Account is that Mrs Smith started the year with a stock of goods valued at £5 000. During the year she has added £50 000 worth of goods, making £55 000. By deducting her closing stock of £8 000, however, we see that the cost of the goods which she has sold for £75 000 amounted to £47 000. This gives her a gross profit of £28 000.

Look more carefully at Mrs Smith's Trading Account. We already know the opposite entries in the accounts for purchases and sales. Both the opening and closing stocks need to be entered into the Stock Account that was opened at the end of the first year's trading; it has a debit balance brought down of £5 000 on 1 January 19–2. Stock Account is completed thus:

Stock

19–2	£	19–2	£
1 Jan. Balance b/d	5 000	31 Dec. Trading Account	5 000
31 Dec. Trading Account	8 000		

You can see that the opening stock for 19–2 (which was, of course, the closing stock for 19–1) is taken out of Stock Account at 31 December 19–2 by a credit entry, the opposite debit entry being in the Trading Account. As Mrs Smith's closing stock is worth £8 000 at the end of 19–2, this amount has to be debited to the Stock Account (and credited in the Trading Account, or shown as a deduction on the debit side). This closing stock of £8 000 will then form the opening stock for the financial year commencing 1 January 19–3, and will be transferred to the Trading Account at 31 December 19–3.

Operating a Stock Account may seem complicated, but it simply follows the basic rules of double-entry book-keeping. When we prepare a Trading Account, we enter the opening stock on the debit side; this means that a credit entry must be made on Stock Account. With closing stock, we make a deduction on the debit side of the Trading Account, and the opposite entry to this is a debit to Stock Account.

Point to notice:
As closing stock is an asset of a business at the year-end, it must be entered on the balance sheet prepared at that date, just like any other asset. Stock is listed on the balance sheet as a current asset (see Unit 9.5(*b*)).

10.5   More About the Trading Account

(*a*)   Returns Inwards and Returns Outwards
In Units 4.8 to 4.10 we saw how returns accounts are used to store up the total returns for a year. Returns Inwards Account records the return of goods previously sold by the business, that is, sales returns. Returns Outwards Account, on the other hand, deals with the return of goods previously bought by the business and then found to be unsuitable, that is, purchases returns. At the end of a firm's financial year the information contained in these two accounts must be taken out and transferred to the Trading Account. In the Trading Account the total of returns outwards is deducted from purchases, while the total of returns inwards is deducted from sales. This then gives us *net figures* for both purchases and sales (the figure for net sales is often called the *turnover* of the business). The Trading Account, using example figures, now takes the following form (notice the use on both sides of *marginal columns* to list amounts which are to be subtotalled):

Trading Account of Mr Jones for the year ended 30 June 19–5

	£	£		£	£
Opening stock			Sales	25 000	
(1 Jul. 19–4)		3 500	*Less* Returns inwards	600	
Purchases	16 500		Net sales (or turnover)		24 400
Less Returns outwards	750				
Net purchases		15 750			
		19 250			
Less Closing stock					
(30 Jun. 19–5)		4 000			
Cost of goods sold		15 250			
Gross profit c/d		9 150			
		24 400			24 400

We already know the opposite entries in the accounts for purchases, sales, opening stock, closing stock and gross profit (entered on the credit side of Profit and Loss Account). To complete double-entry book-keeping, entries must be made in the two returns accounts, and in this example these accounts will appear as:

Returns inwards

19–5	£	19–5	£
30 Jun. Balance b/d	600	30 Jun. Trading Account	600

Returns outwards

19–5	£	19–5	£
30 Jun. Trading Account	750	30 Jun. Balance b/d	750

The returns accounts, just like purchases and sales, store up money amounts during the course of the financial year. In our example, Returns Inwards Account has a debit balance of £600, that is, goods to this value have been sent back to Mr Jones's business. This balance is transferred to the Trading Account by crediting Returns Inwards Account, and by debiting Trading Account—shown as a deduction from sales to give a net sales figure. Returns Outwards Account has a credit balance of £750, that is, Mr Jones has returned goods to his suppliers. This balance is transferred by debiting Returns Outwards Account and crediting Trading Account—deducting from the figure for purchases.

(*b*) Carriage Expenses

Carriage is the expense incurred in delivering goods; it is paid to firms that specialize in providing a delivery service, such as the Post Office, Roadline and Securicor. In book-keeping we need to distinguish between *carriage inwards* and *carriage outwards*.

Carriage in is the charge paid *by the buyer* to the carrier to deliver goods *to the firm*, that is, it is the cost of delivering the firm's purchases. As such it is shown in the Trading Account and added to purchases to show a 'delivered to the door' price for all purchases. Carriage in is not always paid directly by the buying firm: many goods are quoted at a price that includes delivery. Sometimes, though, a buying price is quoted as being 'ex-works', that is, the price at the supplying firm's works, and a carriage charge (carriage in) must be paid to obtain delivery of the goods. Thus one supplier of goods might quote an 'ex-works' price of £75 for goods and then charge carriage of £5, while another supplier might quote, for identical goods, £80 'delivered to your door'. Clearly, where carriage inwards is charged separately it should be added to purchases so that all goods purchased are recorded at 'delivered to the door' prices.

Carriage out is the charge paid *by the firm* to a carrier to deliver goods that it has sold to its customers: it is a cost borne by the supplier who is selling to customers on a 'delivered to the door' basis. It is recorded in the Profit and Loss Account, just like the other expenses of the business.

To summarize, both carriage in and carriage out are expenses, but carriage in is charged in the Trading Account, being added to purchases, while carriage out is charged in the Profit and Loss Account.

(c) Other Expenses Charged to Trading Account

Any other expenses incurred in connection with putting the goods in which a business trades into a saleable condition should be charged to the Trading Account. *Wages*, particularly *warehouse wages*, are an example of such an expense and are considered to be a trading cost (contrasting with *salaries* which are an administrative expense charged to Profit and Loss Account). Where such an expense is shown in the Trading Account, it is added to the cost of goods sold figure. The resultant figure—the cost of goods sold plus Trading Account expense—is referred to as the *cost of sales* (see the Trading Account in Unit 10.6).

(d) Goods Taken for Own Use

We saw in Unit 7.4 that where the owner of a business takes goods for his or her own use without payment, an accounting entry should be made in the books. This is carried out by debiting Drawings Account and crediting Purchases Account with the selling price of the goods.

If you are working from a trial balance to produce year-end accounts and are told that an amount of goods has been taken by the owner of the business but is not recorded in the accounts, you will need to increase the drawings amount and to decrease the amount of purchases; that is, purchases *less* goods for own use.

10.6   A Worked Example

This example shows a number of accounts as they might appear at the end of a financial year, indicating the ledger transfers to produce a Trading Account.

Books of J. Hardcastle

Sales

19–8	£	19–8	£
31 Dec. Trading Account	48 500	31 Dec. Balance b/d	48 500

Purchases

19–8	£	19–8	£
31 Dec. Balance b/d	27 300	31 Dec. Trading Account	27 300

Returns inwards

19–8	£	19–8	£
31 Dec. Balance b/d	470	31 Dec. Trading Account	470

Returns outwards

19–8	£	19–8	£
31 Dec. Trading Account	210	31 Dec. Balance b/d	210

Stock

19–8	£	19–8	£
1 Jan. Balance b/d	2 400	31 Dec. Trading Account	2 400
31 Dec. Trading Account	3 700		

Carriage inwards

19–8	£	19–8	£
31 Dec. Balance b/d	520	31 Dec. Trading Account	520

Warehouse wages

19–8	£	19–8	£
31 Dec. Balance b/d	4 650	31 Dec. Trading Account	4 650

Trading Account of J. Hardcastle for the year ended 31 December 19–8

	£	£		£	£
Opening stock (1 Jan.)		2 400	Sales	48 500	
Purchases	27 300		*Less* Returns inwards	470	
Less Returns outwards	210		Net sales (or turnover)		48 030
	27 090				
Add Carriage in	520				
Net purchases		27 610			
		30 010			
Less Closing stock (31 Dec.)		3 700			
Cost of goods sold		26 310			
Warehouse wages		4 650			
Cost of sales		30 960			
Gross profit c/d		17 070			
		48 030			48 030

10.7 Questions

*1. From the following information draw up a Trading and Profit and Loss Account:

> Stock at start £5 000
> Stock at close £4 500
> Purchases £25 000
> Sales £37 000
> Returns inwards £250
> Carriage inwards £750
> Carriage outwards £1 050
> Warehouse wages £9 500
> Expenses £750
>
> [*South-East Regional Examinations Board*]

2. On 1 August you have 15 items in stock which cost £3 each. During the month you buy 35 more of the same item which also cost £3 each. Your sales for the month were 38 items at £7 each. In simple terms what profit have you made?

> [*Pitman Examinations Institute*]

3. Enter the following transactions for the month into the accounts of Henry Mills, balance each account at the month-end, extract a trial balance, and prepare Trading and Profit and Loss Accounts for the month (showing appropriate transfers):

19–4

1 Feb.	Started in business with £1 000 in the bank and a stock of goods worth £450.
3 Feb.	Bought goods on credit from K. Stone £220; A. Powell £140; M. Lake £120.
4 Feb.	Cash sales £85.
6 Feb.	Returned goods £50 to K. Stone.
7 Feb.	Sold goods on credit to J. Mellor £126; L. Adams £84.
9 Feb.	Paid salaries by cheque £75.
11 Feb.	J. Mellor returns goods £22.
12 Feb.	Paid rent by cheque £100.
13 Feb.	Cash sales £124.
14 Feb.	Sold goods on credit to L. Adams £136.
16 Feb.	Paid the amounts owing by cheque to K. Stone and A. Powell.
17 Feb.	Cash sales £114.
19 Feb.	A cash sales customer returns unsatisfactory goods £9—refund made in cash.
21 Feb.	L. Adams pays the amount owing by cheque.
23 Feb.	Paid salaries by cheque £110.
24 Feb.	Sold goods £108 on credit to J. Mellor.
27 Feb.	Cash sales £121.
28 Feb.	Paid salaries by cheque £97.

On 28 February, the stock of goods is valued at £362.

*4.   Reconstruct in good form the following balance sheet after taking into account the transactions for December.

Balance sheet as at 30 November

Assets:	£	Liabilities:	£
Cash	500	Capital	3 000
Machinery	1 000	+ Net profit	1 000
Vans	2 000		4 000
Debtors	1 500	− Drawings	300
Stock	1 000		3 700
		Creditors	2 300
	£6 000		£6 000

1 Dec.	Received a cheque from debtors £200.
5 Dec.	Took drawings in cash £150.
10 Dec.	Sold goods which cost £100 for £300 cash.
15 Dec.	Purchased goods on credit for £200.
21 Dec.	Took a loan from the bank to buy machine costing £2 000.
31 Dec.	Paid £25 cash into bank.

[*Pitman Examinations Institute*]

*5.   On 1 April 19–3 D. Hall had 200 articles in stock valued at £8 each.
During April he purchased 300 articles at £10 each and a further 50 articles at £12 each.
His sales for the month were 320 articles at £12 each and 200 articles at £15 each.
His stock on 30 April 19–3 consisted of some of the articles from his most recent purchases.

Calculate (*a*) opening stock, (*b*) total purchases, (*c*) total sales and (*d*) closing stock, and (*e*) show the Trading Account of D. Hall for the month ended 30 April 19–3.

[*East Midland Regional Examinations Board*]

6.   From the information below, you are required to extract the necessary details to work out the gross profit on September's trading of David Tomms (Wholesalers) Ltd.

	£
Stock 1 September	620
Stock 30 September	640
Cash balance	120
Drawings	150
Purchases for month	2 160
Sales for month	3 275
Carriage inwards	30

[*Pitman Examinations Institute*]

7.   On 1 March 19–3, M. Bullough had 25 articles in stock valued at £10 each. On 13 March, she purchased 20 articles for £15 each and on 21 March, a further 30 articles for £16 each.

During March, she sold 50 articles for £20 each and 20 articles for £22 each. Her closing stock consisted of some of the items purchased on 21 March.

Calculate (a) opening stock (1 March 19–3), (b) total purchases, (c) total sales, (d) closing stock (31 March 19–3) and (e) show the Trading Account of M. Bullough for the month ended 31 March 19–3.

[*West Midlands Examinations Board*]

8. From the following figures, which relate to the financial year ended 31 January 19–1, prepare the Trading Account of James Gaul. The account should clearly show net purchases, cost of stock sold, cost of sales and net sales.

	£
Purchases on credit	30 420
Cash purchases of goods for resale	6 840
Goods taken by James Gaul for personal use	500
Sales	60 700
Stock 1 February 19–0	4 320
Returns inwards	480
Returns outwards	240
Carriage inwards	60
Carriage outwards	580
Wages (allocated two-fifths Trading Account and three-fifths Profit and Loss Account)	6 525
Stock 31 January 19–1	3 230

Note: A Profit and Loss Account is *not* required.

[*Royal Society of Arts*]

9. The following list of balances was extracted from the books of L. North at 31 December 19–1. You are required to prepare the Trading and Profit and Loss Accounts for the year ended 31 December 19–1 and a balance sheet as at that date:

	£
Purchases	15 740
Sales	32 830
Stock (at 1 January 19–1)	3 790
Returns inwards	120
Returns outwards	310
Carriage inwards	50
Carriage outwards	140
Drawings	7 360
Premises	38 000
Fixtures and fittings	10 500
Wages and salaries	9 310
Rent received	540
Advertising	1 180
Cash at bank	2 010
Cash in hand	60
Debtors	2 240
Creditors	1 870
Capital	54 950

Stock at 31 December 19–1 was valued at £3 030.

10. The following trial balance was extracted from the books of Jane Walsh, who is the proprietor of a fabric shop, at the end of her financial year 30 April 19–0.

Trial balance as at 30 April 19–0

	Dr. £	Cr. £
Sales		30 000
Purchases	15 700	
Shop fittings	13 000	
Capital		15 000
Opening stock (1 May 19–9)	4 700	
Bank	610	
Cash	100	
Shop wages	4 420	
Debtors	120	
Drawings	3 500	
Creditors		2 030
Light and heat	260	
Rent	4 500	
Insurance	120	
	47 030	47 030

In preparing the year-end accounts, the following should be accounted for:

The stock at the end of the year was valued at £4 400.

You are required to:

(a) Prepare Jane's Trading Account for the year ended 30 April 19–0.
(b) Prepare Jane's Profit and Loss Account for the year ended 30 April 19–0.
(c) Draft Jane's balance sheet as at 30 April 19–0.

[*Pitman Examinations Institute, Level 1*]

Multiple-choice Questions—3

Read each question carefully. Choose the *one* answer you think is correct. Answers are given on page 411.

1. **The amount of a firm's gross profit is calculated in the:**

   A Trading Account   C balance sheet
   B Profit and Loss Account   D Capital Account

2. **Net profit equals:**

   A bank balance less expenses   C Capital Account less expenses
   B gross profit less expenses   D gross profit add expenses

3. The correct heading for a Profit and Loss Account is:

    A Profit and Loss Account for the year ended . . . .
    B Profit and Loss Account of . . . . as at . . . .
    C Profit and Loss Account of . . . . for the year ended . . . .
    D Profit and Loss Account as at . . . .

4. Which one of the following does *not* appear in the Profit and Loss Account?

    A capital   **C** rent received
    B salaries   **D** commission paid to salesmen

5. The balance sheet equation is:

    A assets = capital + liabilities
    B capital = assets + liabilities
    C capital = assets + liabilities + net profit
    D liabilities = assets + capital

6. Which one of the following is a current liability?

    A debtors   **B** loan   **C** bank overdraft   **D** capital

7. List the following in increasing order of liquidity:
    (i) bank   (ii) stock   (iii) cash   (iv) debtors

    A (ii), (iv), (iii), (i)   **C** (iv), (ii), (i), (iii)
    B (iii), (i), (iv), (ii)   **D** (ii), (iv), (i), (iii)

8. The capital of a business is £22 000 at the beginning of the year and £26 000 at the
    end. The owner has withdrawn £6 000 during the year. The net profit for the year
    is:
    A £28 000   **B** £26 000   **C** £4 000   **D** £10 000

9. Gross profit is:

    A sales, less cost of sales
    B purchases, plus opening stock, less closing stock
    C sales, less closing stock
    D purchases, plus cost of sales

10. Cost of goods sold is:

    A opening stock, plus purchases, less closing stock
    B purchases, less closing stock
    C purchases, plus closing stock
    D opening stock, plus sales, less closing stock

11. A trader buys £16 000 worth of goods and sells three-quarters of them for £20 000.
     His gross profit is:

    A £4 000   **B** £8 000   **C** £12 000   **D** £16 000

12. A trader operates a free delivery service to customers. The cost of this service is
     recorded in his accounts as:

    A carriage in, debited to the Profit and Loss Account
    B carriage out, debited to the Profit and Loss Account
    C carriage in, debited to the Trading Account
    D carriage out, debited to the Trading Account

Accruals and Prepayments of Expenses and Income; Capital and Revenue Expenditure

11.1 Introduction

The word *accruals* refers to amounts that are owing; *prepayments* clearly means amounts that have been paid in advance. In book-keeping these two words are usually used in connection with expenses and income.

We saw in Unit 8.3 that, at the end of a financial year, an expenses account or an income account which has been storing up information during the course of the year is 'emptied out' by transferring the balance to Profit and Loss Account. For example:

	Rent paid			
19–3	£	19–3		£
25 Mar. Bank	500	31 Dec. Profit and Loss		
30 Jun. Bank	500	Account		2 000
28 Sep. Bank	500			
31 Dec. Bank	500			
	2 000			2 000

The system works well provided that expenses and income are respectively paid or received *during the financial year to which they relate.* In this example it would seem that the business has rented premises for £2 000 a year, with the rent payable at the end of each quarter. Supposing, though, that the actual date of the fourth rent payment had been 3 January 19–4. If we prepare the Rent Paid Account as we have learnt so far it will appear as:

	Rent paid		
19–3	£	19–3	£
25 Mar. Bank	500	31 Dec. Profit and Loss	1 500
30 Jun. Bank	500	Account	
28 Sep. Bank	500		
	1 500		1 500

19–4	£
3 Jan. Bank	500

Something is wrong here: although the business paid £1 500 for rent during the course of the year, it is clear from the Rent Paid Account that the amount should have been £2 000—the payment due at the end of December wasn't paid until early January, that is, at 31 December 19–3 rent of £500 is accrued. To correct such 'timing differences', we need to make adjustments in the expenses and income accounts for *accruals* and *prepayments*.

11.2 Accruals of Expenses

With accruals we are concerned with expenses that are owing by a business at the end of an accounting period. Suppose that the following account appears in the books of a business at 31 December 19–1:

	Telephone	
19–1	£	
2 Apr. Bank	85	
27 Jun. Bank	92	
2 Oct. Bank	90	

The owner of the business tells you that he has received another bill for £102 covering his telephone expenses up to 31 December. He tells you that he has not yet paid this (he finally does so on 10 January 19–2).

When preparing the Profit and Loss Account for this business, we cannot transfer only the amounts that have been paid during the course of the year, that is, (£85 + £92 + £90) = £267. The last bill, even though it has not been paid within the accounting year, nevertheless forms a part of telephone expenses for 19–1. The transfer to Profit and Loss Account will amount to £369 (£267 already paid, plus £102 accrued, and relating to the financial year). This leaves a balance on the Telephone Account at 31 December 19–1 as follows:

	Telephone			
19–1	£	19–1		£
2 Apr. Bank	85	31 Dec. Profit and Loss Account		369
27 Jun. Bank	92			
2 Oct. Bank	90			
31 Dec. Balance c/d	102			
	369			369
		19–2		
		1 Jan. Balance b/d		102

This credit balance of the amount owing will be cleared when the bill is paid:

	Telephone		
19–2	£	19–2	£
10 Jan. Bank	102	1 Jan. Balance b/d	102

The account is now ready to receive payments made in 19–2.

A further point to note concerns the credit balance on Telephone Account at 31 December 19–1. We already know that all accounts with balances remaining at the year-end, after making transfers to the Trading and Profit and Loss Accounts, are entered on the balance sheet. An accruals account is no different and, as it has a credit balance, it is entered as a current liability:

Balance sheet (extract) of . . . as at 31 December 19–1		
Current liabilities:		£
Creditors		x
Bank overdraft		x
Accrual (telephone)		102

To summarize:

(*a*) For an expense, the transfer to Profit and Loss Account includes both the amounts that have been paid, and any amount owing at the year-end—that is, the amount that the business *should have paid*, rather than the amount actually paid.

(*b*) On the balance sheet the amount of any expenses accrued are recorded under the heading of current liabilities.

11.3   Prepayments of Expenses

As we have already seen, prepayments are expenses that are paid in advance, that is, although they have been paid in one accounting period, the expense relates to the next.

Consider a business that rents its offices at a rental of £750 each quarter, payable *in advance* on the first day of each quarter. If all went according to plan we would expect rent payments to be made by the firm on 1 January, 1 April, 1 July and 1 October. But supposing the Rent Paid Account for 19–6 looks like this:

	Rent paid
19–6	£
2 Jan. Bank	750
30 Mar. Bank	750
3 Jul. Bank	750
30 Sep. Bank	750
31 Dec. Bank	750

This shows us that during the year the business has paid £3 750 for rent. But we know that rent payable for the year is £3 000, so clearly the full amount should not be charged to Profit and Loss Account, but only the actual rent payable, £3 000:

	Rent paid			
19–6	£	19–6		£
2 Jan. Bank	750	31 Dec. Profit and Loss Account		3 000
30 Mar. Bank	750	31 Dec. Balance c/d		750
3 Jul. Bank	750			
30 Sep. Bank	750			
31 Dec. Bank	750			
	3 750			3 750
19–7	£			
1 Jan. Balance b/d	750			

At 1 January 19–7 there is a debit balance on the account, because the rent payment due on that date was prepaid on 31 December 19–6. This debit balance is entered on the balance sheet at 31 December 19–6 as a current asset:

Balance sheet (extract) of . . . as at 31 December 19–6

Current assets:	£
Stock	x
Debtors	x
Bank	x
Prepayment (rent)	750

The debit balance will be transferred to the Profit and Loss Account at the end of 19–7, together with the three further payments due in that year (subject to any accruals or prepayments!).

To summarize:

(a) For prepayment of expenses, the transfer to Profit and Loss Account is the amount showing on the expense account *less* the amount of the prepayment, that is, the amount that *should have been paid* for the year.

(b) On the balance sheet, prepaid expenses are shown as a current asset.

11.4   Accrual of Income

Just as expenses can be accrued or prepaid, so too can income, using the same rules.

Suppose that George Payne receives a commission for selling double glazing manufactured by another firm. As amounts of commission are received they are credited to a Commission Received Account. At the end of a year this account might appear as follows:

Commission received

19–3		£
2 Apr. Bank		120
5 Jun. Bank		210
17 Oct. Bank		150

At the end of Payne's financial year (31 December) he knows that a further commission payment of £140 is due in respect of double glazing already sold, and a cheque for this amount is received on 10 January 19–4. This means that the amount to be credited to Profit and Loss Account is £620 (the £480 actually received, together with the £140 due but not yet received). Commission Received Account will be balanced at the end of 19–3 in the following way:

Commission received

19–3	£	19–3	£
31 Dec. Profit and Loss Account	620	2 Apr. Bank	120
		5 Jun. Bank	210
		17 Oct. Bank	150
		31 Dec. Balance c/d	140
	620		620
19–4			
1 Jan. Balance b/d	140		

The debit balance on the account of £140 will feature in Payne's balance sheet:

Balance sheet (extract) of G. Payne as at 31 December 19–3

Current assets:	£
Stock	x
Debtors	x
Bank	x
Commission receivable	140

Alternatively, the amount of commission receivable could be included with debtors.

When the cheque for the commission is received on 10 January 19–4, the account will be cleared and is ready to receive amounts in respect of that financial year:

Commission received

19–4	£	19–4	£
1 Jan. Balance b/d	140	10 Jan. Bank	140

Point to notice:

Many accountants would argue that it is incorrect to anticipate income in this way, since there is no certainty the money will be received. This depends on circumstances, however, and if an examination question implies that the money certainly will be received or, indeed, already has been received during the period between the financial year-end and the date of preparation of the accounts, the amount should be included as an accrual of income.

11.5   Prepayment of Income

We have just seen that a business which receives money for providing a service is often owed amounts at the end of a financial year. In the same way, income amounts due to the business could be paid in advance.

Suppose that a firm rents out part of its premises, that is, it has a rental income which will be credited to Rent Received Account, and that the rent is £1 000 for each quarter of the year, payable on the first day of each quarter. Thus, if all goes according to plan, the business ought to receive rent of £1 000 on 1 January, 1 April, 1 July and 1 October, and would transfer £4 000 to the credit side of Profit and Loss Account. On 31 December 19–1, however, Rent Received Account is as follows:

Rent received

19–1	£
2 Jan. Bank	1 000
30 Mar. Bank	1 000
2 Jul. Bank	1 000
30 Sep. Bank	1 000
30 Dec. Bank	1 000

Clearly, the tenant has paid the first quarter's rent of 19–2 a few days early. The transfer to Profit and Loss Account for the year ended 31 December 19–1 will be £4 000, and the additional £1 000 will be carried down to 19–2:

Rent received

19–1	£	19–1	£
31 Dec. Profit and Loss		2 Jan. Bank	1 000
Account	4 000	30 Mar. Bank	1 000
31 Dec. Balance c/d	1 000	2 Jul. Bank	1 000
		30 Sep. Bank	1 000
		30 Dec. Bank	1 000
	5 000		5 000
		19–2	
		1 Jan. Balance b/d	1 000

On the balance sheet at 31 December 19–1 the amount of rent received in advance will appear under the heading 'current liabilities', either added to creditors or shown as a separate item described as 'rent receivable prepaid'.

As one quarter's rent has been paid in advance the tenant will need to make only three payments during 19–2. Therefore the transfer to Profit and Loss Account at the end of that year will be £4 000, and Rent Received Account will have a nil balance (assuming that there are no amounts paid in advance or owing by the tenant).

11.6   Stocks of Office Supplies

When a business buys items such as stationery, postage stamps and so forth, it usually charges the entire cost to the year's Profit and Loss Account. Technically the stock of such items should be valued at the year-end and the valuation carried down into next year's accounts, thus reducing the charge for the expense in the current year's accounts. In practice this is done only where the stock of such items is sufficient to affect the accounts substantially—the firm's accountant will decide the level at which a carry-down will operate.

Example

The Postages Account has the following balance at the financial year-end:

Postages

19–1	£
31 Dec. Balance b/d	325

At 31 December, the stock of postage stamps is found to amount to £105. It is decided to carry this amount down to next year. The account will appear as:

Postages

19–1	£	19–1	£
31 Dec. Balance b/d	325	31 Dec. Profit and Loss Account	220
		31 Dec. Balance c/d	105
	325		325
19–2			
1 Jan. Balance b/d	105		

Thus £220 is charged to the Profit and Loss Account—it represents the amount of postage stamps actually used, while the year-end stock is carried to next year. In the balance sheet at 31 December 19–1 the stock of postage stamps will be shown as a current asset.

11.7   Filling in Missing Figures

There are likely to be four separate figures making up an expense or an income account. These are:

(*a*) amount owing or prepaid at the beginning of the year;
(*b*) amount paid or received during the course of the year;
(*c*) amount that is to be transferred to Profit and Loss Account at the year-end, that is, the amount that should have been paid or received;
(*d*) amount owing or prepaid at the end of the year.

Knowing any three, we can always find the fourth 'missing figure' by constructing the expense or income account. For example, suppose that we are given the following information about insurance for the year:

(*a*) prepaid at beginning of year £55;
(*b*) amount to be transferred to Profit and Loss Account £275;
(*c*) amount owing at the end of the year £20.

If we are asked to calculate how much was paid for insurance during the year, we can prepare an Insurance Account as follows:

Insurance

	£		£
1 Jan. Balance b/d	55	31 Dec. Profit and Loss Account	275
Bank (*missing figure*)	200		
31 Dec. Balance c/d	20		
	275		275
		1 Jan. Balance b/d	20

By filling in the missing figure (bank), we can tell that £200 was paid during the course of the year.

11.8   Private Expenses

Sometimes it is agreed that a proportion of certain expenses of the business shall be charged to the owner as private expenses—examples might include telephone expenses or car running expenses. All the particular expenses are then debited to the expense account during the year in the normal way. At the year-end, the agreed proportion is debited to the owner's Drawings Account, while the balance is debited to Profit and Loss Account in the normal way.

Example

The following is the balance of the Telephone Expenses Account at the financial year-end:

Telephone

19–1	£
31 Dec. Balance b/d	240

It is agreed that one-quarter shall be charged to the owner for private use, and three-quarters to the business. The account then appears as:

Telephone

19–1	£	19–1	£
31 Dec. Balance b/d	240	31 Dec. Drawings	60
		31 Dec. Profit and Loss Account	180
	240		240

11.9 Capital Expenditure and Revenue Expenditure

Capital expenditure is money spent by a business on the purchase of fixed assets for use in the business and not for immediate resale, or on their alteration or improvement; it includes any costs of delivering or installing fixed assets, and the legal costs of buying land and buildings. *Revenue expenditure* is money spent on the running expenses of a business: that is, the *maintenance* of fixed assets, the costs of administering the business and of selling and distributing goods, and the cost of purchase of stock acquired with the intention of resale. Thus the cost of a new van is capital expenditure; money spent on petrol, insurance and repairs, on the other hand, is revenue expenditure. Capital expenditure is shown in the balance sheet, and revenue expenditure in the Profit and Loss Account.

It is important to classify expenditure correctly in a book-keeping system; otherwise net profit will be wrongly stated, or the balance sheet will show incorrect amounts, even though it will still balance. For example, if the cost price of the van was debited to Profit and Loss Account, net profit would be considerably reduced, or even turned into a net loss. At the same time the van would not appear in the balance sheet—this is clearly wrong because the business owns the van as a fixed asset.

Sometimes the distinction between capital and revenue expenditure is not as clear-cut as this. Look at these items of expenditure and decide which they are:

(*a*) *Cost of building an extension to offices £10 000 (includes £500 for repairs to existing offices).*

£500 is recorded in Repairs Account and shown in the Profit and Loss Account, being revenue expenditure;

£9 500 is additional fixed assets.

(b) *Wages (including wages of employees amounting to £1 000 for working on improvements to the premises) £12 000.*

£11 000 is recorded as an expense and debited in Profit and Loss Account as revenue expenditure;
£1 000 is added to the fixed asset of premises as capital expenditure.

(c) *Carriage inwards of £1 000 includes £100 carriage on a new machine.*

£900 is charged to the Trading Account as revenue expenditure;
£100 is added to the cost of the machine.

(d) *Legal costs of £1 500 include £650 relating to the purchase of a piece of land.*

£850 is debited to Profit and Loss Account;
£650 is added to the cost of the land as a fixed asset.

As you can see, the object of distinguishing between capital expenditure and revenue expenditure is to allocate costs correctly between the balance sheet and the Trading and Profit and Loss Accounts. Only if this is done correctly will the final accounts reflect accurately the state of the business.

11.10 Preparing Final Accounts from a Trial Balance

Several exercises at the end of this Unit (and later Units) require you to prepare the final or year-end accounts of a business—Trading and Profit and Loss Accounts, and balance sheet—from a trial balance. At first you will find the trial balance to be fairly short, and there will be two or three adjustments to be made which are given to you as a note to the trial balance. Here is a typical examination question:

The following trial balance was extracted from the double-entry book-keeping accounts of Albert Simmonds on 31 December 19–3:

	£	£
Stock (1 January 19–3)	7 000	
Purchases	30 000	
Sales		40 000
Rates	1 600	
Heating and lighting	1 500	
Salaries	1 700	
Postage and packing	1 400	
Premises	65 000	
Fixtures and fittings	7 500	
Debtors	5 500	
Creditors		3 700
Bank	2 500	
Capital		85 000
Drawings	5 000	
	128 700	128 700

You are required to take the following into consideration on 31 December 19–3:

  (i) Stock   £9 500
  (ii) Rates paid in advance   £ 400
 (iii) Salaries owing   £ 300

Prepare Trading and Profit and Loss Accounts for the year ended 31 December 19–3, and a balance sheet at that date.

When attempting such a question, all we have to do is to rearrange the trial balance, taking the notes into consideration, so that the final accounts are produced: these should mean more to the owner of the business than a trial balance can do. The important rules to follow are:

  (*a*) each item from the trial balance appears in the final accounts *once only*;
  (*b*) each adjustment or note appears—or affects an item—in the final accounts *twice* (if this is not done, the balance sheet will not balance!).

It is a good idea—certainly at first—to go through the trial balance and adjustments marking against each the final account into which it will go. Thus the trial balance figures for stock, purchases and sales can be marked with a 'T' (for Trading Account); rates, heating and lighting, salaries, and postage and packing can be marked with 'P & L' (for Profit and Loss Account); all the other trial balance figures can be marked 'BS' (for balance sheet). The adjustments or notes for this question can be marked as follows:

Stock	T and BS
Rates paid in advance	P & L and BS
Salaries owing	P & L and BS

As the final accounts are prepared, each item can be ticked as it is entered. When the final accounts are completed it is a simple matter to see if each trial balance item is ticked once, and each adjustment or note twice.

  A word now about this particular question:

  (*a*) The opening stock is found in the trial balance, while the closing stock is given as a note—this is often true of questions of this type.

  (*b*) Rates must be adjusted to allow for the prepayment. The trial balance tells us that £1 600 has been paid for rates but the note explains that £400 has been paid in advance for next year. This means that the Profit and Loss Account must be charged with £1 200 (the amount that should have been paid) and the prepayment must be shown in the balance sheet as a current asset.

  (*c*) The trial balance shows that salaries of £1 700 have been paid during the year, but that £300 is owing at the year-end. Thus £2 000 (what should have been paid) must be charged in the Profit and Loss Account, with £300 showing in the balance sheet as an amount owing (accrual).

The answer to this question is as follows:

Trading Account of Albert Simmonds for the year ended 31 December 19–3

	£		£
Opening stock (1 Jan.)	7 000	Sales	40 000
Add Purchases	30 000		
	37 000		
Less Closing stock (31 Dec.)	9 500		
Cost of goods sold	27 500		
Gross profit c/d	12 500		
	40 000		40 000

Profit and Loss Account of Albert Simmonds for the year ended 31 December 19–3

	£		£
Rates	1 200	Gross profit b/d	12 500
Heating and lighting	1 500		
Salaries	2 000		
Postage and packing	1 400		
Net profit	6 400		
	12 500		12 500

Balance sheet of Albert Simmonds as at 31 December 19–3

	£		£
Fixed assets:		Capital:	85 000
Premises	65 000	*Add* Net profit	6 400
Fixtures and fittings	7 500		91 400
	72 500	*Less* Drawings	5 000
Current assets:			86 400
Stock	9 500		
Debtors	5 500	Current liabilities:	
Bank	2 500	Creditors	3 700
Rates prepaid	400	Salaries accrued	300
	90 400		90 400

It is particularly enjoyable when final accounts balance first time and, with care, they should. You will come across further examples later on in this book, getting progressively more complex. If you tackle them logically—like all book-keeping and accounts—you too will find them easy.

11.11 Questions

*1. M. Wallace hires a car from H. Ford at a quarterly rental of £300. During 19–1 Wallace made the following payments to Ford:

January	1	£300 (cheque)
April	8	£300 (cash)
July	5	£100 (cheque)
July	9	£200 (cash)
October	29	£250 (cash)

You are to prepare the Car Hire Account in the books of Wallace, showing clearly the transfer to the Profit and Loss Account on 31 December 19–1.

[*East Anglian Examinations Board*]

2. P. Jones, a sole trader, had the following account balances on 1 January Year 7:

    (i) Rent payable   Cr. £70
    (ii) Insurance   Dr. £40
    (iii) Telephone   Cr. £45
    (iv) Rates   Dr. £210

During the year, the following payments were made by cheque:

Year 7		£
1 Jan.	Rent payable (quarterly, in advance)	210
1 Feb.	Insurance premium for year to 31 January Year 8	600
1 Feb.	Telephone bill	127
1 Mar.	Rent payable (increased amount)	300
1 May	Telephone bill	146
1 May	Rates for half year to 30 September Year 7	540
1 Jun.	Rent payable	300
1 Aug.	Telephone bill	163
1 Sep.	Rent Payable	300
1 Nov.	Rates for the half year to 31 March Year 8	540
1 Nov.	Telephone bill	184
1 Dec.	Rent payable	300

P. Jones calculates that at the end of the financial year, 31 December Year 7, he owes £60 for telephone calls.

Required:

Open the four accounts listed above, and post the necessary entries to them. Balance the accounts and make the appropriate transfers to the Profit and Loss Account for the year ended 31 December Year 7.

[*London Chamber of Commerce*]

3.   (a) On 31 May 19–2 J. Dougall's balance sheet showed that he had paid rates in advance of £600. On 17 November 19–2 J. Dougall paid his rates for the second half of the rating year to 31 March 19–3 £900. On 13 May 19–3 J. Dougall paid an instalment of rates £1 200 which covered the period 1 April to 30 September 19–3. J. Dougall's financial year ended on 31 May 19–3.

Write up his Rates Account for the year, showing clearly the amount to be charged to Profit and Loss Account, and the amount to be carried forward to the next financial year.

(b) On 31 May 19–2 R. Sparrow held in stock packing materials to the value of £621. During the year his purchases of packing material totalled £1 890. On 31 May 19–3 his packing material in stock was valued at £480.

Write up the Packing Materials Account for the year showing clearly the amount to be charged to Profit and Loss Account, and the amount to be carried forward to the next financial year.

[*Royal Society of Arts*]

4. T. Jones has occupied a property since 1 May 19–0. Rent has been paid as follows:

30 May19–0	£150 for the three months ended 31 July 19–0
25 August 19–0	£300 for the six months ended 31 January 19–1
12 February 19–1	£360 for the six months ended 31 July 19–1

During the whole of this period he has sublet part of this property to D. Smith at an annual rent of £360 and has received rent as follows:

31 July 19–0	£90
30 November 19–0	£90
28 February 19–1	£90

Write up separate Rent Receivable and Rent Payable Accounts as they would appear in Jones's books showing the amounts he transferred to his Profit and Loss Account for the year ended 30 April 19–1.

[Royal Society of Arts]

5. (i) L. George rents his premises at an annual rental of £1 200. On June 1 19–3 George had paid his rent up to the end of July, and during the year ended 31 May 19–4 he made the following payments for rent, by cheque:

August 1	£300
November 5	£300
February 1	£300
June 1	£400

(ii) George sublets part of these premises to S. Broke at a rent of £480 per annum, and on June 1 19–3 Broke's rent was one month in arrears. During the year ended 31 May 19–4 George received the following amounts in cash from Broke:

July 25	£40
August 18	£120
December 4	£150
April 9	£60

(iii) On June 1 19–3 George owed the Electricity Board £74 for electricity supplies up to that date, during the year he made the following payments by cheque:

June 1	£74
September 10	£82
December 5	£104
April 7	£81

On 31 May 19–4 there was a balance outstanding on the Electricity Account of £96.

You are required:

(a) to write up George's Rent Payable Account, Rent Receivable Account and Electricity Account for the year ended 31 May 19–4 showing clearly the amounts to be transferred to the Profit and Loss Account in each case, and

(b) to show how the balances brought down would appear in the balance sheet on 31 May 19–4.

[Royal Society of Arts]

*6. Allocate the following between capital and revenue expenditure, giving reasons:

   (*a*) purchase of new vehicle;
   (*b*) fuel for vehicles;
   (*c*) new tyres for vehicles;
   (*d*) vehicle insurance;
   (*e*) radio equipment fitted to vehicle.

[Pitman Examinations Institute]

7.   (*a*) With the use of your own examples, illustrate what is meant by the two terms 'capital expenditure' and 'revenue expenditure'.

   (*b*) As a local sweet and tobacco retailer you pay for the following:

   (i) a new cash register,
   (ii) wages for part-time assistant,
   (iii) the electricity bill,
   (iv) fire insurance premium on the premises,
   (v) a new show case for the shop,
   (vi) new light fittings,
   (vii) repairs to the shop blind.

Which items would you classify as capital expenditure and which as revenue expenditure? Give brief reasons for your answers.

[Royal Society of Arts]

*8. George Price is the proprietor of a small business. He keeps his financial records on double-entry principles and extracted the following trial balance on 31 May 19–3:

	£		£
Stock 1 June 19–2	7 000	Capital 1 June 19–2	85 000
Cash at bank	8 000	Creditors	3 700
Furniture and fittings	7 500	Sales	40 000
Premises	65 000		
Rates	1 600		
Purchases	30 000		
Heating and lighting	1 500		
Cleaning	1 700		
Packing materials	1 400		
Drawings	5 000		
	128 700		128 700

You are required to take the following into consideration on 31 May 19–3:

	£
(i) Stock on hand	9 500
(ii) Rates paid in advance	400
(iii) Stock of packing material	300

and prepare a Trading and Profit and Loss Account for the year ended 31 May 19–3 and a balance sheet at that date.

[Royal Society of Arts]

9. The following trial balance was extracted from the books of Edwina Anderson on 28 February 19–9.

Trial balance on 28 February 19–9

	£	£
Capital		69 890
Drawings	5 400	
Bank overdraft		3 000
Cash in hand	500	
Salaries	9 540	
Purchases and sales	22 100	45 650
Debtors and creditors	10 100	8 700
Office expenses	2 150	
Lighting and heating	1 200	
Rent and rates	1 000	
Premises	50 000	
Equipment	2 100	
Vehicles	12 100	
Stock on 1 March 19–8	10 900	
Returns in and out	800	650
	127 890	127 890

Additional information on 28 February 19–9:

(i)	Stock on 28 February 19–9	£11 800
(ii)	Office expenses owing	£25
(iii)	Rates prepaid	£220
(iv)	There was an outstanding bill for repairs to the motor van £500.	

You are required to:
Prepare the Trading and Profit and Loss Account for the year ending 28 February 19–9 and a balance sheet on that date.

[*RSA Examinations Board*]

10. Compupro is a small computer and data processing bureau. In a certain trading period it enters into the following transactions :

(*a*) The purchase of supplies of computer print-out paper, all of which is expected to be used within the current trading period.

(*b*) The renewal of insurance on the computer hardware.

(*c*) Expenditure on increasing the security to the building in which the bureau's facilities are situated.

(*d*) The wages of the computer operators.

(*e*) The adding of extra storage capacity to a mainframe computer used within the bureau.

Required:
State in respect of each of the above whether you would treat the item as capital expenditure or revenue expenditure, giving the reason for your choice.

[*London Chamber of Commerce*]

Value Added Tax

12.1 Value Added Tax

This form of taxation—abbreviated to VAT—is in use in many countries as a tax on the supply of goods and services. It is eventually borne by the final consumer, but is collected at each stage of the production and distribution chain, wherever 'value' is added.

A wholesaler buying goods from a manufacturer is charged VAT on items purchased (on *input* to the wholesaler); when the goods are sold (on *output*) to retailers, the wholesaler charges VAT calculated on the price of goods. The wholesaler then pays to the tax authorities the *difference* between *tax charged* to customers and *tax paid* to suppliers, that is, the surplus between tax paid on inputs and charged on outputs. (The rate for VAT varies from time to time; most examinations use a rate of 10 per cent and this rate will be used throughout this book.)

Let us look at an example.

Wholesaler

10 Mar. 19–1 Buys goods from manufacturer, AB:	
£1 000 plus VAT at 10 per cent: value of inputs (excluding VAT)	£1 000
18 Mar. 19–1 Sells goods to retailer, CD:	
£1 200 plus VAT at 10 per cent: value of outputs (excluding VAT)	£1 200
Value added	£ 200

VAT movements:	
Paid to manufacturer by wholesaler	£100
Collected from retailer by wholesaler	£120
Paid to tax authorities by wholesaler	£ 20

12.2 The Use of a VAT Account

In the example in Unit 12.1, the wholesaler will not send a cheque to the tax authorities for each individual transaction. Instead, settlement of VAT is made on a quarterly basis and, pending payment, amounts are stored in a *VAT Account*.

The VAT Account is:

(*a*) debited with the amount of VAT paid on purchases from suppliers, and
(*b*) credited with the amount of VAT charged on sales to customers.

We will now see how the two transactions considered in Unit 12.1 would be entered into the double-entry book-keeping accounts. Here are the two transactions again:

10 Mar. 19–1   *Bought goods £1 000 on credit from AB.*
18 Mar. 19–1   *Sold goods £1 200 on credit to CD.*

Both transactions are subject to VAT at 10 per cent.

Purchases

19–1	£
10 Mar. AB	1 000

Sales

		19–1	£
		18 Mar. CD	1 200

AB

		19–1	£
		10 Mar. Purchases	1 100

CD

19–1	£
18 Mar. Sales	1 320

Value Added Tax

19–1	£	19–1	£
10 Mar. AB	100	18 Mar. CD	120

Points to notice:

(*a*) Purchases Account has been debited with the amount of purchases *exclusive* of VAT. Similarly, Sales Account has been credited with the amount of sales *exclusive* of VAT.

(*b*) The personal account of AB, the manufacturer, has been credited with the amount of purchases *inclusive* of VAT. Similarly the account of CD, a retailer, has been debited with the amount of sales *inclusive* of VAT.

(*c*) If these were the only two transactions for March 19–1, the VAT Account would show a credit balance of £20 at the end of the month:

Value Added Tax

19–1	£	19–1	£
10 Mar. AB	100	18 Mar. CD	120
31 Mar. Balance c/d	20		
	120		120
		19–1	
		1 Apr. Balance b/d	20

This means that £20 is owing to the tax authorities, and will be paid to them in due course. If a balance sheet was prepared on 31 March, this amount would be listed among the other creditors.

When a business incurs capital expenditure, such as the purchase of a machine, it is charged VAT on the cost of the asset. When a firm is VAT-registered (small firms with sales below certain amounts are not usually VAT-registered) it can reclaim the VAT paid, or at least set the amount off against VAT payments due to the tax authorities. For example, a machine bought for

£500 will, with VAT included, cost a total of £550. The book-keeping entries will be:

Dr. Machinery Account	£500
Dr. Value Added Tax Account	£ 50
Cr. Bank Account	£550

Here the VAT amount of £50 is debited to VAT Account—if there were no other transactions during the quarter this would be repaid to the firm by the tax authorities. For most firms, however, the £50 simply reduces the amount to be paid to the tax authorities at the end of the quarter.

12.3   Zero-rated Goods

Most goods and services are subject to VAT. Certain goods carry a *zero rate* of VAT, however; at the time of writing, examples in the United Kingdom include food and children's clothing. Where goods are zero-rated a trader cannot charge VAT to the ultimate purchaser, though VAT can be reclaimed on purchased inputs of materials or components for manufacture or assembly into zero-rated goods; this means that the tax authorities will owe money to the trader. In such circumstances, the VAT Account has a debit balance and, on the trader's balance sheet, is included among the debtors.

12.4   VAT Calculations

If the rate of VAT is 10 per cent, then we know that goods which cost £100 excluding VAT will be £110 when VAT is included. If we were told the *VAT-inclusive* amount was £110 and were asked to calculate the *VAT-exclusive* amount, we would carry out the following calculation:

$$£110 \times \frac{10}{11} = \underline{\underline{£100}}$$

Thus, with VAT at 10 per cent, multiplying the VAT-inclusive amount by 10/11 will give the VAT-exclusive amount. The VAT fraction, therefore, at this rate of tax is 1/11 of the VAT-inclusive amount. Later on in this book, you will see that we need to know both the VAT amount and the VAT-exclusive amount for further recording in a cash book (Unit 15.8), a journal (Unit 17.4), and a petty cash book (Unit 21.6).

12.5   Questions

*1.   Enter the following transactions for the month into the accounts of Sandra Burns, balance each account at the month-end, and extract a trial balance at 31 January 19–1. VAT is to be taken at the rate of 10 per cent.

19–1

3 Jan.	Bought goods on credit from S. Hythe £100 + VAT.
5 Jan.	Bought goods on credit from L. Layton £150 + VAT.
6 Jan.	Cash sales £80 + VAT, paid direct into the bank.
8 Jan.	Sold goods on credit to T. Lancaster £100 + VAT.
10 Jan.	Cash sales £110 + VAT, paid direct into the bank.
13 Jan.	Paid S. Hythe the amount owing by cheque.
16 Jan.	Bought a machine £200 + VAT on credit from Machinery Ltd.
19 Jan.	T. Lancaster settles his account by cheque.
24 Jan.	Cash sales £150 + VAT, paid direct into the bank.
26 Jan.	Bought goods on credit from L. Layton £80 + VAT.
30 Jan.	Paid Machinery Ltd the amount owing by cheque.

*2.   (a) Clearly distinguish between VAT inputs and VAT outputs.

(b) A. Wise made the following purchases and sales on credit during the three months ended 31 December 19–1.

Purchases:

19–1	October	£6 000 + VAT
	November	£8 000 + VAT
	December	£9 000 + VAT

Sales:

	October	£9 000 + VAT
	November	£10 000 + VAT
	December	£15 000 + VAT

VAT is to be taken at the rate of 10 per cent.

Prepare the VAT Account of A. Wise for the three months ended 31 December 19–1. Any outstanding amount payable to the Customs and Excise should be remitted by cheque on 31 December 19–1.

[*Royal Society of Arts*]

3.   Enter the following transactions for the month into the accounts of William Elliott, balance each account at the month-end, and extract a trial balance at 30 April 19–4. VAT is to be taken at the rate of 10 per cent.

19–4

2 Apr.	Bought goods on credit from A. Wood £200 + VAT.
4 Apr.	Bought office equipment from A–Z Ltd £150 + VAT.
7 Apr.	Cash sales £100 + VAT, paid direct into the bank.
10 Apr.	Bought goods on credit from S. Hodgson £180 + VAT.
14 Apr.	Cash sales £110 + VAT, paid direct into the bank.
17 Apr.	Paid the amount owing to A. Wood by cheque.
20 Apr.	Sold goods £190 + VAT on credit to P. McCann.
22 Apr.	Cash sales £150 + VAT, paid direct into the bank.
24 Apr.	Paid salaries £85 by cheque.
27 Apr.	P. McCann settles her account by cheque.
30 Apr.	Paid the amount owing to A–Z Ltd by cheque.

4. The following is a summary of purchases and sales and the relevant figures for VAT for the three months ended 31 March 19–4:

Purchases:

		£	VAT £
19–4	January	20 000	2 000
	February	21 000	2 100
	March	22 000	2 200

Sales:

	January	21 000	2 100
	February	20 000	2 000
	March	15 000	1 500

Required:

(a) Write up and balance the VAT Account for the three months to 31 March 19–4.

(b) Explain briefly the significance of the balance and how it will be cleared.

[Royal Society of Arts]

'Have you a card for a small businessman who is being investigated by the
VAT people?'

Multiple-choice Questions—4

Read each question carefully. Choose the *one* answer you think is correct. Answers are given on page 411.

1. A debit balance on the Rates Account after the transfer to Profit and Loss Account indicates:

   A   an asset and a prepayment   **C**   an asset and an accrual
   B   a liability and an accrual   **D**   a liability and a prepayment

2. A credit balance on the Rent Account after the transfer to Profit and Loss Account indicates:

   A   a liability and a prepayment   **C**   an asset and a prepayment
   B   an asset and an accrual   **D**   a liability and an accrual

3. Which one of the following is a current liability?

   A   heating and lighting accrued   **C**   debtor for rent
   B   loan   **D**   rates repaid

4. At the beginning of its financial year, a firm has a debit balance of £50 on its Rent Paid Account. During the year the firm pays rent of £250, and has a credit balance of £25 on the account at the year-end. The amount charged to Profit and Loss Account for rent for the year should be:

   A   £325   **B**   £275   **C**   £175   **D**   £250

5. Which one of the following is revenue expenditure?

   A   purchase of a filing cabinet for the office
   B   a quarterly electricity bill
   C   legal costs for purchase of property
   D   cost of extension to building

6. Which one of the following is capital expenditure?

   A   repairs to motor vehicles
   B   goods taken by the owner for own use
   C   installation costs of a machine
   D   renewing the electrical wiring in the office

7. A machine purchased for use in a business is:

   A   revenue expenditure appearing in the Profit and Loss Account
   B   capital expenditure appearing in the balance sheet
   C   expenditure added to purchases in the Trading Account
   D   capital receipt added to capital in the balance sheet

8. Wages paid to men for redecorating the office are:

   A   credited to Profit and Loss Account   **C**   capital expenditure
   B   debited to Trading Account   **D**   revenue expenditure

9. A typewriter costs £250 excluding VAT. If VAT is at a rate of 10 per cent the price including VAT is:

   A   £265   **B**   £285   **C**   £225   **D**   £275

10. A machine costs £165 including VAT. If VAT is at a rate of 10 per cent the price excluding VAT is:

   A £151.50   **B** £148.50   **C** £150   **D** £181.50

11. A VAT-registered firm buys a machine for £1 000 (excluding VAT) and pays by cheque. If VAT is at a rate of 10 per cent, this transaction should be recorded by:

	Debit	*Credit*
A	Machinery Account £1 000	Bank Account £1 000
B	Machinery Account £1 000	VAT Account £100;
		Machinery Account £900
C	VAT Account £100;	Bank Account £1 100
	Machinery Account £1 000	
D	Machinery Account £1 100	Bank Account £1 100

12. A debit balance on a firm's VAT Account means

   A the firm owes VAT to the tax authorities
   B the tax authorities owe VAT to the firm
   C the firm has made a profit
   D an error has been made: VAT Account can only have a credit balance

Business Documents

13.1 Introduction

A great many money transactions can be completed with the minimum of documentation. For example, buying a newspaper or packet of sweets is a cash transaction for which the only documentation may be a receipt from the shop's cash till. But many goods are bought and sold on credit, and it is therefore usual for other documents to be prepared detailing the money amounts concerned, often including a description of the goods and the terms of sale. Such documents are important in maintaining accurate records.

In this Unit, we will look in turn at the following common business documents: purchase order, invoice, statement, credit and debit notes, and receipts.

13.2 Purchase Order

A purchase order (see Fig. 13.1) is prepared by a firm that wishes to buy certain goods. It is sent to the firm that is to supply them. Details to be found on a purchase order include:

(*a*) name of firm sending the order;
(*b*) name of firm who is to supply the goods;
(*c*) date;
(*d*) full description of goods, often together with price;
(*e*) quantity required;
(*f*) number of purchase order;
(*g*) signature of person ordering the goods.

Most purchase orders are *numbered* so that control is maintained in issuing them; also the order will be *signed* by a person, such as a buyer, who has authority to make purchases on behalf of the firm. These two controls ensure that goods are not ordered by some unauthorized person within the firm who intends, when the goods are delivered, to intercept them and take them for personal use. Those who order goods on behalf of a firm will have different authority levels. Thus the order to purchase stationery would be authorized at a lower level than an order to purchase new machinery or a new factory, which would certainly need approval from the owner or owners of the business. When a firm that is to supply goods receives a purchase order, it will:

(*a*) ensure that the goods are in stock;
(*b*) check the creditworthiness of the customer.

With a customer who is unknown to the firm it is sensible to check his or her creditworthiness by asking for references—much as an employer asks a poten-

```
                    Newtown Manufacturing Co Ltd
PURCHASE            Unit 64, Anfield Industrial Estate
                    Redditch, Worcestershire B98 8HL
ORDER               Telephone: Redditch (0527) 94482
```

Ace Industrial Suppliers Ltd
84 Smallbrook Ringway
Birmingham B2 8AQ

Date of order	Date required	For queries, please contact	Order No
3 January 19-1	31 January 19-1	Mr M. Lloyd	**0621**

Quantity	Description	Product No	Price
50	Electric motors	A 241	£10-50 each

Please quote Order No on delivery advice,
invoice and other correspondence

For Newtown Manufacturing Co Ltd

J. Smith

Buyer

Fig. 13.1 A purchase order

tial employee for references. Suitable referees might include the customer's bank, and other businesses where he or she is known. A letter can then be sent to each referee asking if the customer is good for credit of a certain amount. Assuming satisfactory replies are received, the customer is given a credit limit which should not normally be exceeded. Once a credit limit has been set, a check will be made whenever a further order is received from the customer, to ensure that the credit limit will not be exceeded if this latest order is dispatched.

If everything is in order, the goods are taken from stock and the stock records (see Unit 31) altered. The goods are then packed for dispatch, and an *advice/delivery/consignment note* is prepared, one copy of which is posted to the customer, another copy is sent with the goods, while a third copy may be given to the carrier who can then obtain a receipt for the goods when they are delivered. (The procedures for dealing with the receipt and stockholding of goods by a firm's stores are covered in Unit 31.2.)

INVOICE		**ACE INDUSTRIAL SUPPLIERS LTD** *84 SMALLBROOK RINGWAY* *BIRMINGHAM B2 8AQ* Telephone: (021) 236 47582 VAT No: 471 4719 81			

Newtown Manufacturing Co Ltd
Unit 64, Anfield Industrial Estate
REDDITCH
Worcestershire B98 8HL

Your Order No	Goods sent by	Date sent	Invoice date (Tax Point)	Invoice No
0621	our driver	10 January 19-1	10 January 19-1	**0871**

Quantity	Description	Unit price	Total value	VAT at 10%	Total amount
50	ELECTRIC MOTORS Catalogue no A241	£10-50	£525-00	£52-50	£577-50
				INVOICE TOTAL	£577-50

Terms: Net 30 days from Invoice Date

Fig. 13.2 An invoice

13.3   Invoice

When the goods have been dispatched the supplying firm will prepare an *invoice* (see Fig. 13.2). An invoice contains the following information:

(*a*) name and address of seller;
(*b*) name and address of buyer;
(*c*) date;
(*d*) number of invoice;

(e) customer's order number;

(f) details of goods supplied;

(g) unit costs of goods supplied (taken from the firm's catalogue, or separate price lists) together with total money amount;

(h) amount of trade discount allowed (if any);

(i) carriage charges (if applicable);

(j) terms of settlement, including any cash discount allowed for quick settlement.

Two terms in this list need some explanation.

Trade discount ((h) above) is frequently deducted where the supplying firm is selling goods to another business, rather than to members of the public. For example, if you buy some spare parts for your car from a 'main dealer' garage you will be charged the normal retail price (often known as the *recommended retail price*); however, if you were the owner of a small garage the main dealer would allow you a trade discount on those same parts.

Cash discount (in (j) above) is often allowed by supplying firms to encourage prompt settlement by the buyer. Thus many invoices have printed on them '2½ per cent cash discount if paid within one month'. This means that for an invoice for an amount of £100, say, the buyer can choose either to settle within one month from the date of the invoice and will then pay £97.50, or to settle in more than one month, paying the full £100.

Some invoices—and other business documents—include the letters 'E & OE'. This old-fashioned expression stands for 'Errors and Omissions Excepted', and means that if there are any errors on the document, such as a wrong price, the issuing firm is not bound legally to the incorrect copy and may issue a revised one.

If the firm supplying the goods is VAT-registered, the invoice also shows its VAT registration number. In addition, where the goods supplied are subject to VAT, tax is added to the total amount of the invoice after trade discount has been deducted. Where the terms of trade include cash discount, the VAT amount is always calculated on the *invoice amount less cash discount*. This method of calculating the VAT applies whether or not the cash discount is taken. For example:

Invoice total (after deduction of trade discount, if any) before calculation of VAT	£100.00
Less 2½ per cent cash discount if paid within one month	£ 2.50
	£ 97.50
VAT at 10 per cent	£ 9.75
Amount due, if paid within one month	£107.25

If the buyer chooses not to take advantage of the cash discount and settles after one month, the amount payable will be £109.75 (£107.25 + £2.50 cash discount disallowed). The VAT amount remains unchanged, however: where a cash discount is offered, VAT is calculated on the net amount after deducting the discount, whether it is taken or not.

When a firm that has ordered goods receives an invoice from a supplier it should ensure, before passing it for payment, that:

(a) the goods stated on the invoice have been received, are in good condition, and are as ordered;

(b) the price charged on the invoice agrees with the price on the purchase order, or is the same as that previously agreed with the supplier;

(c) discounts—both trade and cash—are as agreed;

(d) a check has been made on the arithmetic of the invoice, for example, on unit price × number of units ordered, trade discount, VAT amount, cash discount.

13.4   Statement

Sometimes customers will pay a supplier against an invoice. Most customers wait until they receive a *statement of account* (see Fig. 13.3). This is prepared by the supplier at regular intervals—often monthly—and summarizes the transactions (in date order) that have taken place on the customer's account since the last statement. Thus a statement shows:

(a) the balance from the previous month (if any);

(b) money amounts of invoices (including VAT) sent out during the month;

(c) amounts of money received during the month, together with cash discount allowed to the customer;

(d) the amount of credit notes (see Unit 13.5), including VAT;

(e) the balance owing at the end of the month.

In theory, the balance of a statement of account received from a supplier should agree with the balance on the creditor's account showing in the buyer's books. Apart from any errors that may appear either on the statement or on the creditor's (supplier's) account, there are three other main reasons for discrepancies:

(a) goods in transit,

(b) payments in the post, and

(c) returns outwards.

Consider this creditor's account in the books of J. Bull:

A. Smith

19–1	£	19–1	£
16 Jan. Bank	150	1 Jan. Balance b/d	150
29 Jan. Bank	75	15 Jan. Purchases	75
31 Jan. Returns outwards	20	20 Jan. Purchases	90
31 Jan. Balance c/d	70		
	315		315
		1 Feb. Balance b/d	70

```
┌─────────────────────────────────────────────────────────────────┐
│                           ACE INDUSTRIAL SUPPLIERS LTD            │
│                           84 SMALLBROOK RINGWAY                   │
│  STATEMENT                BIRMINGHAM B2 8AQ                       │
│                           Telephone: (021) 236 47582             │
│                           VAT No: 471 4719 81                     │
│                                                                   │
│  Newtown Manufacturing Co Ltd                                     │
│  Unit 64, Anfield Industrial Estate                              │
│  REDDITCH                                                         │
│  Worcestershire B98 8HL                                           │
└─────────────────────────────────────────────────────────────────┘
```

Date	Ref No	Details	Debit	Credit	Balance
19-1					
10 Jan.	0871	Goods	£577-50		£577-50
18 Jan.	0134	Returns		£23-10	£554-40

Last amount in the balance column is amount owing

Fig. 13.3 A statement

The following statement of account is received from A. Smith:

	Statement of account		Account: J. Bull
19–1	*Dr.*	*Cr.*	*Balance*
	£	£	£
1 Jan. Balance b/d			150 *Dr.*
11 Jan. Goods sent	75		225 *Dr.*
15 Jan. Goods sent	90		315 *Dr.*
22 Jan. Cheque received		150	165 *Dr.*
30 Jan. Goods sent	100		265 *Dr.*

Both the creditor's account and the statement of account agreed on 1 January: £150 credit balance in Bull's books, £150 *debit* balance in A. Smith's books (don't forget that Bull's books show that he owes Smith this amount, while Smith's books will record it *from his point of view*, that is, as a debit balance). By the end of the month, however, the two no longer agree. There are several reasons for the discrepancy. First, Bull has sent a payment to Smith of £75 on 29 January, but it obviously hasn't reached him until early in February; secondly, Smith sent Bull goods of £100 on 30 January, but these have not yet been received; lastly, Bull returned goods to Smith on 31 January, but these do not yet appear on the statement from Smith. The discrepancy can be reconciled from Bull's point of view as follows:

Reconciliation of A. Smith's account for the month ended 31 January 19–1

	£	
Balance of account at 31 January 19–1	70	Cr.
Add Payment sent on 29 January, not yet appearing on statement	75	
	145	Cr.
Add Goods dispatched by A. Smith on 30 January, not yet received	100	
	245	Cr.
Add Goods returned to A. Smith on 31 January, not yet appearing on statement	20	
Balance per statement at 31 January 19–1	265	Cr.

Clearly, the discrepancy is only a 'timing' difference; within a matter of days, the transactions will be entered into the recipients' accounts and the account and the statement will then agree.

13.5   Credit Note

A credit note (see Fig. 13.4) is used when a customer returns goods to a supplier. It is issued by the supplier, often being printed in red, and shows the amount of money to be credited to the customer's account, thereby *reducing the amount owing for the goods*. Credit notes can also be used as adjusting documents where an overcharge has been made for goods, or an allowance is to be made to a customer. The top copy of the credit note is sent to the customer, while a further copy is used in the accounts department of the suppliers to make the necessary accounting entries.

13.6   Debit Note

A debit note, like a credit note, is an adjusting document. It is the opposite of a credit note, however, and is used when a supplier discovers that a customer has been *under*charged: perhaps the seller has invoiced for fewer goods than were supplied, or the goods were charged at a lower price than they should have been. In such cases a debit note, usually printed in black, is sent to the customer

```
┌─────────────────────────────────────────────────────────────────────┐
│                              ACE INDUSTRIAL SUPPLIERS LTD              │
│  CREDIT NOTE                 84 SMALLBROOK RINGWAY                     │
│                              BIRMINGHAM B2 8AQ                          │
│                              Telephone: (021) 236 47582                │
│                              VAT No: 471 4719 81                        │
│                                                                        │
│  Newtown Manufacturing Co Ltd                                          │
│  Unit 64, Anfield Industrial Estate                                    │
│  REDDITCH                                                               │
│  Worcestershire B98 8HL                                                │
│                                                                        │
│                                           Credit Note No               │
│                                           0134                         │
```

Quantity	Description	Unit price	Total value	VAT at 10%	Total amount
2	Electric motors A241	£10-50	£21-00	£2-10	£23-10

Reason for credit: returned faulty		TOTAL	£23-10
Original Invoice No 0871 dated 10 January 19-1			

Fig. 13.4 A credit note

showing the amount that will be debited to his or her account, that is, *added to the amount already owing for the goods.* A copy of the debit note is then passed to the accounts department for the accounting entries to be made.

13.7   Receipt

A receipt (see Fig. 13.5) may be requested as proof of payment. When payment is made by cheque, the paid cheque acts as receipt for most purposes nowadays, and most businesses receiving payments by cheque do not issue receipts; they must supply one upon request, however. Many cash tills in shops issue receipts automatically for cash sales.

| 5 February 19-1 | Newtown Manufacturing Co Ltd | £554-40 | |
| Date | Received with thanks | Cheque | Cash |

ACE INDUSTRIAL SUPPLIERS LTD
84 SMALLBROOK RINGWAY
BIRMINGHAM B2 8AQ

0123

Fig. 13.5 A receipt

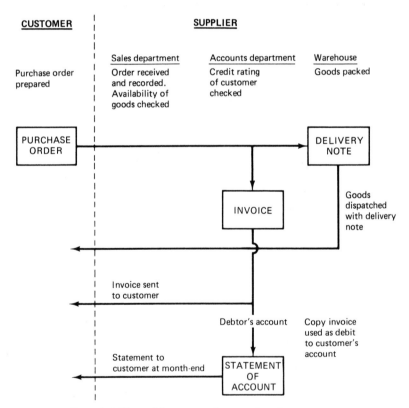

Fig. 13.6 Flow of documents for a credit sale transaction

13.8   Flow of Documents

Fig. 13.6 shows, in simplified form, the flow of documents in a credit sale transaction.

13.9   Profit Margin and Mark-up

When a business sells goods at the recommended retail price, the owner of the business may wish to calculate the *profit margin* or *mark-up*, using the formulae

$$Profit\ margin\ (\%) = \frac{Gross\ profit}{Selling\ price} \times \frac{100}{1} \%$$

$$Mark\text{-}up\ (\%) = \frac{Gross\ profit}{Cost\ price} \times \frac{100}{1} \%$$

For example, suppose that goods cost a business £8, and they are sold for £10. The gross profit is, therefore, £2 for each one sold.

$$Profit\ margin = \frac{£2}{£10} \times \frac{100}{1} = \underline{\underline{20\ per\ cent}}$$

$$Mark\text{-}up = \frac{£2}{£8} \times \frac{100}{1} = \underline{\underline{25\ per\ cent}}$$

Margin is the gross profit compared with the *selling price*, while *mark-up* is the gross profit compared with the *buying price*. When calculating the margin or mark-up for a VAT-registered business, you should use the selling price or the cost price which *excludes* VAT.

A business can compare the margin or mark-up for different products being sold. The more profitable lines can then be more prominently displayed and advertised.

13.10   Questions

1. What steps would you take to check and verify an invoice you had received from a supplier before passing it to your accounts department for payment?

    [Royal Society of Arts]

2. (a) You have been newly appointed as a clerk in your company's credit control department and an order from an old-established customer has been passed to you for clearance. What procedure would you follow before passing the order to the sales department for completion?

    (b) In what way would the procedure be different if the order was for a new customer?

    [Royal Society of Arts]

3.   On 3 May 19–3, you received a statement of account from P. Springfield & Son, one of your suppliers. This showed that the amount outstanding differed from the balance on their account in your ledger.

Assuming that no errors have been made, give and explain *four* possible reasons for this difference.

[*Royal Society of Arts*]

4.   (*a*) You are employed by Thomas Smith and Co of 27 Eastside Downtown. On 21 April 19–3 you received from John Davies of 16 North Parade Uptown, cash in settlement of invoice no 2731 dated 1 April. The amount of the invoice was £150 and Davies has deducted 2½ per cent cash discount from his payment. Prepare the document you would forward to Davies acknowledging receipt of his payment.

(*b*) Under what circumstances might a formal receipt *not* be issued?

[*Royal Society of Arts*]

5.   **Statement**
In account with

T. Wilkinson and Company Ltd
12 Hull Road
Bridlington B3

31 May 19–2

J. W. Joyce,
14 Moor Street,
Bilston.

		(1)	(2)	(3)
		£	£	£
May 1	Balance			120.98
7	Invoice 254	120.14		241.12
8	Cheque		117.37	
	Discount		3.61	120.14
8	Invoice 297	78.10		198.24
10	Returns		15.24	183.00
15	Credit note			
	Overcharge		2.50	180.50
25	Invoice 509	147.00		327.50

Study the above statement and state:
(*a*) the name of the person supplying the goods;
(*b*) the significance of the three columns numbered 1, 2 and 3;
(*c*) the names of the debtor and creditor and the amount owed on 31 May 19–2.

[*Royal Society of Arts*]

*6.   The following supplier's account appears in your book-keeping records:

Smithfield Manufacturing Company Ltd

		£				£
May	1	Returns	1 500	May	1	Balance b/d	8 500
	8	Bank	6 930		8	Purchases	5 650
		Discount	70		19	Purchases	7 310
	29	Bank	11 880				
		Discount	120				
	31	Balance c/d	960				
			21 460				21 460
				June	1	Balance b/d	960

A statement of account received from the Smithfield Manufacturing Company Ltd is as follows:

			£	£	£
May	1	Balance			21 150
	4	Bank		7 000	14 150
	5	Returns		1 500	12 650
	8	Bank		6 930	
		Discount		70	5 650
	12	Sales	7 310		12 960

(a) Reconcile the opening balance of £21 150 on the statement with that of £8 500 in your books.

(b) Reconcile the closing balance of £960 in your books with the figure of £12 960 as shown on the statement.

(c) Why does the entry of £7 310 appear in the statement as sales on May 12, but as purchases on May 19 in your books?

[*Royal Society of Arts*]

'*What do I do? He says his accountant told him always to get a receipt*'

*7. The following is an extract from the trade catalogue of K. E. Stevens who are manufacturers of camping equipment:

Ref.	Sleeping bags		Trade price £	Recommended retail price £
A142	Super	44 oz	8.00	12.00
A143	Standard	38 oz	7.50	10.00

All prices are subject to VAT at 10 per cent.

On 7 April 19–2 P. Burrows of 80 Budge Lane, Northtown, ordered twenty Super sleeping bags and sixteen Standard bags by order number 726. These were dispatched on 8 April 19–2 under invoice number 14631.

You are required to:

(a) prepare the invoice that K. E. Stevens will send to P. Burrows;

(b) assuming that he does not give discounts to customers, calculate the retailer's gross profit on each type of sleeping bag, as a percentage of (i) cost price, and (ii) selling price;

(c) prepare the document that K. E. Stevens will send to P. Burrows on the 21 April 19–2 when Burrows returns two Super sleeping bags as faulty and is allowed full credit for them;

(d) calculate the total gross profit that Burrows will make if he sells all the sleeping bags less the two returned at the recommended price.

[Royal Society of Arts]

8. You are required to complete the following paragraph using words from the list below.

The document a supplier sends to his customer setting out full details of a credit sale transaction is an (i) ———. In order to encourage bulk purchase he may have offered his customer (ii) ——— ———. VAT will be added to the total of the account (iii) ——— deduction of this amount. At the end of the trading period the supplier will send a (iv) ——— to his customer summarizing the transactions which have taken place. If the customer returns goods he will issue a (v) ——— ——— to the supplier and the supplier will acknowledge receipt of these goods by the issue of a (vi) ——— ———.

List of words:

advice note, goods received note, before, after, receipt, statement, invoice, delivery note, credit note, debit note, trade discount, cash discount.

[Royal Society of Arts]

Division of the Ledger

14.1 Introduction

So far in double-entry book-keeping we have opened accounts as and when required. Thus Capital Account might be followed by Bank Account; Purchases Account might be followed by a creditor's account; Motor Vehicles Account might be followed by Sales Account, and so on. Thus the *ledger*, which contains all the accounts, has no sense of order; if we need information contained in, for example, Sales Account, we should have to look through the accounts until we found that particular one. This may be easy when there are twenty or thirty accounts, but as a business expands and the ledger contains more accounts, it needs dividing up into manageable sections. Each of these sections is called a *division of the ledger*.

There are four basic divisions of the ledger:

(*a*) cash book;
(*b*) sales ledger (sometimes known as the debtors ledger);
(*c*) purchases ledger or bought ledger (sometimes known as the creditors ledger);
(*d*) general ledger (often known as nominal ledger).

We will consider each of these in turn.

14.2 Division of the Ledger

(*a*) Cash Book
This section of the ledger contains Cash Account and Bank Account. A business usually appoints a cashier to be responsible for receipts and payments of money—whether in the form of cash or by cheque. The use of the cash book is dealt with in Unit 15.

(*b*) Sales Ledger
Sales ledger contains all the *personal accounts* of the firm's debtors, that is, the customers of the firm who owe money. The sales ledger does *not* contain the Sales Account—this will be found in general ledger. The book-keeping entries of a sales ledger are the responsibility of a sales ledger clerk.

A large firm might divide its sales ledger into smaller sections, so that each section is more readily handled. Such subdivisions can be made in various ways, as may be convenient or appropriate for the firm:

(i) alphabetical, using customers' initials (A–K, L–Z, for instance);
(ii) numerical, using account numbers (account numbers 1–500, 501–1 000, and so on);

(iii) geographical (northern section, southern section, or perhaps by county);

(iv) product basis (paints, chemicals, fertilizers).

A lot of very routine transactions take place on the accounts within the sales ledger and this is therefore an area where nowadays many firms—even small ones—use a computer. Sales ledger accounting by computer is discussed in Unit 20.6.

(c) Purchases Ledger or Bought Ledger

Like sales ledger, the purchases ledger contains personal accounts: in this case, those of a firm's creditors. It does *not* contain the Purchases Account, which is to be found in the general ledger. Like sales ledger, the purchases ledger can be divided, if required, into subsections. The book-keeping entries for a purchases ledger are carried out by a purchases or bought ledger clerk.

Purchases ledger, with its large number of routine transactions, is another area where many firms now use computers—see Unit 20.7.

(d) General Ledger

Also known as *nominal ledger*, this division of the ledger contains all the accounts that do not appear in the other three divisions. It contains, among others, accounts for purchases, sales, expenses and income, for assets such as premises, motor vehicles, machinery and stock, and for liabilities—loans and capital—together with accounts for drawings, trading, and profit and loss. These are often referred to as *impersonal accounts*, because they are the accounts of things rather than of people—in contrast to the *personal accounts* of debtors and creditors found in sales ledger and purchases ledger. Impersonal accounts are sometimes further subdivided into *real accounts*, which relate to assets such as premises, motor vehicles and stock, and *nominal accounts* which are concerned with revenue and expenses, such as wages, sales, rent, discount, purchases and so on.

14.3   More About Division of the Ledger

It may be helpful to think of the division of the ledger in terms of a filing cabinet with four drawers (Fig. 14.1). The whole of the filing cabinet is the ledger, which contains all the accounts of the accounting system. Each of the four drawers contains certain accounts. If we need information from a particular account we know which drawer to look into—the four drawers are labelled respectively cash book, sales ledger, purchases ledger and general ledger. Within each drawer of the filing cabinet are found files for the individual accounts.

The idea of a filing cabinet leads on to other things. If we can devise a way of checking the *total balances* contained in *each section of the ledger* separately then, when a trial balance fails to agree, we can concentrate the search for the error among the accounts in a single ledger section. Thus, as the trial balance

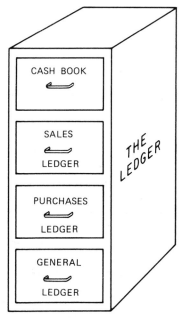

Fig. 14.1 Division of the ledger

contains the balance of *every* account within the ledger, using a device that proves that an error lies in the sales ledger, or that it does not lie in cash book or purchases ledger, will narrow down the search. Such checking devices are considered more fully in Units 23 and 30.

Besides the four divisions of the ledger we have mentioned, the owner of a business may use a further ledger, the *private ledger*, for Capital Account, Drawings Account and the Trading and Profit and Loss Accounts, as these accounts contain information that is private to him- or her-self. This ledger may be available only to the owner and, in a larger business, perhaps to the chief clerk or accountant. Any accounts contained within the private ledger are, of course, part of the double-entry book-keeping system, and cannot be considered in isolation: the balances of these accounts must be included in a trial balance. The owner may nevertheless prefer to keep them out of the mainstream accounting system, so that the information they contain is not available to staff employed in recording routine accounting transactions.

14.4   Questions

1.   (a) Name the divisions of the ledger.
     (b) Give reasons for subdividing the ledger.
     (c) In which division of the ledger would you expect to find each of the following accounts?

Sales; T. Brown, a supplier; Vehicles; the Proprietor's capital; Purchases; D. Jones, a customer; Rates.

[Royal Society of Arts]

2.   G. Christie is a furniture wholesaler and his accounts department subdivides its ledger into five main sections, these being:
The cash book
The bought/purchases ledger
The sales/debtors ledger
The general ledger
The private ledger
     (a) In which of the above ledgers would the following accounts be found?
         (i) C. Hunter, a credit customer of G. Christie;
         (ii) the Stationery Account;
         (iii) Pender and Newry Ltd, suppliers to G. Christie;
         (iv) the Bank Account;
         (v) the Drawings Account of G. Christie;
         (vi) the Sales Account.
     (b) Examine briefly the reasons why a firm should subdivide its ledger in the manner described above.

[Royal Society of Arts]

3.   (a) Name the possible divisions of the ledger and, alongside each, *briefly* specify the types of accounts which would be included therein.
     (b) Suggest four ways in which a business might group its debtor accounts.

[London Chamber of Commerce]

4.   A firm's ledger is subdivided as follows:

Sales ledger	Nominal ledger
Bought ledger	Real ledger
Private ledger	

In which of these ledgers would each of the following accounts appear?

Mortgage	Purchases
T. Jones (customer)	F. Foxhole (debtor)
Bank loan interest	C. Arnold (creditor)
Capital	Stock
Wages and salaries	Office equipment
Drawings	

[Pitman Examinations Institute]

Cash Books and Discount Accounts

15.1 The Two-column Cash Book

We saw in Unit 14 that one of the divisions of the ledger is the cash book, containing transactions on the Cash and Bank Accounts. Previously we have used separate accounts for cash and for bank: the cash book brings both accounts into one book. Such a cash book uses a layout like this:

Cash book

Date	Details	Fol.	Cash	Bank	Date	Details	Fol.	Cash	Bank
			£	£				£	£

As you see, the cash book page is divided into two distinct halves—these are, of course, the debit and credit sides. Each half has columns for date, details, folio, cash and bank. Thus the cash book replaces the separate Cash Account and Bank Account: anything that is entered in the cash or bank columns of the cash book must have an opposite entry elsewhere in the accounting system. The usual rules for double-entry book-keeping apply, and so cash or cheques received by the business are entered on the debit side and listed under the cash or bank headings as appropriate; cash or cheques paid out by the business are listed on the credit side.

Let us consider a few business transactions and see how they are entered in the two-column cash book:

19–4

1 Jan.	Started in business with £1 000 in cash.
4 Jan.	Transferred £500 of the cash into a bank account.
6 Jan.	Paid rent £50 in cash.
8 Jan.	Bought office equipment £250, paying by cheque.
11 Jan.	Cash sales £50.
15 Jan.	Bought goods £200, paying in cash.
17 Jan.	Cash sales £75 paid direct into the bank.
19 Jan.	Cash drawings £105.
23 Jan.	Paid sundry expenses £35 in cash.
27 Jan.	Sold goods to D. Williams for £85, a cheque being received immediately.

The transactions will be entered in the cash book as follows:

Cash book

Date	Details	Fol.	Cash	Bank	Date	Details	Fol.	Cash	Bank
			£	£				£	£
19–4					19–4				
1 Jan.	Capital		1 000		4 Jan.	Bank	C	500	
4 Jan.	Cash	C		500	6 Jan.	Rent		50	
11 Jan.	Sales		50		8 Jan.	Office equipment			250
17 Jan.	Sales			75	15 Jan.	Purchases		200	
27 Jan.	Sales			85	19 Jan.	Drawings		105	
					23 Jan.	Sundry expenses		35	

Points to notice:

(*a*) Just as when separate Cash and Bank Accounts were used, cash or bank transactions must be entered under the correct heading.

(*b*) The transaction on 4 January, the transfer of cash into the Bank Account, involves both sides of the cash book. Here we must credit cash and debit bank, thus completing double-entry book-keeping. As both debit and credit transactions appear in the same book, it is usual to place a 'C' in the folio column against each entry. The 'C' stands for 'contra', indicating that the opposite entry appears in the same account.

(*c*) Some businesses record the receipt of cheques in the cash column (debit side) and, when they are paid into the bank, a contra entry (as explained above) is made. For example, if the cheque received on 27 January was not banked until 30 January, it would be recorded in the *cash column* on the 27th. On the 30th, the amount will be credited in the cash column and debited in the bank column.

15.2   Balancing a Two-column Cash Book

A cash book is easy to balance provided it is done carefully. The best procedure is to subtotal each of the columns in pencil; then, leaving a few clear lines, the totals 'boxes' can be drawn. The cash book from Unit 15.1 then looks like this:

Cash book

Date	Details	Fol.	Cash	Bank	Date	Details	Fol.	Cash	Bank
			£	£				£	£
19–4					19–4				
	Subtotals		1 050	660		Subtotals		890	250

Compare the two cash columns first: we can see that £1 050 was received by the business, while £890 was paid out. This means that, according to our cash book, the balance of cash remaining is £160 (£1 050 minus £890). This is entered on the credit side, just below the subtotal, as 'balance c/d'. It is then entered below the totals boxes on the debit side as 'balance b/d'. The totals for each of the cash columns can now be entered in the boxes previously ruled up.

The same procedure is used for the two bank columns; after this the cash book will appear as follows:

Cash book

Date	Details	Fol.	Cash	Bank	Date	Details	Fol.	Cash	Bank
			£	£				£	£
19–4			1 050	660	19–4			890	250
	Subtotals					Subtotals			
					31 Jan.	Balances c/d		160	410
			1 050	660				1 050	660
1 Feb.	Balances b/d		160	410					

For clarity's sake, the pencilled subtotals can now be rubbed out.

15.3 Is the Cash-book Balance Correct?

The importance of an accurate and up-to-date cash book cannot be stressed too strongly. It is a well-known accounting fact that most businesses that 'go bust' do so not because their service or product is unwanted, but because they simply have not got sufficient cash to keep the business going. Careful maintenance of the cash book enables the business to keep a close watch on its cash position and to be alert to the first sign that cash supplies are falling dangerously low.

We saw in Unit 14 that cash book is one of the divisions of the ledger and that it is helpful if we can check that separate divisions of the ledger do balance. The cash book tells us the balance of cash and the balance at bank, according to the business's accounts. How do we know if these are correct?

The answer for cash is, of course, to count it! Thus we have a very simple checking system in use that can prove the correctness of part of this division of the ledger.

What about the bank balance? Surely we could telephone the bank and ask for the balance of the account or, alternatively, look at the balance shown on the bank statement at the date we have balanced the cash book. Do you think the balance shown on the bank statement would agree with the cash book? It might, but it is doubtful. One reason is that there may well be cheques written out (drawn) by the firm that have been entered in the firm's cash book, but which do not yet appear on the bank statement. Or the bank may have recently made bank charges, or paid a standing order for the business, but these items might not yet appear in the firm's cash book. There are other possible reasons as well. However, we *can* use a bank statement to assist us to agree the bank columns of the cash book—the method for doing this is considered in Unit 23.

15.4   Discount Accounts

Look again at Unit 13.3, and the discussion there of trade discount—which is not entered into the accounts—and cash discount. It is for cash discount that *discount accounts* are used. We shall see how these work by looking at a few business transactions as examples:

14 Nov. 19–3   *Sold goods with a retail price of £500 on credit to T. Smith, allowing him trade discount of 20 per cent and cash discount of 2 per cent for settlement by the end of the month.*

	Sales		
	19–3		£
	14 Nov. T. Smith		400

	T. Smith	
19–3	£	
14 Nov. Sales	400	

Point to notice:

Trade discount does not show in the accounts.

28 Nov. 19–3   *T. Smith settles his account by cheque, deducting cash discount.*

Cash book (bank columns)		
19–3	£	£
28 Nov. T. Smith	392	

T. Smith			
19–3	£	19–3	£
14 Nov. Sales	400	28 Nov. Bank	392

At first glance this would seem to complete the book-keeping transactions with regard to this credit sale: the amount of the sale has been entered in Sales Account and the debtor's account; the cheque received has been entered in the bank columns of the cash book and the debtor's account. Look again at T. Smith's account, however; even after these transactions have been recorded, a debit balance of £8 remains on the account, representing the amount of cash discount he was allowed. A credit for £8 needs to be entered on Smith's account and a corresponding debit entered to *Discount Allowed Account*:

T. Smith			
19–3	£	19–3	£
14 Nov. Sales	400	28 Nov. Bank	392
		28 Nov. Discounts allowed	8
	400		400

Discount allowed	
19–3	£
28 Nov. T. Smith	8

Discount Allowed Account stores up the amount of discount which a business allows to debtors for quick settlement, that is, the cost or expense which a business has to incur in order to obtain faster settlement of debtor's accounts. At the end of a financial year, the balance accumulated on Discount Allowed Account, like those on other expenses accounts, is transferred to the debit of Profit and Loss Account.

Cash discount works in two ways for a business. We have just seen how a business may have to offer cash discount to its debtors to encourage quick settlement and therefore receives a smaller amount than the debt due. But the same firm may *buy* goods on credit. It will receive an invoice from the supplying firm: the invoice may well offer cash discount for quick settlement of the amount. If payment is made quickly to take advantage of the offer, the cash discount thus received represents a reduced cost. The amount gained is called *discount received*. A few transactions will show how Discount Received Account is used:

10 Jan. 19–1   *Bought goods, retail price £400, on credit from B. Jones; he allowed us 10 per cent trade discount, and $2\frac{1}{2}$ per cent cash discount for settlement by the end of January.*

26 Jan. 19–1   *Paid the amount owing to B. Jones by cheque, after deducting cash discount.*

Purchases

19–1	£
10 Jan. B. Jones	360

B. Jones

19–1	£	19–1	£
26 Jan. Bank	351	10 Jan. Purchases	360
26 Jan. Discount received	9		
	360		360

Cash book (bank columns)

		19–1	£
		26 Jan. B. Jones	351

Discount received

		19–1	£
		26 Jan. B. Jones	9

At the end of the financial year, the amount stored up in Discount Received Account is transferred to the *credit* of Profit and Loss Account, where it will add to the gross profit. Thus discount received represents a gain to a business taking advantage of it.

15.5   The Three-column Cash Book

In Unit 15.1 we saw how to use a two-column cash book with columns for cash and bank transactions. Three-column cash books have an extra column which is used as a *memorandum column* to list amounts of cash discount received or allowed. Here are some business transactions:

19–5

1 Mar.	Balances b/d: cash £150, bank £350.
5 Mar.	Received a cheque for £57 from P. Wood—we have allowed him £3 cash discount.
11 Mar.	Paid a cheque for £95 to B. Jones—he has allowed us £5 cash discount.
16 Mar.	We paid by cheque the account of E. Williams £120, deducting 2½ per cent cash discount.
19 Mar.	W. Wilson settles in cash his account of £80, deducting 5 per cent cash discount.
22 Mar.	Received a cheque for £45 from W. Harris in full settlement of his account of £50.
26 Mar.	Paid cash of £62 to R. Field in full settlement of our account of £65.

These transactions are entered in a three-column cash book as in Fig. 15.1. The cash and bank columns record the actual amounts of cash or cheques received or paid. The amount of cash discount, allowed or received, is entered in the discount column. To balance a three-column cash book, the cash and bank columns are dealt with in the same way as for a two-column cash book (see Unit 15.2). The discount columns are simply totalled at the end of the month: no attempt should be made to balance them, and no total should be carried forward to next month. When balanced, the cash book appears in Fig. 15.2.

When balancing a three-column cash book, the discount columns are totalled. These totals are then transferred to discount accounts: the total of the *left-hand column is debited to Discount Allowed Account*; the total of the *right-hand column is credited to Discount Received Account*. Thus, in the case of discount allowed, we are receiving monies on the debit side of the cash book and are allowing an amount of cash discount for quick settlement. As we saw in Unit 15.4, discount allowed costs our business money and, like all expenses, is recorded on the debit side of the appropriate account. Discount Received Account records the amount of cash discount a business gains because it has settled its debts quickly. Using the cash book example above, the discount accounts would appear as:

General Ledger:

Discount allowed

	£
19–5	
31 Mar. Monthly total	12

Discount received

		£
	19–5	
	31 Mar. Monthly total	11

Cash book

Date	Details	Fol.	Discount	Cash	Bank	Fol.	Discount	Cash	Bank	Date	Details
19–5			£	£	£		£	£	£	19–5	
1 Mar.	Balances b/d			150	350		5		95	11 Mar.	B. Jones
5 Mar.	P. Wood		3		57		3		117	16 Mar.	E. Williams
19 Mar.	W. Wilson		4	76			3	62		26 Mar.	R. Field
22 Mar.	W. Harris		5		45						

Fig. 15.1

Cash book

Date	Details	Fol.	Discount	Cash	Bank	Fol.	Discount	Cash	Bank	Date	Details
19–5			£	£	£		£	£	£	19–5	
1 Mar.	Balances b/d			150	350		5		95	11 Mar.	B. Jones
5 Mar.	P. Wood		3		57		3		117	16 Mar.	E. Williams
19 Mar.	W. Wilson		4	76			3	62		26 Mar.	R. Field
22 Mar.	W. Harris		5		45			164	240	31 Mar.	Balances c/d
			12	226	452		11	226	452		
1 Apr.	Balances b/d			164	240						

Fig. 15.2

In Unit 15.4 we entered individual amounts in the discount accounts. Here we are achieving the same objective by entering a total. The third column in the cash book headed 'discount' has acted as a memorandum device, storing up information until it is ready to be put into the accounting system. Thus the two memorandum columns are not part of the double-entry book-keeping system, but the discount accounts are. (Don't forget that cash discount must also be recorded in the personal accounts of debtors and creditors.)

Using a memorandum column to reduce the number of book-keeping transactions passing through the accounts is a device you will meet again later in this book.

15.6   A Worked Example

This worked example shows the use of a three-column cash book, with appropriate double-entry accounts. The ledger is divided up into cash book, sales ledger, purchases ledger and general ledger; all transactions are fully cross-referenced using the folio column.

Transactions:

19–4			£
1 Feb.	Balances b/d:		
	Cash		110
	Bank		385
	Debtors:	A. Smith	160
		P. Green	100
		B. Beecham	120
	Creditors:	H. Bull	120
		T. Gerrard	200
		A. Stuart	280

3 Feb.	P. Green settles her account by cheque, after deducting 5 per cent cash discount.
7 Feb.	Paid amount owing to H. Bull by cheque, less $2\frac{1}{2}$ per cent cash discount.
10 Feb.	Withdrew £150 in cash from the bank for business use.
15 Feb.	Sold goods £240 on credit to P. Green.
17 Feb.	A. Smith paid amount owing by cheque, less $2\frac{1}{2}$ per cent cash discount.
20 Feb.	Paid wages by cheque £315.
22 Feb.	Paid amount owing to T. Gerrard by cheque, after deducting 5 per cent cash discount.
25 Feb.	B. Beecham paid the amount owing by cheque, less $2\frac{1}{2}$ per cent cash discount.
28 Feb.	Paid the amount owing to A. Stuart by cheque, after deducting $2\frac{1}{2}$ per cent cash discount.

Cash book

Date	Details	Fol.	Discount	Cash	Bank	Date	Details	Fol.	Discount	Cash	Bank
19–4			£	£	£	19–4			£	£	£
1 Feb.	Balances b/d			110	385	7 Feb.	H. Bull	PL28	3		117
3 Feb.	P. Green	SL264	5		95	10 Feb.	Cash	C			150
10 Feb.	Bank	C		150		20 Feb.	Wages	GL47			315
17 Feb.	A. Smith	SL101	4		156	22 Feb.	T. Gerrard	PL132	10		190
25 Feb.	B. Beecham	SL82	3		117	28 Feb.	A. Stuart	PL64	7		273
28 Feb.	Balance c/d				292	28 Feb.	Balance c/d			260	
			12	260	1 045				20	260	1 045
1 Mar.	Balance b/d			260		1 Mar.	Balance b/d				292

Fig. 15.3

Answer

Cash book: see Fig. 15.3.

Sales Ledger:

		A. Smith		**Account no 101**	
19–4		£	19–4		£
1 Feb. Balance b/d		160	17 Feb. Bank	CB27	156
			17 Feb. Discount		
			allowed	CB27	4
		160			160

		P. Green		**Account no 264**	
19–4		£	19–4		£
1 Feb. Balance b/d		100	3 Feb. Bank	CB27	95
15 Feb. Sales	GL21	240	3 Feb. Discount		
			allowed	CB27	5
			28 Feb. Balance c/d		240
		340			340
1 Mar. Balance b/d		240			

		B. Beecham		**Account no 82**	
19–4		£	19–4		£
1 Feb. Balance b/d		120	25 Feb. Bank	CB27	117
			25 Feb. Discount		
			allowed	CB27	3
		120			120

Purchases Ledger:

		H. Bull		**Account no 28**	
19–4		£	19–4		£
7 Feb. Bank	CB27	117	1 Feb. Balance b/d		120
7 Feb. Discount					
received	CB27	3			
		120			120

		T. Gerrard		**Account no 132**	
19–4		£	19–4		£
22 Feb. Bank	CB27	190	1 Feb. Balance b/d		200
22 Feb. Discount					
received	CB27	10			
		200			200

		A. Stuart		**Account no 64**	
19–4		£	19–4		£
28 Feb. Bank	CB27	273	1 Feb. Balance b/d		280
28 Feb. Discount					
received	CB27	7			
		280			280

General Ledger:

Sales — Account no 21

19–4		£	19–4		£
28 Feb. Balance c/d		240	15 Feb. P. Green	SL264	240
			1 Mar. Balance b/d		240

Wages — Account no 47

19–4		£	19–4		£
20 Feb. Bank	CB27	315	28 Feb. Balance c/d		315
1 Mar. Balance b/d		315			

Discount allowed — Account no 61

19–4		£	19–4		£
28 Feb. Monthly total	CB27	12	28 Feb. Balance c/d		12
1 Mar. Balance b/d		12			

Discount received — Account no 62

19–4		£	19–4		£
28 Feb. Balance c/d		20	28 Feb. Monthly total	CB27	20
			1 Mar. Balance b/d		20

Point to notice:
In this example, the bank balance at 1 March is brought down on the credit side. This indicates a bank *overdraft*, that is, the business owes money to the bank.

The Use of the Folio Column
The worked example is fully cross-referenced and this is largely self-explanatory. The following 'codes' are in use:

CB = Cash Book
GL = General Ledger
SL = Sales Ledger
PL = Purchases Ledger

The number following the 'codes' refers to the account number in that particular division of the ledger. Like the details column, the folio reference refers to the other account concerned in the transaction: thus PL28 refers to account number 28 in the purchases ledger, which is the account of H. Bull. The cash book also contains a contra item on 10 February: this is indicated by 'C' in the folio column to show that both sides of the transaction appear in the same book.

15.7 Analysed Cash Books

Many firms use an analysed cash book to divide both receipts and payments between main categories. For example, receipts might be divided into Sales Ledger, Cash Sales and Miscellaneous; payments might use Purchases Ledger,

Cash Purchases and Expenses. The subdivisions used can be tailored to meet the needs of the business: for example, the sales ledger receipts could be divided alphabetically—Sales Ledger A–K, and Sales Ledger L–Z, perhaps—or by product—Sales Ledger (Paints) and Sales Ledger (Chemicals), or as appropriate.

The headings for the *receipts side* of such a cash book, including a few sample transactions, could be as shown in Fig. 15.4. The analysis column 'Sales Ledger' records the total amount received from debtors. The month-end total, together with the total of discount allowed, can be used in a special 'checking' account called a *control account* (see Unit 30.3).

In a similar way the payments side of the cash book can be ruled up in analysis form, as in Fig. 15.5. Again, the total of the column 'Purchases Ledger', with the total of discount received, can be used as an aid to checking by using a control account (see Unit 30.2).

Point to notice:

The analysis columns, like the discount columns, are simply memorandum columns and are not part of the double-entry book-keeping system. Nevertheless the month-end totals for cash sales and cash purchases can be entered in Sales and Purchases Accounts respectively (instead of entering each individual transaction): this is the same procedure that we have applied to the totals of the discount columns.

15.8   Analysed Cash Book Incorporating VAT

An analysed cash book is easily extended to incorporate VAT. The receipts side of the cash book (with some sample transactions) appears as in Fig. 15.6.

'A penny plus VAT for your thoughts, dear?'

Cash book (debit side only)

Date	Details	Folio	Discount	Cash	Bank	Sales Ledger	Cash Sales	Miscellaneous
			£	£	£	£	£	£
19–1								
14 Jan.	B. Smith	SL41	10		190	190		
17 Jan.	Sales	GL72			50		50	
20 Jan.	Rent received	GL84		25				25

Fig. 15.4

Cash book (credit side only)

Date	Details	Folio	Discount	Cash	Bank	Purchases Ledger	Cash Purchases	Expenses
			£	£	£	£	£	£
19–1								
11 Jan.	A. Williams	PL25	4		156	156		
14 Jan.	Telephone	GL97			47			47
20 Jan.	Purchases	GL73			35		35	
22 Jan.	Purchases	GL73		12			12	

Fig. 15.5

Cash book (debit side only)

Date	Details	Folio	Discount	Cash	Bank	1 Sales Ledger (incl. VAT)	2 Cash Sales (excl. VAT)	3 Miscellaneous (excl. VAT)	VAT[1] (on columns 2 and 3)
			£	£	£	£	£	£	£
19–1									
3 Feb.	J. Adams	SL57	3		57	57			
5 Feb.	Sales	GL72		55			50		5
10 Feb.	Commission received	GL107			22			20	2

[1] Rate of VAT assumed to be 10 per cent

Fig. 15.6

Cash book (credit side only)

Date	Details	Folio	Discount	Cash	Bank	1 Purchases Ledger (incl. VAT)	2 Cash Purchases (excl. VAT)	3 Expenses (excl. VAT)	4 VAT (on columns 2 and 3)
			£	£	£	£	£	£	£
19–1									
4 Feb.	Telephone	GL97			77			70	7
7 Feb.	G. Young	PL102	3		102	102			
8 Feb.	Purchases	GL73			44		40		4
10 Feb.	Stationery	GL64		11				10	1

Fig. 15.7

Points to notice:

(*a*) As J. Adams is a debtor of our business, VAT will have been charged to him on his invoice and the amount credited to VAT Account at that time; the amount debited to his account in the sales ledger will be the price of the goods plus VAT. Therefore nothing should appear for this receipt in the VAT column of the cash book.

(*b*) For the cash sales made on 5 February, £50 will be credited to Sales Account (or, more likely, the total of the cash sales column—including the £50—will be credited to sales) while VAT of £5 charged to the customer will be credited to VAT Account. Again the month-end total of the VAT column is likely to be credited to VAT Account as 'total VAT received for the month'— this will avoid having too many transactions on VAT Account.

(*c*) Commission Received Account will be credited with £20, while the £2 will be credited to VAT Account in the month-end total.

The payments side of the cash book (with some sample transactions) is shown in Fig. 15.7 (page 128).

Points to notice:

(*a*) As with sales ledger transactions, payments to purchases ledger suppliers, such as G. Young, are not entered in the VAT column, because VAT will have been charged on Young's invoice to us and already debited to VAT Account.

(*b*) VAT on cash purchases is shown in the memorandum VAT column, while the amount excluding VAT is recorded in the purchases column. The month-end total of the cash purchases column will be debited to Purchases Account, while the month-end total of VAT paid will be debited to our VAT Account.

(*c*) For expenses like telephone and stationery, the VAT-exclusive amount will be debited to the respective accounts, while the VAT amount will be debited to VAT Account.

15.9   Questions

*1. During the month of October the following transactions took place in the firm of H. Bunker:

1 Oct.	Bank balance £420; Cash in hand £25.
3 Oct.	Paid debt of £400 owing to P. Franks by cheque, less 2½ per cent cash discount.
6 Oct.	Received a cheque for £195 from K. Kendall, being in payment of account for £200.
9 Oct.	Paid debt of £200 owing to B. Wooster by cheque, deducting 5 per cent cash discount.
12 Oct.	Drew cash from bank £50.
14 Oct.	Received a cheque from M. Faraday for £55 in full settlement of his account for £60.
16 Oct.	G. Greenaway paid his debt of £100 by cheque, less 5 per cent discount.

Draw up a three-column cash book, enter the above transactions and balance and prepare it for use on October 17.

[*South Western Examinations Board*]

2. (*a*) Enter the following balances and transactions in the three-column cash book of M. Armitage:

		£
1 Apr.	Balances: Cash	21.82
	Bank overdraft	41.96

4 Apr.   Received £195 in cash from A. Slessor.
Paid £170 into bank from cash.

5 Apr.   M. Armitage withdrew £50 by cheque for personal use.
Received cheque from R. Lister in settlement of his account for £640 less 2½ per cent cash discount.

6 Apr.   Withdrew £350 from bank for office cash.
Paid wages £336 in cash.

7 Apr.   Cash sales £218.
Paid electricity account in cash £63.19.
Paid all cash into bank except for £20.

8 Apr.   Paid L. Baker by cheque his account for £300 less 2½ per cent cash discount.
Balance the cash book and bring down the balances.

(*b*) Why might M. Armitage have granted cash discount to R. Lister on April 5?

[*West Midlands Examinations Board*]

*3.   Bertram Walters is a sole trader who records all his cash and bank transactions in a three-column cash book. The following are his transactions for the month of October 19–2:

19–2
1 Oct.   Cash in hand £29; Bank overdraft £276.

4 Oct.   Received a cheque for £72 from A. Church, in full settlement of a debt of £76. This was paid into the bank.

8 Oct.   Received cash £43 from H. Wise, in full settlement of a debt of £46.

13 Oct.   Paid to F. Layton by cheque £55, in full settlement of a debt of £60.

16 Oct.   Paid wages in cash £31.

19 Oct.   Received a cheque for £62 from H. Bishop in full settlement of a debt of £67. This was paid into the bank.

25 Oct.   Paid to G. Shipley by cheque £36, in full settlement of a debt of £40.

28 Oct.   Paid cash into bank £30.

30 Oct.   Bank advised Walters that they had debited his account with £31 in respect of bank interest.

Required:

(*a*) Draw up Walters' three-column cash book for the month of October 19–2. Balance the cash and bank columns and carry down the balances as at 31 October 19–2.

(*b*) Total the two discount columns (which should be correctly headed) and state to which ledger accounts the totals should be posted, and to which side.

[*London Chamber of Commerce*]

4. Frank Moore, a sole trader, enters all his cash and bank transactions in a three-column cash book. His transactions for the month of May 19–3 are as follows:

1 May   Cash in hand £27. Cash at bank £493.
4 May   Received from J. Jones cash amounting to £46 in full settlement of a debt of £50.
10 May   Paid wages in cash £53.
12 May   Issued a cheque for £63 in favour of W. Jackson being in full settlement of a debt of £70.
17 May   Drew a cheque for £60 for office cash.
20 May   Paid cash £37 to L. Bishop in full settlement of a debt of £40.
24 May   Received a cheque for £72 from J. Crowther in full settlement of a debt of £80. *This cheque was paid direct into Moore's banking account the same day.*
26 May   Paid salaries by cheque £88.

Required:

(*a*) Draw up the three-column cash book of F. Moore for the month of May 19–3. Balance the cash book and carry down the balances of cash in hand and cash at bank.

(*b*) The discount columns should be totalled and you should state to which ledger accounts the two totals should be posted and also on which side of the ledger each entry should be made.

[*London Chamber of Commerce*]

5.   (*a*) Write up the three-column cash book of C. Keller from the following details:

1 May   Cash in hand: £17.91.
1 May   Bank overdraft: £47.87.
1 May   Paid R. Froude, by cheque, his account of £500 less 2½ per cent cash discount.
2 May   C. Keller withdrew £25, by cheque, for personal expenses.
2 May   Cash sales £417.56 from which a telephone account for £48.26 was paid. Paid the balance of the cash sales into the bank.
3 May   Received cheque from K. Brereton for £396.55.
4 May   Received cheque from M. Arnold for £195 in settlement of her account of £200.
5 May   Withdrew £250 from bank for office cash.
5 May   Paid wages £238.75 in cash.
8 May   K. Brereton's cheque (received May 3) returned by bank marked 'refer to drawer'.
9 May   Balance the cash book and bring down the balances.

(*b*) Open accounts for M. Arnold, R. Froude, Discount allowed and Discount received and post the necessary items to them from the cash book completed in (*a*).

[*East Midland Regional Examinations Board*]

Journals in Accounting—1

16.1   What is a Journal?

We saw in Unit 14 that, as the number of accounts increases, we must divide the ledger into several sections—cash book, sales ledger, purchases ledger and general ledger. A further step, as the accounting system grows, is to use *journals*, which are often referred to as *day books*. A journal or day book is a listing device which is not part of double-entry book-keeping: it stores up details and money amounts of business transactions until they are entered into the accounting system. (We have already seen this technique in use with the discount column of a three-column cash book, where amounts of discount received or allowed are stored up until being transferred, as a total, to the appropriate account at the month-end.)

16.2   When are Journals Used?

Journals and day books are used under two different circumstances:

(*a*) when there is a large volume of regular transactions, such as sales and purchases;
(*b*) for non-regular transactions, such as the purchase of fixed assets or the correction of errors.

For (*a*), a business may use:

> sales journal/day book
> purchases journal/day book
> returns inwards journal/day book
> returns outwards journal/day book

For (*b*) (non-regular transactions), a *general journal* is used. This is often referred to as 'the' journal, reserving the term 'day books' to describe collectively the sales, purchases and returns journals.

Journals and day books are often known as *books of original entry* because they record the first details of business transactions, before they are entered into the double-entry book-keeping system. Cash book and petty cash book (see Units 15 and 21) are also books of original entry, but for cash, as opposed to credit transactions.

This Unit is concerned with the use of basic journals for sales, purchases and returns; Unit 17 deals with more advanced journals which incorporate analysis columns; Unit 24 deals with the general journal.

16.3   Sales Journal

A large number of business transactions are concerned with selling on credit the goods in which a firm trades. As you know, to record such transactions in the accounts, we must credit Sales Account and debit the personal account of the debtor, our customer. Thus, we have a transaction in the general ledger section, that is, in Sales Account, and a transaction in the sales ledger section, in the debtor's account. The entry on the debtor's account should be recorded when the credit sale is made. General ledger is a very busy section, however; it contains heavily used accounts such as sales, purchases and returns. Instead of making the entry in Sales Account immediately we can, for the time being, record the Sales Account part of the book-keeping entry on a separate list of transactions called the *sales journal*. If each credit sales transaction is entered on this list, then at regular intervals—often at the month-end—the total for credit sales shown by the list can be transferred to Sales Account, thus completing double-entry book-keeping for credit sales.

Journal paper is ruled with two, sometimes three or more, columns for money amounts:

Date	Details: Name	Invoice no	Folio	£	£

The two money columns do not represent debit and credit when this type of paper is used for sales, purchases and returns journals. Instead the left-hand column is used as a 'marginal' column for carrying out calculations—such as listing several amounts for the same customer or supplier, or calculating trade discount—the total being carried into the right-hand column.

Worked example

Here are a few credit transactions:

19–3
2 Apr.	Sold goods £245 on credit to L. Jones, invoice no 1234.
7 Apr.	Sold goods £137 on credit to J. Hart, invoice no 1235.
12 Apr.	Sold goods £58 on credit to B. Harris, invoice no 1236.
15 Apr.	Sold goods £96 on credit to D. Williams, invoice no 1237.
22 Apr.	Sold goods £212 on credit to B. Kerr, invoice no 1238.
24 Apr.	Sold goods £35 on credit to J. Hart, invoice no 1239.

Using a sales journal as a 'listing device', the transactions will appear as:

Sales journal

19–3	Name	Invoice no	Folio	£	£
2 Apr.	L. Jones	1234	SL91		245
7 Apr.	J. Hart	1235	SL84		137
12 Apr.	B. Harris	1236	SL82		58
15 Apr.	D. Williams	1237	SL232		96
22 Apr.	B. Kerr	1238	SL102		212
24 Apr.	J. Hart	1239	SL84		35
30 Apr.	Total transferred to Sales Account		GL25		783

Page 21

The accounts appear as:

General Ledger:

Sales   **Account no 25**

19–3		£
30 Apr. Credit sales for month	SJ21	783

Sales Ledger:

L. Jones   **Account no 91**

19–3		£
2 Apr. Sales	SJ21	245

J. Hart   **Account no 84**

19–3		£
7 Apr. Sales	SJ21	137
24 Apr. Sales	SJ21	35

B. Harris   **Account no 82**

19–3		£
12 Apr. Sales	SJ21	58

D. Williams   **Account no 232**

19–3		£
15 Apr. Sales	SJ21	96

B. Kerr   **Account no 102**

19–3		£
22 Apr. Sales	SJ21	212

As you see, a journal has more room for information than is available in an account. For example, the invoice number for each sale can be included so that, if there is a query, the whole transaction can be traced. The sales journal is prepared from a copy of the invoice; the copy invoice then goes to the sales ledger section in order that the debtor's account may be debited. Our example is fully cross-referenced: if there is a query on, say, B. Kerr's account, the personal account is referenced SJ21; on page 21 of the sales journal we can find the invoice number, 1238, and we can then look up the copy invoice.

Notice that in a sales journal, double-entry book-keeping is completed only when the month-end total is transferred to Sales Account. (Remember that entries on individual debtors' accounts are made at the date of sale.) Only one entry is made in Sales Account instead of the six that we should need if we did not use a journal: indeed, there would still be only one entry on Sales Account if sixty, or six hundred, sales transactions were recorded for the month in the sales journal. In the accounts department of a business, the work can be divided up—one person can be given the job of maintaining the sales journal, while another can concentrate on recording general ledger transactions, including the total from sales journal at the month-end.

We have talked about transferring the total of sales journal to Sales Account at the end of each month. The accountant in a firm could decide to make the transfer more frequently, however—daily, say, or weekly. However often the transfer is made, the sales to the date of transfer are then incorporated into the double-entry book-keeping system, and sales journal starts again from nothing. (Do *not* try extracting a trial balance until the transfer from the journal has been made—clearly it cannot balance, because the book-keeping is incomplete!)

Cash Sales

The sales transactions put through the sales journal in our examples have all been credit sales—so far, no cash sales have been entered in the journal. There is no rigid rule of accounting which states that only credit sales can be entered in a sales journal. It is often best to restrict the use of a sales journal to credit sales, however, mainly because the sales journal totals can help us check the accuracy of the sales ledger section, that is, the debtors' accounts. This checking method is known as a *control account* and is dealt with in Unit 29. A busy firm doing a lot of cash sales may well operate a sales journal for cash sales only; modern cash tills in shops are a type of sales journal, because they keep a running total of sales which can then be transferred at the end of the day or the week to Sales Account. Many such tills also keep a record of sales for different departments. Where a business does not keep a separate sales journal for cash sales, then such sales must be entered individually into the accounts, that is, debiting Cash/Bank Account, and crediting Sales Account.

16.4 Purchases Journal

A firm with a large number of credit purchases will use a purchases journal, in much the same way that it uses sales journal. When goods are bought on credit from another firm, an invoice will be received from the supplying firm. The number of this supplier's invoice may be recorded in the details column of the purchases journal; alternatively the number of the purchase order could be shown. (We saw in Unit 13.2 the importance of ensuring that all goods bought have been ordered in the correct manner by a person authorized to make purchases for the firm.)

Worked example

Example transactions for April 19–3:

3 Apr.	Bought goods £250 on credit from P. Thomas, invoice no 783.
6 Apr.	Bought goods £180 on credit from J. Shaw, invoice no A102.
12 Apr.	Bought goods £55 on credit from H. Clark, invoice no 2780.
15 Apr.	Bought goods £105 on credit from S. James, invoice no Y47.
22 Apr.	Bought goods £208 on credit from M. Bartlett, invoice no 241/T.
26 Apr.	Bought goods £160 on credit from S. Preece, invoice no 361.

	Purchases journal				Page 54
19–3	Name	Invoice no	Folio	£	£
3 Apr.	P. Thomas	783	PL354		250
6 Apr.	J. Shaw	A102	PL320		180
12 Apr.	H. Clark	2780	PL54		55
15 Apr.	S. James	Y47	PL127		105
22 Apr.	M. Bartlett	241/T	PL26		208
26 Apr.	S. Preece	361	PL286		160
30 Apr.	Total transferred to Purchases Account		GL33		958

General Ledger:

	Purchases		Account no 33
19–3		£	
30 Apr. Credit purchases for month	PJ54	958	

Purchases Ledger:

	P. Thomas		Account no 354
	19–3		£
	3 Apr. Purchases	PJ54	250

	J. Shaw		Account no 320
	19–3		£
	6 Apr. Purchases	PJ54	180

	H. Clark		Account no 54
	19–3		£
	12 Apr. Purchases	PJ54	55

	S. James		Account no 127
	19–3		£
	15 Apr. Purchases	PJ54	105

	M. Bartlett		Account no 26
	19–3		£
	22 Apr. Purchases	PJ54	208

	S. Preece		Account no 286
	19–3		£
	26 Apr. Purchases	PJ54	160

In the same way as with sales journal, the total of purchases for the month is transferred to Purchases Account—thus only one entry appears on Purchases Account instead of the six that would be needed if a journal was not used. This will reduce the chance of errors creeping into the accounts.

16.5   Returns Journals

We can use a journal wherever it is necessary to record repeated transactions of the same type, such as purchases or sales. A firm may decide to use journals for returns inwards and returns outwards. (Many businesses consider that they have an insufficient number of returns to require the use of returns journals, and make the normal accounting entries instead.) Where returns are frequent, separate journals can be used for returns inwards and returns outwards. As you know, the adjusting document used for returns is a credit note (see Unit 13.5); this is issued when goods are returned and is put through the accounts in the books of both buyer and seller to adjust the previous entries recording the purchase or sale.

Point to notice:

A return outwards to one business is a returns inwards to another—always consider such transactions *from the point of view of the firm whose accounts you are preparing.*

Worked example

Example transactions for April 19–3:

6 Apr.	L. Jones returns goods £50; we issue credit note no 568.
12 Apr.	We return goods £40 to J. Shaw; he issues credit note no Y24.
16 Apr.	We return goods £55 to H. Clark; he issues credit note no 102.
17 Apr.	W. Harris returns goods £58; we issue credit note no 569.
30 Apr.	We return goods £10 to S. James; she issues credit note no 99/83.

Using returns journals and appropriate ledgers, the transactions will appear as:

	Returns inwards journal				Page 84
19–3	Name	Credit note no	Folio	£	£
6 Apr.	L. Jones	568	SL91		50
17 Apr.	W. Harris	569	SL82		58
30 Apr.	Total transferred to Returns Inwards				
	Account		GL56		108

Returns outwards journal					Page 86

19–3	Name	Credit note no	Folio	£	£
12 Apr.	J. Shaw	Y24	PL320		40
16 Apr.	H. Clark	102	PL54		55
30 Apr.	S. James	99/83	PL127		10
30 Apr.	Total transferred to Returns Outwards Account		GL58		—— 105

General Ledger:

	Returns Inwards Account			**Account no 56**
19–3		£		
30 Apr. Returns inwards for month	RIJ84	108		

	Returns Outwards Account			**Account no 58**
		19–3		£
		30 Apr. Returns outwards for month	ROJ86	105

Sales Ledger:

	L. Jones			**Account no 91**
19–3		£	19–3	£
2 Apr. Sales	SJ21	245	6 Apr. Returns inwards RIJ84	50

	B. Harris			**Account no 82**
19–3		£	19–3	£
12 Apr. Sales	SJ21	58	17 Apr. Returns inwards RIJ84	58

Purchases Ledger:

	J. Shaw			**Account no 320**
19–3		£	19–3	£
12 Apr. Returns outwards	ROJ86	40	6 Apr. Purchases PJ54	180

	H. Clark			**Account no 54**
19–3		£	19–3	£
16 Apr. Returns outwards	ROJ86	55	12 Apr. Purchases PJ54	55

	S. James			**Account no 127**
19–3		£	19–3	£
30 Apr. Returns outwards	ROJ86	10	15 Apr. Purchases PJ54	105

(The amounts of sales and purchases shown on the debtors' and creditors' accounts above are taken from the previous worked examples in Units 16.3 and 16.4.)

16.6   Questions

*1.   Enter up the purchases journal/day book from the following details. The transactions are to be entered in the relevant accounts in the purchases ledger, and the transfer to Purchases Account in the general ledger from the journal is to be shown.

19–1

1 Mar.	Bought goods £105 on credit from T. Berry.
3 Mar.	Bought goods £84 on credit from D. Sinclair.
7 Mar.	Bought goods £220 on credit from R. Nelson.
10 Mar.	Bought goods £52 on credit from D. Mills.
14 Mar.	Bought goods £76 on credit from W. Roberts.
19 Mar.	Bought goods £35 on credit from T. Berry.
22 Mar.	Bought goods £102 on credit from D. Mills.
25 Mar.	Bought goods £61 on credit from J. Clarke.
28 Mar.	Bought goods £57 on credit from R. Nelson.

*2.   Enter up the sales journal/day book from the following details. The transactions are to be entered in the relevant accounts in the sales ledger, and the transfer to Sales Account in the general ledger from the journal is to be shown.

19–2

1 May	Sold goods £38 on credit to H. Bridges.
5 May	Sold goods £71 on credit to C. Clements.
7 May	Sold goods £34 on credit to M. Gibbs.
10 May	Sold goods £89 on credit to C. Walker.
12 May	Sold goods £33 on credit to G. Price.
15 May	Sold goods £68 on credit to M. Gibbs.
20 May	Sold goods £105 on credit to M. Bradley.
24 May	Sold goods £44 on credit to C. Walker.
28 May	Sold goods £65 on credit to G. Price.

3.   Enter up the sales, purchases, returns inwards and returns outwards journals/day books from the following details. The transactions are to be entered in the relevant accounts in the sales and purchases ledgers. The totals of the journals are to be transferred to the relevant accounts in the general ledger.

19–8

1 Aug.	Bought goods £250 on credit from D. Clifford.
3 Aug.	Bought goods £110 on credit from R. Howard.
5 Aug.	Sold goods £45 on credit to R. Brown.
6 Aug.	Returned goods £35 to D. Clifford.
7 Aug.	Sold goods £21 on credit to G. Gregory.
10 Aug.	R. Brown returns goods £15.
12 Aug.	Bought goods £135 on credit from J. Evans.
14 Aug.	Sold goods £89 on credit to C. Joyner.
17 Aug.	Bought goods £135 on credit from R. Howard.
20 Aug.	C. Joyner returns goods £29.
21 Aug.	Sold goods £68 on credit to R. Brown.
24 Aug.	Returned goods £15 to R. Howard.
26 Aug.	Sold goods £25 on credit to G. Gregory.
28 Aug.	Bought goods £98 on credit from J. Evans.
29 Aug.	Sold goods £30 on credit to C. Joyner.
30 Aug.	Returned goods £15 to J. Evans.

4. Using the following information, (*a*) draw up a sales day book, and (*b*) transfer the entries to the appropriate ledger accounts.

1 Dec.	Goods were sold to A. Wills & Co Account No 1 on credit:
	3 boxes of nuts and bolts at £12 per box,
	2 engine parts at £10 each.
3 Dec.	Sold goods to B. Carlton Account No 2 on credit:
	1 special unit at £175.
5 Dec.	Sold to C. Winterman Account No 3 on credit:
	2 spanners at £50 each.

[South Western Examinations Board]

5. On 1 December 19–8 the sales and purchases ledgers of C. Morgan contained the following debtors and creditors:

	Debtors	Creditors
	£	£
L. Bullivent	150	
S. Griffiths	120	
G. Mayhew	100	
A. Waller		70
R. Shale		90

Transactions during December are summarized below.

Purchases Day Book

		£
Dec. 14	A. Waller	80
Dec. 16	R. Shale	130

Sales Day Book

		£
Dec. 8	G. Mayhew	80
Dec. 15	S. Griffiths	140
Dec. 22	L. Bullivent	50
Dec. 24	G.Mayhew	70

Returns Inwards Book

		£
Dec. 19	L. Bullivent	10
Dec. 25	G. Mayhew	20

Returns Outwards Book

		£
Dec. 15	A. Waller	15

Cheques received from debtors

		£	£
		Discount	Bank
Dec. 5	S. Griffiths	5	115
Dec. 8	L. Bullivent	10	140
Dec. 9	G. Mayhew	2	98
Dec. 20	S. Griffiths	5	135

Cheques paid to creditors

		£	£
		Discount	Bank
Dec. 8	R. Shale		90
Dec. 18	A. Waller	3	67

You are required to:

(*a*) Write up the accounts in C. Morgan's sales and purchases ledgers for December 19–8 and bring down any closing balances.

(*b*) Make suitable entries in the Sales, Purchases, Returns Inwards, Returns Outwards, Discount Received and Discount Allowed Accounts for December 19–8.

[RSA Examinations Board]

Journals in Accounting—2

17.1 Introduction

This Unit deals with more advanced journals/day books. It shows trade discount, analysed or columnar journals, and VAT incorporated into journal books. It also deals with an accounting system known as the 'slip' system.

17.2 Journals and Trade Discount

Where trade discount is deducted from the retail price, this is usually shown within the journal.

Example

19–1

20 Jan.   Sold goods, retail price £120, on credit to T. Hall, less 20 per cent trade discount.

25 Jan.   Sold goods, retail price £200, on credit to L. Kershaw, less 25 per cent trade discount.

	Sales journal				Page 25
19–1	Name	Invoice no	Folio	£	£
20 Jan.	T. Hall:				
	Goods			120	
	Less 20% trade discount			24	
		108	SL41		96
25 Jan.	L. Kershaw:				
	Goods			200	
	Less 25% trade discount			50	
		109	SL48		150
31 Jan.	Total transferred to Sales Account		GL25		246

Point to notice:

The left-hand money column is used here for showing the gross amount, and for calculating trade discount; the right-hand money column is used only for the net amount.

The personal accounts of Hall and Kershaw will be debited with the net amounts of £96 and £150 respectively. Sales Account will be credited with the total of the net amounts (£246, assuming these are the only two transactions for the month). Thus trade discount appears in the book of original entry (and on the invoice) but is not shown elsewhere in the accounts. Clearly, if any goods are subsequently returned, the entry in the accounts to record this will be at the discounted price.

Purchases journal can also be used to show the trade discount received when a firm buys goods on credit. As before, net amounts only are recorded in Purchases Account and the creditors' accounts.

17.3   Analysed or Columnar Journals

A *columnar* journal or day book is used whenever a business needs to analyse its purchases, sales and returns, distinguishing between different categories of, say, products or departments of the same business.

Example

A business sells two products, X and Y. Transactions for February 19–4 are:

2 Feb.	Sold £200 of product X on credit to J. James.
4 Feb.	Sold £100 of product Y on credit to T. Lewis.
7 Feb.	Sold £150 of product Y on credit to M. Snow.
15 Feb.	Sold £210 of product X on credit to R. Perrin.
20 Feb.	Sold £520 of product Y on credit to A. Appleby.

The analysed journal or day book will appear as:

Sales journal						Page 45
19–4	Name	Invoice no	Folio	Total £	X £	Y £
2 Feb.	J. James	210	SL25	200	200	
4 Feb.	T. Lewis	211	SL30	100		100
7 Feb.	M. Snow	212	SL54	150		150
15 Feb.	R. Perrin	213	SL43	210	210	
20 Feb.	A. Appleby	214	SL10	520		520
29 Feb.	Totals transferred to Sales Accounts			1 180	410	770
					GL84	GL85

As you see, the analysed sales journal is *cross-cast*, that is, it adds up both down and across with the total sales for each product, £410 and £770, adding up to the total sales for the month, £1 180.

At the end of the month the total sales for each product can be transferred to separate sales accounts:

General Ledger:

Sales: Product X		**Account no 84**	
	19–4		£
	29 Feb. Credit sales for month	SJ45	410

Sales: Product Y		**Account no 85**	
	19–4		£
	29 Feb. Credit sales for month	SJ45	770

Alternatively, they may be transferred to an analysed sales account:

Sales

19–4			X £	Y £
29 Feb. Credit sales for month		SJ45	410	770

Either way, the sales figures for each product or department can, at the end of the financial year, be used to prepare *departmental accounts* (see Unit 36).

Analysed journals or day books can be used in the same way for purchases, returns inwards and returns outwards, in each case entering up the debtors' or creditors' accounts as before.

17.4 Journals and VAT

Unit 12 has already introduced you to Value Added Tax. When dealing with both purchases and sales transactions for a VAT-registered business, remember that the general ledger accounts of purchases and sales must show the relevant amounts *without* the addition of VAT. The personal accounts of debtors and creditors must record the VAT-inclusive amount, however; the amount of VAT on purchases and sales is entered on VAT Account.

Journals are adapted to record VAT by using an additional column.

Worked example

The following transactions are the credit purchases and credit sales for March 19–2:

1 Mar.	Bought goods £250 on credit from J. Adams, invoice no 53.
3 Mar.	Sold goods £200 on credit to M. Green, invoice no 541.
5 Mar.	Sold goods £300 on credit to L. Carpenter, invoice no 542.
12 Mar.	Bought goods £70 on credit from P. Jarvis, invoice no 1081.
16 Mar.	Sold goods £250 on credit to B. Black, invoice no 543.
23 Mar.	Bought goods £220 on credit from W. White, invoice no X24.
26 Mar.	Bought goods £100 on credit from P. Wood, invoice no A234.

In each case amounts shown are before the addition of VAT, which is at a rate of 10 per cent.

		Purchases journal					Page 33
19–2	Name	Invoice no	Folio	Net of VAT £	VAT £	Total invoice £
1 Mar.	J. Adams	53	PL28	250	25	275
12 Mar.	P. Jarvis	1081	PL129	70	7	77
23 Mar.	W. White	X24	PL374	220	22	242
26 Mar.	P. Wood	A234	PL392	100	10	110
31 Mar.	Transferred to General Ledger			640	64	704
				GL68	GL101	

		Sales journal					Page 28

19–2	Name	Invoice no	Folio	Net of VAT £	VAT £	Total invoice £
3 Mar.	M. Green	541	SL220	200	20	220
5 Mar.	L. Carpenter	542	SL103	300	30	330
16 Mar.	B. Black	543	SL68	250	25	275
31 Mar.	Transferred to General Ledger			750	75	825
				GL29	GL101	

General Ledger:

	Purchases			**Account no 68**
19–2		£		
31 Mar. Credit purchases for month	PJ33	640		

	Sales			**Account no 29**
		19–2		£
		31 Mar. Credit sales for month	SJ28	750

	VAT				**Account no 101**
19–2		£	19–2		£
31 Mar. Tax on credit purchases for month	PJ33	64	31 Mar. Tax on credit sales for month	SJ28	75
31 Mar. Balance c/d		11			
		75			75
			1 Apr. Balance b/d		11

Purchases Ledger:

	J. Adams			**Account no 28**
		19–2		£
		1 Mar. Purchases	PJ33	275

	P. Jarvis			**Account no 129**
		19–2		£
		12 Mar. Purchases	PJ33	77

	W. White			**Account no 374**
		19–2		£
		23 Mar. Purchases	PJ33	242

	P. Wood			**Account no 392**
		19–2		£
		26 Mar. Purchases	PJ33	110

Sales Ledger:

		M. Green	Account no 220
19–2		£	
3 Mar. Sales	SJ28	220	

		L. Carpenter	Account no 103
19–2		£	
5 Mar. Sales	SJ28	330	

		B. Black	Account no 68
19–2		£	
16 Mar. Sales	SJ28	275	

Point to notice:

VAT Account has a credit balance of £11, being the amount due to the tax authorities in respect of these transactions. If a balance sheet was prepared for this firm at 31 March 19–2, this balance would be shown as a current liability.

The ultimate in journal books is one which is analysed *and* includes a column for VAT. A suitable ruling with a sample transaction is:

		Sales journal						Page 64
19–1	Name	Invoice no	Folio	X	Y	Net of VAT	VAT	Total invoice
				£	£	£	£	£
6 Aug.	A. Webb	341	SL102	40	60	100	10	110

There is plenty of scope for cross-casting in this journal! The total invoice amount will be debited to the customer's account. VAT Account will be credited with the total of the VAT column. Sales Account will be credited with the total of the 'net of VAT' column (or separate sales accounts will be used for the totals of the analysis columns, in this case X and Y).

17.5   A Worked Example

The following is a worked example showing the use of analysed/columnar journals; it is fairly typical of some of the more advanced examination questions on this topic.

Andrews is a wholesaler, buying 'do-it-yourself' goods from manufacturers and supplying smaller shops. The business is divided into two main departments: household and garden.

Sales on credit during May 19–4 were:

4 May	*To Hampstead Handyman*
	Wallpapers @ list price £250, less trade discount 20 per cent.
	Paint @ list price £400, less trade discount 15 per cent.

12 May   *To Southam Garden Centre*
         8 barbecue sets @ list price £25 each, less trade discount 25 per cent.
         5 lawn mowers @ list price £100 each, less trade discount 10 per cent.

20 May   *To Droitwich DIY*
         Electrical sundries @ list price £150, less trade discount 20 per cent.

Cash discount is not allowed for prompt payment, and all transactions are subject to VAT at 10 per cent.

Required:
   Write up the sales journal/day book for the month and enter the relevant payments to the personal and nominal accounts concerned.

Answer:
(Note: invoice and folio numbers are not shown.)

Sales Journal   Page . . . .

19–4	Name			Household	Garden	Net of VAT	VAT	Total invoice
		£	£	£	£	£	£	£
4 May	Hampstead Handyman:							
	Wallpaper at list price	250						
	less trade discount 20%	50						
			200					
	Paint at list price	400						
	less trade discount 15%	60						
			340					
				540		540	54	594
12 May	Southam Garden Centre:							
	8 barbecue sets @ list							
	price £25 each	200						
	less trade discount 25%	50						
			150					
	5 lawn mowers @ list price							
	£100 each	500						
	less trade discount 10%	50						
			450					
					600	600	60	660
20 May	Droitwich DIY:							
	Electrical sundries at							
	list price		150					
	less trade discount 20%		30					
				120		120	12	132
31 May	Transferred to General Ledger			660	600	1 260	126	1 386

General Ledger:

Sales

		Household	Garden
	19–4	£	£
	31 May Credit sales for month	660	600

Value Added Tax

	19–4	£
	31 May Tax on credit sales for month	126

Sales Ledger:

Hampstead Handyman

19–4	£
4 May Sales	594

Southam Garden Centre

19–4	£
12 May Sales	660

Droitwich DIY

19–4	£
20 May Sales	132

17.6   The 'Slip' System

Journal books represent one method of collecting totals which, at the end of the week or month, are transferred to Sales Account, Purchases Account or the appropriate returns account; the *slip system* represents another method. Using the slip system, the journal books and personal ledgers of debtors and creditors are dispensed with, and in their place the original documents and their copies ('slips' of paper) are used to carry out their functions.

(a) Sales

Under the slip system, no sales journal and sales ledger (debtors' accounts) are used. Their place is taken by folders, one representing the sales journal, and others each representing a debtor's account. When an item is sold on credit, three or more copies of the invoice are prepared—one is sent to the customer, a second is placed in the 'sales journal' folder, and a third in the folder for that particular debtor.

At the end of the week or month, the sales journal folder is taken and a listing made on a calculator of the money amounts of the copy invoices; the copy invoices are then withdrawn from the folder and filed. This total, which is the total of credit sales for the week or month, can then be entered to the credit of Sales Account and the debit of a *Sundry Debtors Account* (an account used here to show the total amount of debts due to the business). As each payment is received from a debtor, the invoice relating to the payment is withdrawn from the debtor's personal folder and filed—the book-keeping entries are a debit to

Cash or Bank Account in respect of the cash or cheque received, and a credit to Sundry Debtors Account. At any time the invoices remaining in each individual folder represent the amount owing by that debtor, while the total of all invoices held in the folders represents the total debtors figure. This should agree with the balance on Sundry Debtors Account.

Fig. 17.1 shows the method of using the 'slip' system for credit sales.

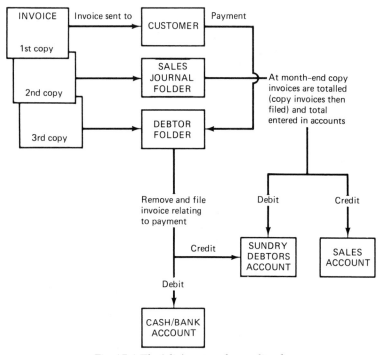

Fig. 17.1 The 'slip' system for credit sales

(b) Purchases

A similar procedure can be used for purchases, with one copy of the invoice received from the supplier being placed in a 'purchases journal' folder, and a second copy being placed in a folder for that particular creditor. At the end of the month the money amounts of copy invoices are totalled and the amount debited to Purchases Account and credited to a Sundry Creditors Account. As creditors are paid, the copy invoices are withdrawn from the individual creditor's folders and a debit passed to Sundry Creditors Account, with a credit to Cash or Bank Account. At any time the folder for each creditor will show the amount owing to that person, while the total of the creditors' folders should equal the Sundry Creditors Account.

(c) **Advantages and Disadvantages**

The *advantages* of the slip system are:

(i) there is a saving in time and labour, because there is no need to maintain day books and personal ledgers for debtors and creditors;

(ii) with less work required, the accounting records are more easily kept up to date;

(iii) the risk of error is reduced—much copying into intermediate books is eliminated;

(iv) there is always a ready reference direct to the original document;

(v) it is a simple system for a small business with a low number of credit transactions, and particularly for the type of business where the owner maintains the book-keeping records.

The *disadvantages* are:

(i) it is unsuitable for larger businesses;

(ii) the system is more susceptible to fraud because full double-entry book-keeping records are not kept.

17.7   Questions

*1.   A. Kinder is a sole trader in the business of selling furniture.

1 Feb.	Kinder bought 8 chairs at £17 each from B. Moran on credit and was allowed a trade discount of 25 per cent.
2 Feb.	Kinder bought 7 tables at £150 each from J. James.
3 Feb.	Kinder returned 2 tables to James because they were damaged.
4 Feb.	Kinder paid Moran the amount due by cheque.
	Kinder paid James half the amount outstanding by cheque.

Prepare the necessary day books and J. James's and B. Moran's accounts and balance them off.

[Pitman Examinations Institute]

2.   Write up the appropriate journals of A. Charlesworth for the month of March 19–2, from the following information (ledger accounts are not required):

6 Mar.	Received invoice from S. Lyons:
	3 oak tables at £180 each,
	3 fireside chairs at £80 each.
	All subject to 25 per cent trade discount.
9 Mar.	Sent invoice to H. Lambert:
	2 oak tables at £215 each,
	2 occasional tables at £45 each.
	All subject to 20 per cent trade discount.
14 Mar.	Invoiced to L. Saxby:
	5 carpet squares at £120 each.
	Subject to 20 per cent trade discount.
21 Mar.	Received an invoice from B. Sharp:
	2 oak sideboards at £350 each,
	4 oak corner cupboards at £90 each.
	All subject to 20 per cent trade discount.

30 Mar.   Received credit note from B. Sharp:
1 oak corner cupboard, damaged, as invoiced on 21 March.
[East Midland Regional Examinations Board]

3. J. Brooks, a sole trader, has the following transactions during the month of September 19–3.

6 Sep.   Bought on credit from S. Knight 3 carpets at £90 each less 10 per cent trade discount.

9 Sep.   Sold on credit to M. Toft 2 carpets at £140 each less 5 per cent trade discount.

14 Sep.   Purchased on credit from F. Church 4 carpets at £85 each less 5 per cent trade discount.

16 Sep.   Sold on credit to J. Aspin 1 carpet at £135 and 1 at £100—no trade discount allowed.

21 Sep.   Purchased on credit from K. Good 2 carpets at £120 each less 10 per cent trade discount.

28 Sep.   Sold on credit to A. Best 1 carpet at £105 and 1 at £115 less 5 per cent trade discount on the complete sale.

Required:

(*a*) Enter the above transactions in the sales day book and purchases day book as appropriate.

(*b*) Post the transactions from the day books to the personal accounts concerned in the ledger.

(*c*) Total the two day books and post the totals to the appropriate impersonal accounts in the ledger.

[London Chamber of Commerce]

4. A. Rankin deals in furniture and carpeting.

During March 19–2 he made the following credit purchases and sales. Enter these items in the appropriate books of original entry with separate columns for furniture, carpeting, and total. Total the books but do not post to the ledger.

10 Mar.   Received an invoice from F. Robinson:
2 occasional tables at £40 each,
6 carpet squares at £80 each.

15 Mar.   Invoiced A. Sutton with
2 oak dining suites at £250 each,
3 Axminster carpets at £120 each.

22 Mar.   Sent an invoice to K. Hanvey for
3 fire screens at £30 each,
20 yards carpeting at £10 per yard.

26 Mar.   I. Robins sent his invoice for
2 oak wardrobes at £90 each,
4 fireside rugs at £40 each.

[West Midlands Examinations Board]

*5. Enter the following transactions in the sales day book. At the end of the month total the day book and indicate the amounts to be posted to the general ledger. All transactions are subject to VAT at 10 per cent.

    1 Apr.   Sold office furniture to Ajax Services, list price £240 allowing them 20 per cent trade discount. Invoice No 8723.

    8 Apr.   Sold 4 filing cabinets to Markups at list price of £50 each. Invoice No 8726.

    18 Apr.   Sold 6 typewriters to Jones Machines list price £90 each. Trade discount of 15 per cent was allowed. Invoice No 8728.

    28 Apr.   Sold office furniture to Wye Products list price £300. Trade discount of 20 per cent was allowed. Invoice No 8734.

Note. Ledger accounts are not required.

[Royal Society of Arts]

6. K. Lynn runs a store which sells camping equipment and sports goods. Credit purchases for the month of May 19–8 were:

    4 May   Canvas Products Ltd, Invoice No CP1916
                4   2-person ridge tents at £20 each
                4   4-person frame tents at £110 each

    9 May   Holiday Products Ltd, Invoice No IP1624
             100   beach balls at £1 each
              20   sleeping bags at £11 each
               6   3-man inflatable dinghies at £25 each

    25 May   T. Wang, Invoice No TW1735
               6   tennis racquets at £10 each
               4   badminton racquets at £5 each
              20   boxes shuttlecocks at £2 per box

    30 May   Anglian Campers, Invoice No AN742
               5   camping stoves at £8 each

On 14 May

    1 ridge tent was returned to Canvas Products Ltd,
    Advice Note AN27, damaged in transit.

All transactions are subject to VAT at 10%.
All suppliers' prices are net and trade discount is not allowed.

You are required to:
Prepare analysed columnar day books for Purchases and Purchases Returns to record these transactions. Note: ledger accounts are not required.

[RSA Examinations Board]

7. Give a full description of the 'slip' system of book-keeping and explain how the system operates.

List three main advantages resulting from the use of the 'slip' system.

[Royal Society of Arts]

8. On 1 May 19–9 Tom Williams was owed the following amounts by his debtors:

	£
R. Blackmore	140
U. Heap	210

On the same day his creditors were:

	£
D. Beanland	88
J. Higgins	670

and he had a debit balance on his bank account of £450.

His day books for the month ending 31 May 19–9 are shown below.

Sales day book

	Invoice no	Folio no	Total £	VAT £	Net £
May 6 R. Blackmore	8952	SL45	110	10	100
May 23 U. Heap	8953	SL46	275	25	250
May 31 Transferred to general ledger			385	35	350

Purchases day book

	Invoice no	Folio no	Total £	VAT £	Net £
May 4 D. Beanland	DB145	PL37	143	13	130
May 23 J. Higgins	JH136	PL38	440	40	400
May 31 Transferred to general ledger			583	53	530

Sales returns day book

	Credit note	Folio no	Total £	VAT £	Net £
May 17 R. Blackmore	CN27	SL45	22	2	20
May 31 Transferred to general ledger			22	2	20

During the month the following transactions took place on his bank account.

May 15 U. Heap paid £150 on account.
May 18 Williams paid Beanland's account in full.
May 30 R. Blackmore paid £200 on account.

You are required:
To write up and balance all the necessary accounts to record the above transactions for the month of May 19–9 in Williams' ledger (use either three-column running balance method or the two-sided format).

[*RSA Examinations Board*]

Multiple-choice Questions—5

Read each question carefully. Choose the *one* answer you think is correct. Answers are given on page 411.

1. Which of the following business documents is used as the source document for credit sales into the firm's accounting records?

    A credit note   **C** copy of the sales invoice
    B sales invoice   **D** delivery note

2. A business buys goods from a supplier at a retail price of £1 000. The terms stated on the invoice are trade discount 20 per cent, and cash discount 5 per cent for payment within seven days. If the invoice is settled within the seven-day period the supplier will receive a cheque for:

    A £760   **B** £800   **C** £950   **D** £755

3. The cost price of an article is £4, and the selling price is £5. The gross profit margin is:

    A 20%   **B** 80%   **C** 25%   **D** 30%

4. An article costs a retailer £8 and the selling price is £10. The mark-up is:

    A 80%   **B** 30%   **C** 25%   **D** 20%

5. The sales ledger of a business contains:

    A the personal accounts of customers   **C** the Sales Account
    B creditors' accounts   **D** the accounts of suppliers

6. The purchases ledger of a business contains:

    A Capital Account   **C** nominal accounts
    B creditors' accounts   **D** debtors' accounts

7. Which one of the following is a 'nominal' account?

    A Machinery Account   **C** H. Bull's account (a debtor)
    B Drawings Account   **D** Wages Account

8. The discount column of the cash book records:

    A discount for trade customers   **C** discount for bulk buying
    B discount for prompt payment   **D** VAT on discount

9. Cash discount allowed to a customer should be recorded by:

	Debit	*Credit*
A	Discount Received Account	customer's account
B	Discount Allowed Account	customer's account
C	customer's account	Discount Received Account
D	customer's account	Discount Allowed Account

10. Which one of the following is *not* a book of original entry?

    A returns inwards journal   **C** sales ledger
    B purchases journal   **D** cash book

11. The total of sales journal is transferred to:

    A the credit side of Sales Account   **C** the debit side of Sales Account
    B the credit side of sales ledger   **D** the debit side of cash book

12. The main source of information for returns inwards journal is:

    A sales invoices   **C** debit notes
    B credit notes   **D** cash till roll

The Accounting System: a Fully Worked Example

This Unit brings together most of the aspects of handwritten double-entry book-keeping that we have considered so far. A month's transactions are put through the books of original entry (sales journal, purchases journal and returns journals) and then entered in the accounts—the ledger is divided into cash books, sales ledger, purchases ledger and general ledger. At the month-end a trial balance is extracted, and Trading and Profit and Loss Accounts, together with a balance sheet, are prepared: transfers to close appropriate accounts are made. The financial year ends on 31 December. (In order to keep the book-keeping fairly simple, VAT has been ignored, and invoice numbers and purchase order numbers are omitted.)

Trial balance of H. Sanderson as at 1 December 19–1

	Dr. £	Cr. £
Sales		33 500
Purchases	11 240	
Returns inwards	100	
Returns outwards		140
Salaries	10 400	
Vehicle running expenses	1 560	
Heating and lighting	750	
Rates	975	
Discount allowed	33	
Discount received		48
Buildings	25 000	
Vehicles	7 500	
Stock (at 1 Jan. 19–1)	4 500	
Debtors: E. Scott	240	
T. Hall	400	
H. Lewis	300	
Creditors: A. Parry		160
J. Stephens		200
G. Young		80
Capital		33 000
Drawings	3 500	
Bank	530	
Cash	100	
	67 128	67 128

Transactions for December 19–1:

1 Dec.	Bought goods £40 on credit from G. Young.
2 Dec.	Received a cheque from E. Scott in full settlement of the amount owing, less 2½ per cent cash discount.
3 Dec.	Sold goods £100 on credit to H. Lewis.
4 Dec.	Paid heating and lighting £125 by cheque.
5 Dec.	Sold goods £750 on credit to E. Scott.
6 Dec.	Bought goods £320 on credit from J. Stephens.
7 Dec.	Owner's drawings £75 in cash.
8 Dec.	Paid amount owing to A. Parry by cheque, after deducting 2½ per cent cash discount.
8 Dec.	E. Scott returns £50 of goods because they are unsuitable.
10 Dec.	Withdrew £200 cash from bank for use in the business.
11 Dec.	Paid salaries in cash £135.
11 Dec.	Sold goods £100 on credit to T. Hall.
12 Dec.	We return unsuitable goods £40 to J. Stephens.
13 Dec.	Paid vehicle running expenses £30 in cash.
14 Dec.	Bought a delivery van for £2 500, paying by cheque.
14 Dec.	H. Lewis pays the amount owing by cheque, less 2 per cent cash discount.
15 Dec.	Bought goods on credit £185 from A. Parry.
16 Dec.	Sold goods on credit £150 to H. Lewis.
17 Dec.	Paid salaries by cheque £520.
18 Dec.	H. Lewis returns unsuitable goods £20.
18 Dec.	T. Hall pays the amount owing by cheque, less 2 per cent cash discount.
19 Dec.	Paid amount owing to G. Young by cheque, less 2½ per cent cash discount.
19 Dec.	Sold goods on credit to T. Hall £500.
21 Dec.	Paid vehicle running expenses in cash £25.
22 Dec.	Bought goods £350 on credit from G. Young.
23 Dec.	Returned unsatisfactory goods £30 to G. Young.
28 Dec.	Sold goods £300 on credit to E. Scott.
29 Dec.	Paid salaries by cheque £625.
29 Dec.	Sold goods £400 on credit to H. Lewis.
30 Dec.	Bought goods £210 on credit from A. Parry.
31 Dec.	Received a cheque from E. Scott for £700.
31 Dec.	Owner's drawings £380 by cheque.

At 31 December, the closing stock is valued at £3 850.

Sales journal			**Page 48**
19–1		£	£
3 Dec. H. Lewis	SL103		100
5 Dec. E. Scott	SL101		750
11 Dec. T. Hall	SL102		100
16 Dec. H. Lewis	SL103		150
19 Dec. T. Hall	SL102		500
28 Dec. E. Scott	SL101		300
29 Dec. H. Lewis	SL103		400
31 Dec. Monthly total transferred to			
Sales Account	GL310		2 300

Purchases journal			**Page 35**
19–1		£	£
1 Dec. G. Young	PL203		40
6 Dec. J. Stephens	PL202		320
15 Dec. A. Parry	PL201		185
22 Dec. G. Young	PL203		350
30 Dec. A. Parry	PL201		210
31 Dec. Monthly total transferred to			
Purchases Account	GL302		1 105

Returns inwards journal			**Page 12**
19–1		£	£
8 Dec. E. Scott	SL101		50
18 Dec. H. Lewis	SL103		20
31 Dec. Monthly total transferred to			
Returns Inwards Account	GL303		70

Returns outwards journal			**Page 15**
19–1		£	£
12 Dec. J. Stephens	PL202		40
23 Dec. G. Young	PL203		30
31 Dec. Monthly total transferred to			
Returns Outwards Account	GL304		70

General Ledger:

			Sales			**Account no 301**
19–1		£	19–1			£
31 Dec. Trading			1 Dec. Balance b/d			33 500
Account	GL316	35 800	31 Dec. Monthly total	SJ48		2 300
		35 800				35 800

Purchases   Account no 302

19–1		£	19–1		£
1 Dec. Balance b/d		11 240	31 Dec. Trading		
31 Dec. Monthly total	PJ35	1 105	Account	GL316	12 345
		12 345			12 345

Returns inwards   Account no 303

19–1		£	19–1		£
1 Dec. Balance b/d		100	31 Dec. Trading		
31 Dec. Monthly total	RIJ12	70	Account	GL316	170
		170			170

Returns outwards   Account no 304

19–1		£	19–1		£
31 Dec. Trading			1 Dec. Balance b/d		140
Account	GL316	210	31 Dec. Monthly total	ROJ15	70
		210			210

Salaries   Account no 305

19–1		£	19–1		£
1 Dec. Balance b/d		10 400	31 Dec. Profit and Loss		
11 Dec. Cash	CB10	135	Account	GL317	11 680
17 Dec. Bank	CB10	520			
29 Dec. Bank	CB10	625			
		11 680			11 680

Vehicle running expenses   Account no 306

19–1		£	19–1		£
1 Dec. Balance b/d		1 560	31 Dec. Profit and Loss		
13 Dec. Cash	CB10	30	Account	GL317	1 615
21 Dec. Cash	CB10	25			
		1 615			1 615

Heating and lighting   Account no 307

19–1		£	19–1		£
1 Dec. Balance b/d		750	31 Dec. Profit and Loss		
4 Dec. Bank	CB10	125	Account	GL317	875
		875			875

Rates   Account no 308

19–1		£	19–1		£
			31 Dec. Profit and Loss		
1 Dec. Balance b/d		975	Account	GL317	975

	Discount allowed		**Account no 309**
19–1	£	19–1	£
1 Dec. Balance b/d	33	31 Dec. Profit and Loss	
31 Dec. Monthly total CB10	24	Account GL317	57
	57		57

	Discount received		**Account no 310**
19–1	£	19–1	£
31 Dec. Profit and Loss		1 Dec. Balance b/d	48
Account GL317	55	31 Dec. Monthly total CB10	7
	55		55

	Buildings		**Account no 311**
19–1	£	19–1	£
1 Dec. Balance b/d	25 000	31 Dec. Balance c/d	25 000
19–2			
1 Jan. Balance b/d	25 000		

	Vehicles		**Account no 312**
19–1	£	19–1	£
1 Dec. Balance b/d	7 500	31 Dec. Balance c/d	10 000
14 Dec. Bank CB10	2 500		
	10 000		10 000
19–2			
1 Jan. Balance b/d	10 000		

	Stock		**Account no 313**
19–1	£	19–1	£
		31 Dec. Trading	
1 Dec. Balance b/d	4 500	Account GL316	4 500
31 Dec. Trading			
Account GL316	3 850	31 Dec. Balance c/d	3 850
19–2			
1 Jan. Balance b/d	3 850		

	Capital		**Account no 314**
19–1	£	19–1	£
31 Dec. Drawings GL315	3 955	1 Dec. Balance b/d	33 000
31 Dec. Balance c/d	36 743	31 Dec. Profit and Loss	
		Account	7 698
	40 698		40 698
		19–2	
		1 Jan. Balance b/d	36 743

	Drawings		**Account no 315**
19–1	£	19–1	£
1 Dec. Balance b/d	3 500	31 Dec. Capital GL314	3 955
7 Dec. Cash CB10	75		
31 Dec. Bank CB10	380		
	3 955		3 955

Sales Ledger:

			E. Scott		**Account no 101**	
19–1		£	19–1			£
1 Dec. Balance b/d		240	2 Dec. Bank	CB10		234
5 Dec. Sales	SJ48	750	2 Dec. Discount			
			allowed	GL309		6
28 Dec. Sales	SJ48	300	8 Dec. Returns			
			inwards	RIJ12		50
			31 Dec. Bank	CB10		700
			31 Dec. Balance c/d			300
		1 290				1 290
19–2						
1 Jan. Balance b/d		300				

			T. Hall		**Account no 102**	
19–1		£	19–1			£
1 Dec. Balance b/d		400	18 Dec. Bank	CB10		490
11 Dec. Sales	SJ48	100	18 Dec. Discount			
19 Dec. Sales	SJ48	500	allowed	GL309		10
			31 Dec. Balance c/d			500
		1 000				1 000
19–2						
1 Jan. Balance b/d		500				

			H. Lewis		**Account no 103**	
19–1		£	19–1			£
1 Dec. Balance b/d		300	14 Dec. Bank	CB10		392
3 Dec. Sales	SJ48	100	14 Dec. Discount			
16 Dec. Sales	SJ48	150	allowed	GL309		8
29 Dec. Sales	SJ48	400	18 Dec. Return			
			inwards	RIJ12		20
			31 Dec. Balance c/d			530
		950				950
19–2						
1 Jan. Balance b/d		530				

Purchases Ledger:

			A. Parry		**Account no 201**	
19–1		£	19–1			£
8 Dec. Bank	CB10	156	1 Dec. Balance b/d			160
8 Dec. Discount			15 Dec. Purchases	PJ35		185
received	GL310	4	30 Dec. Purchases	PJ35		210
31 Dec. Balance c/d		395				
		555				555
			19–2			
			1 Jan. Balance b/d			395

		J. Stephens			**Account no 202**
19–1		£	19–1		£
12 Dec. Returns			1 Dec. Balance b/d		200
outwards	ROJ15	40	6 Dec. Purchases	PJ35	320
31 Dec. Balance c/d		480			
		520			520
			19–2		
			1 Jan. Balance b/d		480

		G. Young			**Account no 203**
19–1		£	19–1		£
19 Dec. Bank	CB10	117	1 Dec. Balance b/d		80
19 Dec. Discount			1 Dec. Purchases	PJ35	40
received	GL310	3	22 Dec. Purchases	PJ35	350
23 Dec. Returns					
outwards	ROJ15	30			
31 Dec. Balance c/d		320			
		470			470
			19–2		
			1 Jan. Balance b/d		320

For cash book, see page 161.

Trial balance of H. Sanderson as at 31 December 19–1

	Dr.	Cr.
	£	£
Sales		35 800
Purchases	12 345	
Returns inwards	170	
Returns outwards		210
Salaries	11 680	
Vehicle running expenses	1 615	
Heating and lighting	875	
Rates	975	
Discount allowed	57	
Discount received		55
Buildings	25 000	
Vehicles	10 000	
Capital		33 000
Drawings	3 955	
Cash	35	
Bank		2 277
Debtors: E. Scott	300	
T. Hall	500	
H. Lewis	530	
Creditors: A. Parry		395
J. Stephens		480
G. Young		320
Stock (at 1 Jan. 19–1)	4 500	
	72 537	72 537

Cash book

Date	Details	Folio	Discount £	Cash £	Bank £	Date	Details	Folio	Discount £	Cash £	Bank £
19–1						19–1					
1 Dec.	Balances b/d			100	530	4 Dec.	Heating and lighting	GL307			125
2 Dec.	E. Scott	SL101	6		234	7 Dec.	Drawings	GL315		75	
10 Dec.	Bank	C		200		8 Dec.	A. Parry	PL201	4		156
14 Dec.	H. Lewis	SL103	8		392	10 Dec.	Cash	C			200
18 Dec.	T. Hall	SL102	10		490	11 Dec.	Salaries	GL305		135	
31 Dec.	E. Scott	SL101			700	13 Dec.	Vehicle running expenses	GL306		30	
31 Dec.	Balance c/d				2 277	14 Dec.	Vehicles	GL312			2 500
						17 Dec.	Salaries	GL305			520
						19 Dec.	G. Young	PL203	3		117
						21 Dec.	Vehicle running expenses	GL306		25	
						29 Dec.	Salaries	GL305			625
						31 Dec.	Drawings	GL315			380
						31 Dec.	Balance c/d			35	
			24	300	4 623				7	300	4 623
19–2			£	£	£	19–2			£	£	£
1 Jan.	Balance b/d			35		1 Jan.	Balance b/d				2 277

Trading Account of H. Sanderson for the year ended 31 December 19–1

				(Account no 316)
	£	£		£
Opening stock		4 500	Sales	35 800
Purchases	12 345		*Less* Returns inwards	170
				35 630
Less Returns outwards	210			
		12 135		
		16 635		
Less Closing stock		3 850		
		12 785		
Gross profit c/d		22 845		
		35 630		35 630

Profit and Loss Account of H. Sanderson for the year ended 31 December 19–1

			(Account no 317)
	£		£
Discount allowed	57	Gross profit b/d	22 845
Salaries	11 680	Discount received	55
Vehicle running expenses	1 615		
Heating and lighting	875		
Rates	975		
Net profit	7 698		
	22 900		22 900

Balance sheet of H. Sanderson as at 31 December 19–1

	£	£		£	£
Fixed assets:			Capital		33 000
Buildings		25 000	*Add* Net profit		7 698
Vehicles		10 000			40 698
		35 000	*Less* Drawings		3 955
					36 743
Current assets:			Current liabilities:		
Stock	3 850		Creditors	1 195	
Debtors	1 330		Bank overdraft	2 277	
Cash	35				3 472
	5 215				
	40 215				40 215

Modern Accounting Methods

19.1 Introduction

So far in this book, the method of recording business transactions in accounts we have studied is a basic handwritten system. While this is perfectly acceptable in accounting terms, other methods are also in use. These include

(a) special handwritten accounting books;
(b) simultaneous or 'write-it-once' handwritten accounting records;
(c) mechanized accounting;
(d) computerized accounting (see Unit 20).

A firm may start in business using the type of handwritten accounting records with which we have become familiar, or perhaps special preprinted handwritten accounting books. As it expands, it might begin using simultaneous accounting records and, later on, move to a computerized accounting system. Do not think that there is anything 'old-fashioned' about using a handwritten book-keeping system: well over half of all businesses use a handwritten system of one type or another. The larger businesses were, not unnaturally, the first users of computerized accounting systems, but nowadays a wide range of business packages is available for use on microcomputers, and these are used by many small firms.

There is a 'halfway house' between handwritten accounting and computerized accounting: this is *mechanized accounting*, which means the use of machines specifically designed to carry out certain aspects of double-entry book-keeping.

19.2 Handwritten Accounting Books

The book-keeping system we have used so far requires some knowledge of accounting procedures, such as the names of accounts to be used, whether something should be entered on the debit side or credit side, and so on. Though many people starting in business are knowledgeable in their own specialist areas, they may know little or nothing about maintaining books of account. To help them, office stationers supply a variety of books and loose-leaf binders that contain preprinted pages ready to be filled in by the business. The preprinted pages often include:

(a) a sales sheet, which may also allow for the analysis of sales between different products or different sales areas;
(b) a purchases sheet, which may allow for analysis in the same way as sales;
(c) a bank account record, which may also allow for cash receipts and payments;

(*d*) a petty cash record (see Unit 21), used for recording small cash payments for various items;

(*e*) an account for each debtor;

(*f*) an account for each creditor;

(*g*) a Value Added Tax (VAT) summary, which takes VAT information from the other accounting sheets and records;

(*h*) a wages summary (see Unit 32);

(*i*) a record of fixed assets, such as plant, machinery and office equipment.

With the guidance notes supplied, this type of accounting book or binder provides an excellent way for a small business to keep accurate book-keeping records. At the end of a financial year the entire records can be passed to the firm's accountant who then prepares the firm's Trading and Profit and Loss Account and balance sheet, and deals with the taxation aspects. In the meantime the firm opens a new set of records for the next financial year, bringing forward balances such as debtors, creditors, fixed assets, bank and cash.

Next time you visit a stationer's shop, look at the types of handwritten book-keeping systems they stock.

19.3   Simultaneous Handwritten Accounting Records

One problem with most handwritten book-keeping systems is that they are time-consuming to maintain. Another is that they are rather liable to errors: for example, if we wish to enter credit sales of £50 to J. Brown, we must make an entry in Sales Account, and then switch to J. Brown's account and make the second entry there. Thus to record the transaction we have had to locate two separate accounts correctly and make two separate entries for the same amount.

A solution to both these problems can be the use of *simultaneous accounting records* or 'write-it-once' systems, which are marketed by several firms. The principle behind all simultaneous records systems is that, by placing carbon paper between the documents and records connected with a certain transaction, the accounts can be brought up to date in one operation. There are difficulties in using carbon paper, however—it is awkward to handle, and messy if it is inadvertently placed the wrong way round. Instead, firms marketing this type of accounting system now use a special type of 'no-carbon-required' paper which copies the information written on it on to the sheet or sheets below. This is used with a 'posting board' on which the accounting sheets are usually held in place by means of a row of pegs on the left-hand side which match up with holes punched in the special stationery (see Fig. 19.1). The pegs on the board and the holes in the stationery allow accurate positioning of the sheets and hold them steady while the transaction is being recorded.

Simultaneous accounting records are available for most accounting functions, the most popular being:

(*a*) sales ledger accounting (see Unit 19.4);

(*b*) purchases ledger accounting;

(*c*) wages and salaries systems (see Unit 32).

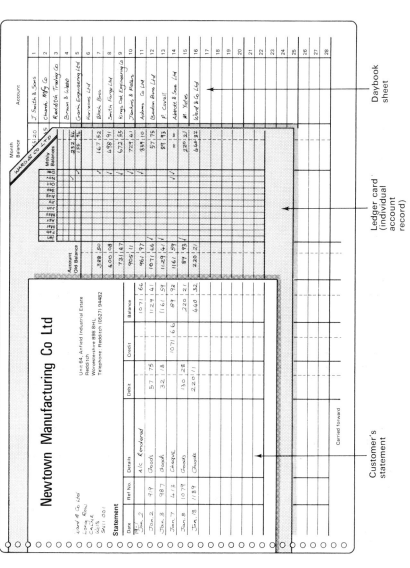

Fig. 19.1 Simultaneous records system

Customer's statement

Ledger card (individual account record)

Daybook sheet

Newtown Manufacturing Co Ltd

Unit 64, Anfield Industrial Estate
Redditch
Worcestershire B98 8HL
Telephone Redditch (0527) 94482

Ward & Co Ltd
Long Road
Calne
Wilts
SN11 001

Statement

Date	Ref No.	Details	Debit	Credit	Balance
19—1					
Jan. 2		A/c Rendered			1071 66
Jan. 2	919	Goods	57 75		1129 41
Jan. 3	987	Goods	32 18		1161 59
Jan. 7	413	Cheque		1071 66	89 93
Jan. 8	1079	Goods	130 28		220 21
Jan. 18	1189	Goods	220 11		440 32
		Carried forward			

Month
WARD & CO LTD
Balance 5120 5125

Mthly Balances 232.56
155.96

Account	Old Balance	Jan	Feb	Mar	Apr	May	Jun	July	Aug	Sep	Oct	Nov	Dec	Balance
	388 50											✓		167 52
	400 08											✓		498 91
	731 67											✓		672 55
	905 11											✓		729 41
	961 97											✓		839 10
	1071 66	✓												57 75
	1129 41	✓												89 93
	1161 59	✓												— —
	89 93	✓												220 21
	220 21													440 32

Account	No.
J. Smith & Sons	1
Church Mfg Co	2
Redditch Trading Co	3
Brown & Webb	4
Garn Engineering Ltd	5
Horizons Ltd	6
Black Bros	7
Smith Forge Ltd	8
Kings Oak Engineering Co	9
Jenkins & Pallas	10
Adams Co Ltd	11
Buxton Bros Ltd	12
P. Cavell	13
Abbott & Son Ltd	14
W. Yates	15
Ward & Co Ltd	16
	17
	18
	19
	20
	21
	22
	23
	24
	25
	26
	27
	28

19.4   Sales Ledger: Simultaneous Accounting

Using a simultaneous accounting system for sales ledger, the statement, the ledger card and the sales journal/day book are written up in one transaction. An accounts clerk has a special tray in which are kept the ledger cards for each customer and the current month's statements. The procedure for operating the system is as follows:

(*a*) A sales journal sheet is placed on the posting board, using the pegs on the board to align it.

(*b*) The clerk then takes the ledger card and statement of the customer to whom the transaction refers. These are placed on the posting board with the statement on top of the ledger card, which is itself on top of the sales journal sheet. They are positioned carefully so that the next clear line on each will be written on.

(*c*) Details of the transaction, from the invoice or copy invoice, are entered on the statement; the transaction is automatically copied on to the ledger card and sales journal sheet.

(*d*) The updated statement and ledger card are removed from the posting board and returned to the tray, and the same process is repeated for the next account.

(*e*) At the end of the day, week or month, the total from the sales journal sheet is transferred to Sales Account.

(*f*) At the month-end the statements are sent out to the customer, and new statements prepared for the next month. The ledger cards form a permanent record of transactions with each customer. When a card is full it is filed away and the balance transferred to a new card.

The *advantages* of this system are as follows:

(*a*) Less clerical time and labour is required than with conventional double-entry book-keeping—each transaction is entered once only.

(*b*) The three accounting records—statement, ledger card and journal— are updated simultaneously, and therefore all show the same transactions. Information is readily available to the owner of the business.

(*c*) There is less risk of numerical errors.

(*d*) Statements are ready for dispatch at the end of the month.

(*e*) Controls can be 'built-in' to the system to provide additional checks on the accuracy of the work.

But there are certain *disadvantages*:

(*a*) Simultaneous accounting systems need to be operated carefully and with a high degree of accuracy.

(*b*) Because one person posts the statement, ledger and journal, there can be difficulties due to errors such as misposts to a wrongly named account or badly written figures.

(*c*) Fraud is more likely because one person is operating the entire ledger section.

A similar procedure can be used for recording credit purchases but, of course, the journal is then the purchases journal. Returns—inwards and outwards—are recorded using the appropriate journal. For receipts and payments in cash and by cheque, a 'cash received' or 'cash paid' summary takes the place of the journal sheet.

As with most book-keeping systems, when using 'write-it-once' records it is best to 'batch' the work, that is, to deal with a run of, say, invoices, then perhaps a run of returns inwards, and so on. Efficiency is thus improved because the clerk repeats the same task a number of times before going on to a different one, and time and effort are saved.

Several fairly elaborate simultaneous accounting systems are available. They are particularly suitable for the smaller business as an early book-keeping system. As a firm expands, it may move on to computerized accounting—see Unit 20.

19.5 Mechanized Accounting

Until the widespread introduction of computers in business, large organizations used accounting machines that were mechanical rather than electronic. Perhaps the most common was the *ledger posting machine* for debtors' accounts and creditors' accounts, and this is still quite widely used. A ledger sheet or card is maintained for each debtor or creditor. Where a transaction is to take place on an account, the operator inserts the current ledger sheet, picks up the balance showing on the account by keying it into the machine and enters the current transaction; the machine automatically performs the appropriate addition or subtraction and prints the resultant closing balance. The ledger sheet is then removed from the machine, and the next required sheet entered into it. Thus the machine is carrying out mechanically the same functions that we have been performing by hand.

The ledger posting machine usually has a full numerical keyboard and a limited number of additional keys which can be pressed to provide an abbreviated 'narrative' for each transaction, with CSH standing for cash, GDS for goods, and so on. The operator usually works from original documents and posts batches of entries to debtors' accounts and then to creditors' accounts— transactions cannot be mixed between the different types of accounts. The machine keeps a carbon copy of the batch of postings and the totals from each batch can be used as a 'check' device within the accounting system.

Machine-posted accounts take a different form from the usual handwritten ledgers and have three money columns, showing a balance after each transaction:

Date	Details	Dr.	Cr.	Balance
		£	£	£

You have already seen this type of account in Unit 5.4.

A disadvantage of these machines is that picking up the current balance of an account—the first operation before posting an item—is a time-consuming and error-prone operation. A new generation of accounting machines has been developed which employ the best features of ledger posting machines while at the same time using computer technology. These machines, often known as *visible record computers* (VRC), use *magnetic stripe ledger cards*. The cards, which look like ordinary ledger cards or sheets containing the appropriate information in printed form, also carry a strip of magnetic material, which is used for the electronic storage of information such as name and address, account number, credit limit (if a debtor), and current balance. When the operator places the ledger card in the machine, there is no need to key in the current balance—the machine picks it up automatically by 'reading' the magnetic stripe. All the operator has to do is to key in the transaction data and the ledger card is updated both in print and electronically. Thus time is saved, and a VRC machine is much quicker to operate than an ordinary accounting machine; it can moreover also be used to produce documents such as invoices and statements.

19.6   Computers in Accounting

The use of computers in accounting is nowadays so extensive that it requires a whole Unit to itself—Unit 20.

19.7   Questions

1. What is meant by 'simultaneous accounting records'?

2. What are the advantages and disadvantages of using simultaneous records for sales ledger accounting?

3. Using simultaneous records enter the following sales ledger transactions under today's date (VAT is levied on each transaction at a rate of 10 per cent):

    Sold goods £120.50 on credit to J. Brown: invoice no 3640.
    Sold goods £155.45 on credit to W. Harris: invoice no 3641.
    Sold goods £95.10 on credit to P. Smith: invoice no 3642.
    Sold goods £84.60 on credit to N. Jarvis: invoice no 3643.
    Sold goods £138.45 on credit to W. Harris: invoice no 3644.
    Sold goods £45.68 on credit to P. Smith: invoice no 3645.
    Sold goods £98.76 on credit to N. Jarvis: invoice no 3646.

Computers in Accounting

20.1 Computer Systems

Nowadays computers, and particularly microcomputers, are becoming more and more common for business and other applications. You may have a microcomputer at home, or you may have used one at school or at work. You will know that microcomputers can be used for a variety of purposes—from graphics and playing games to word-processing. Book-keeping is just one of these uses, and a most important one.

For business use a complete computer system is required consisting, in the main, of four items of equipment (*hardware*) and a number of computer programs (*software*).

20.2 Computer Hardware

For most business systems, this consists of:

(*a*) microcomputer,
(*b*) visual display unit,
(*c*) printer,
(*d*) disc drive.

The *microcomputer* comprises the central processing unit or CPU—the heart of the machine, where all operations are carried out and where information is stored—and a keyboard, which broadly follows the standard typewriter lay-out. The keyboard is an *input device* which places information into the memory of the computer where it is stored and where calculations can be carried out on it.

The *visual display unit* (VDU) or *monitor* or *screen*, is very similar to a television set—in fact most home computers can be linked to an ordinary television set. A business computer system will include a purpose-built VDU designed to give a good-quality display. The VDU converts information sent to it by the computer into a form that can be read by the user.

A *printer* is an *output device* that gives a 'hard copy' of results produced using the computer. For high-quality printing a laser printer is used, while a cheaper 'dot matrix' printer is used for fast printing of lower quality. Some printers can print in different colours.

In order to reduce the cost, the memory of a microcomputer is limited in size and, when the machine is switched off, everything within the memory is lost. However, large amounts of information can be stored in a permanent or semi-permanent form on a *magnetic disc*. *Floppy discs* are generally used with home and small business microcomputers, but the amount of information that can be stored on a floppy disc may be insufficient for business applications, and so *hard discs*, which have a far greater capacity, may be used. A *disc drive* provides a means of reading the information on the disc and passing it rapidly into the computer's memory. (Instead of a disc and disc drive, a home computer often uses a cassette tape and cassette recorder, but though they have the advantage of cheapness these operate far too slowly for business purposes.)

Fig. 20.1 shows the hardware of a computer system.

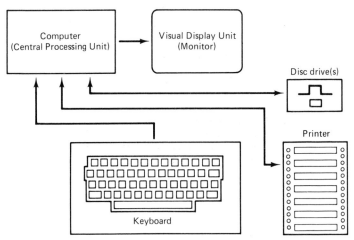

Fig. 20.1 Hardware components of a typical microcomputer system

20.3   Computer Software

Computer hardware is operated by a set of instructions, or *programs*, called *software*. Software has been described as 'the bit that curbs the horse' because, while it is the least visible part of the computer system, you can't go anywhere without it. Under the control of software, an otherwise useless computer will work busily at whatever task is assigned. Software for microcomputers is usually supplied on a floppy disc or, if you are using a home computer, on a cassette tape. Both of these are magnetic devices, carrying information which, by running them in a disc drive or cassette recorder, respectively, can be read and passed into the computer's memory.

Two kinds of software guide a computer. *System software* controls the basic equipment of the computer, such as the memory, and either is built into the computer or comes with it. *Application software* is the concern of the user and allows specific tasks of his or her choice to be performed—in accounting, for example, to enter invoices into debtors' accounts or to prepare payroll (wages and salaries). For carrying out accounting functions by computer most applications software is available in 'off-the-shelf' programs called *packaged software*. Packaged software is rather like a factory-built car: it is relatively inexpensive (at least when compared with one that is hand-built), readily available, reliable and easy to use, even by those without previous computer experience. It comes complete, with an operating manual, giving full instructions.

Most packaged software is *menu-driven*. This means that at every point at which the program is waiting for an instruction, the user is presented with a menu, that is, a series of options on the monitor screen, and then selects the appropriate instruction by pressing a single key. An example from a sales ledger program might look like this:

```
SALES LEDGER

Customer Maintenance

Create new account ........................... 1
Amend account .................................. 2
Delete account ................................... 3
Print alphabetical customer list ......... 4
Return to main menu ......................... 5

SELECT A FUNCTION
```

The user would then press the appropriate number (some systems use letters instead). As choice 5 indicates, a typical package will contain many such menus and submenus; the user works through them until the point is reached where actual data needs to be entered. Most programs also have a HELP command—if you get lost or are unsure how to operate the program, this will give further information and may also refer you to the appropriate page in the instruction manual.

20.4   Computerized Processing of Data

The basis for all computerized processing is the *data file*. This is simply a collection of records, each of which is set out in a standard pattern, so that each can be processed by the computer in the same way. For example, one data file in accounting is the sales ledger, which contains the individual records of each customer. Each individual record in the sales ledger will comprise the name of the customer with his or her address, account number and credit limit, details of transactions and the balance. Using a computerized system, the data file is stored on a floppy or hard disc, and the computer program that uses the file will have access to one record at a time.

From time to time we shall need to *update* the records held in the data file. This is done by first accessing the record so that it appears on the monitor screen, and then keying in the new data to make changes to that record. When this has been done, the next record can be accessed, and so on.

Most computerized accounting systems use *codes* in order that the computer can identify a particular record. Generally these take the form of account or stock item numbers. When updating files it is necessary for all data to bear the appropriate code number so that it can be input to the correct record. Coding all items at source makes for speedier data processing; a good example of this is bank paying-in books and cheques—each bears the number of the account and all the computer operator has to do is to key in the number for the item to be posted to the correct account. Wherever possible the customer should indicate the code number; for instance, when John Smith sends a remittance to a business he should always quote his account number. If Mr Smith does not do this himself, then someone within the firm must look up the number and enter it on a remittance slip, ready to be input to the computer. There is always a danger, particularly with a common name, that the wrong account number will be entered, resulting in a mispost.

Most computer accounting programs print *reports*, perhaps reports for management on a particular aspect of the program, after updating has been carried out. These usually take the form of hard copy produced by a printer.

Most programs also allow *enquiries* to be made at any time while the program is running, so that immediate access is available to any of the records held on the disc—this helps when dealing with problems and queries over the telephone, such as enquiries about particular items of stock or transactions on a certain customer's account.

20.5   Standard Business Accounting Packages

Most software companies offer a range of accounting packages at a reasonable cost. Each package comprises the program, generally in the form of a floppy disc, plus a book of operating instructions. Packages are available to handle a range of standard accounting applications, such as sales ledger, purchases ledger, general (or nominal) ledger, invoicing, stock control and payroll, as well as some specialist applications.

20.6   Sales Ledger

The sales ledger section, as you know, contains the debtors' accounts—the records of the firm's customers. Sales ledger and its effective control are therefore very important to a business. A computerized sales ledger system (also known as *accounts receivable*) does the same things that a manual system does—maintains customer records and keeps a history of each account—but with greater accuracy and in a fraction of the time. A computerized system can significantly improve customer service with prompt and accurate monthly statements, which should reduce the time debtors take to pay their accounts.

Such a computer system usually includes a twin disc drive. Two discs with information stored on them are inserted into separate slots on the disc drive. One disc contains the accounting program, that is, the instructions to the computer. The other disc contains the information to be worked on (the data file)—in the case of sales ledger, information about the debtors' accounts: for each record, the customer's name, address, account number, credit limit, balance brought forward, and transactions posted to the account in the form of invoices, payments réceived and credit notes. With both discs inserted into the drive, the computer can read the information on the discs as needed, depending on what aspect of sales ledger accounting is to be handled.

A typical menu for carrying out sales ledger transactions is:

```
                    SALES LEDGER

                   Post Transactions

        Start invoice batch ............................ 1
        Start credit note batch ....................... 2
        Start payment batch .......................... 3
        Print batch ......................................... 4


                 SELECT A FUNCTION
```

As this indicates, each type of transaction is processed in batches at regular intervals. This is because the computer needs to read the different instructions from the program disc to carry out different tasks: having set the computer up ready to post invoices to debtors' accounts, for example, it is sensible to complete a whole batch of invoices, perhaps a single day's. As you will discover, once the computer is set up to carry out a certain task, accounting by computer is very straightforward: don't just read about it, try it!

Besides maintaining customer accounts by entering invoices, payments received and credit notes, other submenus will cover customer maintenance (opening accounts, or amending customer semi-permanent details such as address or credit limit), management reporting (producing information such as an ageing schedule of debtors—see Fig. 20.2), printing of customer statements, printing of journal transactions, and dealing with enquiries (showing the customer's account on the monitor screen). Naturally, for sales ledger accounting, such a program will be designed to handle and record Value Added Tax.

Sales ledger programs can be linked to nominal or general ledger by the addition to each transaction posted of a nominal ledger account number, that

Customer
account
number

Action to be
taken: send
letter etc.

Analysis of each
account by months
outstanding

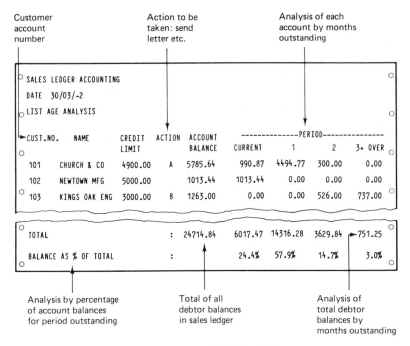

```
SALES LEDGER ACCOUNTING
DATE  30/03/-2
LIST AGE ANALYSIS

CUST.NO.    NAME        CREDIT    ACTION  ACCOUNT    --------------PERIOD--------------
                        LIMIT             BALANCE   CURRENT     1         2      3+ OVER
   101    CHURCH & CO   4900.00     A     5785.64    990.87   4494.77   300.00    0.00
   102    NEWTOWN MFG   5000.00           1013.44   1013.44     0.00     0.00     0.00
   103    KINGS OAK ENG 3000.00     B     1263.00      0.00     0.00   526.00   737.00


TOTAL                           : 24714.84   6017.47 14316.28 3629.84   751.25

BALANCE AS % OF TOTAL           :             24.4%    57.9%    14.7%    3.0%
```

Analysis by percentage
of account balances
for period outstanding

Total of all
debtor balances
in sales ledger

Analysis of
total debtor
balances by
months outstanding

Fig. 20.2 Ageing schedule of debtors

is, the number of the other account involved in the double-entry book-keeping transaction. With a fully integrated computer accounting system (see Unit 20.11), the nominal accounts are posted automatically; otherwise a list of nominal ledger transactions is printed.

20.7   Purchases Ledger

This is basically the same operation as sales ledger, except that it is dealing with the firm's suppliers' accounts, that is, the creditors. In computer accounting terms, the handling of purchases ledger (also known as *accounts payable*) is very much the same as for sales ledger, but with different headings. Suppliers' accounts are maintained by entering the information from invoices, credit notes and payments made, again using batch techniques. Most purchases ledger programs can also print payment cheques and bank giro credits ready to be sent or advised to the creditor, and in addition a journal or day book can be printed as required. Management information is available in the form of total purchases from various suppliers, a creditors' report showing amounts 'aged' according to length of time outstanding, together with other details. Purchases ledger programs can also be linked to nominal or general ledger by the addition of the appropriate account number. With a fully integrated computer accounting system, the nominal accounts are posted automatically; otherwise, a list of nominal ledger transactions can be printed.

20.8   General Ledger

General or nominal ledger contains all the accounts in the business, except for the debtors' and creditors' personal accounts which are to be found in sales ledger and purchases ledger respectively. (Cash book may be dealt with separately; in computer systems, it is often included in general or nominal ledger.)

Using computerized accounts, a general ledger program can enter transactions to the accounts and provide a trial balance. Most programs can also produce a Trading Account, Profit and Loss Account, and balance sheet. A submenu for this might appear as:

```
                  GENERAL LEDGER

              Account Period End Processing

       Trial balance ........................................ 1
       Print Trading Profit & Loss Account .. 2
       Print balance sheet ............................ 3


                  SELECT A FUNCTION
```

20.9   Invoicing

The point at which a transaction is entered into the computerized system varies from one business to another. For example, an invoice can be prepared by hand, and a copy then passed to the computer operator to be entered into the computerized sales ledger. Alternatively, and increasingly nowadays, production of invoices themselves can be carried out using computers, with automatic updating of the sales ledger from the invoice.

To prepare an invoice, two data files are required: one is a customer file, containing name, address and account number; the other is the product file containing details of product descriptions, code, unit quantities and prices. The computer operator enters the code number of the customer to whom the goods are being invoiced, then the product code and the quantity of goods being sold.

In pricing the goods for the invoice, the program takes the information from the product file and carries out the calculations, allowing trade and cash discount as appropriate. In such a way the invoice is built up on the monitor screen and, when complete, can either be stored on disc for later printing, or printed immediately. With an integrated computer accounting system, the sales ledger can then be updated automatically without having to re-key the customer account numbers and invoice totals.

20.10   Stock Control and Payroll

Programs for computerizing these accounting operations are described in the appropriate section of this book: stock control in Unit 31 and payroll in Unit 32.

20.11   Integrated Accounting Systems

Many software firms advertise their accounting programs as being *integrated*. By this is meant that, as each business transaction is entered into the computer, it is immediately reflected right through the accounting system. For example, as a transaction recording a credit sale is entered to the debtor's account, it is at the same time recorded in the Sales Account in general or nominal ledger.

With an accounting system having few transactions, this is advantageous. For a larger system it is necessary for work to be dealt with in batches and, when each batch has been agreed as being correct, the transactions can be integrated into the entire accounting system.

20.12   Trying Out Computerized Accounts

It is difficult within a few pages to do more than sketch the role of computers in accounting. It is moreover impossible to describe in detail how accounting programs work, because all programs differ. There is only one way to learn how to operate computerized accounting systems, and that is to stop reading this book and to go over to a computer, load an accounting program, and operate it using some examples. Don't worry if you go wrong; you will be learning all the time. Here are a few hints to help you through.

(*a*) Load the program into the computer. This involves placing the disc on which the program is stored in the slot on the disc drive and closing the flap. Most accounting programs need a double (twin) disc drive to operate, and you will most probably put the program disc into Drive A or 1. You will need to follow the computer manufacturer's instructions to enable the information contained on the program disc to be read and transferred to the computer's memory—if you are unsure what to do next, refer to the manual supplied with the machine.

(*b*) The program may start to run automatically, or you may need to key in the word RUN or press the RETURN key. Whatever procedure is to be used, you will hear the disc drive operating, and a red light will probably come on. Under no circumstances should you attempt to remove the program disc while the disc drive is operating.

(c) The monitor will display the name of the program. At this stage you may need to enter the correct password in order to continue—this prevents unauthorized users entering transactions, perhaps fraudulently.

(d) The monitor will, by now, be showing the main menu for the program you are operating. You are ready to enter some transactions, and the accounting program will 'prompt' you with instructions. For example, you may be asked to insert the data file disc into the second slot on the disc drive. This disc is designed to contain information on accounts already open and on which you can carry out transactions—your teacher may have prepared material for this disc, or you may be required to open a number of new accounts and then enter certain transactions.

(e) At all times a well-written accounting program will guide you with further prompts by asking you to enter certain details at various stages. If you are in any doubt, one of the function keys (above or to one side of the main keyboard) is usually a 'help' key: pressing this will direct the program to give you some basic instructions. Alternatively, you can consult the manual supplied with the program as part of the 'package'.

(f) As each transaction is completed, so the screen will clear—rather like turning over the page in an accounts book—and you can enter the next transaction; however, earlier transactions will be retained by the computer.

(g) When you have finished a batch of transactions, the computer may ask if you want them printed out: this will produce a hard copy of the book-keeping entries.

'Really; your invoice still hasn't been paid? I'm afraid our computer must be on the blink again'

20.13   Questions

1.   (a) Distinguish between computer hardware and computer software.
      (b) Describe each of the main hardware components necessary for a small business computer system.

2.   What aspects of book-keeping are covered by the different accounting packages available for the microcomputer-user in a small business?
      Choose an accounting package available to you and work through it. Then describe in note form, in terms suitable for a reader with no computer knowledge, the way in which it is operated.

3.   Why is it important to 'code' documents in a computer accounting system?

4.   Using a sales ledger program in a microcomputer, enter the following transactions under today's date, adding VAT at a rate of 10 per cent. (Unless the account names are already held on the data file, you will have to open new accounts filling in as necessary details such as address, account number, credit limit and so on.)

      Sold goods £138.58 on credit to P. Bond: invoice no 2941.
      Sold goods £110.40 on credit to A. Moffatt: invoice no 2942.
      Sold goods £84.32 on credit to T. Lewis: invoice no 2943.
      Sold goods £124.39 on credit to A. Moffatt: invoice no 2944.
      Sold goods £68.98 on credit to P. Bond: invoice no 2945.
      Sold goods £38.60 on credit to T. Lewis: invoice no 2946.

5.   Using a purchases ledger program in a microcomputer, enter the following transactions under today's date, adding VAT at the rate of 10 per cent. (As with Question 4, you may have to open new accounts.)

      Bought goods £163.50 on credit from G. Street: our purchase order no 1263; his invoice no 4751.
      Bought goods £134.25 on credit from T. Hale: our purchase order no 1251; her invoice no 2781.
      Bought goods £84.36 on credit from E. Doyle: our purchase order no 1284; his invoice no 9987.
      Bought goods £78.38 on credit from T. Hale: our purchase order no 1256; her invoice no 2784.
      Bought goods £161.84 on credit from G. Street: our purchase order no 1265; his invoice no 4746.
      Bought goods £41.64 on credit from E. Doyle: our purchase order no 1287; his invoice no 0015.

Petty Cash Book

21.1 What is a Petty Cash Book?

Having just looked at computerized accounting systems, we shall now turn our attention to a type of accounting record that is usually still handwritten: the petty cash book. In Unit 15 we looked at the use of a cash book which includes both Cash Account and Bank Account. While a large number of business payments are made by cash or cheque through the main cash book, a lot of business expenses for very small money amounts are better paid out of a float of *petty cash* drawn from the main cash book, and are recorded in a *petty cash book*. Examples might include small items of postages, stationery and travel expenses.

21.2 The Imprest System

The petty cash book is kept by the *petty cashier* who is responsible for keeping accurate accounting records and for the security of the cash float. Most petty cash books work on the *imprest system*. Using this system the petty cashier starts off with an agreed amount of cash and at regular intervals, perhaps weekly or monthly, sufficient cash is drawn from the main cash book to return the balance of petty cash back to the imprest amount. For example:

	£
Opening balance (imprest amount)	50.00
Less Amounts paid out during week	34.57
Balance of petty cash at end of week	15.43
Add Amount drawn from main cash book	34.57
Balance carried down to next week (imprest amount)	50.00

As you can see, to bring the balance of cash back to the imprest amount, the petty cashier must draw the same amount of cash from the main cash book as has been paid out in expenses.

Under this system, the imprest amount is set at a suitable figure to ensure that the petty cashier does not normally run out of cash between reimbursement dates. If this should happen a transfer can be made from the main cash book; if it happens regularly then the imprest amount might need to be increased.

21.3   Petty Cash Vouchers

Before the petty cashier pays out for various expenses, he or she will wish to see proof that the expenditure has been made. A standard form of petty cash voucher is often used—see Fig. 21.1—to which documentary evidence such as bus tickets, postage receipts or shop till receipts may need to be attached. The petty cashier will follow the regulations of the firm with regard to vouchers, such as a rule that all petty cash claims need signing by a supervisor, or that the person claiming the cash is required to sign for it.

Petty Cash Voucher

Required for	TOTAL		GOODS etc		VAT	
	£	p	£	p	£	p
Envelopes	1	65	1	50	–	15
Staples	2	20	2	00	–	20
Signature A. Brown	3	85	3	50	–	35

Passed by J. Smith

Date 15 April 19 - 2

Fig. 21.1 A petty cash voucher

21.4   Example of a Petty Cash Book Kept on the Imprest System

On returning from holiday you are told to take over the petty cash book. This is kept on the imprest system, the float being £75 at the beginning of each month. The following transactions take place:

19–1

2 Aug.	Voucher no 39: taxi fare £3.80
4 Aug.	Voucher no 40: parcel postage £2.35
7 Aug.	Voucher no 41: pencils £1.26
10 Aug.	Voucher no 42: travel expenses £5.46
12 Aug.	Voucher no 43: window cleaner £8.50
14 Aug.	Voucher no 44: large envelopes £2.45
17 Aug.	Voucher no 45: donation to charity £5

(*continued on page 182*)

Petty cash book

Receipts	Folio	Date	Details	Voucher no.	Total	Travelling	Postages	Stationery	Meals	Miscellaneous	Ledger Fol.	Ledger £
£					£	£	£	£	£	£		£
75.00		19–1										
		1 Aug.	Balance b/d									
		2 Aug.	Taxi fare	39	3.80	3.80						
		4 Aug.	Postages	40	2.35		2.35					
		7 Aug.	Stationery	41	1.26			1.26				
		10 Aug.	Travel	42	5.46	5.46						
		12 Aug.	Window cleaner	43	8.50					8.50		
		14 Aug.	Envelopes	44	2.45			2.45				
		17 Aug.	Charity	45	5.00					5.00		
		18 Aug.	Rail fare/lunch	46	10.80	5.60			5.20			
		20 Aug.	Recorded delivery	47	0.75		0.75					
		23 Aug.	Packing tape	48	1.50			1.50				
		25 Aug.	Excess postage	49	0.55		0.55					
		27 Aug.	Taxi fare	50	5.40	5.40						
		29 Aug.	J. Smith	51	5.00						PL151	5.00
					52.82	20.26	3.65	5.21	5.20	13.50		5.00
						GL36	GL47	GL26	GL69	GL78		
52.82	CB43	31 Aug.	Cash									
		31 Aug.	Balance c/d		75.00							
127.82					127.82							
75.00		1 Sep.	Balance b/d									

Fig. 21.2 A petty cash book kept on the imprest system

18 Aug.	Voucher no 46: rail fare £5.60; lunch £5.20
20 Aug.	Voucher no 47: recorded delivery envelope £0.75
23 Aug.	Voucher no 48: roll of packing tape £1.50
25 Aug.	Voucher no 49: excess postage paid £0.55
27 Aug.	Voucher no 50: taxi fare £5.40
29 Aug.	Voucher no 51: paid J. Smith, a creditor, £5 (his account no is 151)
31 Aug.	Cash received from main cash book to restore imprest amount

The petty cash book appears as in Fig. 21.2 (page 181).

The receipts column is the debit side, while the totals column is the credit side. Analysis columns are used to categorize the various expenses—travelling, postage, stationery and so on: the column headings can of course be varied to suit the needs of the business. The *ledger column* on the right is used where payments are made to a creditor who has a personal account in the purchases ledger. This column would also be used to record purchases out of petty cash for small items of office equipment.

'Will one book of petty cash vouchers be sufficient to cover our capital spending plans for next year?'

21.5   The Petty Cash Book and Double-entry Book-keeping

In the example petty cash book just considered each analysis column has been totalled, and under each total (except for that of the ledger column) appears a general ledger account number. The total of each column is debited to the relevant account in the general ledger, thus:

General Ledger:

	Travelling expenses	Account no 36
19–1	£	
31 Aug. Petty cash book PCB10 20.26		

Thus, from our example, debits are passed to:

	£
Travelling expenses	20.26
Postages	3.65
Stationery	5.21
Meals	5.20
Miscellaneous	13.50

Each item in the analysis column marked 'ledger' must be debited to the appropriate account—in this case, the account of J. Smith in the purchases ledger section must be debited with £5. If an asset such as a small item of office equipment is purchased out of petty cash, the appropriate ledger account— Office Equipment Account—must be debited.

Total debits in our example are £52.82 and this is the amount withdrawn from the cash book on 31 August, that is, credited in cash book, thus completing double-entry book-keeping. If a trial balance is extracted on 31 August (after the analysis column totals have been debited to expenses accounts, and a credit passed to cash book to restore the imprest amount), the balance of petty cash account, £75, must be included as a debit balance.

Using a petty cash book saves a lot of small transactions from being passed through the double-entry accounts. One total, each made up of a number of smaller transactions, is debited to each expenses account.

21.6   The Petty Cash Book and VAT

It is a simple matter to record VAT in a petty cash book. The layout is altered as follows:

Petty cash book

Receipts	Folio	Date	Details	Voucher no	Total (inc. VAT)	VAT	Stationery (exc. VAT)	etc
£					£	£	£	

The total amount paid for each petty cash expense is entered in the total column. This amount is then split between the VAT amount and the remainder of the expense. Thus if we bought a packet of envelopes costing £2 exclusive of VAT, the amounts would be entered as follows (assuming VAT to be 10 per cent):

Receipts	Folio	Date	Details	Voucher no	Total (inc. VAT)	VAT	Stationery (exc. VAT)	etc
£		19–1 10 Apr.	Envelopes	101	£ 2.20	£ 0.20	£ 2.00	

At the end of the week or month, when the totals of the analysis columns are debited to the appropriate expenses account in the general ledger, the total of the VAT column is likewise debited to VAT Account.

This assumes that the VAT-exclusive amount is always known and that the amount of VAT can then be added. For petty cash items this is rarely the case—for example, if you buy some stationery from a shop the only cash record you receive is the shop's till receipt detailing the total amount, which includes VAT. It is then necessary to calculate the VAT amount from the total, using the method described in Unit 12.4: to calculate the *VAT-exclusive amount* when VAT is at 10 per cent, simply multiply the total by 10/11; to calculate the *VAT amount*, multiply the total by 1/11. For example, for stationery at a total cost of £3.85 including VAT:

$$\text{VAT-exclusive amount is £3.85} \times \frac{10}{11} = \text{£3.50}$$

$$\text{Amount of VAT is £3.85} \times \frac{1}{11} = \underline{\text{£0.35}}$$
$$\underline{\underline{\text{£3.85}}}$$

With VAT at 15 per cent, the VAT-exclusive amount is found by multiplying the total by 20/23; the VAT amount is 3/23.

21.7 Questions

*1. Rule a petty cash book with four columns for Cleaning, Postages, Carriage and Office expenses, and enter the items listed below. The book is kept on the imprest system.

		£
1 June	Received £50 from the cashier	
	Bought postage stamps	6
2 June	Paid carriage on parcels	4
3 June	Bought office stationery	12
	Paid bus fares	2
4 June	Bought postage stamps	5
	Bought typewriter ribbons	6
5 June	Paid for cleaning	4
6 June	Paid carriage on parcels	4
	Received cash from cashier to make up the imprest amount	

Balance the book as on 6 June.

[*Pitman Examinations Institute*]

*2. Simon Williams is a sole trader who keeps his petty cash on the imprest system—the imprest amount being £50. His transactions for the month of February 19–1 were:

1 Feb.   Petty cash in hand £7.37.
2 Feb.   Petty cash restored to the imprest amount.

4 Feb.   Purchased envelopes £4.34.
7 Feb.   Paid wages £8.10.
10 Feb.   Purchased postage stamps £4.25.
14 Feb.   Paid £8.72 to F. Jones, a creditor.
17 Feb.   Cost of postages £3.38.
21 Feb.   Paid wages £8.33.
25 Feb.   Purchased note paper £5.24.

Required:

(*a*) Draw up the petty cash book for the month of February 19–1 with analysis columns for Stationery, Wages, Postages and Ledger.

(*b*) Balance the petty cash book as at 28 February 19–1, carry down the balance and show the restoration to the imprest amount on 1 March 19–1.

[*London Chamber of Commerce*]

3.   John Crowther is a sole trader who keeps his petty cash on the imprest system, the imprest amount being £40. During the month of April 19–1 the following petty cash transactions took place:

1 Apr.   Petty cash in hand £3.75.
1 Apr.   Petty cash restored to imprest amount.
4 Apr.   Paid wages £5.36.
7 Apr.   Postages £3.14.
10 Apr.   Cost of postages £3.20.
11 Apr.   Envelopes purchased £2.60.
14 Apr.   Paid to J. Smith, a creditor, £5.50.
18 Apr.   Paid wages £6.20.
20 Apr.   Postages £3.32.
24 Apr.   Purchased carbon paper £3.90.
25 Apr.   Envelopes purchased £2.19.
28 Apr.   Cost of postages £2.18.

Required:

Draw up the petty cash book to record the above transactions, carry down the balance on 30 April 19–1 and, on 1 May 19–1, restore the petty cash to the imprest amount.

Note: The analysis columns are Wages, Postages, Stationery, Ledger.

[*London Chamber of Commerce*]

4.   Thomas Brown is a sole trader who keeps his petty cash on the imprest system and the imprest amount is £50. His petty cash transactions for the month of February 19–3 are as follows:

1 Feb.   Petty cash in hand £6.34.
1 Feb.   Petty cash restored to imprest amount.
4 Feb.   Bought postage stamps £4.25.
8 Feb.   Paid wages £8.72.
11 Feb.   Bought envelopes £3.60.
15 Feb.   Bought typing paper £5.60.
15 Feb.   Paid wages £8.20.
18 Feb.   Bought postage stamps £3.90.
22 Feb.   Paid wages £8.10.
24 Feb.   Paid to C. Jones, a creditor, £4.30.

Required:

Draw up the petty cash book to record the above transactions.

You should balance the petty cash book as on 28 February 19–3, carry down the balance, and give the entry on 1 March restoring the petty cash to the imprest amount.

Note: Your analysis columns should be for Wages, Stamps, Stationery and Ledger.

[London Chamber of Commerce]

5. You are responsible for keeping the cash book and petty cash book of J. Swallow. The petty cash book has three analysis columns: Postages; Stationery; Sundry expenses. Balances at 1 May 19–2 were:

> *Cash book:* Cash in hand £47.13; Bank overdraft £16.79.
>
> *Petty cash book:* £25 (Imprest).

Enter these balances and the following transactions:

1 May	Received cheque from A. Hassall for £97.50 in full settlement of his account for £100.
1 May	Petty cashier sent a recorded delivery letter £1.16.
2 May	Paid S. Sharp, by cheque, his account of £150 less 2½ per cent cash discount.
2 May	Paid through the petty cash for cleaning materials £1.35.
3 May	Bought stamps £2.47 from petty cash.
3 May	Cash sales £248.19, out of which £36.19 was paid for rates and the balance was paid into the bank.
4 May	Petty cash used to buy envelopes £3.87.
5 May	Withdrew £56 from the bank for the office cash (not petty cash).
5 May	Paid wages £87. 23 in cash.
7 May	Balance both books and bring down the balances.
8 May	Petty cash imprest restored.

[East Midland Regional Examinations Board]

*6. Alfred Robertson pays all receipts into the bank and makes all cash payments out of petty cash. At the end of each week the petty cashier is given a cheque to restore the imprest.

At the close of business on 18 April 19–1, Robertson's bank balance according to his cash book was £935.75, and his cash in hand stood at the imprest amount of £50.

The counterfoils of his paying-in book for the next week showed:

20 April	Total paid in £308.65 consisting of cash from sales £250.15 and a cheque from D. Preston for £58.50 in full settlement of £60 owed by him.
22 April	Total paid in £260.90 consisting of a cheque from F. Ives of £22.75 and £238.15 cash from sales.
24 April	Total paid in £210 consisting entirely of cash from sales.

The counterfoils of his cheque book show:

21 April	Midlands Electricity Board for lighting £165.92.
22 April	G. Lamb & Son in settlement of £100 owing to them £95.00.
25 April	Petty cash £29.50.
	Self £50.00.

Payments out of petty cash were as follows:

20 April   Paid cleaner £8.00.
22 April   Postage stamps £2.90.
24 April   Stationery £7.00.
24 April   Cleaning materials £3.00.
25 April   Travelling expenses £3.00.
25 April   Letterheaded paper £5.60.

You are required to write up

(a) the bank cash book (the detail columns of the bank cash book should indicate clearly which ledger account is to be debited or credited in respect of each entry) and

(b) the petty cash book with analysis columns for cleaning, postages, travelling and stationery.

[*Royal Society of Arts*]

7. Alexander Field runs his own small business, and he makes all payments of under £30 through his petty cash book which is operated on an imprest system. At the end of each week he restores the imprest to its nominated figure of £100. All other payments are made by cheque, and all receipts are paid into the bank.

The balance at the bank was £1 605.27, and the petty cash balance was £48.83 at the beginning of the final week of April, and the following receipts and payments occurred:

24 April   The petty cash imprest was restored from the bank, not having been done at the end of the previous week.
Paid amount owing to P. Simpson of £200, less 7½% cash discount.
Paid taxi fare—£6.80.
Paid 15% salary advance on £500 to A. Roe, a new employee.
Paid rail fare of £15.60 and parcel post of £5.20 (grouped on one voucher).

26 April   M. Roe settled his credit account of £100 less 5% cash discount.
Purchased large envelopes £2.45, pencils £3.69 and packing tape £1.93 (grouped on one voucher).
J. Lowbridge settled his account of £120, less 2½% discount.
Paid C. Bell, a creditor, £10.95 (his account number is 251).

28 April   Paid cleaner £12.65 for work done in the office.
E. Gillard paid his credit account of £160, less 5% cash discount.
Received 28% of annual rent income of £200.
Purchased postage stamps—£7.45.
Restored imprest account from bank cash book.

You are required to:

(a) Write up the bank cash book for the week ending 30 April, and balance the book at that date. The name of the ledger account to be debited or credited in respect of each transaction should appear in the 'Particulars' column.

(b) Write up the petty cash book for the week ending 30 April using analysis columns for travelling, cleaning, postage and stationery, and ledger, and using petty cash voucher numbers with a separate voucher number for each transaction, except where otherwise indicated (the last voucher number issued in the previous week was 44).

Balance the petty cash book at the end of the week and restore the imprest figure.

[*RSA Examinations Board*]

Banking Transactions

22.1 Types of Bank Account

Most banks offer two main types of account: current account and deposit account.

A *current account* customer is issued with a cheque book and may make use of most of the services of the bank, including standing orders, direct debits, cheque cards, cash dispensers and so on. No interest is allowed on a current account and charges may be made by the bank for operating the account. Overdrafts and loans are available by prior arrangement with the bank. Bank customers use a current account as a 'working account', which means that their wages and salaries are paid into the account—often directly by their employer—and that they draw their living expenses out of the account.

A *deposit account* is used for savings and the bank pays interest on the amount deposited. Current account facilities—particularly cheque books, standing orders, direct debits and overdrafts—are not permitted. Most banks nowadays operate a variety of savings/deposit accounts: for example, one type of account is designed for regular monthly savings, another is for those who have a lump sum of money to invest. Many customers maintain both a current and a deposit account.

At regular intervals, perhaps monthly, a current account customer receives a *statement of account*. This is a summary showing the balance at the beginning of the month, amounts credited to the account (such as salary) and amounts debited (such as cheques, standing orders and direct debits). In business, a bank statement is reconciled with the firm's cash book (see Unit 23). Statements are issued less frequently for deposit accounts.

22.2 Paying-in Books

All business customers of a bank, and many personal customers, are issued with a paying-in book. An example page from a paying-in book is shown in Fig. 22.1. Notice how the cash is analysed into the different categories of notes or coins: the numbers of these are not entered in the cash columns, however, but the amounts of money in each category. The completed paying-in book is handed to the bank cashier together with the notes, coins and cheques: the cashier counts the cash, ticks off the cheques and, if all is correct, stamps and initials both paying-in slip and counterfoil. The slip is retained by the bank for the amount to be credited to the account-holder, while the rest of the book, including the stamped counterfoil, is handed back.

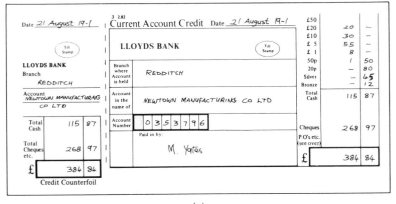

(a)

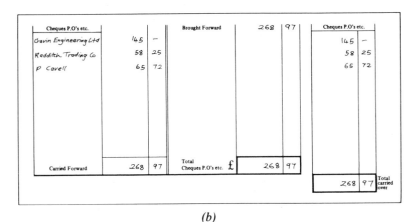

(b)

Fig. 22.1 A paying-in slip: (a) front, (b) reverse

22.3 Cheques

Cheques are well known to most people, and a specimen is shown in Fig. 22.2.

When drawing (writing out) a cheque, care should always be exercised to ensure that all details are completed: the date, name of payee, amount in words and figures, and the drawer's signature. Cheques should be written in ink (large firms often use special cheque-writing machines), and no room should be left for possible fraudulent additions or alterations, any blank spaces being ruled through. Naturally, sufficient funds should be available in the drawer's account; if not, overdraft facilities should have been arranged, to meet cheques when they are presented for payment.

(a)

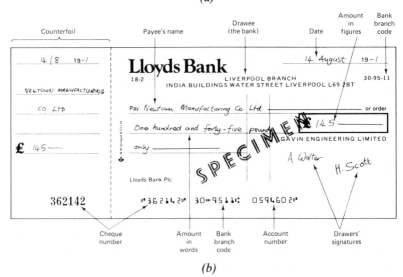

(b)

Fig. 22.2 A specimen cheque: (a) blank, (b) completed

22.4   Crossings on Cheques

Nowadays most cheques are *crossed*, that is, two parallel lines are drawn across the cheque. This indicates that the cheque cannot be cashed at a bank (except by the drawer) but must be paid in for the credit of an account. An uncrossed or *open* cheque can be cashed at the bank on which it is drawn. Crossed cheques provide a safer method of payment than open cheques do.

While most cheques are paid into the account of the payee, a cheque can be transferred to someone else by *endorsement*, that is, the payee signs his or her name on the reverse of the cheque. Small shops sometimes cash cheques for their regular customers: the cheques are endorsed by the payee and can then be paid in to the shop's bank account.

Besides two parallel lines, crossings on cheques may include certain words within the crossing. Two common crossings are shown in Fig. 22.3.

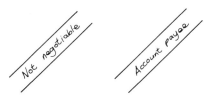

Fig. 22.3 Cheque crossings

(*a*) A 'not negotiable' crossing still allows the cheque to be transferred by the payee to someone else by endorsement. But if the cheque was stolen and then passed to an innocent shopkeeper who agreed to cash it in exchange for goods, the shop could not obtain a 'good title' to the cheque, nor seek reimbursement from the drawer of the cheque.

(*b*) The crossing 'account payee' means that the cheque should normally be paid into the payee's own account, and not transferred to someone else.

22.5 The Cheque-clearing System

The process of clearing a cheque is perhaps most easily studied by monitoring the route followed by an imaginary example.

(*a*) On Monday morning Smith, a customer of Midwest Bank, Norton, pays into his account a cheque for £10 sent to him by a debtor, Williams, who banks at Barminster's Bank, Westport. At the end of the day Midwest Bank, Norton, send the cheque, along with others, to their head office in London.

(*b*) On Tuesday, Midwest Bank head office exchange the cheque, along with others, with the head office of Barminster's. It is now sent by Barminster's head office to their Westport branch.

(*c*) On Wednesday morning, Westport branch of Barminster's Bank receive the cheque from head office, and Williams' account is debited with £10.

This is a simplification of the clearing procedures: in practice, a high degree of automation has been introduced, involving cheque sorting and listing equipment and the banks' computer systems. In the example, clearing has taken three working days; this assumes that there have been no delays and represents the fastest time in which a cheque can normally be cleared. From an accounting point of view, the important point is that there is usually a delay between a cheque being written out and its appearance as a debit on the drawer's bank statement. We shall use this information in Unit 23 when we reconcile a firm's cash book with its bank statement.

22.6   Methods of Payment

There are several ways in which payment may be made for amounts owing—not all use the banking system. We shall consider several of these in turn.

(a) Cash

Notes and coin are an obvious method of payment for small money amounts. For larger sums, however, it is not very convenient because it is bulky to carry, liable to loss, and a temptation to theft. Payment in foreign currency banknotes may be appropriate under some circumstances, but it suffers from the same disadvantages as the domestic currency.

(b) Postal Orders

These are purchased from post offices in certain fixed values, although stamps may be affixed to increase their value within narrow limits. A poundage charge is made on each postal order for the service, and varies according to the value.

The sender of the postal order enters the payee's name and may also indicate the post office of payment. If a postal order is crossed, it can only be paid through a bank. The payee signs the postal order as a form of receipt.

A postal order is a convenient method of sending money through the post for those who do not have a bank account. It is restricted by the maximum value postal order available although, of course, several orders may be sent to one payee.

(c) Cheque

Perhaps the most common method of payment for all but the smallest amounts is the cheque. The risks of cash handling are eliminated and, if a cheque should be lost, the bank can be given instructions to 'stop' payment.

In order to increase the acceptability of cheques, banks issue *cheque cards* to suitable customers. This plastic 'card' acts as a guarantee that the drawer's cheque will be paid up to a certain amount. Cheque cards have been useful in persuading retailers and others to accept cheques from strangers in payment for goods. A cheque card can also be used with a cheque book to draw cash from banks and branches away from the account-holding branch.

Sometimes a cheque is *dishonoured*, that is, the bank on which it is drawn refuses to pay it. We have seen in Unit 22.5 the way in which the cheque-clearing system operates, and it is for the bank on which the cheque is drawn (the paying bank) to decide whether the cheque can be debited to their customer's account. There are two main reasons why a cheque may not be paid:

(i) technical causes, such as being postdated (dated ahead in time) or the amount in words differing from the amount in figures; or
(ii) the drawer of the cheque has insufficient money in his or her account, and has not arranged overdraft facilities.

Whichever the reason, the paying bank must return the dishonoured cheque direct to the bank where it was originally paid in; often it is marked 'refer to drawer' or 'R/D'. This bank then normally debits the account of the person who paid it in and returns the cheque to that customer, who will then take up the matter with the drawer of the cheque.

(d) Bank Giro Credit

This method of payment—also known as a *credit transfer* or a *trader's credit* (see Fig. 22.4)—enables a person to pay money into someone else's bank account. This system is particularly useful for paying accounts such as gas, electricity, telephone or community charge, and often the bills for these services have a suitable form preprinted on them. Hire purchase companies, home shopping clubs and building societies often issue their customers with books of bank giro credit slips. Businesses, too, may include a bank giro credit slip when sending out statements of account to their debtors. Employers can use the system for paying wages and salaries: a credit slip is made out for each employee with details of the name and number of the account to be credited, the bank and branch where it is maintained and the money amount. These slips, together with a summary sheet detailing all the wage and salary payments, are handed to the bank with one cheque for the total amount. This method of making wage and salary payments has the obvious advantage of not requiring large quantities of cash to be withdrawn from the bank on pay day, with the attendant security problems; however, the system can only operate if each employee has a bank account and agrees to be paid in this way.

An increasing number of firms, instead of making out a slip or voucher for each payment through the bank giro credit system, prepare computer tapes containing details of all payments to be made. The tapes are passed to the banking system for processing, thus cutting out a large amount of paperwork.

(e) Standing Orders (Bankers' Orders)

Where a bank customer has regular payments to make for fixed amounts—a mortgage, for instance, or insurance premiums or hire purchase payments—

Fig. 22.4 A bank giro credit

the bank can be given written instructions to make the payments. The bank will do this by debiting the customer's account and sending a credit to the bank and branch of the beneficiary, either by using a bank giro credit voucher or by putting the payment details on a computer tape.

(*f*) **Direct Debit**

Direct debits, like standing orders, are used for regular payments but they differ from standing orders in two ways:

(i) they can be used for either fixed or variable amounts and/or where the time intervals between payments vary;

(ii) it is the beneficiary of the payment who prepares the computer transaction that acts as a debit to the payer's bank account and is passed through the banking system; this contrasts with the standing order system where the payer's bank originates a credit transaction which is passed to the bank and branch of the beneficiary.

Many bank customers are wary of signing the necessary authority to allow direct debit payments to be taken out of their accounts, particularly where the payments are for variable amounts. The banks have introduced a number of safeguards to prevent irregular use of the system, however. These safeguards include restricting the system to organizations approved by the banks, and the immediate reimbursement by banks to a customer whose account is charged with a direct debit that does not conform with the instructions held.

The direct debit system is particularly useful to businesses such as insurance companies, building societies, hire purchase companies and indeed any organization that receives large numbers of payments. The system's operation is rather like that for bank giro credits or trader's credits in reverse: the beneficiary prepares the direct debit transactions, usually on computer tape, and takes or sends them to the bank together with a credit for the total amount. The debits are distributed through the banking system to the banks and branches to which they are addressed and the payers' accounts are debited. At the same time, the beneficiary company receives the funds, without having to wait for bank giro credits to be received.

(*g*) **Credit Cards**

Credit cards, of which Access and Barclaycard are examples, provide a means of obtaining goods and services immediately but paying for them later. A credit limit is set on each cardholder's credit card account, which is entirely separate from his or her normal bank account. Goods and services can only be obtained at outlets having the special machine for preparing sales vouchers to record the transaction, and retailers usually display the signs of the credit cards they are prepared to accept.

Each month a cardholder is sent a statement of purchases made and can choose either to pay the full balance of the account, or to pay part only (subject to a certain minimum amount), carrying forward the remaining balance to next month. Cardholders are charged interest on outstanding balances. The card

'See! I told you it didn't grow on trees'

can also be used to draw cash at bank branches displaying the relevant credit card sign, and from the increasing number of automated teller machines installed outside bank premises.

Many businesses issue company credit cards to their sales representatives and delivery van drivers so that they may buy petrol with the card. Using this method no cash has to be reimbursed to these staff and, at the month-end, the company will receive a full statement of credit card purchases of fuel.

(h) Debit Cards

Debit cards are issued to bank customers to enable them to make payment for goods and services from their bank account without the need to write a cheque. Payments are handled by retailers using EFTPOS (Electronic Funds Transfer at Point of Sale) computer-linked check-out tills. Examples of debit cards are 'Switch' and 'Connect' cards.

(i) Bills of Exchange

In broad terms a bill of exchange is a document requiring a debtor to pay an amount owing by a certain date or at a specified date in the future. When it is signed or *accepted* by the debtor it becomes legally binding. A bill of exchange meets the needs of both debtor and creditor: the debtor often receives a period of credit before payment has to be made under the bill, and the creditor receives a legal promise to pay.

There is more information about bills of exchange in Unit 37, which also deals with the accounting procedures to be followed.

22.7 Questions

1. You are employed by Bell and Charm Ltd. Your employers keep a current account with the Loamshire Bank PLC at their Barr Lane branch. The account is number 0734554.

You are to bank on their behalf the following:

4 notes of £20 each
8 notes of £10 each
35 notes of £5 each
25 coins of £1 each
3 bags of £10 each in 50-pence pieces
14 bags of £5 each in silver
24 bags of 50p each in bronze
One cheque for £189.56
One postal order for £1.00

Copy and write up the paying-in slip shown in Fig. 22.5.

[*Royal Society of Arts*]

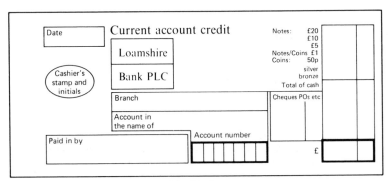

Fig. 22.5

2. (*a*) On 1 April 19–1 you received an account from Anglian Garages for motor repairs. The account is for £180 and is subject to a discount of 2½ per cent if paid within 14 days. You pay the account on 7 April 19–1. Copy and complete the cheque and counterfoil shown in Fig. 22.6, settling the account.

Your balance at bank before this transaction was £470.83.

(*b*) How would you make an alteration to a cheque which you have made out incorrectly?

[*Royal Society of Arts*]

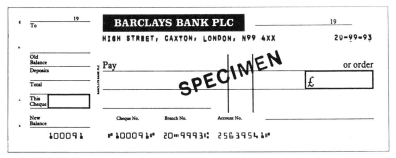

Fig. 22.6

P. Wiseman in account with EAST MIDLAND BANK PLC				
Date	Description	Debits	Credits	Balance
19–2				
Apl. 1	Brought forward			275Cr.
14	Cash and cheques		300 (a)	(b)
20	126 (c)	720 (d)		(e)
30	S/O (f)	20		(g)

Fig. 22.7

*3. Study the statement in Fig. 22.7.

(a) Was the amount labelled (a) paid in or withdrawn?

(b) What was the balance (b) on 14 April?

(c) To what do the figures labelled (c) refer?

(d) Was the amount (d) paid in or withdrawn?

(e) What was the balance (e) on 20 April?

(f) To what do the letters labelled (f) refer?

(g) What was the balance (g) on 30 April?

(h) Provided balance (g) and P. Wiseman's cash book agree, this figure will appear in his balance sheet. Under which heading will it be shown?

[East Midland Regional Examinations Board]

4. (a) Mr S. Matthews has a current account with the Western Bank PLC, King Street, Oban. During the month of October 19–2, he had the following transactions:

On 1 October 19–2, Mr Matthews had a bank balance in hand of £226.00 and during the month of October his paying-in book counterfoils showed the following:

19–2
 2 Oct.   Cash £15.00
10 Oct.   Cheque £90.20
21 Oct.   Cash £17.85
30 Oct.   Cash £34.25

He issued the following cheques:

3 Oct.	86870	£20.00
8 Oct.	86871	£12.16
11 Oct.	86872	£ 4.00
22 Oct.	86873	£75.25
28 Oct.	86874	£19.40

Notes:

(i) On 31 October, the bank paid on Mr Matthews' behalf by standing order an amount of £10.00 to cover his monthly life assurance premium.

(ii) Mr Matthews' salary of £650.00 per month is paid directly into his current account by credit transfer on the last day of each month.

Draw up a bank statement with changing balances showing the above transactions *in date order* and the balance of his account of the 31 October 19–2.

(*b*) What does 'Account Payee Only' mean on a cheque?

(*c*) What is a dishonoured cheque?

[*Associated Lancashire Schools Examining Board*]

Bank Reconciliation Statements

23.1 Introduction

If you have a bank account, you will know that any record you keep invariably disagrees with the balance shown by the bank statement. This is not because you have made an error—usually it is simply that you have recently written cheques that do not yet appear on the bank statement. These cheques have not yet been presented to the bank for payment: either they have not yet been paid in by the payee, or they are still passing through the banks' clearing system. Therefore, for the time being, the bank statement shows a higher balance than your records. Clearly you can't go out and spend the 'extra' money appearing on your bank statement because the cheques *will* be presented for payment, perhaps a few days after receiving your statement, and they will appear on the next statement. To make your records agree with the bank statement, you must add the unpresented cheques to the balance shown by your records.

This method of agreeing your records with the bank statement is a simple type of *bank reconciliation statement*. A business will prepare exactly the same sort of statement, but on a more formal basis: the bank columns of the cash book record payments into and out of the firm's bank account *from the firm's point of view*, and the balance of these bank columns must be reconciled with the balance shown by the firm's bank statement. Fig. 23.1 shows the place of the bank reconciliation statement as a 'checking' device.

Fig. 23.1 The place of the bank reconciliation statement

23.2 Debit, Credit and Bank Statements

In this book we have carried out many double-entry book-keeping transactions. We have said that debtors are those who owe money to our firm, while creditors are those to whom we owe money. Many students find this idea unfamiliar: they argue that, if you have money in the bank, it is described on your bank statement as a credit balance; if you are overdrawn it is called a debit balance. But these students fail to grasp that the bank is showing the position in their books *from the bank's point of view*. Thus a credit balance from the bank's point of view is that it owes the balance of the account to the customer, who is a *creditor* of the bank; on the other hand, a customer who is overdrawn owes money to the bank, and the bank has a *debtor*.

For example, suppose I set up in business and open a bank account with £100. The entries in my accounts will be:

Dr. Bank   £100
Cr. Capital   £100

These show that I have a debtor, that is, the bank owes £100 to my business. (Also my business owes the money back to me in the form of capital.) In the bank's accounting, the book-keeping entry will be:

Dr. Cash/cheques   £100
Cr. Account in name of
      my business   £100

Thus the bank has gained cash or cheques to the value of £100, and records the fact that it owes my business this amount by giving the account a credit balance.

23.3   Reasons for Differences Between Cash Book and Bank Statement

(i)   **Cheques drawn, not yet presented for payment.** We discussed this situation in Unit 23.1. The result is that the cash book will show all cheques drawn and will have a lower balance than that on the bank statement.

(ii)   **Cash or cheques paid in to the bank, but not yet credited on the bank statement.** This happens when cash or cheques are paid into the bank on the same day that the bank statement is sent. The payment into the bank is recorded in the firm's cash book but is received by the bank too late to be included on the current statement: it will appear on the next. This means that the firm's cash book shows a higher balance than that on the bank statement.

Discrepancies of this kind can also occur when amounts are paid in at bank branches other than the account-holding branch, using the bank giro credit system (see Unit 22.6(e)). It will take a few days—usually three working days—before the funds are credited to the bank account, because they have to pass through the banks' credit-clearing system.

(iii)   **Standing orders and direct debits paid by the bank, but not yet entered in the firm's cash book.** Banks are often given instructions to make payments by means of standing orders and direct debits (see Unit 22.6 (*f*) and (*g*)). It sometimes happens that, while the bank makes the payment on behalf of its customer, no entry is made in the firm's cash book until after the payment has been made. The bank statement often serves as a reminder to a firm that payment has been made, and an entry must be made in the firm's cash book and, of course, in the other account concerned in the transaction, to bring them up to date.

In the same way, a business *receiving* standing order payments will find that they have been credited to the bank account, and accounting entries need to be made in the firm's cash book, as well as in the other account concerned in the transaction.

(iv) Receipt of giro credits by the bank, but not yet entered in the firm's cash book. The bank giro credit system is often used by businesses to collect money owing to them. Many firms include a bank giro credit slip as part of the bill or statement sent out to their customers. Firms using this system extensively arrange with their banks for details of credits received to be passed on to them, and the accounting entries can then be completed. A smaller firm receiving only a few credits each month, however, may know nothing about what has been received until its bank statement arrives. Therefore such credits must be entered in the cash book to bring it up to date (and, of course, entries made in the debtors' accounts).

(v) Bank charges and interest charged, not yet entered in the cash book. Banks make charges for operating accounts on behalf of customers (although under certain circumstances private customers can avoid paying them). When a customer is overdrawn, interest is charged on the amount borrowed—the interest is often combined with bank charges. Where charges, including interest, are made, the first a customer may know of them is when a debit appears on the bank statement. For a business, the cash book needs to be written up to date to show that an amount has been taken out of the bank account (and an entry made in the expenses account, 'bank charges and interest').

(vi) Dividends received by the bank, not yet entered in the cash book. Many individuals and businesses own shares in limited companies. From time to time companies pay their shareholders a dividend and these are, by arrangement, often credited direct to the shareholder's bank account. In double-entry book-keeping, a dividend received is debited to the bank column of the cash book and credited to Dividends Received Account. If a dividend is shown on the bank statement, therefore, a book-keeping transaction must be passed in the accounts of the recipient to bring the cash book up to date.

(vii) Dishonoured cheques, not yet entered in the cash book. Where a business has paid in a cheque from one of its customers that is subsequently dishonoured (unpaid—see Unit 22.6(*d*)), the bank will debit the account of the business with the amount of the cheque. In double-entry book-keeping, a customer's unpaid cheque is debited to the customer (to re-establish the debit balance in the account) and credited in the bank columns of the cash book. If an unpaid cheque is shown on the bank statement, book-keeping entries must be passed to bring the cash book up to date.

'Can you provide funds to effect a reconciliation between you and us?'

23.4   Preparing a Bank Reconciliation Statement

There are usually two distinct steps in reconciling a cash book with a bank statement:

(*a*)   write the cash book up to date;
(*b*)   prepare a bank reconciliation statement.

Before starting on either step we must identify *all* the differences between the cash book and bank statement, by 'ticking off' those transactions that appear in both cash book and bank statement. Anything not 'ticked' needs further investigation and will be either an item that needs to be written up in the cash book, such as bank charges, or an item that will correct itself on the next bank statement, such as cheques drawn but not yet presented for payment.

In Unit 23.3, some of the differences between cash book and bank statement refer to items 'not yet entered in the cash book', such as:

standing orders paid by the bank;
direct debits paid by the bank;
bank giro credits and interest credits received by the bank;
bank interest and charges made;
dividends received by the bank;
dishonoured cheques.

If such items appear on the bank statement, they must be entered in the cash book.

When the cash book has been brought up to date, the next step is to prepare the bank reconciliation statement. This takes the following format:

Bank reconciliation statement of . . . as at . . .	
	£
Balance at bank as per cash book	x
Add Cheques drawn, not yet presented for payment	x
	x
Less Cash/cheques paid in to bank, but not yet credited on statement	x
Balance at bank as per bank statement	x

23.5   Bank Reconciliation Statements: a Worked Example

The following are the cash book and bank statement of D. Lane for the month of June 19–7:

Cash book (bank columns)

19–7	£	19–7	£
1 Jun. Balance b/d	150	9 Jun. P. Stone	88
7 Jun. Cash	62	14 Jun. Alpha Ltd	50
16 Jun. C. Brewster	80	17 Jun. P. Watson	20
17 Jun. A. Kennedy	9	25 Jun. H. Williams	15
24 Jun. Cash	60	30 Jun. A. Wright	105
30 Jun. Cash	40	30 Jun. Balance c/d	123
	401		401
30 Jun. Balance b/d	123		

Bank statement

19–7	Payments £	Receipts £	Balance £
1 Jun. Balance			150 Cr.
7 Jun. Cash		62	212 Cr.
15 Jun. P. Stone	88		124 Cr.
19 Jun. C. Brewster		80	204 Cr.
20 Jun. Dividend		46	250 Cr.
22 Jun. Standing order: insurance	66		184 Cr.
23 Jun. P. Watson	20		164 Cr.
23 Jun. A. Kennedy		9	173 Cr.
25 Jun. Alpha Ltd	50		123 Cr.
29 Jun. Cash		60	183 Cr.
30 Jun. Bank charges	10		173 Cr.

Required:
(a) Bring the cash book up to date at 30 June 19–7.
(b) Prepare a bank reconciliation statement at 30 June 19–7.

Answer

To bring the cash book up to date, we must enter the following items which are on the bank statement, but not in the cash book:

20 Jun. Dividend received   £46
22 Jun. Standing order paid   £66
30 Jun. Bank charges   £10

The cash book (with the additional transactions entered under date 30 June) will then appear as:

Cash book (bank columns)

19–7	£	19–7	£
30 Jun. Balance b/d	123	30 Jun. Standing order:	
30 Jun. Dividend	46	insurance	66
		30 Jun. Bank charges	10
		30 Jun. Balance c/d	93
	169		169
1 Jul. Balance b/d	93		

The reconciliation is made as follows:

Bank reconciliation statement of D. Lane as at 30 June 19–7

	£	£
Balance at bank as per cash book		93
Add Cheques drawn, not yet presented for payment: H. Williams	15	
A. Wright	105	
		120
		213
Less Cash paid in to bank, but not yet credited on statement		40
Balance at bank as per bank statement		173

23.6   More About Bank Reconciliation Statements

(a) Starting from the Bank Statement Balance

The specimen bank reconciliation statement in Unit 23.4 and the worked example in Unit 23.5 both start with 'balance at bank as per cash book' and work towards 'balance at bank as per bank statement'. There is no reason why we could not have presented the bank reconciliation statement the other way round, and *started* with the bank statement balance, working to the cash book balance. If it is presented in this way, then we must work the other way round, *deducting* unpresented cheques, and *adding* cash and cheques paid in but not yet credited, so that the bank reconciliation statement in Unit 23.5 appears as:

Bank reconciliation statement of D. Lane as at 30 June 19–7

	£	£
Balance at bank, as per bank statement		173
Less Unpresented cheques	15	
	105	
		120
		53
Add Cash paid in, not yet credited		40
Balance at bank, as per cash book		93

Both methods are correct and, of course, prove the same thing: that cash book and bank statement are reconciled. A business can choose which method to follow because it has both cash book and bank statement to work from. However, an examination question may ask you to present the statement in a certain way, for example, by saying 'starting with the cash book balance ...' or by giving only limited information about the entries on the bank statement.

(b) Bank Overdrafts
When a business has an overdraft, the procedures you have learnt are still valid; you will find it helpful to use brackets to indicate overdraft figures. You need to be careful with the mathematics: when you add to an overdrawn balance, the amount of the overdraft is reduced; when you deduct from an overdrawn balance, the amount of the overdraft is increased. For example:

	£
Balance at bank, as per cash book	(533)
Add Cheques drawn, not yet presented for payment	120
	(413)
Less Cash/cheques paid into bank, but not yet credited	
on statement	40
Balance at bank, as per bank statement	(453)

If you find this hard to follow, try using a calculator on the figures.

(c) Filing the Bank Reconciliation Statement
A bank reconciliation statement is *not* part of double-entry book-keeping. It is prepared either on a sheet of paper or in a separate book. Once completed, the statement should be filed and retained for possible future use: it proves that, at a certain date, the bank columns of the cash book and bank statement were reconciled.

(d) Balance Sheets
When preparing a balance sheet, remember to enter the *balance from the cash book* as the figure for 'bank'—never the bank statement balance.

23.7   Questions

1. When comparing the balance at the bank as shown in the cash book with that given in the bank statement issued by the bank it is more than likely that these two balances will not agree. Give, and explain clearly, three reasons why this is so.

    [*East Anglian Examinations Board*]

*2. The bank columns of your cash book for the month of February 19–2 are shown below.

	£		Cheque no	£
1 Feb. Balance	480	4 Feb. Wages	335	180
22 Feb. A. Ball	250	5 Feb. F. Lowe	336	60
22 Feb. C. Lamb	136	11 Feb. G. Dow	337	110
22 Feb. E. Mann	208	J. Iles	338	244
26 Feb. L. Day	85	23 Feb. K. Peel	339	401
		28 Feb. Balance		164
	1 159			1 159
1 Mar. Balance	164			

The following bank statement was received for the month of February:

	Dr.	Cr.	Balance
1 Feb. Balance			600
3 Feb. Cheque no 334	120		480
8 Feb. 335	180		300
16 Feb. 338	244		56
17 Feb. 336	60		4 o/d
23 Feb. Sundries		594	590
26 Feb. D. May credit transfer		65	655
Ace Insurance standing order	26		
Charges	18		611

(*a*) Make the necessary entries in the cash book and ascertain the correct balance as on 28 February 19–2.

(*b*) Reconcile your revised cash book balance with the balance shown in the bank statement.

[*Royal Society of Arts*]

*3. William Tanner received the following bank statement on 31 May 19–3:

19–3	Debit £	Credit £	Balance £
1 May Balance			332
7 May 110119	102		230
11 May Cash		518	748
18 May Credit transfer investment dividends		600	1 348
19 May 110121	340		1 008
26 May Direct debit insurance	78		930

William Tanner checked the statement against his cheque counterfoils and found that cheques numbered 110118 for £235 and 110120 for £136 had not been presented. The names of the payees of the cheques are:

110118	S. Line
110119	N. Farden
110120	K. O'Connor
110121	A. Brown

As William Tanner has not written up his cash book for the month of May 19–3, you are required to

(a) write up the bank columns for that month,
(b) balance the bank columns, and reconcile that balance with the amount shown on the bank statement at the end of the month.

[Royal Society of Arts]

4. On 28 February 19–1 the bank column of W. Payne's cash book showed a debit balance of £600.

A bank statement written up to 28 February 19–1 disclosed that the following items had not been entered in the cash book:
(i) the sum of £1 500 received from P. Jones by credit transfer,
(ii) the transfer of £1 000 from Payne's private bank deposit account into his business bank account,
(iii) bank charges £180.

When the bank statement was further checked against the cash book the following items were discovered:

(i) cheques drawn in favour of creditors totalling £8 300 had not yet been presented,
(ii) cash and cheques £4 100 had been entered in the cash book but not yet credited by the bank,
(iii) a cheque for £50 drawn by W. Payne in respect of drawings had been correctly entered in the cash book but debited twice in the bank statement.

You are required to prepare as at 28 February 19–1:
(a) a statement showing the adjusted cash book balance,
(b) a bank reconciliation statement showing the balance appearing in the bank statement.

[Royal Society of Arts]

5. Below is the cash book (bank columns only) of Andrew Clark for the month of May 19–0 together with his bank statement for the same period.

Andrew Clark Cash Book			
19–0	Bank £	19–0	Bank £
May 1 Bal b/d	4 200	May 2 Cheque no 422	136
14 Sales	1 414	7 Cheque no 423	204
21 Sales	1 240	27 Cheque no 424	214
28 Sales	1 160		

Bank Statement

Southern Bank plc
Northbrook Branch

In account with:
Mr Andrew Clark

Date	Detail	Debit £	Credit £	Balance £
19–0				
May 1				4 200
May 5	Cheque no 422	136		4 064
May 10	Cheque no 423	204		3 860
May 15	Counter credit		1 414	
May 15	National Insurance Company	284		5 274
May 22	Counter credit		1 240	6 230
May 31	Services charges	100		6 130

You are required to:

(a) Rewrite the cash book making any adjustments you consider necessary.
(b) Balance the cash book and bring the balance down.
(c) Prepare a bank reconciliation statement as at 31 May 19–0.

[*Pitman Examinations Institute, Level 1*]

Multiple-choice Questions—6

Read each question carefully. Choose the *one* answer you think is correct. Answers are given on page 411.

1. A petty cash book is:

   A not part of the double-entry book-keeping system
   B used to pay suppliers' invoices
   C a replacement for a three-column cash book
   D used to pay small expenses

2. Which one of the following would be used as the source document for a petty cash book transaction?

   A copy of a sales invoice   **C** bill for window cleaning
   B credit note   **D** delivery note

3. A petty cash book is kept on the 'imprest' system with a balance at the start of each week of £50. Petty cash expenses during the week amount to £38; the amount received from the cashier at the start of next week will be:

   A £38   **B** £12   **C** £88   **D** £50

4. A request to a bank to make payments at regular intervals is known as a:

   A standing order   **C** bill of exchange
   B bank giro credit   **D** paying-in slip

5. A crossed cheque:

    A can be cashed by payee   **C** is guaranteed to be paid by the bank
    B must be paid into a bank account **D** is the same as an open cheque

6. A cheque crossed 'not negotiable':

    A cannot be transferred by endorsement
    B is the same as one crossed 'account payee'
    C can be transferred by endorsement
    D cannot be 'stopped' by the drawer

7. Which one of the following methods of payment is available only to a person having a current bank account?

    A cash   **C** bill of exchange
    B postal order   **D** direct debit

8. A bank reconciliation statement agrees:

    A the bank statement with the cash book
    B the statement received from a creditor with the personal account
    C the cash book and net profit
    D the cash columns of the cash book with the petty cash book

9. The bank statement of a trader shows a credit balance of £405. Unpresented cheques total £54; cash paid in not yet credited, £38. The trader's cash book should have a balance of:

    A £389   **B** £421   **C** £497   **D** £313

10. Which one of the following will be entered in the cash book, but not appear on the bank statement?

    A wages cheque   **C** payments to the petty cashier
    B bank giro credit from customer **D** dishonoured cheque

11. You are asked to prepare a bank reconciliation statement and the following items have to be taken into account: (i) unpresented cheques, (ii) cash and cheques paid in to the bank, but not yet appearing on the bank statement.
    Starting from the 'balance as per bank statement' which will you add and which will you subtract in preparing the bank reconciliation statement?

    A add (i); subtract (ii)   **C** add (i) and (ii)
    B subtract (i); add (ii)   **D** subtract (i) and (ii)

12. The following information is available:

	£
Bank balance shown in cash book	650
Amounts paid in not yet credited on bank statement	150
Bank charges not yet entered in cash book	50
Credit transfer received by bank, not yet entered in the cash book	100

    The bank statement balance should be:

    A £750   **B** £450   **C** £850   **D** £550

Uses of the General Journal

24.1 Introduction

In Units 16 and 17, we used journals (or day books) for sales, purchases, returns inwards and returns outwards. Such journals are used where there is a large volume of transactions, and are books of original entry which store up information until it is transferred in the form of a total to the appropriate general ledger accounts. For irregular transactions a *general journal* is used, again as a book of original entry.

24.2 Uses of the General Journal

The general journal is used for all items not appearing in any other journal, for example:

(*a*) the transactions which open the books of account of a business;
(*b*) purchase or sale of fixed assets;
(*c*) correction of errors;
(*d*) other transfers.

We shall look at each of these in turn.

The general journal, which does not form part of the double-entry bookkeeping system, can be thought of as a place where transactions can be explained in more detail than is possible in an account. It gives the accounting entries that are then passed in respect of certain transactions. Thus when the accounts are checked, more information about unusual transactions can be found in the journal.

A ruled journal page has two columns for money amounts on the right-hand side. When used for general journal, these two columns represent debit and credit respectively (this is unlike the use they are put to in other journals—see Unit 16.3):

Journal

Date	Details	Folio	Dr.	Cr.
			£	£

24.3 The Use of a Journal for Opening Entries

Opening entries relate to the first transactions which open the accounts of a business. For example, a first business transaction might read:

1 Jan. 19–3   Started in business with £500 in cash.

To record this transaction in the accounts, as you know, we must debit Cash Account and credit Capital Account. As this is a non-regular transaction it needs to be entered in the journal:

Date	Details	Folio	Dr.	Cr.
19–3			£	£
1 Jan.	Cash	CB1	500	
	Capital	GL1		500
	Introduction of opening capital			

Points to notice:

(*a*) The names of the two accounts concerned are given in the 'details' column.

(*b*) A few words of explanation, or *narrative*, are usually included.

(*c*) Each entry in the journal is complete in itself and should be ruled off so as not to confuse it with the next entry.

(*d*) Most journal entries balance, that is, debit amount(s) equal credit amount(s). Very occasionally a journal entry does not balance; this sometimes happens, for instance, when correcting certain types of error.

(*e*) After each journal entry has been made, appropriate entries must be made in the accounts described in the journal.

Now we look at a further example of opening entries for a firm that starts in business with several assets and liabilities.

Example

On 1 January 19–5 Mr Smith sets up in business with the following assets and liabilities: cash £50; bank £250; stock £500; fixtures and fittings £700; creditors £350.

The opening journal entry will read:

Date	Details	Folio	Dr.	Cr.
19–5			£	£
1 Jan.	Cash	CB1	50	
	Bank	CB1	250	
	Stock	GL1	500	
	Fixtures and fittings	GL2	700	
	Creditors	PL		350
	Capital	GL3		1 150
			1 500	1 500
	Assets and liabilities at the commencement of business			

Here, Capital Account provides the balancing figure: Mr Smith's assets minus his liabilities equals his capital.

The individual accounts will then need to be written up.

24.4   Purchase or Sale of Fixed Assets

This, too, is a non-regular business transaction, and therefore should be recorded in the journal.

Example

15 Apr. 19–6   *Bought a new machine for £2 000 plus VAT at 10 per cent, payment made by cheque.*

The journal entry is:

Date	Details	Folio	*Dr.*	*Cr.*
19–6			£	£
15 Apr.	Machinery	GL47	2 000	
	VAT	GL96	200	
	Bank	CB48		2 200
			2 200	2 200
	Purchase of new lathe: capital purchase order no 24/86			

24.5   Correction of Errors

This is an important topic in its own right, and is considered in detail in Units 28 and 29.

24.6   Other Transfers

Any other business transactions of a non-regular nature should be recorded in the journal. There are good reasons for doing this. First, experience shows that the precise details of an unusual transaction are quite likely to be forgotten soon after the event; the journal will indicate the book-keeping entries that were made, and why they were made. Secondly, the owner or the accountant of a business can keep a close watch on such transactions by insisting that they are entered in the journal.

The category of 'other transfers' includes transactions for:

(*a*) all transfers to Trading and Profit and Loss Accounts;
(*b*) charging expenses to Owner's Drawings Account;
(*c*) provision for bad debts (see Unit 27.3);
(*d*) bad debts written off (see Unit 27.2);
(*e*) provision for depreciation (see Unit 25);
(*f*) disposals of fixed assets (see Unit 26).

Examples

(Examples of journal transactions for (c) to (f) are shown in the relevant Units.)

1. *31 Dec. 19–4   The debit balance of Insurance Account is £250. Of this, £200 relates to 19–4, while £50 is a prepayment for 19–5. (The financial year-end is 31 December.)*

Journal entry:

Date	Details	Folio	Dr.	Cr.
19–4			£	£
31 Dec.	Profit and Loss Account	GL106	200	
	Insurance	GL54		200
	Transfer to Profit and Loss Account of expenditure for year			

2. *31 Dec. 19–1   Motor Vehicle Expenses Account has a debit balance of £1 350. Of this £250 represents the cost of the owner's private motoring. (The financial year-end is 31 December.)*

Journal entry:

Date	Details	Folio	Dr.	Cr.
19–1			£	£
31 Dec.	Profit and Loss Account	GL106	1 100	
	Drawings	GL210	250	
	Motor vehicle expenses	GL61		1 350
			1 350	1 350
	Transfer to Profit and Loss Account of expenditure for business use for year; transfer of private use to Drawings Account			

3. *28 Oct. 19–4   A letter is received from G. Glover stating that he has taken over the business of J. Jones, a debtor of your firm for £150, and will be responsible for settlement of Jones's debt.*

Journal entry:

Date	Details	Folio	Dr.	Cr.
19–4			£	£
28 Oct.	G. Glover	SL348	150	
	J. Jones	SL174		150
	Transfer of balance upon take-over of business by G. Glover—see letter dated 24 October 19–4			

4. 14 Dec. 19–6   *J. Smith, a debtor for £100, being unable to settle his*
account in cash offers a typewriter instead; this is
accepted and placed for use in the general office.

Journal entry:

Date	Details	Folio	Dr.	Cr.
19–6			£	£
14 Dec.	Typewriter	GL82	100	
	J. Smith	SL46		100
	Typewriter, Olivetti no 752841, taken in full settlement of Smith's account			

24.7   Questions

*1.   Ron Weller owns a small electrical business. He decides to keep his books in the future by means of the double-entry system. On 1 March 19–3 his financial position was as follows:

	£
Petty cash in hand	86
Shop premises	15 000
Equipment	9 640
Stock-in-trade	7 860
Rates of shop paid in advance	134
Bank overdraft	1 220
Trade creditor—B. Ihle	860
Trade debtors—C. Box £20, D. Dawes £190	210
Electricity account unpaid	120

You are required to set out the journal entry necessary to open the books under the double-entry system.

[Royal Society of Arts]

2.   On 1 June 19–4 T. Jones had the following assets and liabilities:

Freehold premises £25 000; Mortgage on premises £12 500; Motor vehicle £2 700; Amount owing on motor vehicle £1 400; Fixtures and fittings £2 000; Stock £2 750; Debtors £1 580; Bank overdraft £920; Unpaid electricity bill £72.

On 1 April 19–4 Jones had paid rates £180 for the half-year ending 30 September 19–4 and on 1 February 19–4 had paid one year's insurance premium £60.

You are required to prepare an opening journal entry as at 1 June 19–4 showing clearly the capital of Jones at that date.

[Royal Society of Arts]

3. Your firm trades in office machinery and on 1 March 19–1 its financial position was as follows:

	£
Freehold land and buildings	15 000
Cash at bank	12 000
Trade debtors	250
Trade creditors	200
Fixtures and fittings	4 000
Stock on hand	14 000

(*a*) Enter the above in the journal showing the capital at that date.

(*b*) Enter the following transactions for the month of March in the appropriate day books. All are subject to VAT at 10 per cent.

1 Mar. Sold 4 typewriters to Super Office Services, list price £80 each, allowing them 10 per cent trade discount.

4 Mar. Bought 6 calculators from Wye Accessories at £12 each net.

12 Mar. Sold a duplicating machine to J. Smithers at £350 net.

16 Mar. Sold 4 calculators to Markov Ltd list price £20 each allowing them 10 per cent trade discount.

20 Mar. Bought 6 typewriters from Acme Products Ltd list price £40 each. We were allowed trade discount of 15 per cent.

25 Mar. Sold 2 duplicating machines to Murgatroyds, list price £350, allowing them trade discount of 10 per cent.

Note. Entries in the ledger accounts are not required.

[Royal Society of Arts]

Fixed Asset Depreciation

25.1 What is Depreciation?

A dictionary definition of depreciation is 'a fall in value'. Although you may not use the formal term depreciation, you know all too well that the things you own on a long-term basis will, almost certainly, fall in value. Your car, motor-bike, cycle or hi-fi will each depreciate during the time you own them. (Of course, there are some exceptions: antiques, stamp collections, even certain makes of car, may increase in value as time goes by.)

Most assets held for any length of time depreciate because, first, they get older and, secondly, as they are used they wear out. This applies to almost all of the fixed assets of a business: motor vehicles, machinery, office equipment, buildings. Buildings?—yes, they wear out too and, in the longer term, have a limited useful life: think of the rows of leaky, decaying houses that have to be demolished, or the shabby little shops that are knocked down to make way for new shopping centres. Generally, land is the one fixed asset that does not depreciate. It is always there to be used, except when it contains mineral wealth, such as coal, oil or iron ore—then it has a limited life for that particular purpose and will depreciate as the minerals are extracted.

25.2 The Role of Depreciation in an Accounting System

In accounting, when a fixed asset is bought, it is recorded in the accounts at cost. For example:

1 Jan. 19–1   Bought a van for £5 000, paying by cheque.

The accounts will appear as:

Van

19–1	£
1 Jan. Bank	5 000

Cash book (bank columns)

	19–1	£
	1 Jan. Van	5 000

(Don't forget that costs of delivery and installation and also legal charges can be included in the cost of a fixed asset—see Unit 11.9.)

The Van Account tells us that this business owns a van which cost £5 000 on 1 January 19–1. The business has the use of the van to make deliveries and so forth, but after a few years it will be sold. If, when it is bought in 19–1, it is thought that the van will be sold after four years' use (on 31 December 19–4) for £1 400, then clearly it is expected to depreciate by a total of £3 600 (£5 000–£1 400) during the time the firm owns it. We can therefore say that the van is expected to depreciate by £900 each year (£3 600 ÷ 4 years). Remember that this is the amount of *depreciation*—the expected fall in value—of the van each year: it is not a cost of operating the van, like the costs of fuel, oil, road fund licence, insurance, servicing and repairs. Into which account would such operating costs be placed? The answer is Van Running Expenses Account and, as we know with expenses accounts, the total for the year will be debited to Profit and Loss Account. Using the same logic, we need to debit the Profit and Loss Account with the expense of depreciation. There is an important difference between van running expenses and depreciation, however. Although both are debited to Profit and Loss Account at the end of the financial year, money has been paid out to meet van running expenses during the year, while no money is paid for depreciation—no cheque payable to 'depreciation' has been drawn. Certainly, money has to be paid out to buy a fixed asset, but the annual depreciation charged to Profit and Loss Account does not require any payment in cash: hence depreciation is often referred to as a 'non-cash expense'.

As we have seen, a business normally depreciates all its fixed assets, except land. This means that the debit side of Profit and Loss Account contains, besides the other expenses of the business, depreciation amounts for such items as buildings, machinery and motor vehicles. The effect of these is to increase the total expenses of the business, and thus to reduce net profit. Look at the following:

Before charging depreciation:

Profit and Loss Account of . . . for year ended 31 December 19–1

	£		£
Various expenses (not		Gross profit b/d	20 000
including depreciation)	12 000		
Net profit	8 000		
	20 000		20 000

After charging depreciation:

	£		£
Various expenses	12 000	Gross profit b/d	20 000
Depreciation for year on			
motor vehicles	3 000		
Depreciation for year on			
machinery	2 000		
Net profit	3 000		
	20 000		20 000

25.3   Depreciation Methods

In Unit 25.2 we looked at the depreciation on a van that cost £5 000 and was expected to be sold, after four years' use, for £1 400. The total amount of depreciation was expected to be £3 600, or £900 each year. Where the expected selling price (*residual value*) of the asset at the end of the period of use can be estimated fairly accurately, an annual amount is easily calculated:

$$\frac{(Cost\ price - Residual\ value)}{Number\ of\ years} = Depreciation\ each\ year$$

For example, the annual depreciation of a machine which costs £10 000 and will be sold for £2 000 after five years is:

$$\frac{(£10\,000 - £2\,000)}{5} = £1\,600\ depreciation\ each\ year$$

A business must make an estimate of the fall in value of each class of fixed assets each year, or *provision for depreciation*. It is this provision for depreciation that is charged to Profit and Loss Account each year. When a fixed asset is finally sold or scrapped, an adjustment can be made for any under- or over-provision for depreciation (see Unit 26).

There are three main ways of calculating a provision for depreciation:

(*a*) straight-line method;
(*b*) reducing-balance (or diminishing-balance) method;
(*c*) revaluation method.

We shall consider these in turn.

25.4   Straight-line Depreciation

Using this method, *a certain percentage of the original cost* of the fixed asset is taken each year. The money amount is the depreciation for the year, and the cost of the fixed asset less the *total* depreciation to date is known as the *net book value*.

Example
A machine is purchased for £6 000 on 1 January 19–1; it is to be depreciated by the straight-line method at 10 per cent each year. The firm's financial year-end is 31 December.

The machine will depreciate as follows:

	£
Cost at 1 January 19–1	6 000
Depreciation for 19–1	600
Net book value at 31 December 19–1	5 400
Depreciation for 19–2	600
Net book value at 31 December 19–2	4 800
Depreciation for 19–3	600
Net book value at 31 December 19–3	4 200

As you see, this method provides the *same* money amount for depreciation each year.

25.5   Reducing-balance (or Diminishing-balance) Depreciation

With this method, *a certain percentage of the reduced (or diminished) balance* (that is, the balance at the start of each year) is taken as the depreciation for the year.

Example

The machine in the example in Unit 25.4 is to be depreciated using the reducing-balance method at 12½ per cent each year.

The machine will depreciate as follows:

	£
Cost at 1 January 19–1	6 000
Depreciation for 19–1 (12½% of £6 000)	750
Net book value at 31 December 19–1	5 250
Depreciation for 19–2 (12½% of £5 250)	656
Net book value at 31 December 19–2	4 594
Depreciation for 19–3 (12½% of £4 594)	574
Net book value at 31 December 19–3	4 020

The reducing-balance method provides a *decreasing* amount of depreciation each year; in the second year the amount is less than in the first, in the third year it is less than in the second, and so on.

25.6   Straight-line and Reducing-balance Methods Compared

We have used the two methods of calculating depreciation for the same machine but at different rates. The depreciation amounts for each year are:

Year	Straight-line method (10%)	Reducing-balance method (12½%)
19–1	£600	£750
19–2	£600	£656
19–3	£600	£574

The straight-line method, which provides the same amount of depreciation each year, is likely to be used for fixed assets such as buildings, machinery and fixtures and fittings. The reducing-balance method, providing for larger amounts of depreciation in the first year but decreasing in later years, is often used for vehicles because it reflects the way in which their value will fall. A business chooses the method of calculating depreciation that suits it best, and applies appropriate percentage rates for different classes of assets—one rate for vehicles, say, and another rate for buildings, reflecting the difference in the ways their values are expected to change.

25.7   Revaluation Method of Depreciation

The two previous methods of calculating depreciation applied a certain percentage each year either to the cost of the asset (straight-line depreciation), or to the reduced balance (reducing-balance depreciation). A third method for calculating depreciation is to value the fixed assets each year, and the resultant fall in value during the year is the amount of depreciation for that year. (We are not concerned here with any increase in value—*appreciation*—of fixed assets, such as may take place with land.)

Example

Office equipment is bought for £2 000 on 1 January 19–1. It is revalued as follows:

31 December 19–1	£1 600
31 December 19–2	£1 350
31 December 19–3	£1 000

Therefore depreciation amounts will be:

for 19–1	£400
for 19–2	£250
for 19–3	£350

The revaluation method is often used for low-cost fixed assets, such as stock of workshop tools or small items of office equipment, which are frequently added to during the year, and some of which are 'lost'. For items like these, it would be pointless to keep detailed depreciation records for each and every fixed asset.

25.8   Depreciation and Double-entry Book-keeping

Once a business has decided which method of depreciation is to be used, and the rate to be applied, the next step is to record the entries in the books of account. There are two different ways of doing this: the *traditional method* and the *modern method*.

(a)   Traditional Method

Here a fixed asset account is maintained for each class of asset, and the amounts provided for depreciation each year are credited to the account. We will use the example from Unit 25.4 of the machine costing £6 000 on 1 January 19–1 and being depreciated at 10 per cent each year using the straight-line method. The Machinery Account appears as follows for the first three years of ownership:

Machinery

19–1	£	19–1	£
1 Jan. Bank	6 000	31 Dec. Profit and Loss Account	600
		31 Dec. Balance c/d	5 400
	6 000		6 000
19–2		19–2	
1 Jan. Balance b/d	5 400	31 Dec. Profit and Loss Account	600
		31 Dec. Balance c/d	4 800
	5 400		5 400
19–3		19–3	
1 Jan. Balance b/d	4 800	31 Dec. Profit and Loss Account	600
		31 Dec. Balance c/d	4 200
	4 800		4 800
19–4			
1 Jan. Balance b/d	4 200		

The balance at the end of each year is the net book value of the asset, that is, the cost of the asset, less depreciation to date. You can see how the net book value decreases as the machine gets older, by each extra year's depreciation amount.

In the fixed asset account—machinery in this example—amounts of annual depreciation are entered on the credit side. The double-entry book-keeping to this credit entry is completed with a debit to Profit and Loss Account. The book-keeping, therefore, is:

Dr. Profit and Loss Account   } with the annual amount
Cr. Fixed asset (machinery) account } provided for depreciation

A journal entry must be made for annual depreciation amounts along the following lines:

Date	Details	Folio	Dr. £	Cr. £
	Profit and Loss Account	GL	x	
	Fixed asset (machinery) account	GL		x
	Annual provision for			
	depreciation on ...			
	Method of depreciation ...			
	Percentage ...			

The Profit and Loss Account extract for each year, using the same example figures as before, will appear as:

For the year ended 31 December 19–1

	£		£
Expenses	x	Gross profit b/d	x
Provision for depreciation:			
machinery	600		

For the year ended 31 December 19–2

	£		£
Expenses	x	Gross profit b/d	x
Provision for depreciation:			
machinery	600		

For the year ended 31 December 19–3

	£		£
Expenses	x	Gross profit b/d	x
Provision for depreciation:			
machinery	600		

As we have seen, the effect of the entry for depreciation in Profit and Loss Account is to reduce the net profit (or increase any net loss). This is because an extra expense has been incurred, being an estimate of the fall in value of certain fixed assets which the firm has had the benefit of using during the course of the year. When a firm makes a provision for depreciation, it is *not* setting aside an amount of cash. Depreciation is simply a book-keeping entry to make an allowance for the estimated fall in value of fixed assets—as we said in Unit 25.2, it is a 'non-cash' expense.

Provision for depreciation must be shown on the balance sheet. The best way of doing this is to show the *fixed asset at cost*, and then deduct from this the full amount of *provision for depreciation to date* (not just this year's amount, but including amounts from previous years). The balance sheet extracts, again using the same example, will be:

As at 31 December 19–1

	£
Fixed assets:	
Machinery at cost	6 000
Less Provision for depreciation to date	600
	5 400

As at 31 December 19–2

	£
Fixed assets:	
Machinery at cost	6 000
Less Provision for depreciation to date	1 200
	4 800

As at 31 December 19–3

	£
Fixed assets:	
Machinery at cost	6 000
Less Provision for depreciation to date	1 800
	4 200

In this way, depreciation is shown as an increasing amount being deducted from the cost price of the asset. The amount to be added in to the assets side of the balance sheet is the net book value, that is, £5 400 at 31 December 19–1, £4 800 at 31 December 19–2, and so on.

(b) Modern Method

While the traditional method shows the fixed asset account with provisions for depreciation included on it, the modern method uses two separate accounts for the same transactions:

    (i) a fixed asset account, which records the cost price of the asset;

    (ii) a Provision for Depreciation Account, which records the amount of depreciation set aside each year.

Again we will use the example from Unit 25.4 of the machine costing £6 000 on 1 January 19–1 and being depreciated at 10 per cent each year using the straight-line method. Machinery Account and Provision for Depreciation Account appear as follows for the first three years of ownership:

Machinery

19–1	£	19–1	£
1 Jan. Bank	6 000	31 Dec. Balance c/d	6 000
19–2		19–2	
1 Jan. Balance b/d	6 000	31 Dec. Balance c/d	6 000
19–3		19–3	
1 Jan. Balance b/d	6 000	31 Dec. Balance c/d	6 000
19–4			
1 Jan. Balance b/d	6 000		

Provision for depreciation—Machine

19–1	£	19–1	£
31 Dec. Balance c/d	600	31 Dec. Profit and Loss Account	600
19–2		19–2	
31 Dec. Balance c/d	1 200	1 Jan. Balance b/d	600
		31 Dec. Profit and Loss Account	600
	1 200		1 200
19–3		19–3	
31 Dec. Balance c/d	1 800	1 Jan. Balance b/d	1 200
		31 Dec. Profit and Loss Account	600
	1 800		1 800
		19–4	
		1 Jan. Balance b/d	1 800

Study these two accounts carefully and note the following:

    (i) The fixed asset account—Machinery Account—remains 'at cost'.

    (ii) Provision for Depreciation Account stores up the amounts provided for depreciation year by year.

(iii) Both accounts are balanced at the end of each financial year—this is a good habit to get into when preparing depreciation accounts.

(iv) A separate Provision for Depreciation Account is maintained for each class of fixed asset.

Annual depreciation amounts are credited to Provision for Depreciation Account, and this account *always has a credit balance*. The double-entry book-keeping is:

Dr. Profit and Loss Account } with the annual amount
Cr. Provision for Depreciation Account } provided for depreciation

Of course this will require a journal entry to be passed, very similar to the one in (*a*) above.

The Profit and Loss Account and balance sheet extracts will be the same as with the 'traditional' method.

25.9   Depreciation in Examination Questions

(*a*) In examination questions relating to depreciation you will always be given the appropriate information concerning the rate and method of depreciation to be used. The question will also tell you if depreciation is to be provided for part-years when fixed assets are bought or sold during a financial year. For example, suppose that a firm with a financial year-end of 31 December buys a machine on 1 July: this business may decide to provide for depreciation for half a year, or it may choose to provide for depreciation for the whole year on all assets held at the end of the year. The examiner will always give you sufficient information to enable you to tackle the question.

(*b*) Most examination questions will guide you as to whether the 'traditional' or the 'modern' method is to be used. For example, a question that says 'using the straight-line method of depreciation, show the Machinery Account ...' implies that the 'traditional' method, recording provisions for depreciation on the fixed asset account, is to be used. On the other hand, a question that states '... show the Machinery Account and the Provision for Depreciation Account ...' requires the 'modern' method, using separate accounts.

(*c*) When attempting a question concerning several fixed assets of the same class—for example, a number of machines—acquired on different dates, it is often helpful to prepare a schedule of depreciation amounts.

Example

XYZ Ltd acquired machines as follows:

1 Jan.	19–1	machine costing £1 000
1 Jul.	19–1	machine costing £800
1 Apr.	19–2	machine costing £1 200
1 Oct.	19–3	machine costing £1 600

Depreciation is at the rate of 10 per cent per annum, straight-line method, machines being depreciated for each proportion of a year.

Schedule of depreciation:

		19–1	19–2	19–3
		£	£	£
1 Jan. 19–1	Machine purchased	100	100	100
1 Jul. 19–1	Machine purchased	40 (½ year)	80	80
1 Apr. 19–2	Machine purchased	–	90 (¾ year)	120
1 Oct. 19–3	Machine purchased	–	–	40 (¼ year)
Total depreciation for year		140	270	340

Such a schedule makes the calculation of depreciation totals an easy matter.

25.10   Questions

*1.   (*a*) What is the meaning of 'depreciation'?

(*b*) A machine was purchased on 1 January for £2 000 and was estimated to be worth £200 at the end of its working life after three years. Show the Asset Account and the Provision for Depreciation Account with the entries for each of the three years using the straight-line method of depreciation.

(*c*) Show how the asset would be valued on the balance sheet at the end of the third year.

[*South Western Examinations Board*]

*2.   The financial year of W. Hastings ends on 30 June. On 1 January 19–9 he purchases for cash a machine worth £3 000 and decides to depreciate it at the rate of 10 per cent per annum using the straight-line method. Prepare his Machine Account for the three years ending 30 June 19–1.

[*East Anglian Examinations Board*]

3.   A car worth £4 000 is purchased for cash by M. Dowding on 1 January 19–9. Dowding decides to depreciate it at the rate of 10 per cent per annum using the reducing-balance method. Show the Car Account and Provision for Depreciation Account for the three years ending 30 June 19–1.

[*East Anglian Examinations Board*]

4.   William Prentice, a sole trader, bought a new delivery van for his business on 1 January 19–2. He wishes to write off depreciation of the van over three years but cannot decide whether to use the straight-line method or the diminishing-balance method. The cost of the new van was £2 800 and Prentice's year-end is 31 December.

Notes:

(i) Identify each account clearly—'straight-line method' and 'reducing-balance method'.

(ii) Each account should be balanced at the end of each year.

(iii) The rate of depreciation in both cases is to be 10 per cent and calculations should be made to the nearest £.

Required:

To assist Prentice in making his decision, draw up the Delivery Van Account as it would appear in the ledger of William Prentice for three years from the date on which the van was acquired, using (a) the straight-line method, (b) the reducing-balance method.

[London Chamber of Commerce]

*5. Prepare final accounts for N. Sharma using the trial balance and additional information given below.

Trial balance of N. Sharma as at 30 June 19–2

	£	£
Debtors and creditors	1 500	700
Buildings, at cost	5 000	
Rates	500	
Bank	600	
Fixtures, at cost	1 200	
Heating	500	
Returns inward and outward	50	100
Provision for depreciation of buildings on 1 July 19–1		500
Discount allowed	100	
Commission received		200
Purchases and sales	8 000	12 900
Drawings	300	
Salaries	1 200	
Stock, 1 July 19–1	900	
Carriage inward	200	
Goodwill	1 000	
Capital		6 650
	21 050	21 050

Additional information:
1. Closing stock £1 100.
2. Buildings are to be depreciated at the rate of 10 per cent per annum on cost.
3. Fixtures are to be depreciated at the rate of $33\frac{1}{3}$ per cent per annum on cost.
4. Rates paid in advance £150.

[East Anglian Examinations Board]

6. From the following list of balances in the books of B. Smallweed at 31 December 19–2, you are required to draw up a Trading and Profit and Loss Account for the year and a balance sheet as at that date.

	£
Cash at bank	8 000
Carriage inwards	400
Wages and salaries	8 400
Stock at 31 December 19–2	3 000
Purchases	12 000
Sales	30 000
Sundry creditors	4 000
Sundry debtors	3 000
Depreciation on vehicles	600

	£
Vehicles before depreciation	6 000
Office expenses	2 500
Rates and rents	600
Discounts received	500
Capital at 31 December 19–2	15 400

[*London Regional Examining Board*]

7. From the following trial balance extracted from the books of Paulo Gavinci, restaurateur, you are required to prepare the Trading and Profit and Loss Account for the year ended 30 April 19–0 and the balance sheet as at that date.

Trial balance as at 30 April 10–0

	Dr.	Cr.
	£	£
Capital		75 000
Fixtures and fittings	95 000	
Delivery vehicle	8 000	
Opening stock	2 000	
Cash	450	
Bank		4 300
Bank loan (long-term)		30 000
Purchases	190 250	
Sales		300 000
Creditors		5 000
Wages	45 000	
Drawings	25 000	
Purchases returns		400
Rent	31 800	
General expenses	17 200	
	414 700	414 700

You should also take the following additional information into account:

(i) Closing stock at 30 April 19–0 was £1 600.
(ii) Depreciation is to be provided as follows on a straight-line basis:

Fixtures and fittings	20 per cent on cost
Delivery vehicle	25 per cent on cost

(iii) Paulo took goods for personal use amounting to £250 at cost and an adjustment needs to be made for this.
(iv) Provide for:

	£
Rent prepaid	2 000
Wages accrued	1 000

[*Pitman Examinations Institute, Level 2*]

Disposals of Fixed Assets

26.1 Introduction

Fixed assets—such as buildings, machinery or vehicles—are usually purchased with the intention that they will be used in the business for some time to come: they are depreciated in order to take account of their fall in value over that time. When a fixed asset is sold, we find out if our provision for depreciation has been accurate. Until the asset is sold and its price is known, the provisions are estimates; the sale 'crystallizes' the situation and we can work out the 'gain' or 'loss' on sale. For example:

	£
Cost price of machine	2 500
Less Provision for depreciation to date	1 750
Net book value at date of sale	750
Selling price	650
'Loss' on sale	100

A 'gain' or a 'loss' is a book-keeping difference only. In this example depreciation has been underprovided; it should have been £1 850 which would give a net book value equal to the selling price. Where there is a 'profit' on sale, depreciation has been overprovided, that is, too much depreciation has been provided during ownership of the asset.

26.2 The Use of Disposals Account

A *Disposals Account*, known also as a *Sale of Assets Account*, is used to bring together:

    (i) the cost price of the asset being sold;
    (ii) depreciation to date relating to the asset;
    (iii) sale proceeds of the asset.

The book-keeping entries are as follows (each needing a journal entry):

    (*a*) The fixed asset account—machinery, vans or as the case may be—is 'emptied' of the cost price of the asset sold, which is transferred to Disposals Account:

    Dr. Disposals Account } with the cost price of the
    Cr. Fixed asset account } asset now sold

    (*b*) Provision for Depreciation Account is 'emptied' of the depreciation 'stored up' in the account that relates to the asset now sold:

    Dr. Provision for Depreciation Account } with depreciation to date
    Cr. Disposals Account } relating to the asset

(*c*) The sale proceeds of the asset are entered in the accounts:

Dr. Bank/Cash Account ⎱ with the sale proceeds
Cr. Disposals Account ⎰

After these transactions have been carried out, any balance remaining on Disposals Account is transferred to Profit and Loss Account. Using the figures from Unit 26.1, for example, after carrying out steps (*a*), (*b*) and (*c*) above Disposals Account appears as:

Disposals

	£		£
Machinery	2 500	Provision for depreciation	1 750
		Bank (sale proceeds)	650

The account does not balance; it is balanced by transferring the difference to Profit and Loss Account:

Disposals

	£		£
Machinery	2 500	Provision for depreciation	1 750
		Bank (sale proceeds)	650
		Profit and Loss Account	100
	2 500		2 500

To complete double-entry book-keeping the £100 is debited to Profit and Loss Account and described as a 'loss on sale of machinery'. This shows that the business has underprovided for depreciation during ownership of the asset. With a loss on sale, therefore, the book-keeping entries to close off Disposals Account are:

Dr. Profit and Loss Account ⎱ with amount of loss on sale
Cr. Disposals Account   ⎰

Journal entries for this complete transaction are:

Date	Details	Folio	*Dr.*	*Cr.*
			£	£
	Disposals	GL	2 500	
	Machinery	GL		2 500
	Provision for depreciation	GL	1 750	
	Disposals	GL		1 750
	Bank	CB	650	
	Disposals	GL		650
	Profit and Loss Account	GL	100	
	Disposals	GL		100
			5 000	5 000
	Sale of machine no XYZ 123			

If the machine had been sold for £800 instead of £650, Disposals Account would be shown as:

Disposals

	£		£
Machinery	2 500	Provision for depreciation	1 750
Profit and Loss Account	50	Bank (sales proceeds)	800
	2 550		2 550

Here Profit and Loss Account will be *credited* with £50, described as 'profit on sale of machinery'. This indicates an *overprovision* of depreciation. The book-keeping entries for a profit on sale are:

> *Dr.* Disposals Account   }
> *Cr.* Profit and Loss Account   }   with amount of profit on sale

26.3   Questions

*1. On 1 January 19–1, F. Smith bought a small machine costing £85. Its working life is estimated to be four years, and it is estimated that at the end of that time its scrap value will be £5. It is decided to depreciate the asset by the straight-line method. At the end of three years the machine was sold for £20.

Prepare (*a*) the Machinery Account, (*b*) the Provision for Depreciation Account and (*c*) the Disposals Account, for the years 19–1, 19–2 and 19–3. Show also how the asset would be shown in the balance sheet at 31 December 19–2.

2. On 1 January 19–1 N. Johnson bought a car for £8 500. She estimates that, after four years' use, she will be able to sell it for £2 500. It is decided to depreciate the car by the straight-line method. At the end of four years it is sold for £3 000.

Prepare (*a*) the Car Account, (*b*) the Provision for Depreciation Account and (*c*) the Disposals Account, for the years 19–1, 19–2, 19–3 and 19–4. Show also how the car would be shown in the balance sheet at 31 December 19–3.

*3. From the following information, prepare (*a*) the Machinery Account, (*b*) the Provision for Depreciation Account and (*c*) the Machinery Disposal Account, up to and including the year ending 31 December 19–4.

1 Jan. 19–1	Purchased a machine at a cost of £500.
1 Apr. 19–2	Purchased a machine at a cost of £800.
1 Jul. 19–3	Purchased a machine at a cost of £600.
1 Jul. 19–4	The machine purchased in 19–1 was sold for £290.

Depreciation is to be provided at the rate of 10 per cent per annum (straight-line method) for each month of ownership.

4. A company depreciates its plant at 20 per cent per annum, straight-line method, for each month of ownership. From the following details, draw up a Plant Account and the Provision for Depreciation Account fof each of the years 19–1, 19–2, 19–3 and 19–4.

    19–1   Bought plant costing £2 000 on 1 January.
            Bought plant costing £800 on 1 October.

    19–3   Bought plant costing £3 000 on 1 July.
            Sold plant which cost £1 000 on 1 January 19–1 for £550 on 30 September 19–3.

    19–4   Bought plant costing £1 000 on 1 January.
            Sold plant which cost £500 on 1 January 19–1 for £250 on 30 September 19–4.

You are also required to draw up the Plant Disposal Account and the extracts from the balance sheet at the end of each year.

Bad Debts and Provision for Bad and Doubtful Debts

27.1 Introduction

We must now turn our attention to the *debtors* of a business, that is, the amounts due to it from its customers. We shall consider two aspects of debtors here:

(*a*) *Bad debts*—these are amounts which a firm is unable, for various reasons, to collect from customers; the amount is written off in the firm's accounts as being irrecoverable.

(*b*) *Provision for bad and doubtful debts*—this is the amount or proportion of the debtors that the firm considers may not pay in the future, but as yet it is not certain that these debts will become bad.

The objective in writing off bad debts, and in making a provision for bad and doubtful debts, is to be able to show in the balance sheet a figure for *net debtors* that fairly represents a collectable amount. American accountants refer to net debtors as *receivables* and this very well expresses the idea—the amount of the total debtors figure that is receivable.

27.2 Bad Debts Written Off

Look at the following account, which appears in the sales ledger section:

	J. Smith		
19–1	£	19–1	£
15 Apr. Sales	95	20 Jun. Bank	50
		28 Sep. Cash	15
		31 Dec. Balance c/d	30
	95		95
19–2		19–2	
1 Jan. Balance b/d	30	2 Feb. Cash	5

It is now mid-November 19–2 and you have been given the task of going through the debtors' accounts to see if there are any bad debts that should be written off before the financial year-end on 31 December. What about J. Smith's account? It tells us that goods to the value of £95 were sold to this customer on credit on 15 April 19–1. In the eighteen months since then we have received payments totalling £70. The balance of the account is now £25 debit, and you discover that the last statement sent was returned by the Post Office marked 'not known at this address'. What is your firm to do? On enquiry, you find that the firm's procedures for attempting to recover debts have been exhausted (we shall discuss these in Unit 27.6). If nothing has persuaded Smith to pay, then the firm should write this account off as a bad debt. This is done by making the following book-keeping entries:

Dr. Bad Debts Account ⎱ with amount of debt
Cr. Debtor's personal account ⎰ being written off

Using the example of J. Smith's account, the effect will be:

J. Smith

19–2	£	19–2	£
1 Jan. Balance b/d	30	2 Feb. Cash	5
		15 Nov. Bad debts	25
	30		30

Bad debts

19–2	£
15 Nov. J. Smith	25

What has happened is that the firm has paid off Smith's account itself (although Smith will not be advised of this!). A journal entry will be required along the following lines:

Date	Details	Folio	*Dr.*	*Cr.*
19–2			£	£
15 Nov.	Bad debts	GL	25	
	J. Smith	SL		25
	Smith's account written off as a bad debt—see correspondence file reference 82/151			

Bad Debts Account acts as a 'holding account', that is, it stores up all the debtors' accounts that have gone bad during the course of a year (it is to be hoped there are not too many). At the end of the financial year, the total of Bad Debts Account is transferred to Profit and Loss Account as follows:

Dr. Profit and Loss Account ⎱ with total bad debts written
Cr. Bad Debts Account ⎰ off during the year

The transactions for this particular firm might be:

Bad debts

19–2	£	19–2	£
12 Feb. M. Green	12	31 Dec. Profit and Loss Account	116
1 Apr. A. Day	20		
26 May T. Owen	8		
6 Aug. D. Mills	30		
17 Oct. L. Willis	6		
15 Nov. J. Smith	25		
20 Dec. D. Williams	15		
	116		116

Profit and Loss Account (extract) for year ended 31 December 19–2

	£		£
Expenses	x	Gross profit b/d	x
Bad debts written off	116		

The journal entry will read:

Date	Details	Folio	Dr.	Cr.
19–2			£	£
31 Dec.	Profit and Loss Account	GL	116	
	Bad debts	GL		116
	Total of bad debts written off for year transferred to Profit and Loss Account			

The effect of debiting Profit and Loss Account with bad debts written off is, of course, to reduce net profit.

27.3 Provision for Bad and Doubtful Debts

The creation of a provision for bad and doubtful debts (frequently referred to as provision for bad debts) is best regarded as a completely separate operation from the writing-off of bad debts. Suppose that at the year-end, Tom Piper has debtors totalling £20 500 before writing off bad debts and creating a provision for bad debts. Piper's first step is to go through the debtors' accounts to see if any should be written off as bad (although ideally this should be a continuous process carried on throughout the year, rather than once a year at the year-end). This first step might lead to the writing-off of debtors totalling, say £500. Piper is then left in the following position:

	£
Gross debtors at 31 December 19–1	20 500
Less Bad debts written off	500
	20 000

Would Piper be correct in showing debtors in the balance sheet at a figure of £20 000? If he were to do so, this would imply that he expected to collect all £20 000, that is, that none of the debts would later go bad. Most firms realize that, of all their debtors at any time, some will not pay the amount due. Piper cannot predict which particular debtors will go bad—if he knew this he would not have sold to those people on credit in the first place!—but past experience informs him that a certain percentage of debtors will not pay, and consequently he needs to reflect this in the accounts. This percentage varies from business to business, and from trade to trade: for example, a hire purchase company is likely to have a larger percentage of bad debts than that of a bank.

The accounting procedures to create a provision for bad debts are:

Dr. Profit and Loss Account $\left.\begin{array}{l}\\\end{array}\right\}$ with amount of provision
Cr. Provision for bad debts

A journal entry will be necessary. This will read:

Date	Details	Folio	*Dr.*	*Cr.*
			£	£
	Profit and Loss Account	GL	x	
	Provision for bad debts	GL		x
	Creation of a provision for bad debts			

Point to notice:

The amount of the provision for bad debts is calculated on the balance of debtors outstanding *after* deducting bad debts written off.

Example

On 31 December 19–1 Tom Piper has debtors of £20 000, after writing off £500 as bad debts. Past experience shows that 2 per cent of debtors will not pay, and it is decided to create a provision for bad debts.

Piper needs to create a provision for bad debts of £400 (2 per cent of £20 000). The accounts appear as:

Profit and Loss Account (extract) for the year ended 31 December 19–1

	£		£
Expenses	x	Gross profit b/d	x
Bad debts written off	500		
Provision for bad debts	400		

Provision for bad debts

		19–1	£
		31 Dec. Profit and Loss Account	400

Balance sheet (extract) as at 31 December 19–1

	£	£
Fixed assets:		
Current assets:		
Debtors	20 000	
Less Provision for		
bad debts	400	
		19 600

(The journal entries and Bad Debts Account are not shown.)

The effect of creating a provision for bad debts reduces the net profit—in this example by £400. On the balance sheet, the amount of provision for bad debts is deducted from debtors, thus giving a reasonable estimate of collectable debts.

27.4   Increases and Decreases in Provision for Bad Debts

Having created a provision for bad debts based on a certain percentage of debtors, the firm needs to ensure that the money amount of the provision is adjusted at each financial year-end as the figure for debtors changes.

(*a*) Increase in Provision for Bad Debts

In Unit 27.3, Tom Piper created a 2 per cent provision. If, at 31 December 19–2, debtors have risen to £25 000 after writing off bad debts, Piper needs a total provision for bad debts of £500 (2 per cent of £25 000). As the firm already has a provision of £400, it needs to make an *increase in the provision of £100*. As well as the appropriate journal entry, the accounting entries to record an *increase* in the level of provision for bad debts are:

Dr. Profit and Loss Account
Cr. Provision for bad debts } with the *amount of the increase*

In Piper's accounts they will appear as:

Profit and Loss Account (extract) for the year ended 31 December 19–2

	£		£
Expenses	x	Gross profit b/d	x
Bad debts written off	x		
Increase in provision for			
bad debts	100		

Provision for bad debts

19–2	£	19–2	£
31 Dec. Balance c/d	500	1 Jan. Balance b/d	400
		31 Dec. Profit and Loss Account	100
	500		500
		19–3	
		1 Jan. Balance b/d	500

Balance sheet (extract) as at 31 December 19–2

	£	£
Fixed assets:		
Current assets:		
Debtors	25 000	
Less Provision for bad debts	500	
		24 500

Points to notice:

(i) Only *the amount of the increase*, that is, £100, has been debited to Profit and Loss Account and credited to Provision for Bad Debts Account.

(ii) Once created, the provision account only needs increasing (or decreasing—see (*b*) below) to bring it into line with the change in the level of a firm's debtors.

(iii) As you see, the balance of Provision for Bad Debts Account at 31 December 19–2 is £500, and it is this amount that is shown in the balance sheet as a deduction from debtors.

(*b*) Decrease in Provision for Bad Debts

Suppose that at 31 December 19–3, Piper finds that the debtors figure, after writing off bad debts, has fallen to £23 000. This means that the balance of Provision for Bad Debts Account should now be £460 (2 per cent of £23 000). As the current balance of the account is £500, a reduction of £40 is needed. As well as the journal entry, the accounting entries to record a *decrease* in the level of provision for bad debts are:

Dr. Provision for bad debts ⎱
Cr. Profit and Loss Account ⎰ with the *amount of the decrease*

Piper's accounts will then appear as:

Profit and Loss Account (extract) for the year ended 31 December 19–3

	£		£
Expenses	x	Gross profit b/d	x
Bad debts written off	x	Decrease in provision for bad debts	40

Provision for bad debts

19–3	£	19–3	£
31 Dec. Profit and Loss Account		1 Jan. Balance b/d	500
	40		
31 Dec. Balance c/d	460		
	500		500
		19–4	
		1 Jan. Balance b/d	460

Balance sheet (extract) as at 31 December 19–3

	£	£
Fixed assets:		
Current assets:		
Debtors	23 000	
Less Provision for		
bad debts	460	
		22 540

As before, only the *amount of the change*—the reduction of £40—has been passed to Profit and Loss Account. The balance of the Provision for Bad Debts Account, now £460, is deducted from debtors.

27.5   A Worked Example

This worked example shows the accounting treatment for bad debts written off and for provision for bad debts. (Journal entries are not shown.)

A business has a year-end of 31 December. Gross debtors, before writing off debts and creating provisions for bad debts are:

£50 750 at 31 December 19–5
£60 875 at 31 December 19–6
£56 025 at 31 December 19–7

Bad debts to be written off at the end of each year are £750, £875 and £1 025 respectively. At 31 December 19–5 the company decides to make a provision for bad debts equal to $2\frac{1}{2}$ per cent of debtors, and to keep the provision at the same percentage at each year-end thereafter. Show (*a*) Bad Debts Account, (*b*) Provision for Bad Debts Account, (*c*) Profit and Loss Account (extracts), and (*d*) balance sheet (extracts) for each of the three years.

Answer

(*a*)	**Bad debts**			
19–5	£	19–5		£
31 Dec. Sundry debtors	750	31 Dec. Profit and Loss Account		750
19–6		19–6		
31 Dec. Sundry debtors	875	31 Dec. Profit and Loss Account		875
19–7		19–7		
31 Dec. Sundry debtors	1 025	31 Dec. Profit and Loss Account		1 025

(b)   **Provision for bad debts**

19–5	£	19–5	£
31 Dec. Balance c/d	1 250	31 Dec. Profit and Loss Account	1 250
19–6		19–6	
		1 Jan. Balance b/d	1 250
31 Dec. Balance c/d	1 500	31 Dec. Profit and Loss Account	250
	1 500		1 500
19–7		19–7	
31 Dec. Profit and Loss Account	125	1 Jan. Balance b/d	1 500
31 Dec. Balance c/d	1 375		
	1 500		1 500
19–8		1 Jan. Balance b/d	1 375

(c)   **Profit and Loss Account (extract) for the year ended 31 December 19–5**

	£		£
Expenses	x	Gross profit b/d	x
Bad debts written off	750		
Provision for bad debts	1 250		

For the year ended 31 December 19–6

	£		£
Expenses	x	Gross profit b/d	x
Bad debts written off	875		
Increase in provision for bad debts	250		

For the year ended 31 December 19–7

	£		£
Expenses	x	Gross profit b/d	x
Bad debts written off	1 025	Decrease in provision for bad debts	125

(d)   **Balance sheet (extracts)**
                       as at 31 December 19–5

	£	£
Fixed assets:		
Current assets:		
Debtors	50 000	
Less Provision for bad debts	1 250	
		48 750

As at 31 December 19–6

	£	£
Fixed assets		
Current assets:		
Debtors	60 000	
Less Provision		
for bad debts	1 500	
		58 500

As at 31 December 19–7

	£	£
Fixed assets		
Current assets:		
Debtors	55 000	
Less Provision		
for bad debts	1 375	
		53 625

27.6   Avoidance of Bad Debts

We have just looked at the accounting entries in connection with both bad debts written off and the creation or adjustment of a provision for bad debts. But no business wants bad debts; the question therefore arises as to how they can be kept to a minimum.

The simple way to avoid bad debts is always to insist upon payment in cash at the time of sale. This is probably only practicable for a retail shop, and even retail customers may ask for credit. For most firms selling to other firms, credit sales are customary. One way to reduce the incidence of bad debts is to ask each prospective credit customer for two references (see also Unit 13.2)—a bank reference and a trade reference. These should both be taken up (for the bank reference the firm's own bank must be asked to take it up on the firm's behalf—another bank cannot be approached direct). Only when satisfactory replies have been received should credit be granted, and a credit limit established for the customer. The amount due from the customer should not exceed this limit.

It is important in avoiding bad debts to send out regular statements of account (see also Unit 13.4)—probably at the month-end. If this method does not produce results then the business must follow its chosen procedure for dealing with debtors. The information about the overdue account should be passed to a particular person who is responsible for taking action. This action usually takes the form of a series of 'chaser' letters which start by pointing out politely that the account is overdue, and progress to the threat of legal action. Whether legal action is taken or not will depend on the amount of the debt—a small amount owing is not usually worth the legal costs involved although action may still be taken on a matter of principle. Whenever legal action is to be taken, the matter will be passed to the firm's solicitors or, in a large organization, to the legal department.

In an attempt to avoid long overdue debts, many firms prepare a schedule of their debtors at the month-end, showing how long the accounts have been outstanding. Such an 'ageing' schedule of debtors might look like that shown in Fig. 20.2 (page 174).

27.7   Questions

*1.   T. Pitt owes you £59.00 on 1 January. He pays you £29.00 on 31 January but ignores all further requests for payment. On 6 May you hear that he has been made a bankrupt, and his trustee in bankruptcy announces that a dividend of 25 per cent in the £ will be paid on 30 September. This payment was received in due course.

Show Pitt's ledger account and the Bad Debts Account at 31 December, the end of your financial year.

[Pitman Examinations Institute]

*2.   During the months of March and April the following transactions took place on Micawber's account in the books of Pickwick.

		£
1 Mar.	Micawber owes Pickwick	400
3 Mar.	Micawber paid the balance on his account by cheque being allowed cash discount of 2½ per cent	
10 Mar.	Micawber obtained further goods on credit value	250
14 Mar.	Micawber returned goods to Pickwick value	50
21 Mar.	Pickwick received cash on account	100
30 Apr.	You are informed that Micawber has gone out of business due to financial difficulties, and it is decided to write off the balance on his account as a bad debt.	

(*a*)   Write up Micawber's account for the months of March and April.

(*b*)   Show the entry in the Bad Debts Account caused by the above transactions.

[Royal Society of Arts]

3.   During the year ended 31 May 19–1 Thomas Church, a sole trader, incurred the following bad debts:

William Smith £25
Arthur Edwards £31
Frank Williams £18
John Frost £43
David Parsons £52

At the close of business on 31 May 19–0, Thomas Church's provision for bad and doubtful debts had a balance of £130. At the close of business on 31 May 19–1 his debtors totalled £3 840 and on this date he decided to increase the provision for bad and doubtful debts to 5 per cent of the debtors figure of £3 840.

Required:

Draw up the Bad Debts Account and the Provision for Bad and Doubtful Debts Account for the year ended 31 May 19–1, showing the amounts to be transferred to the Profit and Loss Account.

[London Chamber of Commerce]

4.   John Doe, a sole trader, extracted the following trial balance from his ledgers at the close of business on 30 June Year 6, the end of his financial year.

	Dr. £	Cr. £
Fixtures and fittings	2 100	
Purchases and sales	25 160	39 210
Wages	8 140	
Office furniture	1 200	
Capital Account 1 July Year 5		44 260
Bad debts written off	70	
Rates and insurance	1 090	
Discounts allowed	420	
Sales and purchases returns	270	315
Carriage inwards	720	
Postage and stationery	255	
Stock at cost 1 July Year 5	3 160	
Discounts received		290
Debtors and creditors	3 620	1 750
Provision for bad/doubtful debts		150
Carriage outwards	450	
Drawings	1 800	
Miscellaneous expenses	320	
Balance at bank	2 150	
Cash in hand	50	
Freehold premises	35 000	
	£85 975	£85 975

The following additional information is available:
   (i) Closing stock at 30 June Year 6 was valued at cost £4 200.
   (ii) Accrued wages, unpaid at 30 June Year 6, were £150.
   (iii) Prepayments of rates at 30 June Year 6 amounted to £120.
   (iv) John Doe wishes to increase his provision for bad/doubtful debts to £180.
   (v) Provide for depreciation as follows:
       Fixtures and fittings   £200
       Office furniture   £80

Required:
Draw up John Doe's Trading and Profit and Loss Accounts for the year ended 30 June Year 6 and a balance sheet as at that date.

[*London Chamber of Commerce*]

*5.   Edward Thomas, a sole trader, extracted the following trial balance from his books at the close of business on 30 April 19–1:

	Dr. £	Cr. £
Capital Account 1 May 19–0		11 100
Debtors and creditors	3 460	2 090
Office furniture	700	
Discounts	680	280
Fixtures and fittings	600	
Purchases and sales	9 450	16 330
Sales and purchases returns	760	410
Wages and salaries	2 960	
Bank	750	
Cash	70	
Bad debts written off	190	
Rates and insurance	270	
Freehold premises	6 000	
Carriage outward	520	
Drawings	1 700	
Sundry expenses	120	
Stock 1 May 19–0	1 980	
	£30 210	£30 210

Notes:

1. Stock 30 April 19–1 £2 050.
2. Wages and salaries accrued 30 April 19–1 £50.
3. Provide for depreciation as follows:
   Office furniture   £70;
   Fixtures and fittings   £20.

Required:

Draw up the Trading and Profit and Loss Accounts for the year ended 30 April 19–1 together with a balance sheet as at that date.

[*London Chamber of Commerce*]

*6.   The following trial balance was extracted from the books of T. Revie, a retailer, on 31 December 19–1. You are to prepare from it a Trading and Profit and Loss Account for the year ended 31 December 19–1, and a balance sheet as at that date.

Trial balance of T. Revie as at 31 December 19–1

	Dr.	Cr.
	£	£
Business premises	9 600	
Fixtures and fittings	1 400	
Cash at bank	1 112	
Debtors and creditors	480	2 340
Stock, 1 January 19–1	3 940	
Purchases and sales	11 468	22 440
Returns	1 124	100
Carriage inwards	160	
Carriage outwards	80	
Rates	320	
Discounts	48	72
Salaries and wages	1 800	
Printing and stationery	268	
Bad debts	148	
Telephone and postages	360	
Insurance	84	
Capital, 1 January 19–1		10 040
Drawings	2 600	
	£34 992	£34 992

Note: Take into account the following matters:
1. Stock on hand at 31 December 19–1, £2 064.
2. Rates paid in advance at the end of December 19–1 amounted to £80.
3. Printing and stationery due at 31 December 19–1 was £18.
4. Depreciate business premises by 5 per cent and fixtures and fittings by 20 per cent.

[*Associated Lancashire Schools Examining Board*]

Multiple-choice Questions—7

Read each question carefully. Choose the *one* answer you think is correct. Answers are given on page 411.

1.   Which one of the following is entered in the general journal?

   A   purchase of goods for resale   **C**   returns inwards
   B   purchase of fixed assets   **D**   sale of goods on credit

2. Which one of the following is *not* entered in the general journal?

   A opening entries
   B depreciation of fixed assets
   C purchase of goods for resale on credit
   D correction of errors

3. Smith, a debtor for £85, is unable to settle his account in cash and offers you a typewriter instead. The journal entry to record this in your accounts should be:

	Debit	*Credit*
A	Smith's account	Typewriter Account
B	Typewriter Account	Bank Account
C	Typewriter Account	Smith's account
D	Cash Account	Smith's account

4. A machine costing £1 000 is expected to have a working life of five years and a scrap value of £100 at the end of that time. Using the straight-line method of depreciation, the depreciation charge each year will be:

   A £200   **B** £100   **C** £220   **D** £180

5. A machine was purchased on 1 January 19–1 for £1 250. Depreciation is charged at 20 per cent per year using the reducing-balance method, the financial year-end being 31 December. At 31 December 19–3 the machine will have a written-down value of:

   A £750   **B** £512   **C** £500   **D** £640

6. A van was purchased on 1 January 19–1 for £5 000. After two years it has a written-down value of £2 500. The straight-line depreciation percentage each year is:

   A $12\frac{1}{2}$%   **B** 25%   **C** $33\frac{1}{3}$%   **D** 50%

7. A machine which originally cost £5 000 is sold for £750. The Provision for Depreciation Account relevant to this machine shows a credit balance of £4 350. This means that there is:

   A a loss on sale of £100   **C** a profit on sale of £750
   B a profit on sale of £100   **D** a profit on sale of £4 350

8. The charge for depreciation in Profit and Loss Account will reduce:
   A net profit   **C** gross profit
   B bank balance   **D** current assets

9. If Smith, a debtor, is unable to pay the amount owing and his account is to be written off as a bad debt, this should be recorded by:

	Debit	*Credit*
A	Bad Debts Account	Smith's account
B	Smith's account	Bad Debts Account
C	Cash Account	Smith's account
D	Provision for Bad Debts Account	Smith's account

10. At the end of the financial year a business has debtors of £10 000 and a provision for bad debts of £480. It is proposed to maintain provision for bad debts at 5 per cent. What amount will be passed to Profit and Loss Account for the year?

   A   a debit of £500   **C**   a debit of £20
   B   a credit of £20   **D**   a debit of £480

11. A decrease in provision for bad debts will:

   A   increase the cash/bank balance
   B   increase net profit for the year
   C   decrease net profit for the year
   D   decrease the cash/bank balance

12. The Profit and Loss Account of a business shows a net profit of £5 500. A decrease of £100 in provision for bad debts should have been made, and bad debts of £75 should have been written off. Net profit will now be:

   A   £5 675   **B**   £5 475   **C**   £5 525   **D**   £5 325

Errors Not Shown by a Trial Balance

28.1 Errors Not Shown by a Trial Balance

A trial balance proves only the *arithmetical accuracy* of a set of accounts; some errors, because of their nature, are not shown up by a trial balance. These are:

> error of omission;
> reversal of entries;
> mispost;
> error of principle;
> error of original entry;
> compensating error.

In this Unit we shall explain these one by one.

(a) Error of Omission

This means that a business transaction has been *completely omitted* from the accounts: thus there is no debit entry and no credit entry. The trial balance will balance because the same amount has been omitted from both the debit side of one account and the credit side of another.

(b) Reversal of Entries

Here a transaction has been entered in the correct accounts and for the correct amount, but is recorded on the *wrong side of both accounts*. For example, the purchase of a machine by cheque might have been entered as:

> *Dr.* Bank
> *Cr.* Machinery

This should, of course, be entered the other way round; but the error will not show in the trial balance because there has been both a debit and a credit entry for the same amount.

(c) Mispost

Here a transaction has been entered in the *wrong person's account*: for example, the sale of goods on credit to J. Smith is entered in error to A. Smith's account. The arithmetic of the book-keeping is correct, but A. Smith will not be very pleased at being charged for goods he has never seen and doesn't want. This kind of error can often be revealed by sending out regular statements of account to customers: this makes sure that the customer who has been charged for goods not supplied will soon let you know! Keeping an accurate book-keeping system is better than letting others find the errors for you, however.

This kind of error is often referred to as an *error of commission*.

(*d*) **Error of Principle**

This arises where an item is entered in the *wrong class of account*. For example, the cost of a van must be kept separate from the costs of running it, such as money spent on petrol, oil and repairs, and a business will have both a Van Account and a Van Running Expenses Account; it would be an error of principle if both the cost of the van and the running expenses were combined in the same account. (Although the trial balance would still be arithmetically correct!)

(*e*) **Error of Original Entry**

Here the amount of a transaction has been entered incorrectly in the accounting system, and thus *both debit and credit amounts are incorrect*. This could come about for several reasons: for example, a badly written figure on a document could be entered incorrectly, or an invoice total could be added up incorrectly, or figures could be reversed, such as £65 entered in the accounts as £56. Where such errors affect both the debit and credit entries in the accounts they will not be shown by the trial balance. (If only one entry is made incorrectly, the trial balance will, of course, fail to agree.)

Point to notice:

In a reversal of figures error the discrepancy is either 9, or divisible by 9; for example, the difference between £65 and £56 is £9; the difference between £84 and £48 is £36.

(*f*) **Compensating Error**

Here *two errors cancel each other out*. For example, suppose that an error was made when working out the balance of Purchases Account, producing a calculated balance that was £10 too high, and another error in Sales Account which also produced a balance that was £10 too high: the error in Purchases Account, having a debit balance, would be compensated by the error in Sales Account, which has a credit balance. Compensating errors are likely to be for round amounts such as £10, £100 or even £1 000 and are often found if the casting (adding up) of the account is checked.

Errors not shown by a trial balance can largely be avoided by operating an efficient well-designed accounting system. We have already noted the need to circulate statements of account to customers. Another way of avoiding errors is to divide the book-keeping system into sections, such as division of the ledger (see Unit 14) and the use of journals (see Unit 16), with a different person responsible for each section, so that no one person makes both the debit and credit entries for each business transaction. Many small businesses, however, haven't enough transactions to require more than one book-keeper and so it is not possible to divide the system—one person has to do all the work. Under these circumstances it may help if the owner of the business closely supervises the book-keeper's work.

Using account numbers should avoid many of the problems of the mispost, and the use of computers in accounting also helps to avoid errors in calculating the balances of accounts; but neither numbering of accounts nor using computers will eliminate every type of error in a book-keeping system.

28.2   Correcting Errors Not Shown by a Trial Balance

When an error not shown by a trial balance is found it must be corrected by means of a journal entry, and then passed through the appropriate accounts.

(a) Error of Omission

Credit sales of £45 to J. Lewis omitted from the accounting records.

Date	Details	Folio	Dr.	Cr.
			£	£
	J. Lewis	SL	45	
	Sales	GL		45
	Credit sales, invoice no 12345, omitted from the accounts			

(b) Reversal of Entries

Receipt of £30 cash from B. Mitchell, a debtor, entered in error on the payments side of the cash book and debited to Mitchell's account.

Date	Details	Folio	Dr.	Cr.
			£	£
	Cash	CB	30	
	B. Mitchell	SL		30
	Cash	CB	30	
	B. Mitchell	SL		30
	Correction of error: £30 cash received entered to credit of cash book and debited to B. Mitchell's account			

Point to notice:

When correcting a reversal of entries, it is necessary to 'take out' the incorrect entries, and then 'put through' the correct entries. Therefore *twice the amount* of the error is needed to correct it; if the amount of the error only is used it will merely cancel out the original error, and not correct it. In this example a debit to cash of £60 and a credit to Mitchell of £60 would correct the error; it would not be good accounting practice, however, because £60 is not the amount of the original transaction. It is better to show the amount of the original error being taken out, and then a new correct entry being put through the accounts.

(c) Mispost

Credit sales of £65 entered to the account of J. Smith instead of J. Smith Ltd.

Date	Details	Folio	Dr.	Cr.
			£	£
	J. Smith Ltd	SL	65	
	J. Smith	SL		65
	Invoice no 9876 entered to account of J. Smith instead of J. Smith Ltd — now corrected			

(d) Error of Principle

Motor vehicle expenses of £25 debited in error to Motor Vehicles Account.

Date	Details	Folio	Dr.	Cr.
			£	£
	Motor vehicle expenses	GL	25	
	Motor vehicles	GL		25
	Correction of error: expenses debited in error to Motor Vehicles Account on 10 April 19–2			

(e) Error of Original Entry

Credit purchase of goods £65 from T. Keane entered in the accounts as £56.

Date	Details	Folio	Dr.	Cr.
			£	£
	T. Keane	PL	56	
	Purchases	GL		56
	Purchases	GL	65	
	T. Keane	PL		65
	Correction of error: purchases invoice no 5678 for £65 entered in the accounts as £56			

Point to notice:

Although £9 could have been put through the accounts as a correct amount, it is better to 'take out' the wrong amount and to 'put through' new entries for the correct amount.

(*f*) Compensating Error

Purchases Account is found to be overcast (over-added) by £100, while Rates Account is found to be undercast (under-added) by the same amount

Date	Details	Folio	Dr.	Cr.
			£	£
	Rates	GL	100	
	Purchases	GL		100
	Correction of overcast on Purchases Account and compensating undercast on Rates Account			

We have shown the correcting journal entry for each kind of possible error. Remember that the journal entries must then be entered into the double-entry book-keeping system.

Examination note. When dealing with examination questions that require correction of errors, it is often helpful to work out what has gone wrong by writing the accounts down: it should then be easy to see what needs to be done to make the correction.

28.3   Questions

1. (*a*) Explain briefly four different types of error which the trial balance would not disclose.

(*b*) What checks would you undertake if the trial balance totals did not agree?
[*Pitman Examinations Institute*]

2. (*a*) Explain why a trial balance which agrees is not conclusive proof of the complete accuracy of the books of account. Give examples of three types of errors which can occur but will not be revealed by the trial balance.

(*b*) Outline the procedures to be adopted if the trial balance does not agree.
[*Royal Society of Arts*]

*3. A. Choules is a sole trader who has prepared the following accounts:

K. Haddock

	£
Balance	48
Goods	72

A. Salmon

		£
	Cash	72

Office furniture

	£
Balance	530
Cash	30

Bad debts

	£
Balance	186

Unfortunately, it was discovered that:

(i) goods to the value of £72 already dispatched to A. Salmon were incorrectly charged to K. Haddock;

(ii) in the case of K. Haddock, the amount of £48 has been outstanding for some time and it has been found that he is a bankrupt, and is therefore unable to pay anything towards his debts;

(iii) £30 paid for a repair of furniture entered in the Office Furniture Account, should have been posted to an Office Furniture Repair Account.

You are required to:

(a) show the journal entries to deal with each of the above;

(b) write out the ledger accounts above, post the necessary adjustments to the ledgers, and balance or close the accounts.

[South Western Examinations Board]

4. Show the journal entries to correct the following errors discovered on 28 February in the ledgers of A. Consulate:

4 February	Goods valued at £60 were returned to K. Slate, but the return had been posted to K. Slateson's account.
14 February	The sale of a van for £500 in cash had been wrongly posted to the Sales Account.
15 February	N. Mitten purchased an office safe at £185 on credit from the Stacey Safe Co Ltd and did not enter the transaction in his books.

[South Western Examinations Board]

*5. On 31 May 19–1 the following trial balance was extracted from the books of R. Wilson:

	£	£
Capital 1 June 19–0		50 000
Fixtures and fittings	25 000	
Delivery vans	20 000	
Trade creditors		3 716
Stock 1 June 19–0	8 720	
Trade debtors	5 350	
Cash at bank	4 750	
Cash in hand	376	
Purchases	10 816	
Sales		27 314
Proprietor's drawings	3 000	
Delivery van expenses	3 018	
	81 030	81 030

A check of the accounts revealed the following errors:

(a) a customer's account of £50, long overdue, should have been written off as a bad debt;

(b) no entry had been made for bank charges £100;

(c) a sale of fixtures and fittings at book value £3 000 had been credited to Sales Account;

(d) a customer had paid an account in cash £250; the envelope containing the cash had been left in a desk drawer and no entry had been made in the books;

(*e*) the delivery van expenses includes £500 paid for repairs to R. Wilson's private car;

(*f*) a purchase invoice of £270 had not been entered in the books.

Prepare the trial balance which would be extracted from R. Wilson's books after the corrections have been made.

[Royal Society of Arts]

6. James White on checking his accounting records discovers that he has made the following errors:

(*a*) A filing cabinet recently purchased for £115 had been charged in error to the General Expenses Account.

(*b*) The account of S. Blaker had been debited with goods £75 sold to S. Blakeman.

(*c*) An amount of £172 for machinery repairs had been debited to the Machinery (asset) Account.

(*d*) Discounts allowed £27 had been posted to the debit of Discounts Received Account.

(*e*) When paying G. Hale his account of £60, cash discount of £3 had been deducted in error. Hale has subsequently disallowed this.

(*f*) A payment of £76 for rates had been debited in error to the Rent Account.

You are required to prepare journal entries in the books of James White to correct the above errors.

[Royal Society of Arts]

7. Enter the following in the journal of J. Hicks:

19–8

Dec. 2   J. Hicks put a further £6 000 capital into the business, 15% went into cash and the remainder went to the firm's bank account.

Dec. 4   Purchased a motor vehicle costing £3 000 from A. Brown, paying 50% of the total cost by cheque.

Dec. 9   Returned some unsuitable fixtures and fittings costing £50 to H. Nunan Ltd.

Dec. 15   Rent received of £60 had been posted to the Commission Received Account.

Dec. 15   The motor vehicle purchased on 4 December 19–8 had been debited in error to Purchases Account in the ledger.

Dec. 16   It was found that the £3 000 paid for the motor vehicle purchased on 4 December 19–8 included a road fund licence of £100.

Dec. 18   C. Read, a debtor owing £600, was declared bankrupt. J. Hicks received 25% of the amount outstanding by cheque. The remainder to be written off to Bad Debts.

Dec. 20   An account of £25 for petrol for J. Hick's private car had been posted to the firm's Motor Expenses Account.

Dec. 21   Purchased some more fixtures and fittings on credit from H. Nunan, list price £120 less trade discount of 20%.

(Marks will be awarded for appropriate narrations.)

[RSA Examinations Board]

Unit Twenty-nine

Errors Shown by a Trial Balance

29.1 Introduction

In Unit 28 we looked at errors not shown by a trial balance; here we look at those that a trial balance shows up. These include:

(a) the omission of one half of the double-entry book-keeping transaction: for example, where sale of goods on credit to J. Smith has been entered in the Sales Account, but not in Smith's account;

(b) the entry of different amounts for the same transaction on the debit and credit sides of the accounts concerned: for example, goods bought on credit from A. Jones for £65 and entered correctly in Purchases Account, but as £56 in Jones's account;

(c) errors in the addition of accounts or the calculation of balances, which are not compensated by other errors;

(d) wrong entry of an item as two debits, or as two credits.

'Two debits don't make a credit'

29.2 The Use of a Suspense Account

When a trial balance fails to agree an attempt must be made to locate the errors quickly. If this proves impossible, however, the trial balance must be 'balanced' by placing the difference to a *Suspense Account*. For example:

Trial balance as at 31 May 19–2

	Dr. £	Cr. £
Totals	59 940	60 000
Suspense Account	60	
	60 000	60 000

A Suspense Account is now opened in the general ledger:

Suspense

	£
19–2	
31 May Difference from trial balance	60

The task now is to locate the errors and, when found, to correct them by means of a journal entry and appropriate accounting transactions.

A Suspense Account provides a temporary place for errors until they are found. If a balance sheet has to be prepared before the errors are located, however, the balance of Suspense Account is included under the heading of current assets or current liabilities. In our example, Suspense Account has a debit balance, and so would be included among the current assets; a credit balance would be listed under current liabilities.

When the errors are located a journal entry must be made, and transactions passed through the appropriate accounts. In our example, suppose that two errors are found on 10 June 19–2:

(*a*) Purchases Account is undercast by £100;

(*b*) cash received, £40, from H. Wall, a debtor, has not been entered in Wall's account.

These will be corrected by journal entry as follows:

Date	Details	Folio	Dr. £	Cr. £

19–2
10 Jun.
	Purchases
	  Suspense
	
	Correction of undercast on Purchases
	  Account
		GL
		GL
			100	100

10 Jun.	Suspense
	  H. Wall
	
	Correction of omission of receipt of cash
	  on … in Wall's account
		GL
		SL
			40	40

The entries appearing in the accounts are:

Purchases

	£
19–2	
10 Jun. Suspense	100

H. Wall

		£
	19–2	
	10 Jun. Suspense	40

Suspense

19–2	£	19–2	£
31 May Difference from trial		10 Jun. Purchases	100
balance	60		
10 Jun. H. Wall	40		
	100		100

The error from the trial balance is now cleared, and Suspense Account has a nil balance.

Point to notice:

Only errors shown by a trial balance are corrected through Suspense Account, which is never required for the correction of errors *not* shown by a trial balance.

Examination note. Many questions on this topic present you with a Suspense Account balance and then tell you the errors: you are expected to prepare journal entries and show how the Suspense Account balance will be eliminated, or altered (increased/reduced) if all errors are not found.

29.3 Amendments to Profit After Correction of Errors

If errors are found and corrected after the preparation of the year-end accounts, there is likely to be an effect on gross profit and net profit, and certainly an effect on the balance sheet. For example, if Sales Account is found to be undercast, its correction will increase sales in the Trading Account and also gross profit; net profit will be increased too, which will change the balance sheet. An error affecting a debtor's account will alter the balance sheet only, however.

Examination note. It is quite common to encounter a question that presents a balance sheet, together with a list of errors discovered after its preparation. You are then asked to correct the errors by means of journal entries, and to prepare a statement of corrected net profit, together with a corrected balance sheet.

Example

Balance sheet of M. Fletcher as at 30 June 19–4

	£	£		£
Fixed assets:			Capital	30 000
Premises		20 000	*Add* Net profit	6 280
Machinery at cost	5 000			36 280
Less Provision for			*Less* Drawings	4 320
depreciation to				31 960
date	1 000			
		4 000		
		24 000		
Current assets:			Current liabilities:	
Stock	4 550		Creditors	4 820
Debtors	6 250		Suspense Account	85
Bank	2 065			
		12 865		
		36 865		36 865

Subsequent investigation reveals the following errors:

(*a*) Rates Account is overcast by £20;

(*b*) Sales Account is undercast by £100;

(*c*) a payment to Williams, a creditor, for £35 has been entered in the cash book only;

(*d*) sales of goods on credit to Johnson for £45 has been entered in both accounts as £54.

Write journal entries to correct these errors. Prepare a statement of corrected net profit and a corrected balance sheet.

Answer

The journal entries (without narrative) are:

Details	Folio	Dr.	Cr.
		£	£
(*a*) Suspense	GL	20	
Rates	GL		20
(*b*) Suspense	GL	100	
Sales	GL		100
(*c*) Williams	PL	35	
Suspense	GL		35
(*d*) Sales	GL	54	
Johnson	SL		54
Johnson	SL	45	
Sales	GL		45

Point to notice:
Error (*d*) does not involve the use of a Suspense Account.

Suspense Account is closed as follows:

Suspense

	£		£
Rates	20	Difference from trial balance	85
Sales	100	Williams	35
	120		120

M. Fletcher
Statement of corrected net profit for the year ended 30 June 19–4

	£	£
Net profit from Profit and Loss Account		6 280[1]
Add Rates overcast	20	
Sales undercast	100	
		120
		6 400
Less Sales overstated (Johnson)		9
Corrected net profit		6 391

[1] taken from balance sheet

Point to notice:
The error on Williams' account does not affect the net profit.

Corrected balance sheet as at 30 June 19–4

	£	£		£
Fixed assets:			Capital	30 000
Premises		20 000	*Add* Net profit	6 391
Machinery, at cost	5 000			36 391
Less Provision for			*Less* Drawings	4 320
depreciation to				32 071
date	1 000			
		4 000		
		24 000		
Current assets:			Current liabilities:	
Stock	4 550		Creditors	4 785
Debtors	6 241			
Bank	2 065			
		12 856		
		36 856		36 856

Note: Debtors per unadjusted balance sheet	£6 250
Less Reduction in Johnson's balance	£ 9
Debtors per corrected balance sheet	£6 241
Creditors per unadjusted balance sheet	£4 820
Less Reduction in Williams' balance	£ 35
Creditors per corrected balance sheet	£4 785

29.4   Questions

*1.   A. Bradshaw takes out his trial balance on 30 June and in order to make it balance he opens a Suspense Account with a credit balance of £6. On checking his books he discovers the following errors:

(a) An invoice for £48 has been entered correctly in the sales journal but the double entry to R. Belgrave's account has been made as £84.

(b) The returns inward journal has been overcast by £20.

(c) A credit note for £4 received from H. Singh has been entered twice in his account.

(d) Two payments of £40 each have been made to T. Lewsey but only one has been entered in her account.

(e) A payment of £14 to D. Nash has been entered in the cash book but no corresponding double entry has been made.

Show the Suspense Account as it would appear after the correction of errors.

[*East Anglian Examinations Board*]

*2.   (a) State how each of the following errors, made during the year ending 31 December 19–1, would affect the net profit of M. Peters for that period:

(i) a loan of £2 000 made to Peters was credited to his Profit and Loss Account;

(ii) the omission of credit purchases of £360 from the purchases day book;

(iii) opening stock undervalued by £352;

(iv) discounts received, £740, debited to Profit and Loss Account;

(v) interest on Peters' bank deposit, £56, was treated as interest charged by the bank in the Profit and Loss Account.

(b) If the incorrect net profit obtained after committing these errors was £4 000, calculate what the correct amount should be.

[*Associated Lancashire Schools Examining Board*]

3.   When Daniel Martin prepared his final accounts he calculated his net profit at £8 975. However, on more careful inspection of his accounts he found the following errors. Construct an adjustment of profit statement to show his true net profit.

(a) A bill for rates of £200 had not been paid;

(b) sales of £28 had not been recorded;

(c) closing stock had been overvalued by £48;

(d) depreciation of £200 had not been provided for;

(e) rent receivable of £50 was outstanding;

(f) sales returns of £22 had not been entered;

(g) rent of £10 recorded in the Profit and Loss Account related to next year;

(h) a provision for bad debts of £20 should have been created.

[*Pitman Examinations Institute*]

*4.   J. Jones extracted the following trial balance from his books on 31 January 19–2:

	£	£
Capital		7 450
Drawings	3 000	
Stock 1 February 19–1	2 500	
Trade debtors	2 950	
Trade creditors		2 684
Shop fittings	1 530	
Purchases	5 140	
Sales		7 460
General expenses	860	
Discount received		40
Cash at bank	1 660	
Returns outwards		40
	17 640	17 674

The following errors and omissions were subsequently discovered:

(a) A purchase of shop fittings £320 had been debited to Purchases Account.

(b) A sales invoice of £150 entered in the sales day book had not been posted to the customer's personal account.

(c) A credit note for £30 issued by J. Jones to a customer had been completely omitted from the books.

(d) A credit balance of £16 in the purchases ledger had been omitted from the trial balance.

(e) The sales day book was undercast by £100 in December 19–1.

Draw up a corrected trial balance. Show all workings.

[*Royal Society of Arts*]

5.   George Walters, a sole trader, extracted a trial balance from his books at the close of business on 31 March 19–1. The two sides of this trial balance did not agree but, in spite of this, Walters prepared Trading and Profit and Loss Accounts and these showed a net profit of £1 920.

Subsequent to the above, the following errors were discovered and these accounted for the whole of the trial balance difference:

(i) Wages Account had been debited with £76 in respect of wages paid to workmen engaged in installing new office fixtures.

(ii) A sale of goods—selling price £113—had been entered in *both* the sales day book and personal account of the buyer as £131.

(iii) The discount total of £175 on the Dr side of the three-column cash book had been entered on the *wrong* side of the Discount Account.

(iv) There was an error in the calculations of stock-in-trade at 31 March 19–1— an item listed as £220 should have been listed as £360.

Required:

(a) Indicate briefly the nature of the effect of each of the above errors on the original trial balance.

(b) Calculate the correct net profit. Your calculations (starting with the incorrect figure of £1 920) must be shown or marks will be lost.

[*London Chamber of Commerce*]

*6. At the close of business on 31 October 19–1 James Holt, a sole trader, extracted from his books a trial balance, but this did not agree. Holt entered the difference in a Suspense Account and then prepared his Trading and Profit and Loss Accounts in the usual way. The net profit—as shown by the Profit and Loss Account—was £2 770.

Subsequent to the above it was discovered that the following errors had been made and these accounted for the entire difference in the trial balance:

(i) Sales day book total £7 160 posted to the Sales Account as £7 610.

(ii) Discount received total of £84 had been posted to the *wrong* side of Discount Account.

(iii) Wages paid £66 had been debited to Office Furniture Account in error.

(iv) Purchases of £125 had been correctly entered in the purchases day book but the personal account concerned had been credited with £152.

Required:

(a) State how, and to what extent, each of the above errors would have affected the trial balance, e.g.: 'Debit overstated £ …'.

(b) Calculate the correct net profit and show your calculations.

Note: Journal entries are *not* required.

[*London Chamber of Commerce*]

7. Sally Jones was not able to balance her trial balance at 30 April 19–0 so she opened a Suspense Account to balance the trial balance.

Subsequently she discovered the following errors:

(i) The sale proceeds of an old delivery van amounting to £700 were placed to the Sales Account.

(ii) Discounts allowed amounting to £400 were entered as a credit balance in the trial balance.

(iii) Debtors amounting to £500 had not been included in the trial balance total.

You are required to:

(a) Make appropriate journal entries to rectify the errors.

(b) Draft the Suspense Account after the errors have been corrected showing the original balance.

(c) Sally also wishes to create a provision for bad debts for £500 and write off a bad debt for Simon Joseph for £250. Draft the journal entry for these items.

[*Pitman Examinations Institute, Level 2*]

Multiple-choice Questions—8

Read each question carefully. Choose the *one* answer you think is correct. Answers are given on page 411.

1. If a trial balance agrees this proves that:

    A all the accounting entries are correct
    B the trial balance is arithmetically correct
    C the final accounts prepared at the same date must be accurate
    D neither a profit nor a loss has been made

2. Payment of £16 in cash to M. Holmes has been debited to cash and credited to M. Holmes's account in error. Which entry will correct the error?

	Debit	Credit
A	Cash Account £32	M. Holmes's account £32
B	M. Holmes's account £16	Cash Account £16
C	M. Holmes's account £32	Cash Account £32
D	Cash Account £16	M. Holmes's account £16

3. An error of principle is made if

A a transaction has been completely omitted
B an entry has been made on the wrong side of the two accounts concerned
C an entry has been made in the wrong class of account
D a transaction is entered in both accounts for the wrong amount

4. Credit sales of £48 to N. Lowe are entered in both Sales Account and Lowe's account as £84. This is:

A an error of original entry   C an error of principle
B a compensating error   D a reversal of entries

5. Purchases Account is overcast £100, while Wages Account is undercast by £100. This is:

A an error of omission   C an error of principle
B an error of commission   D a compensating error

6. Which one of the following errors would be shown by a trial balance?

A credit purchase from T. Jones completely omitted from the accounts
B cheque received from I. Lewis debited to Lewis's account
C repairs to van debited to Van Account
D credit sale to J. Smith entered in J. Smythe's account

7. A book-keeper enters an amount of £60 on the debit side of an account when it should have gone on the credit side. Assuming that there are no other errors, the trial balance totals will show:

A £120 less on the credit side than on the debit
B £120 less on the debit side than on the credit
C £60 more on the credit side than on the debit
D £60 more on the debit side than on the credit

8. A Suspense Account is opened when:

A the trial balance does not agree
B the balance sheet does not balance
C the business makes a net loss
D the Profit and Loss Account does not balance

9. A trial balance fails to agree. It is discovered that Purchases Account has been overcast by £100. The correction is made by:

	Debit	Credit
A	Purchases Account £100	Suspense Account £100
B	Suspense Account £200	Purchases Account £200
C	Purchases Account £200	Suspense Account £200
D	Suspense Account £100	Purchases Account £100

10. A trial balance fails to agree and it is discovered that discount received £50 had been entered on the wrong side of the account. The correction is made by:

	Debit	*Credit*
A	Discount Received Account £50	Suspense Account £50
B	Suspense Account £100	Discount Received Account £100
C	Suspense Account £50	Discount Received Account £50
D	Discount Received Account £100	Suspense Account £100

11. A trial balance fails to agree and it is discovered that a cheque for £50 received from I. Finlay, a debtor, has been entered in the cash book only. The correction is made by:

	Debit	*Credit*
A	Suspense Account £50	Finlay's account £50
B	Finlay's account £50	Suspense Account £50
C	Bank Account £50	Finlay's account £50
D	Suspense Account £100	Finlay's account £100

12. A trial balance fails to agree and it is discovered that returns inwards of £45 from P. Johnson have been debited to Returns Inwards Account as £54. The correction is made by:

	Debit	*Credit*
A	Returns Inwards Account £9	P. Johnson's account £9
B	Returns Inwards Account £99	Suspense Account £99
C	Returns Inwards Account £9	Suspense Account £9
D	Suspense Account £9	Returns Inwards Account £9

Unit Thirty

Control Accounts

30.1 The Use of Control Accounts

Control accounts are 'master' accounts which record by means of totals the transactions passing through the accounts that they control; they are sometimes known as *total accounts*. The principle of control accounts is that if the total of the opening balances for a certain number of accounts is known, together with the total amount of entries *increasing* these balances and the total amount of entries *decreasing* them, we can work out the closing balance for the group or section of accounts. For example:

	£
Opening balance for accounts	10 000
Add Entries increasing the balances	5 000
	15 000
Less Entries decreasing the balances	6 000
Closing balance for accounts	9 000

In this example, if the closing balances of the individual accounts total £9 000, then the section balances. On the other hand, if the individual balances total, say, £8 950, there is an error in this section. (Don't forget that if the section balances, it does not of course prove that the accounting entries are completely accurate: for example, there could be misposts or compensating errors—compare Unit 28.1.)

This Unit is concerned with two particular control accounts: Purchases Ledger Control Account and Sales Ledger Control Account.

30.2 Purchases Ledger (or Bought Ledger) Control Account

This account controls the purchases ledger section of the accounting system, that is, the creditors' accounts. It records totals for credit purchases, returns outwards, cash and cheque payments and discounts received, and takes the following form:

Purchases Ledger Control Account

	£		£
Cash paid to creditors		Balance b/d	
Cheques paid to creditors		Credit purchases	
Cash discount received			
Returns outwards			
Balance c/d			

Here are three creditors' accounts which we will assume comprise the entire purchases ledger section of a firm:

A. Adams

	£		£
Bank	95	Balance b/d	100
Discount received	5	Purchases	200
Returns outwards	50		
Balance c/d	150		
	300		300
		Balance b/d	150

B. Brown

	£		£
Cash	50	Balance b/d	50
Balance c/d	100	Purchases	100
	150		150
		Balance b/d	100

C. Clark

	£		£
Bank	285	Balance b/d	250
Discount received	15	Purchases	50
	300		300

The control account for these accounts acts as a 'master' account, recording totals on the individual accounts of the different types of transactions, such as purchases or returns outwards. The control account appears as:

Purchases Ledger Control Account

	£		£
Cash paid to creditors	50	Balance b/d	400
Cheques paid to creditors	380	Credit purchases	350
Discount received	20		
Returns outwards	50		
Balance c/d	250		
	750		750
		Balance b/d	250

Point to notice:

Totals for transactions appear in the control account *on the same side as they appear in the personal accounts.*

In this example the control account balance agrees with the total of the individual accounts contained within the ledger section, proving the arithmetical accuracy of the ledger section.

30.3   Sales Ledger Control Account

The sales ledger section, containing the debtors' accounts, has a control account which takes the following form:

Sales Ledger Control Account

	£		£
Balance b/d		Cash received from debtors	
Credit sales		Cheques received from debtors	
		Cash discount allowed	
		Returns inwards	
		Bad debts written off	
		Balance c/d	

You will notice the inclusion of *bad debts written off* in the control account. This is because the control account summarizes all transactions taking place in the accounts which it controls. The ledger entries to write off a bad debt (see Unit 27.2) are:

Dr. Bad Debts Written Off Account
Cr. Debtor's personal account

As this affects a debtor's personal account, it must be entered on the credit side of the control account. The creation of a *provision for bad debts* does *not* appear in the control account, however; the accounting entries for this (see Unit 27.3) are:

Dr. Profit and Loss Account
Cr. Provision for Bad Debts Account

Thus there is no entry to be made in a debtor's personal account, and therefore no entry to be made in the Sales Ledger Control Account.

30.4   Set-off/Contra Entries

Set-off/contra entries occur when a firm is both buying and selling goods from and to the same person. Under such circumstances there is an account for this person in both the purchases ledger section and the sales ledger section, that is, he is both a creditor and debtor.

For example, E. Green is both a supplier and a customer of N. Brown. Green's accounts in Brown's books are as follows:

Purchases Ledger:

E. Green

	£		£
		Balance b/d	50

Sales Ledger:

E. Green

	£		£
Balance b/d	100		

From these two accounts you can see that Brown must pay Green £50 to clear his account in the purchases ledger, and that Green will have to pay Brown £100 to settle for the goods he has bought. To simplify matters, and with permission from the customer, it is appropriate to set off one account against the other. In this case the account in Brown's purchases ledger is set off against that in the sales ledger, as follows:

Purchases Ledger:

	E. Green		
	£		£
Set-off: sales ledger	50	Balance b/d	50

Sales Ledger:

	E. Green		
	£		£
Balance b/d	100	Set-off: purchases ledger	50

Here we have debited Green's account in Brown's purchases ledger and credited his account in the sales ledger. The result of this is that only one payment has to be made: Green will pay Brown £50.

From the point of view of Purchases and Sales Ledger Control Accounts, set-off is important because transactions are being made in the ledger sections they control. Therefore any balances set off in this way must be entered in the control accounts. The set-off entries in the Purchases and Sales Ledger Control Accounts are always:

> *Dr.* Purchases Ledger Control Account } with amounts set off
> *Cr.* Sales Ledger Control Account }

30.5 More About Control Accounts

Some students find control accounts difficult to understand. Remember that a control account is simply a master debtors or creditors account, and that totals of transactions are entered in the control account *on the same side* on which they appear in the debtors' or creditors' personal accounts. If we are dealing with a Sales Ledger Control Account, therefore, the opening balance appears on the debit side, because we are dealing with debtors. When a firm sells goods on credit, the debtors' totals increase and so the credit sales total should be entered on the debit side of the Sales Ledger Control Account. Cash or cheques received from debtors reduce their balances and are shown on the credit side of the control account. Other items on the control account can similarly be thought out logically.

(a) Balances on Both Sides of a Control Account
Sometimes a control account may have an opening balance on *both sides* of the account. For example, with the Sales Ledger Control Account, the main opening balance will be on the debit side; however, if one or two debtors have

overpaid their accounts, or have returned goods after making payment, they will have a credit balance on their personal accounts. Likewise, at the end of the period covered by the control account there may be closing balances on both sides of the account. In the case of the Sales Ledger Control Account, the main debtor balance is *carried down* on the credit side (and *brought down* on the debit side), while any small balance is *carried down* on the debit side (and *brought down* on the credit side).

With the Purchases Ledger Control Account, the main opening balance will be on the credit side, while if 'our' business has overpaid creditors, or returned goods after making payment, some opening balances will be on the debit side. At the end of the period, the main creditor balance is *carried down* on the debit side (and *brought down* on the credit side), while any small balance is *carried down* on the credit side (and *brought down* on the debit side).

(*b*) Information for Control Accounts

The main sources of information for control accounts are:

total credit sales: sales journal or day book;
total credit purchases: purchases journal or day book;
total returns inwards: returns inwards journal or day book;
total returns outwards: returns outwards journal or day book;
total cash/cheques received from debtors and paid to creditors: cash book (incorporating an analysis column—see Unit 15.7);
total discount allowed: discount allowed column of cash book or Discount Allowed Account;
total discount received: discount received column of cash book or Discount Received Account.

(*c*) Using Control Accounts

Control accounts are used principally as a checking device, that is, they check the arithmetical accuracy of the ledger section they control. If a discrepancy is revealed it will be necessary to check the balances of the individual accounts and perhaps to tick back individual transactions from the listings that make up the totals entered in the control account.

Another use for control accounts is as an aid to the management of a business. If an owner or manager wishes to know the total for debtors or creditors, the balance of the control account will give the figure at once, rather than having to add up the balances of all the debtors' or creditors' accounts.

(*d*) Control Accounts and Double-entry Book-keeping

Used in the way we have described, control accounts do not form part of the double-entry book-keeping system but act as 'checking' devices for a particular ledger section. Some businesses treat control accounts as double-entry book-keeping accounts, however, and the balances of control accounts are entered into the trial balance. Under such circumstances, the personal accounts of debtors and creditors do not form part of double-entry book-keeping but are simply *memorandum accounts* of how much is owed to, and by, the firm. At regular intervals the balances of these personal memorandum accounts are agreed with the total of the appropriate control account.

30.6   Questions

*1. Prepare a Sales Ledger Control Account from the following for the month of April 19–1.

19–1		£
1 April	Sales ledger balances	3 953
30 April	Sales journal	45 742
	Returns inwards	350
	Cheques received from debtors	41 270
	Discounts allowed	450
	Bad debts written off	1 059
	Sales ledger balances	6 566

[*Royal Society of Arts*]

*2. The following balances have been extracted from the books of R. Stevenson at 31 December 19–2:

1 January 19–2:	
Sales ledger balances	6 840
Further balances:	
Sales	46 801
Discounts allowed	420
Bad debts written off	494
Receipts from customers	43 780
Returns inwards	296

Required:

(*a*) Prepare the Sales Ledger Control Account for R. Stevenson, showing clearly the balance carried forward at 31 December 19–2.

(*b*) An explanation of the meaning and use of the final balance.

[*Royal Society of Arts*]

*3. From the following information prepare Purchases Control Account for H. Williamson for the month of June 19–1.

	£
Credit balance, 1 June 19–1	7 000
Payments during the month	5 100
Discount	300
Purchases during the month	4 000
Returns outward	200
Transfer of debit balances in sales ledger to purchases ledger	100

[*East Anglian Examinations Board*]

4. The following figures were extracted from the books of Pevatec & Co for the month of April 19–2.

	£
Sales ledger balances 1 April	4 842
Purchases ledger balances 1 April	2 182
Receipts from customers	84 804
Payments to suppliers	63 294
Sales	86 402
Purchases	64 823
Returns inwards	1 420
Returns outwards	1 210
Bad debts written-off	496
Discounts allowed	1 902
Discounts received	1 048
Sales ledger balances 30 April	2 622
Purchase ledger balances 30 April	1 453

Prepare a Sales Ledger Control Account and a Purchases Ledger Control Account for the month of April from the above information.

[Royal Society of Arts]

5. On 31 March 19–1 the following balances appeared in John Richard's sales ledger (W section):

	£
W. Wilkins	1 200 dr.
T. Wright	750 dr.
L. Williams	325 dr.

During April 19–1 the following transactions took place:

Credit sales:

			£
April	3	W. Wilkins	1 370
	13	T. Wright	600
	23	W. Wilkins	450

Sales returns:

		£
April 15	L. Williams	200
24	T. Wright	30

Payments received and cash discounts allowed:

		£	£
April 10	W. Wilkins	1 170	30
	T. Wright	740	10

You are to:

(*a*) write up the personal accounts of the three customers in John Richard's sales ledger (W section);

(*b*) write up the Sales Ledger (W section) Control Account for the month of April 19–1;

(*c*) reconcile the Control Account balance with the personal account balances.

[Royal Society of Arts]

Stock Records

31.1 Introduction

The *stock* of a business comprises the goods in which it trades. Stock is usually a valuable part of a firm's current assets and it is essential that suitable records are kept and that control is kept over stock movements. A stock control system should:

(*a*) indicate stock availability without the need to inspect the physical stock, so that the stock position of a particular item can be ascertained quickly from the records in response, say, to a telephone enquiry;

(*b*) show the need to re-order when stocks run low, bearing in mind the current rate of usage and the time taken for delivery once a re-order has been placed (the *lead time*);

(*c*) maintain a record which can be used to calculate stock values;

(*d*) act as a deterrent to pilferage;

(*e*) allow the stock holdings and movements to be reviewed easily, in order that money tied up in stock should be minimized.

Not all stock records meet these five points, and both records and the methods of keeping them up to date vary according to the needs of the business. A small shop does not update its stock records after every sale—it would be too time-consuming and customers would be kept waiting—but the increasing use of bar codes and computerized checkouts in the retail trade means, among other things, that stock records can be updated automatically and that stocks, when running low, can be automatically re-ordered from the suppliers. Stock records are essential for most businesses, and especially so where the goods in which the business trades are of a high value and the number sold each day or each week is relatively small, such as cars, typewriters, machines or furniture. A warehouse and a firm's stores alike need to keep accurate records both from the accounting point of view, and in order to give a good service to customers.

31.2 Storekeeping Procedures

When a purchase order (see Unit 13.2) is sent to a suitable supplier by a firm wishing to buy goods, a copy of the purchase order is passed to the stores in the buying firm to await delivery of the goods. Storekeeping involves other documents as well. We shall look at these in turn.

(*a*) Delivery/Advice Note
This is prepared by the supplier and gives details of the supplier, the buyer, the goods, quantity ordered and so on. It is signed by the person receiving the

goods at the buyer's stores. Usually one copy is handed to the carrier for return to the supplier and this acts as proof of delivery.

(b) Goods Received Note (GRN)
This is prepared by the warehouse/storekeeping staff of the buyer. Details included are description of the goods, date of receipt, name of supplier, advice note number, quantity of goods received, damages or shortages (if any), and the storekeeper's signature. The original is sent to the accounts department for payment of the supplier's invoice, a copy is sent to the purchasing department to advise that the goods have been received, and a further copy is passed to the storekeeper for preparation of the stock record card.

(c) Stock Record Card
Using the GRN the storekeeper prepares, or updates, a stock record card for the new stock received. This is a card which records receipts and issues of the stock item and shows the balance of stock on hand. Stock record cards are kept together at the stores office and are discussed more fully in Unit 31.3.

(d) Bin Card
This is a record card kept with the physical stock itself. Bin cards are attached to the bins or racks containing the materials, using a separate card for each item of stock. Bin cards give a description of the goods, receipts and issues, and the balance remaining in the bin.

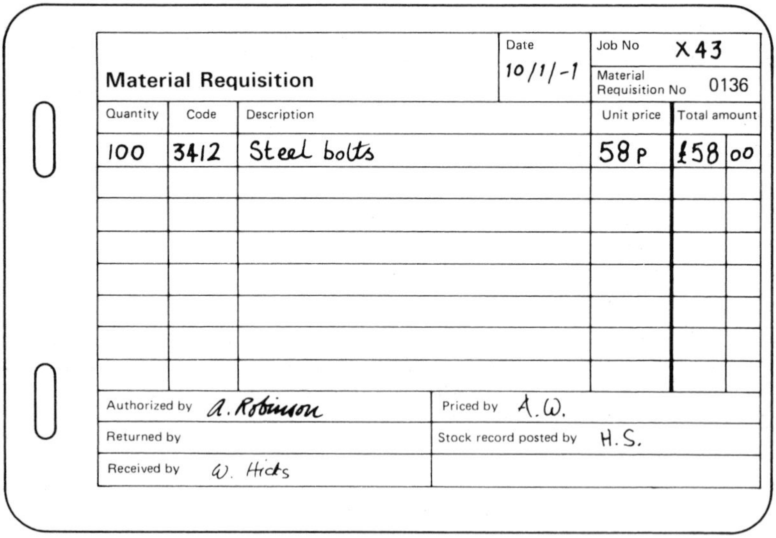

Fig. 31.1 Material requisition note

(*e*) **Material Requisition Note or Issue Note**

This is a basic stores control document which must be completed before goods can be taken from the stores. The information it contains includes item required, quantity, department or person requisitioning the item, date of issue and the signature of the person authorizing the transaction (see Fig. 31.1).

(*f*) **Return Note**

This is a document used when goods withdrawn from the stores are returned for any reason (see Fig. 31.2).

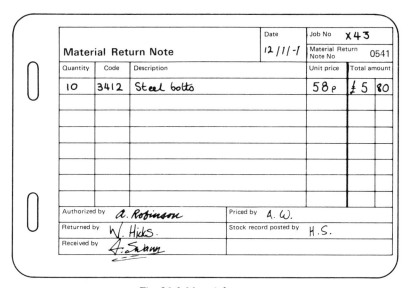

		Date	Job No	**X 4 3**
Material Return Note		$12/1/-1$	Material Return Note No	0541

Quantity	Code	Description	Unit price	Total amount
10	3412	Steel bolts	58 p	£ 5 80

Authorized by *a. Robinson*	Priced by A. W.
Returned by W. Hicks.	Stock record posted by H.S.
Received by [signature]	

Fig. 31.2 Material return note

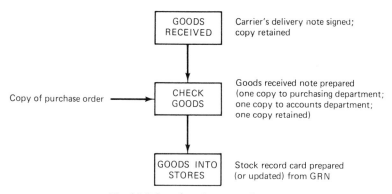

| GOODS RECEIVED | Carrier's delivery note signed; copy retained |

Copy of purchase order → | CHECK GOODS | Goods received note prepared (one copy to purchasing department; one copy to accounts department; one copy retained) |

| GOODS INTO STORES | Stock record card prepared (or updated) from GRN |

Fig. 31.3 Storekeeping procedures

Fig. 31.3 (page 273) summarizes the storekeeping procedures to be followed when goods are delivered by the supplier.

31.3   Manual Stock Record Cards

All non-computerized stock record systems use the same basic method—a separate stock record card is maintained at a central place in the stores for each product held in stock. An example of a stock record card is shown in Fig. 31.4. The reference column is used to record the number of the delivery/advice note, or goods received note, or invoice number, covering stocks received (stocks *in*). When issues of stock are made (stocks *out*), the number of the material requisition note (or issue note) is entered in the reference column. If any stocks issued are subsequently returned to stock then a return note is used, and the number of this goes into the reference column.

Stock Record Card				
Item:				
Date	Ref.	In	Out	Balance

Fig. 31.4 A stock record card

Fig. 31.5 shows diagrammatically the role of the stock record card in recording movements of physical stock.

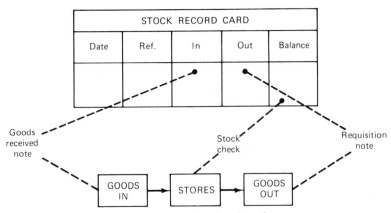

Fig. 31.5 The stock record card and stock movements

Example: Component ABC.

Stock on 1 February 19–2: 300 units.

Transactions for February:

Date	Requisition no	Issues	Receipts
2 Feb.	F22	55	
8 Feb.	F87	100	
10 Feb.			200 (GRN no 5411)
15 Feb.	F125	70	
16 Feb.			10 returns (RN44)
20 Feb.	F172	85	
24 Feb.			100 (GRN no 5485)
27 Feb.	F212	60	

Prepare the stock record card for February.

Answer

Stock Record Card				
Item: ABC				
Date	Ref.	In	Out	Balance
19–2				
1 Feb.	Balance			300
2 Feb.	F22		55	245
8 Feb:	F87		100	145
10 Feb.	5411	200		345
15 Feb.	F125		70	275
16 Feb.	RN44	10		285
20 Feb.	F172		85	200
24 Feb.	5485	100		300
27 Feb.	F212		60	240

31.4   Stock Losses

Ideally the stock record card should agree with a physical stock count (that is, the actual counting up of the number of items held in stock). Sometimes there is a discrepancy between the two. It is then necessary to check the stock record card carefully, looking at the documentation covering receipts and issues. If the source of the discrepancy still cannot be found, the stock loss is recorded on the stock card. Suppose that, using the stock figures in the last example, a physical count of item ABC revealed that 230 items were held in stock on 28 February and that efforts to trace the discrepancy are unsuccessful; the stock card will be completed as follows:

24 Feb.	5485	100		300
27 Feb.	F212		60	240
28 Feb.	Stock loss		10	230

If continual stock losses are detected, the matter may need further investigation to find out if stocks are being pilfered.

31.5　Computerized Stock Records

Stock control, often referred to as *inventory control*, is an important aspect of business that can be handled by a computer program, and many small businesses use microcomputer systems in their stock control.

Central to any computerized stock control system is the *stock file*. This, at its simplest, records the product or stock number, description and stock currently held (*book stock*) of each item of stock carried. Such a program will keep a running balance of the stock of each item, adding as new supplies are received, and deducting as stock is issued. Most programs also allow stock levels to be adjusted (for stock losses, for example) after stocktaking. More elaborate stock control systems can be used to:

(*a*) value the stock on hand;

(*b*) identify the levels at which stock should be re-ordered;

(*c*) hold information on lead times (see Unit 31.1);

(*d*) give immediate information on the quantity of stock in hand, together with the quantity on order;

(*e*) allocate stock currently held for known future uses;

(*f*) advise management of the total of stock issues for the current month or year;

(*g*) hold the supplier's product code number, together with supplier's name and address (this will facilitate the printing of orders);

(*h*) contain the retail price.

Most stock control programs for microcomputers are menu-driven (see Unit 20.3). A main menu, for example, might appear as:

```
                     STOCK CONTROL
                       Main Menu
        ---------------------------------------------
        Stock movements ............................. 1
        Stock enquiries ............................. 2
        Reports ..................................... 3
        Product updating ............................ 4

                    SELECT A FUNCTION
```

The user would then press either 1, 2, 3 or 4, as required, whereupon the *submenu* would appear on the screen. For example, the submenu for stock movements might be:

```
                STOCK CONTROL

                Stock Movements
        -------------------------------------------------

        Stock ordered ...................................... 1
        Stock received ...................................... 2
        Stock issued ........................................ 3
        Stock returned ...................................... 4
        Stock allocated ................................... 5
        Stock count ........................................ 6

                SELECT A FUNCTION
```

Pressing the appropriate number gives the user the information he needs to bring the stock records up to date.

After a number of stock transactions have been entered it might be necessary to produce a report showing the *stock status*, that is, the different types of stock held, together with quantities held and a stock valuation. A report of stock status might appear as follows:

Date: 21/10/–5   STOCK STATUS   Page 1

Product number	Description	Book stock	Re-order level	Unit	Unit cost (£)	Book value (£) at cost
0002001	Widgets	357	200	Each	10.00	3570.00
0002002	Plastic sheet	725	250	Sq.m.	0.25	181.25
0002003	Gnomes—plastic	390	100	Each	2.00	780.00

While a computerized stock control system can be used on its own, many can be linked to other computer programs dealing with a variety of accounting functions. Thus, for example, invoicing, sales ledger and purchases ledger programs can be linked in to update stock records automatically.

31.6   Stock Valuations

At regular intervals, and certainly at the end of a financial year, the owner of a business needs to know the value of stock on hand. As we said in Unit 10.2, stock is normally valued *at the lower of cost and net realizable value*. This means that two different values are compared: cost, and net realizable value. *Cost* is the cost of purchase plus carriage in; *net realizable value* is the amount that the item is expected to sell for.

Where the cost price of stocks changes frequently, many firms adopt a policy known as 'first in, first out' (FIFO). For example, suppose that a firm's stock of widgets at 30 June consists of:

75 units at a cost of £1 each, purchased on 20 May, and
100 units at a cost of £1.25 each, purchased on 15 June.

An issue of 50 widgets on 30 June will be valued at the unit price on 20 May, that is, at £1 each.

Some firms use 'last in, first out' (LIFO), in which case the issue on 30 June would be made at the unit price of £1.25 per widget.

31.7   Questions

1.   (*a*) Rule up a card suitable for recording the quantity of an item in stock. The card should show receipts, issues and balance. The goods received note number should be shown against receipts and the requisition number against issues.

(*b*) Enter the following information relating to component X40 on your stock card.

		Units
April 1	Balance in stock	600
Receipts:		
April 8	Goods received note no GR9	280
April 14	Goods received note no GR14	460
April 20	Goods received note no GR16	500
April 28	Goods received note no GR32	240
Issues:		
April 5	Requisition number R180	550
April 16	Requisition number R207	350
April 27	Requisition number R291	425

[Royal Society of Arts]

*2.   At 1 January 19–1, Brian Jenkins had 1 500 articles in stock which had cost him £2 each. During the month of January, he purchased 2 000 more articles at the same price. He sold 2 500 at £3.00 each and 100 at £2.50 each.

You are required to:

(*a*) draw up a simple stock record to show the number of items in stock at the end of the month;

(*b*) prepare his Trading Account for the month of January to show clearly the cost of sales and gross profit.

[Royal Society of Arts]

3. Rule up a stock ledger card with headings as under:

ITEM X421

Date	Reference	Receipts		Issues		Balance	
		Units	£	Units	£	Units	£

(a) Complete the stock ledger card for May 19–3 from the following information, commencing with an opening balance of 200 units having a total cost price of £1 400. Your firm's policy is to maintain stock records at cost. During the month of May the cost price per unit of all units purchased was £7 per unit.

Date	Reference	Issues	Receipts
1 May	RN 123	60	
4 May	GR 27		100
12 May	RN 180	80	
18 May	RN 260	120	
24 May	GR 38		60
31 May	RN 186	20	

(b) How would you verify that the closing balance of units on 31 May 19–3 was correct?

[*Royal Society of Arts*]

'*Computer records first, then women and children*'

4. Using a stock control program in a microcomputer, enter the following stock movements under today's date. (You will, most probably, need to create a new record on the stock file for this stock item—complete the details required by the program as necessary.)

Stock item no ABC 123

Received	100 units: goods received note number	GRN 1041
Received	50 units: goods received note number	GRN 1052
Issued	28 units: requisition note number	RN 0548
Issued	41 units: requisition note number	RN 0582
Received	75 units: goods received note number	GRN 1071
Issued	55 units: requisition note number	RN 0602

5. Using a stock control program in a microcomputer, enter the following stock movements under today's date. (As with Question 4, you may have to create a new stock record.)

Stock item no XYZ 987

Received	50 units: goods received note number	GRN 7867
Issued	21 units: requisition note number	RN 1731
Received	100 units: goods received note number	GRN 7882
Issued	15 units: requisition note number	RN 1745
Issued	33 units: requisition note number	RN 1760

6. A. Martin keeps a manual record of stock issues and receipts by maintaining a bin card for each item of stock held.

During the month of May the following issues and receipts of stock item ref: JKL/345 took place.

	Receipts	Units		Issues	Units
5 May	Delivery note DN122	140	8 May	Requisition note RN459	135
11 May	Delivery note DN127	160	14 May	Requisition note RN464	120
21 May	Delivery note DN129	150	29 May	Requisition note RN467	200
30 May	Delivery note DN140	100	31 May	Stock loss	5

The number of units in stock on 1 May was 120.

You are required:

To write up the stock record card showing the closing balance of the item in stock after each transaction.

How would Martin have discovered the stock loss on 31 May?

[*RSA Examinations Board*]

Unit Thirty-two

Wages Books and Records

32.1 Wages and Salaries

As we saw in Unit 10.5, *wages* are invariably a cost charged to Trading Account. *Salaries*, on the other hand, are an administrative expense charged in the Profit and Loss Account. Wages are paid (usually on a weekly basis) to employees engaged in producing goods or carrying out work on goods, while those who carry out administrative work—in the office, for instance—are paid salaries (usually monthly). The general term used to describe the calculation of amounts payable to employees is *payroll*.

Wages are usually paid on either a time basis (see Unit 32.2) or a piece-work basis (see Unit 32.3). Salaries, however, are almost always paid on a time basis.

32.2 Time Basis

Where a time basis is used for wages, the employee is paid a certain rate for each hour worked. Employees usually use a weekly time card/record (Fig. 32.1, page 282). When reporting for duty, the employee takes his or her card from the rack and puts it in a slot in the time machine or time clock, which records the arrival time on the card. On leaving at lunch time and at the end of the day the same procedure is used to establish the time of departure. At the end of the week the card then bears a precise record of the time that the employee has spent at work.

The hours are then totalled and the gross pay (the pay before any deductions have been made) is calculated by multiplying the number of hours worked by the hourly rate of pay. If any overtime has been worked this is usually paid at a higher rate than normal hours, such as 'time and a quarter', 'time and a half', or 'double time'.

Example

A firm has a normal working week of 40 hours and employees are paid £5 per hour. Overtime is paid at time and a half for the first ten hours of overtime worked, and after that at double time. Smith worked 45 hours, and Jones worked for 52 hours. Calculate the gross wage for each employee.

Smith:	
40 hours at £5 per hour (normal pay)	£200.00
5 hours at £7.50 per hour (time and a half)	£ 37.50
Gross wage for week	£237.50

Jones:

40 hours at £5 per hour (normal pay)	£200.00
10 hours at £7.50 per hour (time and a half)	£ 75.00
2 hours at £10 per hour (double time)	£ 20.00
Gross wage for week	£295.00

```
        DAILY TIME RECORD

Date  Week ending 24 March 19 - 3
Name  A. Lewis
```

	Details	Hours		
Mon.			ON	8·00
			OFF	12·00
		8	ON	1·00
			OFF	5·00
Tues.			ON	8·00
			OFF	12·00
		8	ON	1·00
			OFF	5·00
Wed.			ON	8·00
			OFF	12·00
	2 hours overtime at Rate 1	10	ON	1·00
			OFF	7·00
Thurs.			ON	8·00
			OFF	12·00
		8	ON	1·00
			OFF	5·00
Fri.			ON	8·00
			OFF	12·00
		8	ON	1·00
			OFF	5·00
		Total Hours		42·00

Fig. 32.1 A time card/record

32.3 Piecework Basis

Under this system each employee is paid for the amount of work that he or she performs. In a factory a certain sum is paid for each unit of goods produced or processed by individual employees: thus faster workers earn more than those who are slower. Where employees are paid on a piecework basis, a minimum wage is usually paid, which is based on an hourly rate; then if piecework earnings fall below hourly rate earnings, the latter will be paid.

Example

The following information relates to two employees:

	Wilson	*Young*
Piecework rate per unit produced	50p	50p
Number of units produced	450	410
Number of hours worked	40	42
Hourly rate of pay	£5	£5

The firm operates its piecework system on the basis that if an employee's piecework earnings fall below earnings at the hourly rate, then the hourly rate earnings are paid. A 40-hour week is in operation and overtime is paid at time and a half. Calculate the gross wage for each employee.

Wilson:	
Piecework rate: 450 units at 50p per unit	£225
Hourly rate: 40 hours at £5 per hour	£200

Therefore the piecework rate will be paid, with a gross wage of £225.

Young:	
Piecework rate: 410 units at 50p per unit	£205
Hourly rate: 40 hours at £5 per hour	£200
2 hours at £7.50 per hour	£ 15
	£215

Therefore the hourly rate will be paid, with a gross wage of £215.

32.4 Deductions from Wages

In the examples in Unit 32.3, we calculated the *gross* wages. An employee's *net* wages are calculated by subtracting from gross wages certain deductions, some compulsory and some voluntary.

Compulsory deductions comprise:

(*a*) income tax,

(*b*) National Insurance contributions (an employer also has to make a National Insurance contribution in respect of each employee).

Voluntary deductions may include:

(*a*) savings and pension/superannuation schemes (some superannuation schemes are compulsory, however),
(*b*) union contributions,
(*c*) social club contributions.

'*You've been beaten to it*'

32.5   Income Tax

The scheme used in Britain for collecting income tax payable by an employee is known as PAYE (Pay As You Earn). The amount of income tax due is calculated and must be deducted by the employer *before* the wages are paid to the employee. Thus most wage- and salary-earners pay a part of their total annual tax liability as a weekly or monthly deduction from wages or salary. The employer then sends the amount of income tax deducted from the pay of the employees to the tax authorities, the Inland Revenue.

The Inland Revenue gives each employee a tax code number, which is used by an employer to calculate the *taxable pay* (the amount on which income tax is levied) of an employee. The code number determines the amount of *allowances* the employee receives, that is, the amount of his or her income which is not subject to income tax. It is in fact the amount of allowances, but without the last digit; for example, allowances of £3 485 are represented by the code 348.

Each individual receives a personal allowance; a married couple receive an additional married couple's allowance which they can choose to allocate to either husband or wife—normally it is allocated to the higher earner. A married person claiming the additional allowance has a higher code number than someone receiving only a personal allowance, and can thus earn more before starting to pay income tax. Using tax code numbers enables allowances against income to be varied according to individual circumstances.

Example
Assume a personal allowance is £2 860 per year (tax code number 286), while a personal allowance plus married couple's allowance is £4 680 per year (tax code number 468). Janet Smith is single and earns a gross wage of £220 each week; her brother John is married and earns £195 gross each week. Calculate the taxable pay for each.

Janet Smith:	
Gross wage	£220
Less allowance per week (£2 860 ÷ 52)	£ 55
Taxable pay	£165

John Smith:	
Gross wage	£195
Less allowance per week (£4 680 ÷ 52)	£ 90
Taxable pay	£105

Once a person's income exceeds his or her allowances, income tax becomes payable at a rate of, say, 25 per cent. As he or she earns more money, a higher rate of tax is levied on the next band of taxable income.

Example
Suppose that the rates of tax and bands of taxable pay per year are:

	£
25%	1–20 000
40%	over 20 001

(These are illustrative figures only: current figures will be found in the current *PAYE Coding Guide* available from the Inland Revenue, or in books on income tax.)

Calculate the income tax paid in a year by the following employees:

G. Wilson, taxable pay £18 000 per year
B. Brown, taxable pay £35 000 per year

G. Wilson:	£18 000 at 25%	£4 500
B. Brown:	£20 000 at 25%	£5 000
	£15 000 at 40%	£6 000
	Total income tax for year	£11 000

The employer works out the amount of income tax to be deducted from each employee's pay by using special tax tables supplied by the Inland Revenue. These consist of two sections: (*a*) Free Pay Table, and (*b*) Taxable Pay Table.

Using the Free Pay Table the wages clerk calculates the total allowances ('free pay') to which the employee is entitled up to that week (or month). Deducting free pay from total pay gives the taxable pay. The wages clerk then uses the Taxable Pay Table to calculate the tax payable. As these calculations are based on cumulative totals of free pay and taxable pay, the employer needs to keep a weekly (or monthly) record of calculations, and also a record for each employee of deductions for income tax and National Insurance contributions, together with the employer's own National Insurance contributions. This record is kept on a form supplied by the Inland Revenue, which is submitted upon completion so that they can check the calculations and ensure that they have received payment of the due amount.

32.6   National Insurance Contributions

Most people working in Britain are required to pay National Insurance contributions. Payment of contributions enables certain benefits to be claimed from the State when needed, such as retirement pension and sickness benefits. The amount contributed by an employee varies according to his or her earnings: the more the earnings, the higher the contribution, up to a certain maximum amount. The employer also contributes an amount on behalf of each employee.

32.7   Superannuation/Pension Contributions

Many employers operate superannuation schemes under which the employee is entitled to certain benefits, including a pension (in addition to the State pension) and often a lump-sum payment upon retirement. In the event of an employee's death before retirement, benefits are usually paid to a surviving wife or husband.

32.8   Calculation of Wages and Salaries Payable

It is the job of a wages department within a firm to calculate the amount of wages or salary payable to each employee. The wages department is also responsible for drawing cash from the bank to make up pay packets where

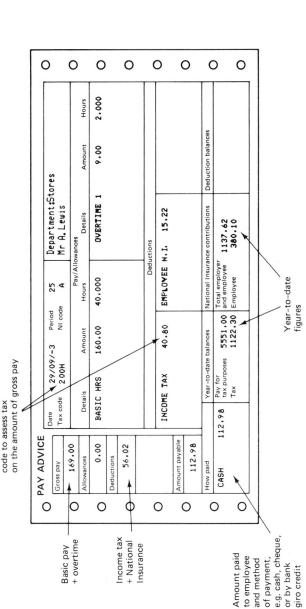

Tax is calculated using the personal code to assess tax on the amount of gross pay

Basic pay + overtime

Income tax + National Insurance

Amount paid to employee and method of payment, e.g. cash, cheque, or by bank giro credit

Year-to-date figures

PAY ADVICE

| | Date | 29/09/–3 | Period | 25 | Department:Stores |
| | Tax code | 200H | NI code | A | Mr A. Lewis |

Gross pay 169.00

Pay/Allowances

Details	Amount	Hours		Details	Amount	Hours
BASIC HRS	160.00	40.000		OVERTIME 1	9.00	2.000

Allowances 0.00

Deductions

| INCOME TAX | 40.80 | | EMPLOYEE N.I. | 15.22 |

Deductions 56.02

	Year-to-date balances	National Insurance contributions	Deduction balances
Amount payable 112.98	Pay for tax purposes 5551.00	Total employer and employee 1137.62	
	Tax 1122.30	Employee 380.10	

How paid

CASH 112.98

Fig. 32.2 A pay slip/advice

employees are paid in cash, and for preparing bank giro credits where their bank accounts are to be credited. In addition, the wages department handle the total amounts deducted from wages for income tax, National Insurance contributions, superannuation, union subscriptions and so on, and accounts for these to the appropriate authorities.

For identification purposes in a large organization, each employee will be given a works reference number. This will appear on the pay slip (Fig. 32.2) distributed to each employee.

Examination note. You may be asked to calculate the gross wage for an employee using either a time basis or a piecework basis. You will then be given the amount of deductions such as PAYE, National Insurance or superannuation, and be asked to prepare a pay slip.

Example (starting from gross wage)

	£
J. Jenkins: Gross wage for week ended 16 March 19–1	145
Income tax (PAYE)	32[1]
National Insurance	16[1]
Sports and welfare fund	2

[1] figures used for illustrative purposes only

J. Jenkins: Payslip for week ended 16 March 19–1

	£	£
Gross wage for week		145
Less: income tax	32	
National Insurance	16	
Sports and welfare fund	2	
		50
Net wage		95

A payslip also includes details of the total amount of deductions made so far during the current tax year for income tax, National Insurance and superannuation.

Example (starting from gross wage)

	£
A. Hughes: Gross wage for week ended 15 October 19–2	180
Income tax (PAYE)	38[1]
National Insurance	18[1]
Superannuation contribution: 5[1] per cent of gross wage	

Cumulative deductions made up to the previous pay day were:
income tax £954
National Insurance £408
superannuation £182

[1] figures used for illustrative purposes only

A. Hughes: Payslip for week ended 15 October 19–2

	£	£
Gross wage for week		180
Less: income tax	38	
National Insurance	18	
superannuation	9	
		65
Net wage		115
Totals to date in current tax year:		
income tax		992
National Insurance		426
superannuation		191

A small firm will maintain the wages records of its employees in a *wages book* or *payroll sheet*; a larger firm will maintain computer records (see Unit 32.10). A simplified payroll sheet is shown in Unit 32.11 (Fig. 32.3). A payroll sheet can be developed into a simultaneous records system by using a series of loose sheets. The record card of each employee's tax and earnings can be placed on top of the payroll sheet, which is itself placed over a perforated sheet, which can then be separated to form the employee's pay slip.

32.9   Notes and Coin Analysis

As we saw in Unit 32.8, the wages department has the task of drawing cash from the bank and making up wage packets for those employees who wish to be paid in cash. It is good accounting practice for a cheque to be drawn for the total of the net wages of all employees; if all the cash is used this provides one check of the accuracy of the contents of the wage packets. It is undesirable to withdraw part of the cash for wages from the bank, taking the rest out of the cash till; it is better for all cash receipts to be banked and for a cheque for the wages cash to be made out separately.

When making up wage packets, the wages department must ensure that it has the appropriate quantities of the different denominations of bank notes and coin to enable all wage packets to be completed. To this end, a *notes and coin analysis* is prepared showing the quantities of notes and coin requiring to be withdrawn from the bank.

Example

Employee	Net wage	£10	£5	£1	50p	20p	10p	5p	2p	1p
A. Andrews	£126.51	12		6	1					1
B. Bloggs	£154.75	14	1	9	1	1		1		
C. Clarke	£147.83	14		7	1	1	1		1	1
D. Duggan	£118.96	11		8	1	2		1		1
	£548.05	51	1	30	4	4	1	2	1	3

The wages clerk can now go to the bank with a cheque for £548.05 and request the following:

51 × £10	=	£510.00
1 × £5	=	5.00
30 × £1	=	30.00
4 × 50p	=	2.00
4 × 20p	=	0.80
1 × 10p	=	0.10
2 × 5p	=	0.10
1 × 2p	=	0.02
3 × 1p	=	0.03
		£548.05

In this example high-value bank notes (£50 and £20) have been avoided as these may not be popular with employees. Also, each employee will receive at least £5 in one-pound coins, so there should be no difficulties in paying the bus fare home on pay day!

32.10   Computerized Payroll

For a business with more than a handful of employees, computerized wage and salary records—payroll—can save considerable amounts of time. Semi-permanent information about each employee (such as employee number, name, tax code, other deductions) is held on disc, together with gross pay to date and tax to date during the tax year. For the computer to calculate gross pay for each employee, the semi-permanent information must include either annual salary or hourly rate, and overtime rates.

For most staff earning a salary, no input is needed from one payment to the next unless the semi-permanent information has changed. For hourly paid employees it will be necessary to key-in either the hours worked from clock card data, or piecework data. Once this has been done the payroll program can calculate gross pay, income tax deductions, National Insurance contributions, other deductions, and net pay. At the same time, gross pay to date and tax to date are brought up to date.

A payroll program produces reports consisting of a printout of the payroll, payslips, bank giro credit slips, and a list for cheque payments (where appropriate). Where wages are paid in cash the program will produce an analysis of notes and coin requirements. At the end of a tax year the payroll program can print the necessary information for employees and the Inland Revenue.

Payroll programs are usually menu-driven, and a main menu might appear as:

```
┌─────────────────────────────────────────────────┐
│                                                  │
│                                                  │
│                      PAYROLL                     │
│                     Main Menu                    │
│         ---------------------------------        │
│                                                  │
│         Data file maintenance .............. 1   │
│         Payroll calculation run ............ 2   │
│         Reports ............................ 3   │
│         Enquiries .......................... 4   │
│         System maintenance ................. 5   │
│             SELECT A FUNCTION                    │
│                                                  │
│                                                  │
│                                                  │
└─────────────────────────────────────────────────┘
```

The main menu appears on the screen at the start of the program. If we wish to change certain information held in the data file (the semi-permanent information), we select function 1 and a submenu then appears. This offers various choices and, according to what we wish to alter, we again select the appropriate function. For example, we might wish to alter the bank account details for an employee paid by bank giro credit, or another employee might be switching from payment in cash to payment by bank giro credit. When all data file maintenance for a pay period has been completed the payroll calculation can be run.

The *payroll calculation run* function enables the payroll to be processed. It prints pay advices, payroll summary, coin analysis, bank giro credits and certain other items. The submenu might appear as:

```
┌─────────────────────────────────────────────────┐
│                                                  │
│                                                  │
│                      PAYROLL                     │
│              Payroll Calculation Run             │
│         ---------------------------------        │
│                                                  │
│         Process payroll ................... 1    │
│         Enquire payroll ................... 2    │
│         Print pay advices ................. 3    │
│         Print payroll summary ............. 4    │
│         Print coin analysis ............... 5    │
│         Print bank giro credits ........... 6    │
│         Update payroll .................... 7    │
│             SELECT A FUNCTION                    │
│                                                  │
│                                                  │
└─────────────────────────────────────────────────┘
```

The *system maintenance function* enables bulk changes to be made in information such as the general level of tax rates or National Insurance contributions. One change made here affects all the wage and salary calculations without each individual employee's records having to be altered.

Enquiries function gives access to the whole payroll program. The submenu for enquiries might appear as:

```
                           PAYROLL

                        Enquiries Menu
        ---------------------------------------------------

        Company payroll data ...................... 1
        Employee permanent data ............... 2
        Employee cumulative data ............... 3
        Employee temporary data ................ 4
        Clock card data ................................. 5

                     SELECT A FUNCTION
```

While a payroll program can be operated by itself, it can also be linked to the general ledger so that the appropriate accounts can be debited or credited (see Unit 32.11 below).

32.11   Wages and Double-entry Book-keeping

The wages book or payroll sheet does not form part of the double-entry book-keeping system. When the calculations for wages have been made it is necessary for the amounts to be entered in the double-entry book-keeping accounts.

Let us consider three employees of a small firm. At the end of a particular week the payroll sheet appears as in Fig. 32.3. From the payroll sheet gross pay totals £555 for the week, employees' deductions total £167 (income tax £115, National Insurance contributions £52), giving total net pay of £388. The journal entry for these transactions is:

Date	Details	Folio	Dr.	Cr.
			£	£
19–4			555	
3 May	Wages	GL		
	Bank	CB		388
	Inland Revenue	GL		167
	Wages for week ending 3 May 19–4			

PAYROLL SHEET

NAME	HOURS WORKED		RATE PER HOUR		GROSS PAY	DEDUCTIONS				NET PAY	EMPLOYER'S NAT. INS.	TOTAL NAT. INS.
	NORMAL	OVERTIME	NORMAL	OVERTIME		INCOME TAX	NAT. INS.	OTHER	TOTAL			
			£	£	£	£	£	£	£	£	£	£
S. ARMSTRONG	40	2	5	7.50	215	45	20	-	65	150	22	42
T. JOHNSON	40	-	4	6.00	160	30	14	-	44	116	16	30
A. WILSON	40	4	4	5.00	180	40	18	-	58	122	20	38
TOTALS	-	-	-	-	555	115	52	-	167	388	58	110

Fig. 32.3 A payroll sheet

As with all journal entries, the appropriate entries must then be made in the accounts.

Clearly, only the amount of net pay—£388— needs to be drawn from the bank; alternatively, bank giro credits will be made out in the name of each employee and will total £388. Total deductions of £167 are credited to an account in the name of Inland Revenue. At the same time, book-keeping entries will be made for the employer's part of the National Insurance contributions:

Dr. Wages   £58
Cr. Inland Revenue   £58

On the due date payment of the total amount due to the Inland Revenue, £225 (£167 + £58), in respect of income tax and National Insurance contributions will be made as follows:

Dr. Inland Revenue   £225
Cr. Bank   £225

If a balance sheet is prepared before payment to the Inland Revenue, then the balance of the account is either shown separately, or included among the creditors under the heading of 'current liabilities'.

32.12   Questions

*1.   The following information relates to four employees:

Name	Basic	Hours worked Overtime Weekdays	Sundays	Number of items produced
M. Groom	38	—	—	3 200
L. Tarrant	40	6	—	4 000
R. Blake	40	8	—	3 800
C. Ford	40	1	4	3 600

The firm pays £1.50 per hour with time and a half for overtime during weekdays and double time on Sundays.

Required:

(*a*) Calculate for each employee: (i) his basic wage, (ii) his overtime earnings and (iii) his total gross weekly earnings.

(*b*) The firm is considering the introduction of piecework at a rate of £2 per 100 items produced. Using the figures shown calculate each employee's wage on the piece rate basis. Indicate for each employee which would result in the lowest costs to the firm.

[*Royal Society of Arts*]

*2.   Peter Price is paid a basic wage of £2.50 per hour for the first 35 hours a week; all hours in excess of this are paid at time and a half. In the week ending 6 May 19–3 he worked a total of 41 hours, and received in addition to his basic pay and overtime a productivity bonus of £5.

His deductions for the week were:

Social and welfare	£1.00 per week
National Insurance	5 per cent of all earnings in excess of £30 per week
Income tax	30 per cent of all earnings in excess of £45 per week

You are required to:
  (a) calculate his gross pay for the week ending 6 May 19–3;
  (b) calculate his take-home pay for the same period.

[*Royal Society of Arts*]

3.   The information below appeared on the wages record of Miss E. Wren for the week ending 5 March 19–2.

Name of employee: Miss E. Wren   *Grade:* Machinist
Works No 3546
                            Piecework rates: Type A units £1 per 100
                                                 Type B units £1 per 150
Week ending: 5 March 19–2

	No of units produced	Type
Monday	1 600	A
Tuesday	1 400	A
Wednesday	1 800	B
Thursday	1 500	B
Friday	1 300	A

No of times late: Nil

Employees work 40 hours per week and an additional bonus of £3 per week is paid to those who commence work on time every day.

You are required to:
  (a) calculate Miss Wren's total piecework earnings showing separately the amount earned for each type of unit produced;
  (b) give the payroll entry for Miss Wren for the week ending 5 March 19–2 taking into account the additional information below:

Contribution to pension fund is at the rate of 5 per cent of the employee's gross earnings
PAYE £7   National Insurance £5.50
Cumulative deductions made up to the previous pay day were:
  Income tax £359   National Insurance £234.50
  Pension fund £280

[*Royal Society of Arts*]

4. The following details relate to the earnings of three employees during the week ending 6 March 19–1.

Employee	A	B	C
Piecework price per			
100 units produced	160p	180p	200p
Number of units produced	2 000	2 700	2 600
Number of hours worked	40	42	38
Hourly rate of pay	90p	95p	100p

If an employee's piecework earnings falls below his earnings at the hourly rate then the hourly rate earnings are paid. A 40-hour week is in operation and overtime is paid at time and a half.

You are required to:
    (a) calculate each employee's wages at (i) hourly rates and (ii) piecework rates;
    (b) prepare the pay slip for the week ended 6 March 19–1 to be handed to employee A, taking into account the additional information below:
        PAYE £6   National Insurance £5
        Deduction for Sports and Welfare Fund 50p

[*Royal Society of Arts*]

5. The following table refers to two employees:

Name	Hours worked w/e 18 June	Rate £
John Brown	42	2.00
Wilson Cap	46	1.50

Their employment has a basic working week of 40 hours, and all overtime is paid at time and a half. Income tax is paid as follows: Brown £5, Cap £3; 5 per cent of gross earnings is to be deducted for social security contributions. All employees make a voluntary contribution towards the social and athletic club of £1.00 per week.

You are required to calculate the net pay of each employee and set out pay slips for the week ending 18 June 19–3.

[*Royal Society of Arts*]

6. The following are the net wages of four employees in your firm for the week ending 26 May 19–8.

P. Hall	£142.70
A. Brewer	£152.76
D. Black	£137.92
R. Green	£158.14

You are required to:
Calculate the number of notes and coins of each denomination that you would need to collect from the bank in order to make up their pay packets. It is company policy to include a minimum of three £1 coins in each wage packet otherwise the minimum number of notes/coins must be used in each pay packet, for example one 20p coin would be used in preference to two 10p coins.
    Your answer should take the form of a table under the headings below:
    Amount   £20   £10   £5   £1   50p   20p   10p   5p   2p   1p

[*RSA Examinations Board*]

Incomplete Records Accounting

33.1 What is Meant by Incomplete Records?

It is a fact of accounting life that a large number of businesses, including many small shops, do not maintain a full set of double-entry book-keeping accounts. Instead, they keep some records—incomplete records—but these are not usually balanced during the course of a financial year. It is the job of the book-keeper or accountant to use these incomplete records and produce the Trading and Profit and Loss Account for the year, together with a balance sheet at the year-end. Information likely to be available to the book-keeper might include:

(a) a list of assets and liabilities at the beginning of the year;
(b) details of purchases, sales and expenses for the year;
(c) bank statements;
(d) details of fixed assets acquired or sold during the year;
(e) a list of assets and liabilities at the year-end.

33.2 Opening Capital

If we know the assets and liabilities of a business at the beginning of the year, we can calculate the owner's opening capital using the formula:

$$Assets - Liabilities = Capital$$

Example

At 1 January 19–1, M. Sankey has the following assets and liabilities:

stock £1 250; debtors £2 300; creditors £1 540; machinery £1 750; balance at bank £225; rent owing by him £40.

His opening capital is calculated:

Statement of assets and liabilities of M. Sankey as at 1 January 19–1

Assets:	£	£
Stock		1 250
Debtors		2 300
Machinery		1 750
Balance at bank		225
		5 525
Less Liabilities:		
Creditors	1 540	
Rent owing	40	
		1 580
Capital		3 945

Examination note. Most questions dealing with incomplete records require the calculation of opening capital. The statement of assets and liabilities (sometimes called a *Statement of Affairs*) can be presented either in the format shown or in the form of a balance sheet (which is, of course, what the statement represents).

If we can calculate opening capital, we can work out closing capital from the assets and liabilities held at the year-end. By comparing the two capital positions we know how much profit has been retained in the business during the year. For example, our calculation shows opening capital to be £3 945; if the capital at 31 December 19–1 is £4 945, we know that £1 000 has been retained in the business. Furthermore, if we also know that, during the year, the owner made drawings of £2 000, then the net profit of the business (that is, before deduction of drawings) is £3 000. The capital position would be set out in the balance sheet as:

Balance sheet (extract) of M. Sankey as at 31 December 19–1

	£
Capital at 1 Jan. 19–1	3 945
Add Net profit for year	3 000
	6 945
Less Drawings for year	2 000
Capital at 31 Dec. 19–1	4 945

33.3   The Use of a Cash/Bank Summary

Comparing the opening and closing capital positions gives us the profit (or loss) for the year, but we may also be required to calculate a figure for purchases or sales. To do this we need to have a list of receipts and payments made during the year. There are two likely sources for such a list:

(i) the firm's own cash book (even a business that does not keep a full set of double-entry accounts usually maintains a cash book); or

(ii) the bank statements (often a most reliable source of accounting information, particularly if all receipts are banked and all payments are made by cheque).

Using either or both of these we should be able to identify, first, the receipts relating to sales and, secondly, the payments relating to purchases, from which we must be careful to exclude payments for the expenses of running the business and for the purchase of fixed assets.

(a) Calculation of Sales

Suppose that we have the following information:

debtors at 1 Jan. 19–4	£4 200
debtors at 31 Dec. 19–4	£4 800
receipts from debtors during the year	£35 600

Can we use the figure for receipts from debtors as the sales figure for the year? If the business had no debtors at both the beginning and the end of the year, the answer would be 'yes'. In this example, however, we cannot use the receipts figure of £35 600 as sales, because it takes no account of the change in the level of debtors. What we must realize is that the debtors at the beginning of the year represent amounts owing from sales made *in the previous year*, that is, in 19–3. If we assume that all debtors have paid what they owe, we can say that this year's receipts of £35 600 include payments for £4 200 in respect of some of the 19–3 sales. So far, then:

receipts from debtors during 19–4	£35 600
less debtors at 1 January 19–4	£4 200
	£31 400

Is this the sales figure for 19–4? It is not, because the figure of £31 400 represents the amount of sales made and paid for in 19–4. As the business has debtors at 31 December 19–4 of £4 800, representing sales that are not yet paid for, these must be added as follows:

receipts from debtors during 19–4	£35 600
less debtors at 1 January 19–4	£4 200
	£31 400
add debtors at 31 December 19–4	£4 800
sales in 19–4	£36 200

An easy way to find the 'missing figure' for sales is to prepare a control account (see Unit 30), as follows:

Sales Ledger Control Account

19–4	£	19–4	£
Balance b/d	4 200	Receipts (cash/bank)	35 600
Sales	?	Balance c/d	4 800
	40 400		40 400
Balance b/d	4 800		

The figure for sales can now be completed as £36 200 (£40 400 – £4 200).

Four main items make up the control account:
  (i) opening balance,
  (ii) closing balance,
  (iii) receipts from debtors during the year, and
  (iv) sales during the year.

The control account can be used to find any one of these where the other three are known. For example, if we know

opening balances	£3 500
sales for year	£10 000
receipts from debtors during year	£9 500

the closing balance for debtors can be calculated thus:

Sales Ledger Control Account

	£		£
Opening balances	3 500	Receipts	9 500
Sales	10 000	Balance c/d	?
	13 500		13 500
Balance b/d	?		

The missing figure is £4 000 (£13 500−£9 500).

(b) Calculation of Purchases

A summary or a control account can be used to calculate purchases for the year.

Example

Calculate purchases for the year if:

creditors at 1 January 19–6	£8 200
creditors at 31 December 19–6	£9 500
payments to creditors during the year	£56 200

We cannot use the payments figure of £56 200 as purchases, because £8 200 will have been used to pay the creditors outstanding at the beginning of 19–6 for purchases made during 19–5. The closing creditors, being the amount of goods purchased but not yet paid for, must be added. Thus the control account appears as:

Purchases Ledger Control Account

19–6	£	19–6	£
Payments (cash/bank)	56 200	Balance b/d	8 200
Balance c/d	9 500	Purchases	?
	65 700		65 700
		Balance b/d	9 500

The figure for purchases is £57 500 (£65 700−£8 200).

33.4   A Worked Example

W. Harris has the following assets and liabilities:

	1 January 19–1	31 December 19–1
	£	£
Machinery at cost	1 000	1 000
Stock	850	1 200
Debtors	710	830
Creditors	540	560
Balance at bank	160	140

All transactions are passed through his bank, and a summary of his bank account is as follows:

	£
Receipts: from debtors	6 890
Payments: to creditors	3 200
business expenses	1 810
drawings	1 900

Depreciation on machinery is to be provided at 10 per cent per year.

Prepare (*a*) a statement of his capital at 1 January 19–1, (*b*) a Trading and Profit and Loss Account for the year to 31 December 19–1, together with a balance sheet at that date.

Answer

(*a*)

W. Harris
Statement of assets and liabilities as at 1 January 19–1

Assets:	£
Machinery	1 000
Stock	850
Debtors	710
Balance at bank	160
	2 720
Less Liabilities:	
Creditors	540
Capital	2 180

(*b*)
Calculation of purchases:

Purchases Ledger Control Account

19–1	£	19–1	£
Payments	3 200	Balance b/d	540
Balance c/d	560	Purchases	3 220
	3 760		3 760

Calculation of sales:

Sales Ledger Control Account

19–1	£	19–1	£
Balance b/d	710	Receipts	6 890
Sales	7 010	Balance c/d	830
	7 720		7 720

W. Harris
Trading Account for the year ended 31 December 19–1

	£		£
Opening stock	850	Sales	7 010
Add Purchases	3 220		
	4 070		
Less Closing stock	1 200		
	2 870		
Gross profit c/d	4 140		
	7 010		7 010

Profit and Loss Account for the year ended 31 December 19–1

	£		£
Expenses	1 810	Gross profit b/d	4 140
Provision for depreciation: machinery	100		
Net profit	2 230		
	4 140		4 140

Balance sheet as at 31 December 19–1

	£	£		£
Fixed assets:			Capital (at 1 Jan. 19–1)	2 180
Machinery		1 000	*Add* Net profit	2 230
Less Provision for				4 410
depreciation		100	*Less* Drawings	1 900
		900		2 510
Current assets:			Current liabilities:	
Stock	1 200		Creditors	560
Debtors	830			
Bank	140			
		2 170		
		3 070		3 070

Point to notice:

The bank balance at 31 December 19–1 can be checked as follows:

	£	£
Opening balance (1 Jan. 19–1)		160
Add Receipts from debtors		6 890
		7 050
Less Payments to creditors	3 200	
Business expenses	1 810	
Drawings	1 900	
		6 910
Closing balance (31 Dec. 19–1)		140

33.5 Questions

*1. John Emery is a sole trader who does not operate a full double-entry system of book-keeping, but the records he does keep are accurate, and from them the following figures have been extracted:

	30 Sept. 19–0 £	30 Sept. 19–1 £
Fixtures and fittings	400	360
Stock	1 280	1 490
Cash at bank	720	940
Cash in hand	30	40

On 30 September 19–0, debtors amounted to £1 460. Cash received from debtors for the year ended 30 September 19–1—£6 390. Sales for the same period totalled £5 950.

On 30 September 19–0, creditors amounted to £1 040. Cash paid to creditors for the year ended 30 September 19–1—£4 130. Purchases for the same period totalled £3 890.

During the year ended 30 September 19–1 no bad debts were incurred. In addition there was no discount allowed or received.

Required:

(a) Calculate debtors and creditors as at 30 September 19–1.

(b) Calculate John Emery's capital as at 30 September 19–0 and 30 September 19–1.

(c) Calculate John Emery's net profit for the year ended 30 September 19–1, allowing for the fact that his drawings during that period amounted to £1 250.

Note: All calculations must be shown.

[London Chamber of Commerce]

*2. Walter Price, a sole trader, keeps accurate records of his business transactions but he does not use the double-entry system. From his records the following information has been obtained:

	30 April 19–1 £	30 April 19–2 £
Stock	2 280	2 760
Debtors	3 170	4 040
Bank	1 160	930
Office furniture (cost)	250	600 (cost)
Creditors	1 980	2 020

During the year ended 30 April 19–2 Walter Price made withdrawals as follows:

Cash £1 300
Goods (cost) £80

The increase in office furniture—£350—is due to the fact that during the year Price purchased from his private banking account additional office furniture for use in his business.

Required:

(*a*) Calculate the amount of Walter Price's capital as at 30 April 19–1 and 30 April 19–2. (Ignore depreciation.)

(*b*) Calculate Walter Price's net profit for the year ended 30 April 19–2.

(*c*) Draw up Walter Price's Capital Account for the year ended 30 April 19–2 as it would have appeared under the double-entry system.

Note. Calculations must be shown.

[*London Chamber of Commerce*]

*3. Smith does not keep proper books of account. On 1 January 19–1 he had the following assets and liabilities: cash at bank and in hand £541, trade debtors £194, stocks on hand £989, furniture and shop fittings £250, van £600, trade creditors £1 240 and £25 was owing for rent.

A summary of his bank account and cash book for the year ended 31 December 19–1 shows the following:

Receipts:	£
Cash sales	6 943
Receipts from debtors	1 236
Payments:	
Payments to creditors	5 988
Drawings	700
Rent, rates and insurance	540
Light and heat	42
Motor van expenses	226
Repairs	17
New shop fittings	50
General expenses	84

On 31 December 19–1, the following information is available:

(i) Stock was valued at cost £910; trade debtors were £136; trade creditors were £1 570.

(ii) Light and heat outstanding was £11.

(iii) Rates and insurance prepaid were £30.

(iv) Depreciation at 10 per cent is to be written off furniture and shop fittings at 31 December 19–1, and at 20 per cent off the value of the van.

Required:

(*a*) a statement of Smith's capital at 1 January 19–1;

(*b*) a Trading and Profit and Loss Account for 19–1;

(*c*) a balance sheet at 31 December 19–1.

Multiple-choice Questions—9

Read each question carefully. Choose the *one* answer you think is correct. Answers are given on page 411.

1. When preparing a control account the total of credit sales for the month should be entered on the:

   A   debit side of Purchases Ledger Control Account
   B   credit side of Purchases Ledger Control Account
   C   debit side of Sales Ledger Control Account
   D   credit side of Sales Ledger Control Account

2. When preparing a control account the total of returns inwards for the month should be entered on the:

   A   debit side of Purchases Ledger Control Account
   B   credit side of Purchases Ledger Control Account
   C   debit side of Sales Ledger Control Account
   D   credit side of Sales Ledger Control Account

3. When preparing a control account the total of discounts received for the month should be entered on the:

   A   debit side of Purchases Ledger Control Account
   B   credit side of Purchases Ledger Control Account
   C   debit side of Sales Ledger Control Account
   D   credit side of Sales Ledger Control Account

4. ABC Company has a credit balance in your purchases ledger of £200 and a debit balance in your sales ledger of £300. If it is agreed to set one account off against the other the entries in your control accounts should be:

	Debit	*Credit*
A	Sales Ledger Control Account £300	Purchases Ledger Control Account £300
B	Purchases Ledger Control Account £200	Sales Ledger Control Account £200
C	Purchases Ledger Control Account £300	Sales Ledger Control Account £300
D	Sales Ledger Control Account £200	Purchases Ledger Control Account £200

5. In preparing control accounts you consider the following:

   (i)   opening balances of debtors
   (ii) discounts received
   (iii) provision for bad debts
   (iv) returns inwards journal

   Which of these will you disregard when preparing the Sales Ledger Control Account?

   A   (i) and (ii)   C   (iii) and (iv)
   B   (ii) and (iii)   D   (ii) and (iv)

6. The valuation of stock is carried out by:

    A   counting the stock and valuing it at selling price
    B   counting the stock and valuing it at cost price
    C   counting the stock and valuing it at the lower of cost price and market price
    D   balancing the Stock Account

7. If stock at the year-end is undervalued, gross profit will be:

    A   understated   **C**   overstated
    B   only affected next year   **D**   not affected

8. Rates of tax and bands of taxable pay are as follows:

    30%   £1 to £15 000
    45%   £15 001 to £20 000
    50%   £20 001 to £25 000

    N. Johnson has taxable pay of £24 000 for the year. She will pay tax for the year amounting to:

    A   £7 200   **B**   £8 750   **C**   £9 250   **D**   £12 000

9. John Jarvis is paid on a piecework basis of 50p for each unit produced, with a guaranteed hourly rate of £6 per hour for a 40-hour week. In week 1 he makes 510 units, and in week 2 he makes 460 units. His wages for these weeks will be:

    A   week 1 £240; week 2 £240   **C**   week 1 £255; week 2 £230
    B   week 1 £240; week 2 £230   **D**   week 1 £255; week 2 £240

10. Which one of the following calculations can be used to give a figure for net profit where full double-entry book-keeping records have not been kept?

    A   increase in value of capital less drawings
    B   increase in value of capital add drawings
    C   this year's net assets, less last year's net assets
    D   increase in bank balance

11. At the beginning of a firm's financial year, debtors were £1 750 and at the year end were £2 100. During the year receipts from debtors by cash and cheque totalled £10 450. What was the figure for sales during the year?

    A   £8 700   **B**   £10 450   **C**   £10 800   **D**   £10 100

12. At the beginning of a firm's financial year, creditors were £1 250 and at the year-end were £840. During the year cash and bank payments to creditors amounted to £130 and £5 190 respectively. What was the figure for purchases during the year?

    A   £4 780   **B**   £4 910   **C**   £5 320   **D**   £5 730

Accounts of Clubs and Societies

34.1 Introduction

So far in this book we have dealt with the year-end accounts of businesses, most of which exist for the purpose of making a profit—hence the use of a Profit and Loss Account. Clubs and societies, on the other hand, do not regard profit as their main objective. Instead they aim to provide facilities and services for their members, meeting expenses from subscription income and other fund-raising activities. The preparation of a Profit and Loss Account is not appropriate to a non-profit-making organization, and in this Unit we shall look at the alternatives.

34.2 The Accumulated Fund

In the balance sheet of a club the term 'capital' is usually replaced by the words *accumulated fund*. This fund is calculated in the same way as for capital, that is:

$$Assets - Liabilities = Accumulated\ fund$$

but using the term 'accumulated fund' helps to free the club from the image of a business organization working primarily to make money. The balance of the fund is the amount that belongs to the members after all liabilities have been met.

Example

The Southtown Social Club has the following assets and liabilities at 30 June 19–2:

	£
Clubhouse	20 000
Furniture and fittings	2 200
Trophies	500
Stocks of food, etc	220
Cash	27
Bank overdraft	575
Creditors (for food)	108

The accumulated fund is calculated as follows:

Southtown Social Club
Statements of assets and liabilities as at 30 June 19–2

Assets:	£	£
Clubhouse		20 000
Furniture and fittings		2 200
Trophies		500
Stocks of food, etc		220
Cash		27
		22 947
Less Liabilities:		
Bank overdraft	575	
Creditors	108	
		683
Accumulated fund		22 264

34.3   Accounting Records

Not many non-profit-making organizations maintain a double-entry book-keeping system. For most clubs the treasurer keeps a cash book, showing cash and bank transactions, a summary of which may well be presented to members under the title *Receipts and Payments Account*. An example of such an account is:

Deansway Sports Club
Receipts and Payments Account for the year ended 31 December 19–1

Receipts:	£	Payments:	£
Bank balance at 1 Jan. 19–1	45	Rent of clubhouse	350
Subscriptions	584	Prizes	50
		Printing, stationery and	
		postages	78
		Sundry expenses	42
		Bank balance at 31 Dec. 19–1	109
	629		629

The treasurer of a very small club might present such information as the 'year-end accounts'. There are, however, two major disadvantages in using a Receipts and Payments Account for this purpose:

(*a*) Only the actual receipts and payments during the year are recorded—no account is taken of prepayments or accruals at the beginning and end of the accounting period.

(*b*) Items of capital expenditure, such as the purchase of a mowing machine or sports equipment, appear in the Receipts and Payments Account of the year in which they are paid for; after that, the accounts will show no record of their existence.

Clearly, a Receipts and Payments Account is not a very suitable way for the treasurer to report to members at the year-end.

34.4   The Use of Income and Expenditure Accounts

The correct method of presenting club accounts is to convert the Receipts and Payments Account (cash book summary) into an *Income and Expenditure Account*. This, together with a balance sheet at the year-end, gives members the same information that a Profit and Loss Account and balance sheet give to the owner of a business.

An Income and Expenditure Account is prepared in the same way as a Profit and Loss Account, although the main source of income is usually subscriptions, and the types of expenditure are different from those of a business. Thus accruals and prepayments at the year-end are noted, and depreciation is charged to the Income and Expenditure Account. Instead of making a net profit or a net loss, a club or society makes a *surplus of income over expenditure* or an *excess of expenditure over income*. In the balance sheet a surplus is added to accumulated fund, while an excess of expenditure over income is deducted—just as net profit or net loss is added to or subtracted from capital.

Examination note. As the main source of accounting information for a club is the treasurer's cash book, most questions start with a summary of this, often presented in the form of a Receipts and Payments Account. From this, to prepare year-end accounts, we must first calculate the balance of accumulated fund (in a similar way to the incomplete records procedure—see Unit 33.2) at the beginning of the year. Using the Receipts and Payments Account, we can then produce the Income and Expenditure Account, being careful to exclude items of capital expenditure, to include accruals and prepayments, and to take account of any provision for depreciation. A balance sheet can then be prepared from the information available, incorporating any capital expenditure made during the year.

34.5   A Worked Example

At 1 January 19–1, Extown Domino Society had the following assets and liabilities:

	£
Furniture	250
Trophies	50
Cash at bank	120
Sundry expenses owing	15

The Receipts and Payments Account for the year to 31 December 19–1 is:

Receipts:	£	*Payments:*	£
Bank balance at 1 Jan. 19–1	120	Rent of clubhouse	110
Subscriptions	215	Secretary's expenses	54
		New furniture	50
		Sundry expenses	38
		Bank balance at 31 Dec. 19–1	83
	335		335

Notes:

(i) Depreciation is to be provided for at 10 per cent on the value of furniture held at the end of the year.

(ii) At 31 December 19–1, £20 is owing to the secretary for expenses.

Prepare an Income and Expenditure Account for the year ended 31 December 19–1, together with a balance sheet at that date.

Answer

Calculation of accumulated fund at 1 January 19–1:

		£
Assets:		
	Furniture	250
	Trophies	50
	Cash at bank	120
		420
Less Liabilities:		
	Sundry expenses owing	15
	Accumulated fund	405

Extown Domino Society

Income and Expenditure Account for the year ended 31 December 19–1

Expenditure:	£	Income:	£
Rent of clubhouse	110	Subscriptions	215
Secretary's expenses	74	Excess of expenditure over	
Sundry expenses	23	income	22
Provision for depreciation			
on furniture	30		
	237		237

Balance sheet as at 31 December 19–1

Fixed assets:	£		£
Furniture	300	Accumulated fund (1 Jan. 19–1)	405
Less Provision for		*Less* Excess of expenditure	
depreciation	30	over income	22
	270		383
Trophies	50		
	320		
Current assets:		Current liabilities:	
Cash at bank	83	Secretary's expenses owing	20
	403		403

Notes:

(i) Secretary's expenses:	amount paid during year	£54
	owing at 31 Dec. 19–1	£20
	shown in Income and Expenditure Account	£74
(ii) Sundry expenses:	amount owing at 1 Jan. 19–1	£15
	amount paid during year	£38
	shown in Income and Expenditure Account	£23
(iii) Depreciation:	furniture at 1 Jan. 19–1	£250
	addition during year	£ 50
	depreciation for year, 10 per cent of	£300
	=	£30

34.6   The Use of a Trading Account

Where a club carries out an activity on a regular basis with the *intention of making a profit*, such as running a bar, then a Trading Account is prepared, and the gross profit on this separate activity is transferred to the club's Income and Expenditure Account. The following is an example of a Bar Trading Account, together with the relevant extract from Income and Expenditure Account:

Battenhall Social Club
Bar Trading Account for the year ended 31 December 19–5

	£		£
Opening stock	1 355	Sales	14 523
Add Purchases	10 278		
	11 633		
Less Closing stock	1 274		
Cost of goods sold	10 359		
Barman's wages	2 350		
Cost of sales	12 709		
Gross profit c/d	1 814		
	14 523		14 523

Income and Expenditure Account (extract) for the year ended 31 December 19–5

	£
Income:	
Gross profit from Bar Trading	
Account b/d	1 814
Subscriptions	*x*

34.7   Profit or Loss on Individual Events

When preparing an Income and Expenditure Account it is usual to link the income and expenses of particular events together. For example, if a society held a raffle, the expenditure can be linked to the income to show the profit or loss on the raffle:

Income and Expenditure Account (extract) for the year ended 31 December 19–9

	£	£
Income:		
Subscriptions		*x*
Raffle:		
sale of tickets	254	
less expenses	138	
profit		116

This method of presentation enables club members to see the profit or loss on individual events, and is the layout you should use if an examination question asks you to show, within the Income and Expenditure Account, the profit on certain events.

'*Let us pray*'

34.8   Subscriptions: a Problem Area

For many clubs and societies, subscriptions form the main source of income. If we were to treat subscriptions in the same way that a business treats debtors then, at the year-end, we would record in the Income and Expenditure Account *the amount that should have been received*, including unpaid subscriptions. At the same time we would show in the balance sheet a figure of 'debtors for subscriptions', representing the amount unpaid for that year at the date of the balance sheet. This is the strictly correct accounting treatment and would be perfectly valid if subscriptions were like the debtors of a commercial firm, that is, if the treasurer could go to non-payers and demand their money. As any club treasurer can confirm, however, membership changes from year to year, as people move away from an area or lose interest in the society—in both cases often leaving their subscriptions unpaid. A club is most unlikely to sue a member for unpaid subscriptions in the same way that a commercial firm might take a debtor to court for non-payment. For most clubs and societies, it is therefore unrealistic to adopt the strict accounting approach which assumes that most debtors will pay eventually. Instead it is better in practice to record subscription income at the amount actually received during the year and to ignore outstanding subscriptions (but see the examination note below).

With *subscriptions paid in advance*, we can adopt the correct accounting treatment of excluding the amount of the prepayment from the current year's subscription income. On the balance sheet at the year-end it will be necessary to record a liability for the club described as 'subscriptions in advance', that is, the club owes these members next year's subscription.

Example

At 1 January 19–2 the Blanktown Social Club has 300 members. The annual subscription is £5. At 31 December 19–2 the treasurer advises that he has received £1 525 for subscriptions during the year, being 285 subscriptions for 19–2 and 20 subscriptions in advance for 19–3. The Income and Expenditure Account will appear as:

Income and Expenditure Account (extract) for the year ended 31 December 19–2

Income:	£
Subscriptions (285 members at £5 each)	1 425

The extract from the balance sheet appears thus:

Balance sheet (extract) as at 31 December 19–2

	£
Accumulated fund	x
Current liabilities:	
Subscriptions prepaid (20 members at £5 each)	100

Point to notice:

As explained, no record is made of unpaid subscriptions—if any should be paid subsequently, they will be included in the income of the year of receipt.

Examination note. In an examination you should always record *the total subscription income that should have been received* and, in the balance sheet, show debtors for subscriptions, *unless you are told otherwise*. Thus, if the above example had been an examination question with no guidance of the treatment for subscriptions, the Income and Expenditure Account would have shown '£1 500 receivable (300 members at £5 each)', while the balance sheet would, additionally, have shown 'debtors for subscriptions £75' as a current asset.

34.9   Questions

*1. The Town Society was formed on 1 July 19–0 and at the end of the first year the Treasurer submitted the following statement to members:

Receipts and Payments Account for the year ended 30 June 19–1

	£		£
Subscriptions	320	Cost of refreshments	20
Sale of dance tickets	80	Printing and stationery	15
Proceeds of sale of		Rent	10
refreshments	30	Furniture	150
		Dance expenses	45
		Sundry expenses	15
		Balance	175
	430		430

You are required to prepare an Income and Expenditure Account for the year ended 30 June 19–1, and a balance sheet as at that date. You are given the following information:

No subscriptions were paid in advance;
No depreciation on the furniture;
Stock of stationery £5;
Rent owing £10.

[Pitman Examinations Institute]

*2. The Treasurer of the Keswick Sports Club drew up the following trial balance on 31 December 19–2:

	Dr.	Cr.
	£	£
Equipment	700	
Land	2 000	
Clubhouse	7 000	
Travelling expenses	112	
Printing and stationery	53	
Repairs	85	
Prizes	150	
Cash at bank	1 350	
Subscriptions 19–2		2 200
Subscriptions 19–3		70
Refreshments		430
Rent received		50
Accumulated fund		8 700
	11 450	11 450

Prepare an Income and Expenditure Account for the year ended 31 December 19–2 and a balance sheet as at that date.

[East Midland Regional Examinations Board]

3. (*a*) From the following Receipts and Payments Account and the 'additional information', prepare an Income and Expenditure Account:

Senior Service Club
Receipts and Payments Account
Year ended 31 December 19–2

	£		£
Balance (1 January 19–2)	200	Expenses	40
Subscriptions	972	Wages	800
Locker rents	496	Telephone	100
		Heating	80
		Lighting	80
		Rates	220
		Balance c/d	348
	1 668		1 668
Balance b/d	348		

Additional information:
  (i) subscriptions due, but unpaid £128;
  (ii) subscriptions paid in advance £200;
  (iii) locker rents due £4;
  (iv) rates paid in advance £20;
(*b*) What does the balance of £348 on the Receipts and Payments Account represent?

[South Western Examinations Board]

4. On 1 January 19–2, Hambleton Sports Club had a clubhouse valued at £10 000 and an accumulated fund of £13 875. The receipts and payments for the year ended 31 December 19–2 were as follows:

Receipts:	£	*Payments:*	£
Balance 1 January 19–2	3 875	Games equipment	400
Subscriptions 19–2	1 400	Land	1 800
Subscriptions 19–3	90	Travelling expenses	187
Fund raising:		Printing and stationery	56
Coffee mornings	260	Postages	23
Bring and buy sales	375	Prizes	175
Dances	512	Repairs	210
		Refreshments (net)	15
		Balance	3 646
	6 512		6 512

Prepare an Income and Expenditure Account for the year ended 31 December 19–2 and a balance sheet as at that date.

[West Midlands Examinations Board]

5. The Treasurer of the Turveydrop Football Club has produced the following accounts and supporting information. You are asked to prepare an Income and Expenditure Account for the year ending 31 May 19–3 and a balance sheet at the same date.

Receipts and Payments Account, year ending 31 May 19–3

	£		£
Balance at 1 June 19–2	320		
Subscriptions	2 460	Groundsman	3 000
Bar income	8 200	Bar purchases	5 600
Raffles	3 500	Advertising	400
Dances	2 000	Secretarial	1 400
Programmes	620	Lawnmower	1 600
Loan from bank	8 000	New clubhouse	9 000
		Dance expenses	800
		Balance at 31 May 19–3	3 300
	25 100		25 100

Subscriptions owing 31 May 19–2 £30.
                       31 May 19–3 £60.
Bar stocks 31 May 19–3 £80.

The lawnmower should be depreciated by 10 per cent.

[*London Regional Examining Board*]

*6. The Shockers Cricket Club was formed on the 1 April 19–0. From their Receipts and Payments Account shown below, you are required to prepare:
    (*a*) an Income and Expenditure Account for the year ended 31 March 19–1, and
    (*b*) a balance sheet as at that date.

Receipts and Payments Account (year ended 31 March 19–1)

	£		£
Loans from Members		Bar refreshments	
@ 8% per annum	450	purchased	203
Bar takings	246	Purchase of lockers	
Subscriptions from		for players	180
members	540	Travelling expenses	96
Match receipts	114	Printing	48
		Stationery and postage	28
		Rent	225
		Cricket league fees	69
		Rates and insurance	150
		Purchase of sporting	
		equipment	152
		Balance c/d	199
	1 350		1 350

Notes at 31 March 19–1:
   (i) A stationery bill of £6 is outstanding.
   (ii) There were bar stocks valued at £48.
   (iii) The interest on loans from members was due for the full year ended 31 March 19–1.
   (iv) Rent was prepaid into the forthcoming year £25.
   (v) £80 is to be paid to the Club Treasurer for his services.

[Royal Society of Arts]

*7. The following trial balance was extracted from the books of the Newtown Social Club as at the close of business on 30 April 19–2:

	Dr. £	Cr. £
Accumulated fund 1 May 19–1		2 120
Subscriptions received		2 920
Bar stocks 1 May 19–1	1 070	
Wages of part-time staff	2 190	
Salary of secretary	750	
Bar purchases	4 280	
Rent and rates	640	
Creditors for bar supplies		440
Postages and stationery	220	
Fixtures and fittings—at cost	900	
Bar takings		6 370
Balance at bank	1 820	
Insurance	140	
Sundry expenses	210	
Accumulated depreciation of fixtures and fittings 1 May 19–1		180
Discount received		260
Cash in hand	70	
	12 290	12 290

Notes:
   (i) Wages accrued at 30 April 19–2 £120.
   (ii) Of the wages total, one-third is to be regarded as an expense of the bar.
   (iii) Bar stocks at 30 April 19–2 £1 150.
   (iv) Rent and rates prepaid at 30 April 19–2 £60.
   (v) No subscriptions were due on 1 May 19–1 but on 30 April 19–2 subscriptions due amounted to £50. No subscriptions had been paid in advance.
   (vi) Provide additional depreciation of fixtures and fittings £90.

Required:
Draw up the Bar Trading Account and Income and Expenditure Account for the year ended 30 April 19–2 together with a balance sheet as at that date.

[London Chamber of Commerce]

8. The Dyble Dance and Social Club was formed on 1 January 19–8. The Treasurer has kept the accounts using the double-entry system of book-keeping. On 31 December 19–8 the following trial balance was extracted:

	Dr. £	Cr. £
Bar takings		3 100
Bar supplies purchased	2 050	
Lighting and heating	250	
Sundry expenses	40	
Rates, rent and insurance	390	
Cleaning expenses	120	
Caretaker's wages	350	
Members' subscriptions		870
Christmas dance expenses	200	
Christmas dance ticket sales		340
Equipment	300	
Cash at bank	540	
Cash in hand	70	
	4 310	4 310

You have been asked by the Treasurer to check his accounting records before presentation to the members at the Annual General Meeting. In checking, you find that the following need to be considered:

(i) Rates prepaid £30 at 31 December 19–8.
(ii) Rent owing £40 at 31 December 19–8.
(iii) There was a bar stock of refreshments at 31 December 19–8 valued at £50.

Required:

(*a*) An Income and Expenditure Account for the year ended 31 December 19–8 clearly showing the profit or loss on the bar and on the Christmas dance.

(*b*) A balance sheet as at 31 December 19–8.

[*RSA Examinations Board*]

Manufacturing Accounts

35.1 The Manufacturing Process

In the preparation of year-end accounts so far, we have produced Trading Accounts, Profit and Loss Accounts and balance sheets. In effect, the Trading Account compares the price at which a firm buys goods with the price at which it sells them: the difference, after adjustments for opening and closing stock, is gross profit. Thus the Trading Account is ideal for businesses such as shops and wholesalers where goods are simply bought in at one price and then sold at a higher one.

Many firms, however, buy raw materials or partly manufactured goods, carry out or complete a manufacturing process, and then sell the finished product to others. Fig. 35.1 gives an indication of the manufacturing process and of the costs incurred at each stage. Let us look at some of the terms in the diagram in more detail.

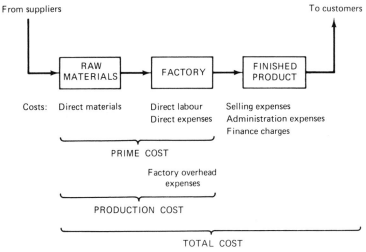

Fig. 35.1 The manufacturing process

(a) Direct Materials

This means the raw materials that are used to make up the finished product. For example, consider a plastic chair with tubular steel legs—the kind that is common in schools and colleges. The direct materials are a quantity of plastic, a length of steel tubing and four rubber feet; they do not include things like, for example, the drop of oil that is given to the machine each time it bends the steel tubing into shape. Thus raw materials are easily identifiable with the finished product, and a 'per unit' cost for materials can be calculated. As with purchases in a Trading Account, the cost of carriage in is added to the cost of direct materials.

(b) Direct Labour

This is the cost of the workforce directly engaged in producing the finished product—people such as machine operators. The labour costs of the foreman or storekeeper are *indirect labour* and are classified under *factory overhead expenses* (see (e) below). The reason for making this distinction is that a machine operator is continuously working at the production process and we can work out his or her costs per unit of production; the foreman is not part of the direct production process, however, and therefore his or her time must be charged to the whole production rather than on a 'per unit' basis.

(c) Direct Expenses

These include any special costs that can be identified with each unit produced. Suppose that you have designed a new children's toy and a manufacturer wishes to produce the product; he may propose that he pays you a royalty, perhaps twenty pence per unit, based on the number made. This is a direct cost to the manufacturer: if he makes no toys he pays you nothing; if he makes 1 000 he pays you £200, and so on.

To take another example: suppose that a manufacturer, to carry out a job for a customer, has to hire special machinery. The hire cost will be charged as a direct expense of the particular job.

You might consider that electricity should be a direct expense, because it is possible to work out the cost of electricity used by the machinery to manufacture each unit of finished product, and it is indeed regarded as such where a lot of electricity is used per unit manufactured. Where electricity is not a significant cost, however, it is included among the factory overhead expenses, since where the cost is not large it is not worth the accounting effort of calculating a 'per unit' cost.

(d) Prime Cost

Prime cost is the basic cost of manufacturing a product before the addition of factory overhead expenses, that is:

Prime cost = Direct materials + Direct labour + Direct expenses

(e) Factory Overhead Expenses

These are all the other *factory* expenses of a manufacturing business and include:

(i) indirect labour: the cost of foremen, storekeepers and others employed at the factory but not directly engaged in the manufacturing process;

(ii) depreciation of fixed assets used in the factory, such as plant and machinery;

(iii) others: factory rent, rates, heating, lighting, power, insurance, repairs and so forth.

(f) Production Cost

This is the sum of all the costs of manufacturing the product, that is:

Production cost = Prime cost + Factory overhead expenses

35.2   The Manufacturing Account

The Manufacturing Account calculates the production cost of goods completed. Other costs of a business, such as selling expenses, administration expenses and finance charges, are recorded in the Profit and Loss Account, so that the sum of production cost plus these other costs gives the total cost for a business. Deducting the total cost from total sales revenues gives its net profit for the period.

The layout of a Manufacturing Account is shown in Fig. 35.2. Work through this layout carefully; it will help when you are preparing year-end accounts for a manufacturing business.

Points to notice:

(a) The Manufacturing Account deals with three types of stock:

raw materials,
work in progress (representing the value of work passing through the factory but incomplete at the financial year-end), and
finished goods.

(b) The cost of raw materials used is calculated as follows:

opening stock of raw materials
add purchases
less closing stock.

(c)   Direct labour and direct expenses are added to the cost of raw materials used to give prime cost.

(d)   To prime cost are added the factory overhead expenses.

(e)   At the end of a Manufacturing Account an adjustment is made for work in progress. This is carried out in the same way as for other stocks, that is: *add* opening stock, *less* closing stock.

(f)   A Manufacturing Account is easily balanced! Simply enter the total of the debit side on to the credit side. This total is then described as 'production cost of goods completed' and is carried down to the Trading Account.

(g)   The Trading Account is prepared in the same way as before, except that (i) the opening and closing stock figures are those for finished goods and (ii) instead of (or in addition to) purchases, the figure for production cost is brought down from the Manufacturing Account.

Manufacturing, Trading and Profit and Loss Accounts of . . . for the year ended . . .

	£	£		£
Opening stock of raw materials		x	Production cost of goods	
Add Purchases of raw materials	x		completed c/d	x
Add Carriage in on raw materials	x			
		x		
		x		
Less Closing stock of raw materials		x		
Cost of raw materials used		x		
Direct labour		x		
Direct expenses		x		
Prime cost		x		
Factory overhead expenses:				
Indirect labour	x			
Depreciation of plant	x			
Factory rent, rates, etc	x			
		x		
		x		
Add Opening stock of				
work in progress		x		
		x		
Less Closing stock of				
work in progress		x		
		x		x
Opening stock of finished goods		x	Sales	x
Add Production cost of goods				
completed b/d		x		
Add Purchases of finished				
goods		x		
		x		
Less Closing stock of finished goods		x		
Cost of goods sold		x		
Gross profit c/d		x		
		x		x
Selling expenses		x	Gross profit b/d	x
Administration expenses		x		
Finance charges		x		
Net profit		x		
		x		x

A balance sheet will then follow in the normal way.

*Fig. 35.2 The layout of a Manufacturing, Trading and Profit and Loss
Account*

(*h*) The Profit and Loss Account is completed in the normal way, with care being taken to ensure that no factory expenses are entered. (**Examination note.** Sometimes a question will ask you to apportion costs between factory and office—clearly the factory part of the costs are included in the Manufacturing Account, while the office part of the costs is shown in the firm's Profit and Loss Account.)

(*i*) A balance sheet will conclude the year-end accounts and will be completed in the normal way. The only slight difference in the balance sheet is that all three types of stock are included in current assets, as follows:

Current assets:	£	£
Stocks: raw materials	*x*	
work in progress	*x*	
finished goods	*x*	
		x
Debtors, etc.		*x*

35.3   Manufacturing Accounts—a Worked Example

Question

The following figures relate to the accounts of YZ Manufacturing for the year ended 31 December 19–0:

	£
Stocks at 1 January 19–0:	
raw materials	3 186
work in progress	2 745
finished goods	4 264
Stocks at 31 December 19–0:	
raw materials	4 479
work in progress	3 621
finished goods	9 651
Purchases of raw materials	23 766
Purchases of finished goods	2 431
Sales of finished goods	102 695
Rent and rates	3 292
Manufacturing wages	33 463
Factory power	1 765
Factory heating and lighting	1 237
Factory expenses and maintenance	1 819
Salaries and wages	22 870
Advertising	4 217
Office expenses	1 786
Depreciation of plant and machinery	2 450
Depreciation of office equipment	750

One-half of salaries and wages and three-quarters of rent and rates are to be treated as a manufacturing charge.

You are required to prepare the Manufacturing, Trading and Profit and Loss Accounts for the year to show clearly (*a*) cost of raw materials used, (*b*) prime cost, (*c*) cost of factory overheads, (*d*) production costs of goods completed, (*e*) cost of goods sold, (*f*) gross profit for the year, and (*g*) net profit for the year.

Answer

Manufacturing, Trading and Profit and Loss Accounts of YZ Manufacturing for the year ended 31 December 19–0

	£	£		£
Opening stock of raw materials		3 186	Production cost of goods completed c/d	76 235
Add Purchases of raw materials		23 766		
		26 952		
Less Closing stock of raw materials		4 479		
Cost of raw materials used		22 473		
Manufacturing wages		33 463		
Prime cost		55 936		
Factory overhead expenses:				
Rent and rates	2 469			
Power	1 765			
Heating and lighting	1 237			
Expenses and maintenance	1 819			
Salaries and wages	11 435			
Depreciation of plant and machinery	2 450			
		21 175		
		77 111		
Add Opening stock of work in progress		2 745		
		79 856		
Less Closing stock of work in progress		3 621		
		76 235		76 235

Opening stock of finished goods	4 264	Sales	102 695
Add Production costs of goods completed b/d	76 235		
Add Purchases of finished goods	2 431		
	82 930		
Less Closing stock of finished goods	9 651		
Cost of goods sold	73 279		
Gross profit c/d	29 416		
	102 695		102 695
Rent and rates	823	Gross profit b/d	29 416
Salaries and wages	11 435		
Advertising	4 217		
Office expenses	1 786		
Depreciation of office equipment	750		
Net profit	10 405		
	29 416		29 416

35.4   Questions

*1. From the following list of balances of Alan Coat at 28 February 19–3, draw up a Manufacturing Account for the year ending that day:

	£
1 March 19–2 Stocks of raw materials	1 000
Work in progress	400
28 February 19–3 Stocks of raw materials	2 000
Work in progress	600
Direct wages	4 000
Supervision wages	2 000
Purchase of raw materials	12 000
Fuel and power	1 000
Direct expenses	200
Rent and rates	400
Depreciation of plant	300
Insurance of factory	100
Carriage inwards	200

[*London Regional Examining Board*]

*2. The following figures relate to the accounts of Hughes Ltd, a manufacturing business, for the year ended 31 December 19–1:

	£
Stocks of raw materials at 1 January 19–1	3 186
Stocks of raw materials at 31 December 19–1	4 479
Stocks of finished goods at 1 January 19–1	4 264
Stocks of finished goods at 31 December 19–1	9 651
Purchases of raw materials	23 766

Sales of finished goods	79 695
Rent and rates	3 292
Manufacturing wages	23 463
Manufacturing power	765
Manufacturing heat and light	237
Manufacturing expenses and maintenance	819
Wages and salaries	13 870
Advertising	2 217
Office expenses	786
Depreciation of plant and machinery	745

One-half of 'wages and salaries' and three-quarters of the 'rent and rates' are to be treated as a manufacturing charge.

Required:

Manufacturing, Trading and Profit and Loss Accounts for the year to show clearly (*a*) prime cost, (*b*) factory cost of goods completed, (*c*) cost of goods sold, (*d*) gross profit for the year and (*e*) net profit for the year.

3. The following balances are taken from the books of David Farr at 28 February 19–4. You are required to draw up a Manufacturing, Trading and Profit and Loss Account for the year ending 28 February 19–4 and a balance sheet as at that date.

	Raw materials £	£	Finished goods £
Stocks at 1 March 19–3	8 400		3 800
Purchases	52 000		——
Stock at 28 February 19–4	2 600		12 400
Work in progress 1 March 19–3	1 500		
28 February 19–4	2 400		
Factory wages		18 000	
Factory power		2 500	
Factory overheads		9 500	
Machinery and plant at cost		30 000	
Office salaries		6 500	
Sales		86 000	
Office heat and light		4 500	
General office expenses		3 500	
Factory premises		60 000	
Debtors		8 500	
Creditors		10 500	
Capital Account		115 700	
Cash at bank		3 500	

Depreciation on machinery and plant is to be calculated at 10 per cent.

[*London Regional Examining Board*]

4. Gordon Dace, a manufacturer, extracted the following trial balance at the end of his financial year, 30 September Year 7:

	Dr.	Cr.
	£	£
Freehold premises (cost)	120 000	
Plant and machinery (cost)	60 000	
Provision for depreciation—plant and machinery		18 000
Office fixtures and fittings (cost)	8 000	
Provision for depreciation—fixtures and fittings		1 600
Stocks at 1 October Year 6:		
Raw materials	8 500	
Finished goods	6 320	
Purchases of raw materials	56 000	
Bad debts	170	
Debtors and creditors	4 820	2 780
Office wages and salaries	30 140	
Rates [factory £610, office £220]	830	
Insurance [factory £450, office £150]	600	
Light/heat and power [factory £1 210, office £210]	1 420	
Miscellaneous expenses	350	
Repairs and renewals [factory £1 070, office £230]	1 300	
Telephone [factory £150, office £250]	400	
Drawings	15 000	
Balance at bank	12 170	
Cash in hand	100	
Manufacturing wages	62 000	
Sales		186 600
Capital Account		179 140
	£388 120	£388 120

The following additional information is available:
  (i) Closing stocks at 30 September Year 7 are as follows:

Raw materials	£10 500
Finished goods	£7 410

 (ii) Provide for depreciation as follows :

Plant and machinery [factory]	£6 000
Fixtures and fittings [office]	£800

Required:
  Prepare Gordon Dace's Manufacturing, Trading and Profit and Loss Accounts for the year ended 30 September Year 7, using such information as is required from the above trial balance.
  Note: A balance sheet is *not* required.

[*London Chamber of Commerce*]

Departmental Accounts

36.1 Introduction

A large store is often divided into several different departments such as furniture, clothes, kitchenware, electrical goods and so on; many businesses trade in several types of products. *Departmental accounts* are used to analyse the trading results of the different departments or divisions within a business.

A department does not usually operate a double-entry book-keeping system of its own. Instead, the book-keeping for the whole business is generally kept by a central department whose accounts distinguish between the purchases and sales made either by different departments, or in respect of different products. This analysis is usually made in analysed journals (see Unit 17.3) for purchases, sales and returns. In a large store departmental sales figures can be readily obtained from the cash tills in the store, the cash receipts being analysed between the various departments by a coding system on the tills. You don't have to go far to see departmental accounting in operation!

36.2 Departmental Trading Accounts

Once an analysis of purchases and sales between departments has been made it only requires a departmental stocktake at the end of the accounting period in order to prepare a Trading Account for each department.

Example

XYZ Store has the following information about its three departments, X, Y and Z, for the year ended 31 December 19–4:

		£
Sales:	X	100 000
	Y	75 000
	Z	125 000
Purchases:	X	78 000
	Y	70 000
	Z	118 000
Stock at 1 Jan. 19–4:	X	12 000
	Y	14 000
	Z	23 000
Stock at 31 Dec. 19–4:	X	12 000
	Y	18 000
	Z	21 000

Prepare a departmental Trading Account for the year.

Answer

XYZ Store
Departmental Trading Account for the year ended 31 December 19–4

	X	Y	Z	Total		X	Y	Z	Total
	£	£	£	£		£	£	£	£
Opening stock	12 000	14 000	23 000	49 000	Sales	100 000	75 000	125 000	300 000
Add Purchases	78 000	70 000	118 000	266 000					
	90 000	84 000	141 000	315 000					
Less Closing stock	12 000	18 000	21 000	51 000					
	78 000	66 000	120 000	264 000					
Gross profit c/d	22 000	9 000	5 000	36 000					
	100 000	75 000	125 000	300 000		100 000	75 000	125 000	300 000

The gross profit figures might be used by management to investigate the poor performance of a particular department (but see Unit 36.4).

36.3   Departmental Profit and Loss Accounts

Some departmental accounting systems attempt to carry the analysis further than a Trading Account by including a departmental Profit and Loss Account. Where this is prepared, each department must be charged with its share of the various expense items along the following lines:

(a) Expenses directly attributable to an individual department should be charged to that department.

(b) Selling expenses, such as advertising, should be charged to departments on the basis of sales. Administration expenses and general expenses are often dealt with in the same way.

(c) For all other business expenses a suitable basis of apportionment should be used. For instance, for rent, rates, building insurance, heating and lighting the expenses could be divided between departments in proportion to the floor areas they occupy. For insurance premiums on stock, the basis might be the average value of stock.

Example
XYZ Store (from the previous example) has the following expenses for the year ended 31 December 19–4:

	£
Rent and rates	8 000
Administration	6 000
Heating and lighting	2 000
Salaries: Department X	8 000
Y	3 000
Z	3 500

Rent and rates, heating and lighting are to be apportioned on the basis of floor area which is X one-quarter, Y one-quarter, and Z one-half. Administration is to be apportioned on the basis of sales.

Prepare a departmental Profit and Loss Account for the year, using the departmental gross profits from the previous example.

XYZ Store
Departmental Profit and Loss Account for the year ended 31 December 19–4

	X	Y	Z	Total		X	Y	Z	Total
	£	£	£	£		£	£	£	£
Rent and rates	2 000	2 000	4 000	8 000	Gross profit b/d	22 000	9 000	5 000	36 000
Administration	2 000	1 500	2 500	6 000					
Heating and lighting	500	500	1 000	2 000					
Salaries	8 000	3 000	3 500	14 500					
Net profit (net loss)	9 500	2 000	(6 000)	5 500					
	22 000	9 000	5 000	36 000		22 000	9 000	5 000	36 000

Point to notice:
Net loss of £6 000 is shown in brackets, and *deducted*.

While departmental Trading and Profit and Loss Accounts are often prepared, it would be unusual to find the assets and liabilities of the balance sheet divided among the departments.

36.4 Loss-making Departments

There are dangers in apportioning fixed expenses such as rent and rates, heating and lighting, and then using the results to decide whether or not a department should close. Should the calculation seem to identify a 'loss-making' department, it must be remembered that closing such a department is unlikely to reduce these expenses significantly, because they will still largely have to be paid. Moreover, closing one department may well affect the sales of others; closing a furniture department, for instance, is likely to result in falling sales in the carpet department. The management should, instead, look for a more profitable use of the floor space occupied by the poor-performing department.

36.5 Questions

*1. (a) Dunhill's Department Store, which has two departments—Department A and Department B—produced the following balances on the 30 April 19–2.

	Department A	Department B
	£	£
Stock (1 April)	600	800
Sales	1 136	1 263
Purchases	1 008	145
Stock (30 April)	810	465

Wages £150, Telephone £114, Lighting £39, Advertising £147.

Note: Expenditure items to be apportioned to Department A—one-third and Department B—two-thirds.

Draw up a Trading, Profit and Loss Account, showing a Department A, Department B and a Total Column.

(b) Why does a departmental store keep separate accounts for its major departments?

[*South Western Examinations Board*]

*2. Dedlock has two departments (A and B).

Some items of income and expenditure are allocated directly to the two departments. The remaining expenses are to be allocated to each department in the ratio: **A** two-fifths, **B** three-fifths.

You are required to draw up a Trading and Profit and Loss Account for the firm in columnar form so as to show the gross and net profit for each department and a balance sheet for the firm as a whole.

Items recorded separately for each department:

	A	B
	£	£
Opening stock	8 000	12 000
Purchases	16 000	20 000
Closing stock	9 000	4 000
Sales	38 000	52 000
Wages	10 000	15 000
Salaries	5 000	8 000

Expenses to be allocated between departments are:

	£
Heat and light	4 000
Rent and rates	1 200
Carriage inwards	1 000
Carriage outwards	500
Office expenses	2 000

Other balances are:

	£
Creditors	8 000
Debtors	2 000
Cash at bank	15 000
Capital	21 700

[*London Regional Examining Board*]

3. From the following list of balances taken from the books of the Albion Department Store, prepare departmental Trading and Profit and Loss Accounts for the year ended 31 December 19–2, so as to show the gross net profits of each department. The expenses are to be apportioned between the departments in proportion to their respective turnovers (sales).

	Dr. £	Cr. £
Stocks 1 January 19–2: A Department	5 040	
B Department	4 560	
Purchases: A Department	14 600	
B Department	11 120	
Wages: A Department	2 608	
B Department	1 640	
Sales: A Department		36 000
B Department		24 000
Shop assistants' salaries and wages	7 980	
Travellers' commissions and expenses	4 000	
Telephone and postages	220	
Rates	660	
Discounts	230	
Display equipment	2 600	

Notes:

(i) Stocks 31 December 19–2:

    A Department   £9 824

    B Department   £6 528

(ii) Depreciate display equipment by 15 per cent per annum.

(iii) Rates prepaid £180.

[Associated Lancashire Schools Examining Board]

Unit Thirty-seven

Bills of Exchange

37.1 What is a Bill of Exchange?

A bill of exchange (Fig. 37.1) is a means of obtaining acknowledgement for a debt which will be paid, usually at a certain date in the future. When a business sells goods on credit to a customer, it normally waits for payment. An alternative would be to ask the debtor to agree to make the payment at a certain date by accepting a bill of exchange. A formal definition of a bill of exchange is: *an unconditional order in writing addressed by one person to another, signed by the person giving it, requiring the person to whom it is addressed to pay on demand, or at a fixed or determinable future time, a sum certain in money to or to the order of a specified person or bearer.*

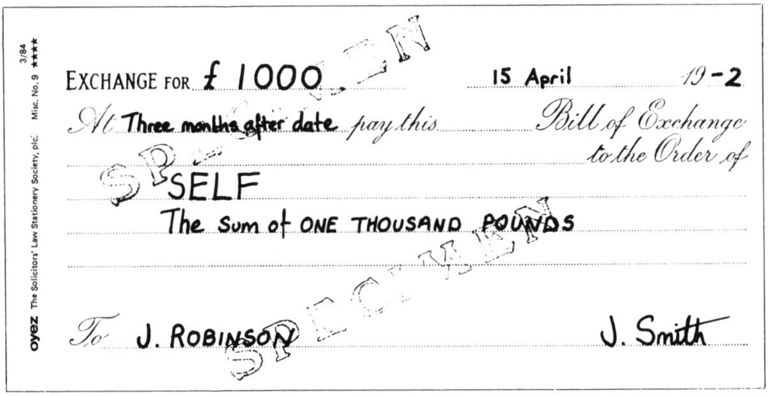
oyez The Solicitors' Law Stationery Society, plc. Misc. No. 9 3/84 ****

EXCHANGE FOR £ 1000 15 April 19-2

At Three months after date pay this Bill of Exchange to the Order of

SELF

The Sum of ONE THOUSAND POUNDS

To J. ROBINSON J. Smith

SPECIMEN

Fig. 37.1 A bill of exchange

Bills of exchange are used widely in international trade, and are also used between buyers and sellers in the same country. In both cases the bill may be either payable on demand, or worded so as to make the payment due at some future date, thus giving the debtor a period of credit.

37.2 Parties to a Bill of Exchange

There are initially three *parties* to a bill of exchange (that is, three people are concerned in the transaction): drawer, drawee and payee. The *drawer* is the person who has drawn up, or prepared, the bill; the *drawee* is the person on whom it is drawn and who has to make payment; the *payee* is the person to whom the money will be paid. On the bill shown in Fig. 37.1, the drawer is Smith, the drawee is Robinson, and the payee is also Smith. In this example, therefore, Smith must have sold goods to Robinson who has agreed to settle by means of a bill of exchange. Here two parties, Smith and Robinson, are concerned, but there can be three different parties to a bill at the start: if Smith owed £1 000 to Harris who was prepared to accept the money direct from Robinson in settlement of the debt due, then the bill would be drawn to read 'three months after date pay to Harris or his order the sum of one thousand pounds'. Harris is now the payee.

A bill that is payable at some definite future date is known as a *term bill*—because it is drawn for a certain term—and must be sent to the drawee for *acceptance*. This is done by the drawee 'accepting' liability by signing the bill and agreeing to pay the bill on the due date. The bill shown in Fig. 37.1 would be sent to Robinson for acceptance; when he has signed it he is known as the *acceptor*. If the bill had been payable at sight—a *sight bill*—there would be no need to obtain the acceptance of Robinson because he would be expected to pay immediately on 'sight' of the bill. If a bill is payable 'three months after sight', it would need to be presented for acceptance and the acceptance date recorded, in order to determine the date of payment.

37.3   The Bill of Exchange in Business

The essential point about a term bill of exchange is that it allows a period of credit—often three months—before payment is made. For example, Ann Black, who deals in jewellery, may supply goods to a buyer and be prepared to allow payment to be postponed until the buyer has had an opportunity of selling the goods and receiving the cash. In order to acknowledge the debt that exists between them, Miss Black may draw a bill of exchange for her customer to accept and return to her. Miss Black, as the holder of an accepted bill of exchange can:

(a) hold the bill until the date of payment;

(b) sell the bill for face value, less a discount amount, to her own bank, to a specialist discount house or to any other person;

(c) ask her bank for a loan against the bill.

So Miss Black, even though she has allowed her customer a period of credit by obtaining acceptance of a bill of exchange, can herself obtain immediate finance against the bill, using options (b) or (c); or, if she does not need the money urgently, she can hold the bill until the date of payment (a). She could also use an accepted bill to settle a debt that she owes to someone else, provided that her creditor is willing to agree to such an arrangement.

A person holding an accepted bill of exchange and due to receive payment has an asset called 'bills receivable'; the acceptor of a bill, who is due to make the payment, has a liability called 'bills payable'.

37.4   Accounting Entries

(a) Holding the Bill until Date of Payment

Example

Adams supplies goods on 1 January 19–1 to Brown who, on that date, accepts a bill of exchange payable in three months' time for £500. Record the entries in the accounts of (i) Adams and (ii) Brown, including the payment made on 1 April.

Answer

(i) *Accounts of Adams:*

Sales

		19–1	£
		1 Jan. Brown	500

Brown

19–1	£	19–1	£
1 Jan. Sales	500	1 Jan. Bills receivable	500

Bills receivable

19–1	£	19–1	£
1 Jan. Brown	500	1 Apr. Bank	500

Bank

19–1	£
1 Apr. Bills receivable	500

(ii) *Accounts of Brown:*

Purchases

19–1	£
1 Jan. Adams	500

Adams

19–1	£	19–1	£
1 Jan. Bills payable	500	1 Jan. Purchases	500

Bills payable

19–1	£	19–1	£
1 Apr. Bank	500	1 Jan. Adams	500

Bank

		19–1	£
		1 Apr. Bills payable	500

You can see that the basic book-keeping entries for bills of exchange are quite simple. The credit sale or credit purchase is dealt with as usual and then, as payment is to be by means of a bill of exchange, the seller transfers the amount from the personal account to Bills Receivable Account, while the buyer transfers it to Bills Payable Account.

If Adams prepared a balance sheet at any time between 1 January and 1 April 19–1, the balance of Bills Receivable Account, £500, would be shown under the heading of 'current assets'; in Brown's balance sheet it would appear under 'current liabilities'.

(b) Discounting the Bill

In (a) above, Adams kept the bill until maturity. But as we saw earlier, the holder of an accepted bill who requires finance may discount it with a bank or discount house and receive the face value, less discounting charges. Suppose that Adams discounts the bill with his bank on 10 January, the discounting charges being £14. The accounts of Brown are unaffected, but those of Adams will appear as follows:

Sales

		19–1	£
		1 Jan. Brown	500

Brown

19–1	£	19–1	£
1 Jan. Sales	500	1 Jan. Bills receivable	500

Bills receivable

19–1	£	19–1	£
1 Jan. Brown	500	10 Jan. Bank	486
		10 Jan. Discounting charges	14
	500		500

Bank

19–1	£
10 Jan. Bills receivable	486

Discounting charges

19–1	£
10 Jan. Bills receivable	14

The balance of Discounting Charges Account is transferred to the debit of Adams' Profit and Loss Account at the end of the accounting period. If Adams prepared a balance sheet after 10 January, no current asset would be shown for bills receivable.

(c) Using the Bill as Security for a Bank Overdraft

If Adams uses a bill of exchange as security for a bank loan or overdraft, the accounting entries remain as in (a), because the current asset of bills receivable still belongs to him. The accounts of Brown are unchanged.

(d) Using an Accepted Bill to Settle Another Debt

Adams could use the accepted bill from Brown to settle, either wholly or in part, an amount owing to a creditor. Suppose that on 20 January he passes on the bill to Clark, a creditor for £700. The accounts of Adams will be:

Sales

		19–1	£
		1 Jan. Brown	500

Brown

19–1	£	19–1	£
1 Jan. Sales	500	1 Jan. Bills receivable	500

Bills receivable

19–1	£	19–1	£
1 Jan. Brown	500	20 Jan. Clark	500

Clark

19–1	£	19–1	£
20 Jan. Bills receivable	500	1 Jan. Balance b/d	700

Brown, the acceptor of the bill, will now pay Clark instead of Adams; otherwise Brown's accounts remain unchanged.

37.5   Dishonour of a Bill of Exchange

Should a bill of exchange be dishonoured (that is, the money is not paid) the debt on the debtor's personal account must be re-established by debiting the account with the amount of the dishonoured bill.

Example

On 15 January 19–3, goods were sold to Davis for £200 and he agreed to accept a bill of exchange payable to us. Upon presentation of the bill on the date for payment (15 April 19–3), it is dishonoured.

The book-keeping entries in our accounts are:

Sales

		19–3	£
		15 Jan. Davis	200

Davis

19–3	£	19–3	£
15 Jan. Sales	200	15 Jan. Bills receivable	200
15 Apr. Bills receivable (bill dishonoured)	200		

Bills receivable

19–3	£	19–3	£
15 Jan. Davis	200	15 Apr. Davis (bill dishonoured)	200

If any charges or costs have to be paid in connection with dishonour of the bill they are passed to the debtor's account as follows:

> *Dr.* Debtor's account ⎫
> *Cr.* Bank Account   ⎬ with amount of charges
>   ⎭

37.6 Questions

*1. Arthur Scott, a sole trader, has the following transactions:

19–1

1 Sept. He owes Frederick Ames £320 in respect of goods supplied. Ames draws a bill of exchange on Scott, payable one month after date, for this amount. The bill is 'accepted' by Scott.

3 Sept. Robert Potter owes Scott £270 in respect of goods supplied and Scott draws a bill of exchange on him for that amount. This is 'accepted' by Potter. The bill is payable one month after date.

7 Sept. Percival Jones owes Scott £190 in respect of goods supplied and Scott draws a bill of exchange on him for that amount. This is 'accepted' by Jones and is payable two months after date.

11 Sept. Scott owes Thomas Jeffries £150 in respect of goods supplied. Jeffries draws a bill of exchange on Scott for that amount. The bill is payable one month after date and is 'accepted' by Scott.

All the bills of exchange are paid on the due dates except that for £190, which was dishonoured. Bank charges £5.

Required:

Draw up the personal accounts, the Bills Receivable Account and the Bills Payable Account as they would appear in the ledger of Arthur Scott. Also required are the entries as they would appear in Scott's cash book.

Note. Journal entries are *not* required.

[London Chamber of Commerce]

*2. Thomas Robinson, a sole trader, had the following transactions:

19–1

2 Jan. Robinson drew a bill of exchange for £470, on Arthur Parsons, payable one month after date. This was accepted by Parsons.

5 Jan. The bill of exchange for £470 was discounted by Robinson at his bankers. Bank interest charged £22.

9 Jan. Norman Martin drew a bill of exchange for £262 on Thomas Robinson payable two months after sight. This was in full settlement of a debt of £274.

14 Jan. Thomas Robinson accepted the bill of exchange drawn by Norman Martin.

On the due dates the bill of exchange for £470 was dishonoured but that for £262 was paid.

Required:

Draw up the journal entries to record the above transactions in the books of Thomas Robinson, including the dishonour of the first bill of exchange and the payment of the second. Cash entries should be journalized.

[London Chamber of Commerce]

3. On 31 March 19–4, Harold Ives, a sole trader, had the following balances in his ledger:–

W. Adams	£470	*Dr.* balance
F. Brown	£260	*Dr.* balance
M. Church	£330	*Cr.* balance

During the month of April 19–4 Ives had the following transactions:

1 Apr. 19–4 Drew a bill of exchange for £400 on W. Adams at 1 month after date (Bill no 1). This was accepted by Adams.

10 Apr. 19–4 Discounted Bill no 1 with his bank. Bank interest £20.

17 Apr. 19–4 Church drew a bill of exchange on Ives at one month after date (Bill no 2). This was for £300 and was in *full settlement* of the amount due by Ives to Church. The bill was accepted by Ives.

24 Apr. 19–4 Drew a bill of exchange for £260 on Brown at one month after date (Bill no 3). This was accepted by Brown.

Bills 1 and 2 were paid on the due dates but Bill no 3 was dishonoured when presented for payment.

Required:

(*a*) Draw up the ledger accounts of Adams, Brown and Church as they should appear in Ives' ledger to record *all* the above transactions.

(*b*) Draw up the appropriate cash book entries.

(*c*) Draw up the Bills Receivable Account and Bills Payable Account as they should appear in Ives' ledger.

[*London Chamber of Commerce*]

Partnership Accounts

38.1 Sole Traders and Partnerships

The year-end accounts of businesses that we have looked at so far in this book have been those of *sole traders*, that is, individuals who are in business on their own. Sole traders run businesses such as shops, factories, farms and garages. Their businesses are generally small because the owner usually has limited capital with which to start; profits are often low and, after the owner has taken out drawings, anything remaining is ploughed back into the business.

A *partnership* may be the logical growth of a sole-trader firm (see Unit 39.1) or it may be formed to set up a new business. A partnership is defined by the Partnership Act of 1890 as *the relation which subsists between persons carrying on a business in common with a view of profit*. As there is more than one owner, a partnership is often larger than a sole-trader business, and there is likely to be more capital.

38.2 Legal Points

A partnership consists of between two and twenty partners, although this maximum can be exceeded by certain types of partnership. In law a partnership can be created orally, by conduct or in writing: however, it is sensible for partners to draw up a written *deed of partnership* setting out their rights and duties. As far as the accounts are concerned, a deed of partnership normally covers the following points:

(*a*) the capital to be contributed by each partner;
(*b*) the division of profits or losses between partners;
(*c*) if any salaries are to be paid to partners;
(*d*) the rate of interest, if any, to be allowed on capital;
(*e*) the rate of interest, if any, to be charged on partners' drawings.

We will consider each of these points more fully later on.

If there is no deed of partnership, or if the deed does not cover a particular point, then the rules laid down in the Partnership Act apply. The accounting points from the Act include the following rules:

(*a*) profits and losses are to be shared equally among partners;
(*b*) no partner is entitled to a salary;
(*c*) a partner is not entitled to interest on capital;
(*d*) no interest is to be charged on drawings;
(*e*) where a partner puts more money into a business than he has agreed to contribute, interest will be paid on the excess at 5 per cent per year.

Examination note. It is important to know and bear in mind the accounting points covered by the Act, particularly points (*a*) and (*b*). If a partnership deed—or the information given to you in a question—does not cover an important accounting point, such as the profit-sharing ratio, then the rules in the Act will apply.

38.3   The Accounts of a Partnership

An important difference between the accounts of a sole trader and those of a partnership is that each partner has a separate *Capital Account*, which records the amount of capital contributed by that partner. The only transactions on this account record any permanent increases or decreases in capital. In addition, in most partnerships each partner has an extra account—a *Current Account*, which records drawings, salary paid (if any), share of profits or losses, interest allowed on capital (if any) and interest charged on drawings (if any). The Capital Account has a fixed balance, while that of the Current Account fluctuates.

By using a Capital Account and Current Account, the capital of each partner is kept separate from transactions involving share of profits, drawings and so on. Normally a partner's Current Account (like the Capital Account) has a credit balance, which represents the amount of profits not yet drawn out of the business. Sometimes, though, the balance of a partner's Current Account can be in debit—this indicates that the account is 'overdrawn', that is, that drawings have exceeded the share of profits.

While most partnerships use separate Capital and Current Accounts for each partner, it is possible to put all the transactions for a partner through his or her Capital Account, without distinguishing between capital and current amounts. This is the way in which a sole trader's Capital Account operates. For a partnership, it is better practice to operate separate Capital and Current Accounts.

A partner's Current Account might look like this:

Partner X: Current Account

	£		£
Drawings		Balance b/d	
Interest charged on		Share of net profit	
drawings[1]		Salary[1]	
Balance c/d		Interest allowed on	
		capital[1]	
	——		——
	═══		═══
		Balance b/d	

[1] assuming that these are allowed by the partnership deed

38.4   Division of Profits and Losses

The Partnership Act states that, in the absence of agreement to the contrary, profits and losses are to be shared equally among the partners, even if partners have contributed different amounts of capital. For example, if A and B are in partnership and the net profit for 19–2 is £12 000, the Partnership Act provides for A and B to take £6 000 each—even if A's capital is £20 000 and B's is £4 000. But this clause from the Partnership Act only applies if the deed of partnership makes no mention of the division of profits and losses. Thus, many partnerships agree to share profits and losses in a certain way—perhaps in the same proportions that capital has been contributed. If this were so with A and B's partnership, they would share profits and losses in the proportions 5:1 respectively. Of the £12 000 profits for the year, A would then receive £10 000 and B £2 000.

Examination note. If a question does not tell you the profit-sharing ratio, you can assume that the Partnership Act applies, and that profit and losses are shared equally.

38.5   Partnership Salaries

We saw in Unit 38.2 that the Partnership Act rules lay down that no partner is entitled to a salary; this too, however, may be varied in the deed of partnership. In practice a salary is usually paid to any partner who devotes the whole or most of his time to the business, while others do not. In the year-end accounts of a partnership a partner's salary must not be included amongst the wages and salaries figure shown in Profit and Loss Account—this figure refers to payments to employees, not to the owners of the business, that is, the partners. Instead, it is shown in the Partnership Appropriation Account (see Unit 38.8) before calculation of the share of profits.

38.6   Interest Allowed on Capital

Although not permitted by the Partnership Act rules, a deed of partnership may allow interest to be paid on partners' Capital Account balances, and may fix the rate that is to be paid. Interest is often allowed on capital in a partnership where profits are shared equally, but where the partners have differing Capital Account balances. Without an allowance for interest on capital, a partner with a small amount of capital would gain in the overall share-out against one who has put a great deal of money into the business.

For example, suppose that partners C and D have Capital Account balances of £5 000 and £10 000 respectively, and that profits and losses are shared equally. If the profits for the year are £5 000, then C and D receive £2 500 each.

If, however, interest is allowed on capital at 10 per cent each year then, using the same profit figure:

	C	D
Interest allowed on capital	£500	£1 000
Remainder of profits (£3 500) shared equally	£1 750	£1 750
	£2 250	£2 750

Thus allowing interest to be paid on capital has enabled a greater share of the profit to go to the partner with the higher Capital Account balance.

38.7 Interest Charged on Partners' Drawings

Sometimes a partnership deed may make provision for interest to be charged at a certain rate on partners' drawings. This is imposed to discourage partners from taking too much money out of the business, in the form of drawings, too early in the financial year. The interest is charged to the partner as a 'penalty' because it is better from the firm's point of view that profits should be left in the business for as long as possible.

Examination note. By now you may be concerned about answering questions on the various accounting matters that could be included in a deed of partnership. A question at this level is most unlikely to include more than two of the points mentioned in Units 38.5 to 38.7. Either it will tell you directly what is required—for example, 'pay a salary of £5 000 to partner X'—or it will require a short calculation using convenient rates of interest, such as 'allow interest on partners' Capital Accounts at the rate of 10 per cent per year'.

38.8 Partnership Year-end Accounts

Preparing the year-end accounts of a partnership is a little different from preparing a sole trader's. The Trading and Profit and Loss Accounts remain the same, however—remember *not* to include a partner's salary in the Profit and Loss Account expenses. The net profit or loss is carried down to an account called an *Appropriation Account*. In this account net profit or loss is *appropriated* (divided) among the partners in accordance with the terms of the partnership deed and/or the requirements of the Partnership Act rules. An Appropriation Account might be laid out as follows:

X, Y and Z in partnership
Appropriation Account for the year ended 31 December 19–9

	£		£
Salary: X		Net profit b/d (from Profit	
Interest allowed on		and Loss Account)	
partners' capitals: X		Interest charged on	
Y		partners' drawings: X	
Z		Y	
Share of remaining profits: X		Z	
Y			
Z			

Points to notice:

(*a*) The following are allowed or charged before calculating the share of remaining profits:

> partners' salaries;
> interest allowed on partners' salaries;
> interest charged on partners' drawings.

(*b*) All profits are shared out among the partners—there is no 'balance c/d' on the account.

The balance sheet of a partnership differs from a sole trader's only in the layout of the capital section. It is necessary to show first the Capital Accounts and then the Current Accounts of each partner. The changes in Current Accounts, such as salaries, profit shares, interest allowed on capital, drawings and so on are usually shown in detail on the balance sheet. Care should be exercised in the layout of this section of the balance sheet, however. A suitable layout of a partnership balance sheet is as follows (imaginary figures have been used, and figures in brackets are deducted):

D and E in partnership
Balance sheet (extract) as at 31 December 19–3

	£			£	£
Fixed assets:	*x*	Capital Accounts:			
		D		20 000	
		E		30 000	
Current assets:	*x*				50 000
		Current Accounts:			
			D	E	
			£	£	
		Balances b/d	750	(250)[1]	
		Share of profits	3 000	4 500	
		Salary	4 000	—	
		Interest on capital	1 000	1 500	
			8 750	5 750	
		Drawings	(8 500)	(4 500)	
		Interest on drawings	(400)	(750)	
		Balances c/d	(150)[1]	500	350
					50 350
		Current liabilities:			*x*
	x				*x*

[1] debit balances

Point to notice:

Where only a Capital Account is in use for each partner, rather than separate Capital and Current Accounts, then all transactions, such as share of profits or drawings, must appear on that Capital Account.

38.9   Partnership Year-end Accounts—a Worked Example

Work through this example carefully—it will help you as a 'guideline' when attempting questions yourself.

Example

The following trial balance was extracted from the books of R, S and T at 31 December 19–9 (a Trading Account has already been prepared):

	Dr. £	Cr. £
Capital Accounts: R		60 000
S		40 000
T		20 000
Current Accounts at 1 Jan. 19–9: R		2 000
S		3 000
T	1 000	
Drawings for year: R	12 000	
S	8 000	
T	10 000	
Gross profit for year		70 000
Expenses	42 500	
Fixed assets	110 000	
Current assets	48 750	
Current liabilities		37 250
	232 250	232 250

Required:

The preparation of a Profit and Loss Account and an Appropriation Account for the year ended 31 December 19–9, together with a balance sheet at that date, after taking the following matters into account:

(i) Interest is to be allowed at 6 per cent per annum on partners' Capital Accounts.

(ii) £5 000 is to be allowed as a salary to T.

(iii) Profits and losses are to be shared between R, S and T in the proportions of one-half, one-quarter and one-quarter respectively.

Answer

R, S and T in partnership
Profit and Loss Account for the year ended 31 December 19–9

	£		£
Expenses	42 500	Gross profit b/d	70 000
Net profit c/d	27 500		
	70 000		70 000

Appropriation Account for the year ended 31 December 19–9

	£	£		£
Salary: T		5 000	Net profit b/d	27 500
Interest allowed on				
partners' capitals:				
R	3 600			
S	2 400			
T	1 200			
		7 200		
Share of profits:				
R (½)	7 650			
S (¼)	3 825			
T (¼)	3 825			
		15 300		
		27 500		27 500

Balance sheet as at 31 December 19–9

	£					£
Fixed assets	110 000	Capital Accounts:				
Current assets	48 750	R				60 000
		S				40 000
		T				20 000
						120 000
		Current Accounts:				
			R	S	T	
			£	£	£	
		Balances b/d	2 000	3 000	(1 000)	
		Share of profits	7 650	3 825	3 825	
		Salary	—	—	5 000	
		Interest on				
		capital	3 600	2 400	1 200	
			13 250	9 225	9 025	
		Drawings	(12 000)	(8 000)	(10 000)	
			1 250	1 225	(975)	1 500
						121 500
		Current liabilities				37 250
	158 750					158 750

Points to notice:

(*a*) The Appropriation Account need not have a separate heading, but can continue as a section of the Profit and Loss Account.

(*b*) Where a question does not mention matters such as partners' drawings, salary, interest on capital and so on, it can be assumed that the Partnership Act rules apply: in this question, therefore, no interest is charged on partners' drawings.

(c) From the trial balance we can see that partner T's Current Account has an opening debit balance; at 31 December 19–9 it remains a debit balance (see balance sheet). Partners' Current Accounts normally have credit balances—a debit balance is indicated in the balance sheet by brackets and must be deducted.

38.10 Questions

*1. F. Shilton and T. Rough are in partnership and the following details were taken from their accounts on the 31 December 19–1.

	£
Capital Accounts: F. Shilton	12 000
T. Rough	16 000
Current Accounts: F. Shilton (Cr.)	224
T. Rough (Dr.)	240
Drawings during 19–1: F. Shilton	1 128
T. Rough	1 016
Gross Profit for the year was:	8 000
Other balances were: Printing and stationery	500
Salaries and wages	1 544
Rent and rates, January 19–1 to March 19–2	600
Insurance	1 200
Discount received	608
Discount allowed	192

Each partner is to receive 3 per cent per annum interest on his capital.

Shilton and Rough share profits and losses in the ratio 5:4.

Prepare:
  (a) the firm's Profit and Loss Account for the year 19–1;
  (b) the firm's Appropriation Account for the year 19–1;
  (c) each partner's Current Account for the year 19–1.
      [*Associated Lancashire Schools Examining Board*]

2. Rogers and Thompson are in partnership. They share profits and losses equally. On 1 January 19–2 the following balances appeared in their personal accounts:

Capital Accounts: Rogers £4 000, Thompson £3 000.
Current Accounts: Rogers £17 (Cr.), Thompson £20 (Cr.).

The net trading profit for 19–2 was £4 028 *before* providing for interest on capital: Rogers £200, Thompson £150.

Draw up a partners' balance sheet as at 31 December 19–2, taking into account the following information:

Drawings: Rogers £2 000, Thompson £2 020.
Creditors: £1 980; Provision for bad debts £160; Petty cash £60;
Cash at bank £1 535; Machinery at cost £2 600; Stock £2 760;
Depreciation of machinery £1 250; Furniture £470; Rent prepaid £30;
Debtors £2 980.

[*South Western Examinations Board*]

3. Kenge and Carboy are in partnership together. A trial balance has been drawn up at 30 April 19–3 and is shown below.

Prepare a Profit and Loss and Appropriation Account for year ended 30 April 19–3 and a balance sheet as at that date. The partners' Current Accounts should be shown *within* the balance sheet.

	£	£
Capital Accounts: Kenge		8 000
Carboy		7 000
Current Accounts: Kenge		4 000
Carboy	2 000	
Drawings: Kenge	3 500	
Carboy	4 500	
Gross trading profit		36 000
Office expenses	7 000	
Discounts allowed	2 000	
Heat and light	1 500	
Salaries	8 500	
Motor vehicles before depreciation	15 000	
Investments	5 000	
Sundry debtors	8 000	
Sundry creditors		2 000
	57 000	57 000

Notes:

(i) Profits and losses are to be shared equally.

(ii) Interest on capital at 10 per cent is to be allowed for each partner.

(iii) Depreciation at 10 per cent is to be provided on the motor vehicles.

[*London Regional Examining Board*]

*4. L. Gibson and H. Powell are in partnership sharing profits and losses in the proportion of two-thirds and one-third respectively. The following trial balance was extracted from their books at the close of business on 28 February 19–2:

		Dr.	Cr.
		£	£
Capital Accounts	Gibson		5 000
1 March 19–1	Powell		3 000
Current Accounts	Gibson		240
1 March 19–1	Powell		190
Drawings	Gibson	1 200	
	Powell	700	
Purchases and sales		7 630	13 990
Stock 1 March 19–1		1 780	
Wages and salaries		2 860	
Debtors and creditors		3 830	1 910
Office furniture		660	
Balance at bank		4 560	
Cash		80	
Discounts		390	170
Rent and rates		440	
Sundry expenses		370	
		24 500	24 500

Notes:
 (i) Stock at 28 February 19–2 is valued at £2 120.
 (ii) Rent and rates prepaid at 28 February 19–2 £60.
 (iii) Wages and salaries accrued at 28 February 19–2 £70.
 (iv) No provision is to be made for depreciation.
 (v) Interest is to be allowed on the Capital Accounts at the rate of 5 per cent per annum.
 (vi) The Capital Accounts are to remain unchanged, at the figures shown in the trial balance. All entries in respect of drawings, interest on capital and share of profits are to be made in the partners' Current Accounts.

Required:
Prepare the Trading and Profit and Loss Accounts of the partnership for the year ended 28 February 19–2, together with a balance sheet as at that date.

[London Chamber of Commerce]

5. North and South are in partnership sharing profits and losses in the ratio 2:1. The following trial balance was extracted from their books at the close of business on 28 February 19–3:

	Dr. £	Cr. £
Capital Accounts 1 March 19–2: North		2 800
South		1 500
Drawings: North	2 900	
South	1 450	
Bank overdraft		310
Cash	70	
Purchases and sales	8 260	17 350
Discounts	510	190
Stock at 1 March 19–2	1 870	
Debtors and creditors	3 920	1 750
Wages and salaries	2 160	
Rent and rates	390	
Fixtures and fittings	500	
Delivery van	700	
Van running expenses	420	
Current Accounts 1 March 19–2: North		270
South		240
Bad debts written off	170	
General expenses	1 090	
	24 410	24 410

Notes:
  (i) Stock 28 February 19–3 £2 280.
  (ii) Rent prepaid 28 February 19–3 £30.
  (iii) Wages accrued 28 February 19–3 £60.
  (iv) Provide for depreciation as follows:
       Fixtures and fittings £50   Delivery van £70.
  (v) No interest is to be allowed on the Capital Accounts.
  (vi) The Capital Accounts are to remain fixed at the figures shown in the trial balance. Entries concerning drawings and share of profit are to be passed through the Current Accounts.

Required:
Prepare the Trading and Profit and Loss Accounts for the year ended 28 February 19–3 together with a balance sheet as at that date.

[London Chamber of Commerce]

Amalgamation of Two Sole Traders

39.1 Introduction

We saw in Unit 38.1 that a sole-trader business may grow into a partnership. Quite commonly, in order to enlarge their business, two sole traders may agree to form a partnership from their two separate businesses. Examination questions will often give you the separate balance sheets of two sole traders who are to form a partnership, and will then ask you to draw up the partnership's opening balance sheet.

39.2 Two Balance Sheets

Here are the balance sheets of two sole traders as at 30 June 19–1:

Balance sheet of Y

	£	£		£
Fixed assets:			Capital	7 700
Machinery	3 250			
Van	2 000			
		5 250		
Current assets:			Current liabilities:	
Stock	1 750		Creditors	770
Debtors	1 050			
Bank	420			
		3 220		
		8 470		8 470

Balance sheet of Z

	£	£		£
Fixed assets:			Capital	4 140
Machinery		2 500		
Current assets:			Current liabilities:	
Stock	1 200		Creditors	540
Debtors	850			
Bank	130			
		2 180		
		4 680		4 680

On 1 July 19–1, Y and Z decide to form a partnership.

Assuming that the figures from the separate balance sheets are to be used, all that is needed to prepare a partnership balance sheet is to add together the various assets and liabilities:

Y and Z in partnership
Balance sheet as at 1 July 19–1

	£	£		£	£
Fixed assets:			Capital:		
Machinery	5 750		Y	7 700	
Van	2 000		Z	4 140	
		7 750			11 840
Current assets:			Current liabilities:		
Stock	2 950		Creditors		1 310
Debtors	1 900				
Bank	550				
		5 400			
		13 150			13 150

A journal entry would be required to record the *opening entries* (see Unit 24.3) in the books of the partnership. This would appear as:

Date	Details	Folio	Dr.	Cr.
19–1			£	£
1 Jul.	Machinery	GL	5 750	
	Van	GL	2 000	
	Stock	GL	2 950	
	Debtors	SL	1 900	
	Bank	CB	550	
	Creditors	PL		1 310
	Capital: Y	GL		7 700
	Z	GL		4 140
			13 150	13 150
	Assets and liabilities at the commencement of the partnership of Y and Z			

Following the opening journal entry, the double-entry book-keeping accounts would then be opened.

39.3 Changes in the Value of Assets

When a partnership is formed from two sole-trader businesses, changes are often agreed in the value of assets taken over by the partnership. Some assets may be increased in value, others may be reduced. Such changes in value will affect the opening capital figure in the partnership of the partner on whose sole-trader balance sheet the items appeared.

Example

In the formation of the partnership described in Unit 39.2, the following changes are made:

(a) Certain debtors are to be written off by the sole traders as bad, and will therefore not be taken over by the partnership. These debts amount to: Y £75; Z £50.

(b) Machinery is to be valued: Y £2 800; Z £2 250.

(c) Van to be valued: Y £1 500.

We can calculate the opening Capital Account balances for the partnership as follows:

	Y	Z
	£	£
Balance from sole-trader balance sheet	7 700	4 140
Less Bad debts written off	75	50
	7 625	4 090
Less Reduction in value of machinery	450	250
	7 175	3 840
Less Reduction in value of van	500	—
Partnership Capital Account balances	6 675	3 840

Reducing the values of the assets concerned for the partnership balance sheet, it will appear as:

Y and Z in partnership
Balance sheet as at 1 July 19–1

	£	£		£	£
Fixed assets:			Capital:		
Machinery	5 050		Y	6 675	
Van	1 500		Z	3 840	
		6 550			10 515
Current assets:			Current liabilities:		
Stock	2 950		Creditors		1 310
Debtors	1 775				
Bank	550				
		5 275			
		11 825			11 825

The appropriate journal entry for opening entries would then have to be made.

In all amalgamations between two sole-trader businesses, the opening Capital Account for each partner shown in the partnership balance sheet is simply the value of the net assets (assets minus liabilities) taken over by the partnership. Sometimes it is agreed that certain assets should be kept by the sole trader and not introduced into the partnership; the opening capital would then be adjusted accordingly. For example, it might be agreed that a private car appearing on a sole trader's balance sheet should not be taken over by the partnership or, where a sole trader has a bank overdraft, that this should not be taken over by the new business.

39.4   Questions

*1. Adams and Brown are two sole traders who decide to enter into partnership as from 1 April 19–2. At the close of business on 31 March 19–2 their respective balance sheets were as follows:

Adams

	£		£
Delivery van	450	Capital Account	2 790
Office furniture	370	Creditors	580
Stock	760		
Debtors	920		
Balance at bank	840		
Cash	30		
	3 370		3 370

Brown

	£		£
Office furniture	560	Capital Account	2 390
Stock	910	Creditors	970
Debtors	2 230	Bank overdraft	380
Cash	40		
	3 740		3 740

The new partnership takes over all the assets and liabilities *except* the bank overdraft of Brown. The partnership values the assets as follows:

Adams: Delivery van £400
　　　　Office furniture £350
　　　　Additionally, bad debts of £60 are to be written off *before* the debtors are taken over by the new firm.

Brown: Office furniture £500
　　　　Additionally, bad debts of £90 are to be written off *before* the debtors are taken over by the new firm.

Required:
　(a) Draw up the journal entries required to open the books of the new partnership. *Note:* Cash entries should be journalized.
　(b) Draw up the opening balance sheet of the new partnership.

[*London Chamber of Commerce*]

2. On 1 November 19–1, two sole traders, David Gardner and Alfred Young, decided to enter into partnership. At the close of business on 31 October 19–1, their separate balance sheets were:

David Gardner

	£	£		£
Fixed assets:			Capital Account	4 410
Office furniture	720		Bank overdraft	360
Delivery van	1 260		Trade creditors	950
		1 980		
Current assets:				
Stock	1 970			
Debtors	1 730			
Cash in hand	40			
		3 740		
		5 720		5 720

Alfred Young

	£	£		£
Fixed assets:			Capital Account	4 850
Office furniture		640	Trade creditors	1 060
Current assets:				
Stock	2 240			
Debtors	2 070			
Balance at bank	960			
		5 270		
		5 910		5 910

The partnership takes over all the assets and liabilities *except* Gardner's bank overdraft.

Additionally, it is agreed that certain debts shall be written off by the sole traders, as bad. Such debts will *not* therefore be taken over by the partnership. These debts are: Gardner £70; Young £60.

For the purpose of the new partnership, the above figures are acceptable, apart from the following:

Office furniture to be valued—Gardner £650, Young £600;
Delivery van to be valued—Gardner £1 100.

Required:

(a) Draw up the journal entries to open the books of the partnership (*Note:* cash should be journalized).

(b) Draw up the opening balance sheet of the partnership.

[*London Chamber of Commerce*]

3.   North and South, two sole traders, decide to enter into partnership as from 1 June 19–3. At the close of business on 31 May 19–3 their respective balance sheets were as follows:

North

	£		£
Office furniture	360	Capital Account	3 170
Delivery van	720	Creditors	550
Stock	1 050		
Debtors	1 130		
Bank	460		
	3 720		3 720

South

	£		£
Office furniture	470	Capital Account	3 220
Stock	1 760	Creditors	1 160
Debtors	2 430	Bank overdraft	280
	4 660		4 660

The new partnership takes over all the assets and liabilities of the two sole traders *except* the bank overdraft of South.

It is also agreed that the above assets taken over by the partnership be at the figures shown in the balance sheets with the following exceptions:

North: Office furniture to be valued at £300
        Van to be valued at   £650
South: Office furniture to be valued at £400
        Stock to be valued at   £1 650

It is also agreed that included in North's debtors are bad debts of £70. These are *not* taken over by the partnership.

Required:

(*a*) Prepare the journal entries necessary to open the books of the new partnership. (*Note:* Narrations need not be given.)

(*b*) Draw up the opening balance sheet.

[*London Chamber of Commerce*]

Unit Forty

Accounting Ratios

40.1 Introduction

This Unit is concerned with the accounting ratios that can be calculated from the year-end accounts of a business. While the owner of a business will be primarily concerned with whether the business has made a profit or loss, the calculation of certain accounting ratios additionally helps to show if the business has improved or worsened its performance as compared with the previous year's.

40.2 Trading and Profit and Loss Account

Here is a Trading and Profit and Loss Account which we will use for the purpose of calculating several accounting ratios:

J. Bloggs
Trading Account for the year ended 31 December 19–1

	£		£
Opening stock	8 000	Sales	150 000
Add Purchases	124 000		
	132 000		
Less Closing stock	12 000		
Cost of goods sold	120 000		
Gross profit c/d	30 000		
	150 000		150 000

Profit and Loss Account for the year ended 31 December 19–1

	£		£
Various expenses	25 000	Gross profit b/d	30 000
Net profit	5 000		
	30 000		30 000

(a) Gross Profit Margin

$$\frac{Gross\ profit}{Sales} \times \frac{100}{1} = Gross\ profit\ as\ a\ percentage\ of\ sales$$

$$\text{that is,}\ \frac{£30\,000}{£150\,000} \times \frac{100}{1} = \underline{\underline{20\ per\ cent}}$$

Here we have calculated the gross profit margin as a percentage of the sales that have been obtained during the year. It means that for every £100 of sales, the business has made a gross profit of £20. Whether that is satisfactory for this business, we cannot say: we should need to compare the result with those for previous years—the figure ought to be about the same each year.

(b) Gross Profit Mark-up

$$\frac{Gross\ profit}{Cost\ of\ goods\ sold} \times \frac{100}{1} = Gross\ profit\ as\ a\ percentage\ of\ cost\ price$$

$$that\ is,\ \frac{£30\,000}{£120\,000} \times \frac{100}{1} = \underline{\underline{25\ per\ cent}}$$

This shows the average percentage that has been added to cost prices to reach the price at which the goods are to be sold; again, this result needs to be compared with values for previous years.

Link between gross profit margin and gross profit mark-up

The two calculations, which we have already looked at briefly in Unit 13.9, use the same information but approach the calculation from different viewpoints. *Margin* is the profit as a percentage of *selling price*, while *mark-up* is the profit as a percentage of *buying price*. To remind you:

$$\begin{array}{ccccc} Cost\ price & + & Gross\ profit & = & Selling\ price \\ £4 & & £1 & & £5 \end{array}$$

Thus the margin is:

$$\frac{£1}{£5} \times \frac{100}{1} = \underline{\underline{20\ per\ cent}}$$

while the mark-up is:

$$\frac{£1}{£4} \times \frac{100}{1} = \underline{\underline{25\ per\ cent}}$$

(c) Stock Turnover

$$\frac{Cost\ of\ goods\ sold}{Average\ stock\ held} = Stock\ turnover\ per\ year$$

This calculation indicates how many times the average stock has been turned over (sold and replaced with new stock) during the year. 'Average stock' is usually calculated by adding the opening and closing stocks, and then dividing by 2; in our example,

Opening stock	£8 000
Add Closing stock	£12 000
	£20 000
Divide by 2: Average stock =	£10 000

Then Stock turnover per year = £120 000 ÷ £10 000 = $\underline{\underline{12}}$

If the stock turnover figure is divided into 12 (12 ÷ Stock turnover), the answer is the number of months, on average, that stock remains in the shop or warehouse before being sold and replaced. In our example, the answer is one month. Dividing the stock turnover figure into 52 gives the answer in weeks—approximately four weeks in our example.

When considering stock turnover, it is often difficult to decide whether the figure calculated is good or bad. The decision depends on the type of business. For example, a stock turnover of six times a year would be good for a furniture dealer, but not for a fresh fish seller! What would you expect the stock turnover to be for a business selling only newspapers? It ought to be about 360 times a year!

(d) Net Profit Margin

$$\frac{Net\,profit}{Sales} \times \frac{100}{1} = Net\,profit\,as\,a\,percentage\,of\,sales$$

that is,

$$\frac{£5\,000}{£150\,000} \times \frac{100}{1} = 3.3\,per\,cent$$

For this calculation we use the net profit from the Profit and Loss Account and the sales figure from the Trading Account. It indicates that for every £100 of sales, this business made a net profit of £3.30 for the owner. This should be compared with the calculations from previous years' accounts: any substantial changes, particularly a fall in net profit margin, would need to be investigated.

40.3 Calculating Missing Information

Some examination questions require you to calculate missing information in a Trading Account.

(a) Sales Figure Missing

We are told the following for a business:

Opening stock (1 Jan. 19–1)	£700
Closing stock (31 Dec. 19–1)	£1 200
Purchases for year	£6 500
Standard rate of gross profit mark-up	30 per cent

We are required to calculate (i) the gross profit and (ii) the sales for the year.

The first step is to put the information we do know into the form of a trading account:

Trading Account for the year ended 31 December 19–1

	£		£
Opening stock	700	Sales	x
Add Purchases	6 500		
	7 200		
Less Closing stock	1 200		
Cost of goods sold	6 000		
Gross profit c/d	x		

As we know that a standard rate of mark-up of 30 per cent applies, the gross profit is:

$$\frac{Cost\ of\ goods\ sold}{1} \times \frac{\%\ Mark\text{-}up}{100} = \frac{£6\,000}{1} \times \frac{30}{100} = £1\,800$$

If gross profit is £1 800, then the debit side total for the Trading Account is £7 800. If the account is to balance, this must be the sales figure. The completed Trading Account appears as:

Trading Account for the year ended 31 December 19–1

	£		£
Opening stock	700	Sales	7 800
Add Purchases	6 500		
	7 200		
Less Closing stock	1 200		
Cost of goods sold	6 000		
Gross profit c/d	1 800		
	7 800		7 800

(b) Purchases Figure Missing

We are told the following:

Opening stock (1 Jan. 19–4)	£1 200
Closing stock (31 Dec. 19–4)	£1 000
Sales for year	£8 800
Standard rate of gross profit margin	25 per cent

We are required to calculate (i) the gross profit and (ii) purchases for the year.

Putting the information into the form of a Trading Account:

Trading Account for the year ended 31 December 19–4

	£		£
Opening stock	1 200	Sales	8 800
Add Purchases	x		
	——		
Less Closing stock	1 000		
Cost of goods sold			
Gross profit c/d	x		
	——		——
	8 800		8 800

Using the standard rate of gross profit margin, we can calculate gross profit as:

$$\frac{Sales}{1} \times \frac{\% \, Margin}{100} = \frac{£8\,800}{1} \times \frac{25}{100} = \underline{\underline{£2\,200}}$$

If we enter this figure for gross profit into the Trading Account, we can 'work back' up the debit side of the account to fill in the figure for purchases:

Trading Account for the year ended 31 December 19–4

	£		£
Opening stock	1 200	Sales	8 800
Add Purchases	6 400		
	7 600		
Less Closing stock	1 000		
Cost of goods sold	6 600		
Gross profit c/d	2 200		
	8 800		8 800

'*I'm thinking of giving up my business—I can't see a future in it*'

40.4   Balance Sheet Ratios and Calculations

The following balance sheet continues on from the Trading and Profit and Loss Account considered in Unit 40.2:

J. Bloggs
Balance sheet as at 31 December 19–1

	£	£		£	£
Fixed assets:			Capital		40 000
At cost		40 000	*Add* Net profit		5 000
Less Depreciation					45 000
to date		10 000	*Less* Drawings		4 000
		30 000			41 000
Current assets:			Current liabilities:		
Stock	12 000		Creditors	15 500	
Debtors	25 000		Bank overdraft	10 500	
		37 000			26 000
		67 000			67 000

From this we can extract some useful information.

(a) Working Capital

(i) $$\text{Working capital} = \text{Current assets} - \text{Current liabilities}$$
$$= £37\,000 - £26\,000 = £11\,000$$

Sufficient working capital ensures that a business is able to pay its creditors without difficulty, hold adequate stocks and allow its debtors a reasonable time for payment. As a business expands so it needs to carry larger stocks and increased debtors, and hence an increase in the amount of its working capital.

Calculating working capital in this way year by year can show the trend of the business.

(ii) $$\text{Working capital ratio (or Current ratio)} = \frac{\text{Current assets}}{\text{Current liabilities}}$$
$$= \frac{£37\,000}{£26\,000} = 1.42:1$$

The figure for working capital as calculated in (i) does not enable us to compare businesses of differing sizes. For example, the working capital requirements of a small shop are totally different from those of a large departmental store; a small manufacturing business needs rather less working capital than does ICI. The current ratio is used in order to make comparisons more meaningful. The balance sheet of J. Bloggs gives us a current ratio of 1.42:1, that is, for every £1 of current liabilities there is £1.42 of current assets. This is rather on the low side—a satisfactory current ratio is usually regarded as being about 2:1, or approximately £2 of current assets for every £1 of current liabilities. Thus, if a creditor demands immediate payment, there should be sufficient current assets to be realized to meet his requirements. A ratio higher than about 3:1, unless there are unusual circumstances, may indicate that the business is not using its working capital to best advantage. It may have cash lying idle in the bank account, or it may be allowing debtors too long a period before payment, or it may be maintaining its stocks at too high a level.

(b) Liquid Capital

(i)   *Liquid capital = (Current assets − Stocks) − Current liabilities*

$$= (£37\,000 - £12\,000) - £26\,000 = -£1\,000 \text{ or } (£1\,000)$$

When referring to the *liquidity* of an asset we mean the ease and speed with which it can be converted into cash. The balance of money in the bank and cash in hand are, of course, perfectly liquid. Debtors are 'near-liquid'—they are only one step away from cash and we await payment from them. Stock, however, is not as liquid as debtors because it generally has to go through the process of being converted into debtors before it becomes cash. Therefore we would recognize debtors, bank and cash as the *liquid assets* of a business. We can then deduct the current liabilities, leaving us with the amount of liquid capital. This indicates what the surplus or deficit would be if all the liquid assets were realized to repay all the current liabilities.

The problem with liquid capital, as with working capital, is that the answer is in pounds. While this may help an individual business to make comparisons from year to year, it does not enable firms of different sizes to be compared. Therefore we must calculate the *liquid ratio*.

(ii) $$Liquid\ ratio = \frac{(Current\ assets - Stock)}{Current\ liabilities}$$

$$= \frac{(£37\,000 - £12\,000)}{£26\,000} = 0.96{:}1$$

In this example the liquid assets almost balance against current liabilities: for every £1 of current liabilities, there is £0.96 of liquid assets. This is about right—a liquid ratio of 1:1 is considered reasonable. A ratio of 1.5:1 is even better, but one that is any higher could indicate that the firm is tying up too much in debtors and bank—idle money that is not working for the business. Any ratio better than 1:1 indicates that the business could, if necessary, cover its current liabilities in full without having to resort to panic measures such as the urgent sale of fixed assets or stocks at bargain prices. (The liquid ratio is also known as the *quick ratio* or the *acid test ratio*.)

Conflict between liquidity and profitability. There is a fundamental conflict between liquidity and profitability. For example, very high current and liquid ratios, while indicating liquidity, may suggest that funds are lying idle. The opposite of this is that low current and liquid ratios are traditionally regarded as an indication of illiquidity, but may reflect a more efficient and profitable use of assets. There are no 'correct' current and liquid ratios for a firm to aim for—each business must find the levels suited to its needs. Clearly very low or very high ratios will be detrimental to any firm.

(c) Credit Allowed to Customers

$$Number\ of\ months'\ credit\ allowed = \frac{Debtors}{Credit\ sales} \times 12$$

$$= \frac{£25\,000}{£150\,000} \times 12 = \underline{\underline{2\ months'\ credit\ allowed}}$$

This calculation gives the number of months' credit allowed to debtors on average—that is, after goods are sold on credit it takes an average of two months for the debtors to pay. If the answer is required in weeks then we must multiply by 52:

$$\frac{£25\,000}{£150\,000} \times 52 = \underline{\underline{8.7\ weeks}}$$

Similarly, multiplying by 365 gives the answer in days.

Calculating this figure for several sets of accounts allows us to reveal the trend for a particular business. In interpreting the trend we must consider if the figures are reasonable, bearing in mind the type of business—if the accounts are those of a sweet shop, say, we would not expect to see any substantial debtors on the balance sheet. If the credit allowed period tends to increase, it may be that the firm's credit controls are inefficient.

(d) Credit Received from Suppliers

$$Number\ of\ months'\ credit\ received = \frac{Creditors}{Credit\ purchases} \times 12$$

$$= \frac{£15\,500}{£124\,000} \times 12 = \underline{\underline{1\tfrac{1}{2}\ months'\ credit\ received}}$$

This calculation, like credit allowed, may also be expressed in weeks or days. Again, the owner will look for a trend: a general increase in credit received may indicate that the firm is finding it difficult to pay its way because of cash shortages.

(e) Return on Capital Employed

$$Return\ on\ capital\ employed = \frac{Net\ profit}{Capital} \times 100$$

$$= \frac{£5\,000}{£40\,000} \times 100 = \underline{\underline{12\tfrac{1}{2}\ per\ cent\ return}}$$

This is an important ratio to calculate because it compares the net profit from Profit and Loss Account with the owner's capital, thus giving a percentage return on the investment made in the business. For a simple balance sheet it is best to use the opening capital balance as the capital employed; an examination question will often tell you how capital employed is to be defined. Return on capital employed can be used in comparing one firm with another, although care should be exercised in making decisions without other evidence in support.

40.5   Questions

1. From the following information for two firms, Firm A and Firm B, calculate:
    (a) the gross profit percentage on sales for *each* firm,
    (b) the net profit percentage on sales for *each* firm.

	Firm A	*Firm B*
Sales	£100 000	£100 000
Gross profit	£20 000	£25 000
Net profit	£5 000	£5 000

   (c) Give *one* reason why the gross profits of the firms differ.
   [*South Western Examinations Board*]

*2. J. Cleary normally takes stock on 31 December of each year. In 19–2, however, it is more convenient for him to take it on 26 December. Calculate the value of his stock on 31 December 19–2 from the following:

	£
Stock at cost on 26 December	5 900
Purchases on 27 December	2 000
Returns inward on 27 December	90
Sales on 28 December	2 700
Goods returned by Cleary on 29 December	40

Note: Cleary earns 33⅓ per cent gross profit on selling price.
   [*East Anglian Examinations Board*]

3. State the formula for each of the following and explain its usefulness to a sole trader.

    (a) return on capital;
    (b) net profit percentage;
    (c) working capital;
    (d) rate of stock turnover.

   [*Pitman Examinations Institute*]

*4. Thieves broke into the warehouse of Brian Carson, a sole trader, on 15 February 19–3, and all his stock in trade was stolen *except* for a quantity of goods which were in a locked room. The value of these goods—at cost price—was £90.
    Carson wishes to submit a claim to his insurance company in respect of his loss and gives the following information:

Purchases: 1 January to 15 February 19–3 £1 520.
            Of the total of £1 520, goods costing £70 were actually in transit at the time of the theft.

Sales: 1 January to 15 February 19–3 £2 460.
               All the goods sold had been delivered to Carson's customers before the
               theft took place.

The following is Carson's Trading Account for the year ended 31 December 19–2:

Trading Account for the year ended 31 December 19–2

	£		£
Stock 1 Jan.	1 280	Sales	7 200
Purchases	6 220		
	7 500		
Less Stock 31 Dec.	1 500		
Cost of goods sold	6 000		
Gross profit	1 200		
	7 200		7 200

Carson states that for the period 1 January 19–3 to 15 February 19–3 the percentage of gross profit to sales was the same as for the year 19–2.

Required:
   To assist Carson with his insurance claim calculate the value—at cost price—of the goods stolen on 15 February 19–3.

Note: Calculations should be shown.

[*London Chamber of Commerce*]

5.   The following is the Trading Account of William Martin, a sole trader.

Trading Account for year ended 31 December 19–1

	£		£
Stock 1 Jan.	3 200	Sales	24 000
Purchases	17 700		
	20 900		
Less Stock 31 Dec.	2 900		
Cost of goods sold	18 000		
Gross profit	6 000		
	24 000		24 000

During the night of 4 June 19–2 Martin's warehouse was broken into and his entire stock in trade was stolen except for a small quantity of goods in an office. The value—at cost price—of the goods which were not stolen was £190.

   The following information is available from Martin's records:

Purchases: 1 January 19–2 to 4 June 19–2 £6 400
           Of this total goods costing £240 had *not* been delivered by 4 June
           19–2.
Sales: 1 January 19–2 to 4 June 19–2 £8 280
           All the goods sold had been delivered from the warehouse by the close
           of business on 4 June 19–2.

Required:
Calculate the value, at cost price, of the goods actually stolen. Calculations must be shown.

Note: Assume that the percentage of gross profit to sales is the same for 19–2 as it was for 19–1.

[*London Chamber of Commerce*]

*6. Here is a Trading Account:

	£		£
Opening stock	5 000	Sales	50 000
Add Purchases	42 500		
	47 500		
Less Closing stock	10 000		
	37 500		
Gross profit	12 500		
	50 000		50 000

From the above calculate:
(*a*) gross profit percentage;
(*b*) stock turnover for the year;
(*c*) number of weeks stock held on average;
(*d*) if debtors are £6 250, the credit that is being taken on average;
(*e*) if creditors are £10 625, the credit that is being received on average;
(*f*) if net profit for this business is £7 500, the net profit percentage.

7. Here is a balance sheet:

	£		£
Premises	13 000	Capital at start of year	30 000
Machinery	5 000	*Add* Net profit for year	10 000
Office equipment	2 500		40 000
Stock	12 000	*Less* Drawings	7 500
Debtors	4 000		32 500
Bank	2 000	Creditors	6 000
	38 500		38 500

From the above calculate:
(*a*) current ratio;
(*b*) liquid, quick or acid test ratio;
(*c*) return on capital employed.

Comment on the figures you have calculated, comparing them with last year's balance sheet which showed a current ratio of 1.5:1, a liquid ratio of 0.8:1, and a return on capital employed of 20 per cent.

8. The following comparative balance sheets show the position of John Smith's
    business as at 31 December 19–1 and 19–2:

Balance sheets as at 31 December

	19–1 £	19–2 £		19–1 £	19–2 £
Fixed assets:			Capital:		
Land and buildings	45 000	70 000	At start of year	50 000	52 500
Plant and machinery	18 000	12 000	*Add* Net profit	10 000	15 000
	63 000	82 000		60 000	67 500
			Less Drawings	7 500	6 000
Current assets:			At end of year	52 500	61 500
Stock	11 000	14 000			
Debtors	13 000	18 000	Long-term loan	30 000	25 000
Bank balance	9 500	—			
			Current liabilities:		
			Creditors	14 000	15 000
			Bank overdraft	—	12 500
	96 500	114 000		96 500	114 000

Calculate the following accounting ratios for each year:
  (*a*) working capital;
  (*b*) working capital ratio;
  (*c*) liquid capital;
  (*d*) liquid capital ratio;
  (*e*) return on capital employed;
  (*f*) net profit/sales percentage (sales figures for the two years were £95 000 and
        £120 000 respectively);
  (*g*) debtors turnover.

Comment briefly on the trends indicated by your calculations.

9. Leo Hua Fen has to pay £2 000 to a supplier, Kang Sai Hoon, tomorrow (25 April
    19–0). Accounting records, as follows, show that Leo Hua Fen does not have the
    funds to do so. No overdraft is available to draw upon either.

Cash book

19–0	Disc. £	Cash £	Bank £	19–0	Disc. £	Cash £	Bank £
24 Apr. Balance b/d		100	400				

Debtors Control Account

19–0	£
24 Apr. Balance b/d	4 200

Creditors Control Account

	19–0	£
	24 Apr. Balance b/d	3 900

A stock-take reveals £8 500 stock at cost.

Leo Hua Fen has spoken to various customers:

(i) Tan Yaw Ming, a debtor for £1 500, will pay in full by cheque on 25 April providing discount of 10 per cent can be claimed. Leo Hua Fen has agreed to this arrangement.

(ii) Loh Yan Yong will purchase, for cash, £500 of the remaining stock, at cost, on 25 April.

Assuming the above are the only transactions taking place on 25 April, and that the creditor is paid, you are required to:

(a) write up the cash book of Leo Hua Fen, transferring sufficient cash to the bank account to balance it at £100 credit at the end of the day;

(b) calculate the working capital after the transactions on 25 April.

You are also required to:

(c) explain the importance of circulating assets.

[Pitman Examinations Institute, Level 2]

Multiple-choice Questions—10

Read each question carefully. Choose the *one* answer you think is correct. Answers are given on page 411.

1. A club's Receipts and Payments Account is similar to a firm's:

   A balance sheet
   B Capital Account
   C Trading, and Profit and Loss Account
   D cash book

2. A club's Income and Expenditure Account is similar to a firm's:

   A Trading, and Profit and Loss Account
   B balance sheet
   C cash book
   D trial balance

3. A society has 100 members and the subscription is £5 per year. During the course of the financial year, all have paid the correct amount except for four members who paid £10 each because they owed for the previous year, and two members who have paid for next year. The subscription income for this year's Income and Expenditure Account is:

   A £470   **B** £480   **C** £500   **D** £530

4. In a club balance sheet, subscriptions paid in advance are recorded as:

   A a current asset   **C** a fixed asset
   B a current liability   **D** added to the accumulated fund

5. Prime cost in a Manufacturing Account is:

   A all factory indirect costs
   B all factory costs
   C direct factory costs only
   D direct materials, plus direct expenses

6. In a manufacturing business, royalties are included under the heading of:

   A raw materials   **C** indirect expenses
   B direct expenses   **D** overheads

7. Which one of the following would not appear in a Manufacturing Account?

   A depreciation on factory machinery
   B foremen's wages
   C depreciation on office equipment
   D royalties

8. Indicate which of the following accounting points for a partnership is not permitted by the Partnership Act:

   A no partner is entitled to a salary
   B no interest is to be charged on drawings
   C profits and losses are to be shared in proportion to capital
   D no partner is entitled to interest on capital

9. Profits of a partnership amount to £3 280 before the following are taken into account:

   (i) interest on partners' capitals, £180
   (ii) interest on drawings, £20
   (iii) salary of one partner, £1 000

   How much profit remains for division between the partners?

   A £2 080   **B** £2 100   **C** £2 120   **D** £2 440

10. The following information is available:

	£
Sales	30 000
Opening stock	5 000
Purchases	20 000
Closing stock	10 000

    The rate of stock turnover for the year is:

    A 4 times   **B** $2\frac{2}{3}$ times   **C** 2 times   **D** $1\frac{1}{2}$ times

11. The following information is available:

	£
Sales	100 000
Purchases	80 000
Opening stock	10 000
Closing stock	15 000
Expenses	10 000

    Gross and net profit margins are respectively

    A 20% and 10%   **C** 15% and 5%
    B 25% and 15%   **D** 10% and 20%

12. Which one of the following would you *not* take into account in calculating working capital?

    A cash   **B** debtors   **C** motor vehicles   **D** creditors

Limited-company Accounts

41.1 Introduction

Many expanding sole-trader and partnership businesses decide to form into limited companies, while many new businesses choose the limited company as their business entity at the outset. There are a number of reasons for this, including:

(a) A sole-trader or partnership business which wishes to raise more finance by way of capital may do so by forming into a company. This enables shares to be issued to the owner(s), family, business associates, and other investors. This small or medium-sized company is often referred to as a 'private company'.

(b) A larger company (with a share capital of over £50 000) can become a 'public limited company' (plc); it may then raise finance from the public by means of a listing on the Stock Exchange (or a related market), although not all plcs do so.

(c) The liability of members—that is, shareholders—for the debts of the company is limited and their personal assets cannot be taken to pay the debts of the company unless pledged as security to a lender.

(d) A limited company has a separate legal identity from its owners and anyone taking legal action proceeds against the company, not against individual shareholders. This contrasts with sole traders and partnerships, where legal action can be taken against the individual or the partners.

In this Unit we shall study the year-end Trading and Profit and Loss Accounts and balance sheets of limited companies. These broadly follow the layout of those prepared for sole traders and partnerships. The Companies Act 1985, however, stipulates that certain annual financial statements must be filed with the Registrar of Companies, and a copy has to be sent to each shareholder. Such 'published accounts', as they are known, will not be discussed here, as they form part of a course of more advanced studies of accountancy. In this Unit we shall concentrate on the basic form of limited-company year-end accounts. Before we examine these in detail, we will look at the principal way in which a company raises finance by means of shares.

41.2 Types of Shares Issued by Limited Companies

We must distinguish, first of all, between the *authorized share capital* and the *issued share capital*.

(a) *Authorized share capital*—this is the maximum amount of capital that the company is legally allowed to raise by issuing shares. The amount of the authorized capital will vary from company to company, and it is a clause in the company's Memorandum of Association (the document setting out the powers and objects of the company) that states the authorized share capital and its division into shares of a fixed amount. A company's Memorandum of Association has to be registered with the Registrar of Companies at Companies House, and so the authorized share capital is often called the *registered capital*.

(*b*) *Issued share capital*—this is the number and total value of shares that a company has actually issued. The issued share capital can never exceed that which has been authorized: if a company wishes to increase its issued share capital beyond the authorized share capital, a general meeting of the shareholders must first pass an appropriate resolution increasing the amount authorized. The increase is then registered with the Registrar of Companies.

The authorized and issued share capitals are divided into two main classes or types of share: *ordinary shares*, and *preference shares*, see Fig. 41.1. Each share has a *nominal value* or face value which is entered in the accounts. Shares can be issued with nominal values of 5p, 10p, 25p, 50p, or £1, or indeed any amount. Thus a company with an authorized share capital of £100 000 might state in its Memorandum of Association that this is divided up into:

100 000 ordinary shares of 50p each	£50 000
50 000 seven-per-cent preference shares of £1 each	£50 000
	£100 000

The nominal value of a share often bears little relationship to its market value. It is easy to find out the market value of shares in a large public limited company—the price may well be listed in the *Financial Times*.

Shareholders receive *dividends* on their shares, being a distribution of a part of the company's profits for a year or half-year. The dividend paid half-way through a financial year is known as an *interim dividend*, while that paid at the end of a financial year is a *final dividend*.

(*a*) Ordinary (or Equity) Shares

These are the most commonly issued class of share. Holders of ordinary shares take a share of the profits available for distribution after allowance has been made for all expenses of the business, including loan interest, and after taxation, and after preference dividends (if any). When a company makes large profits, it will be able to pay higher dividends to the ordinary shareholders. When profits are low or losses are made, the ordinary shareholders may receive a smaller, or even no, dividend. Companies rarely pay out all of their available profits in the form of dividends; most retain some profits as reserves. These can always be used to enable a dividend to be paid in a year when the company makes little or no profit—always assuming that the company has sufficient cash in the bank to make the payment.

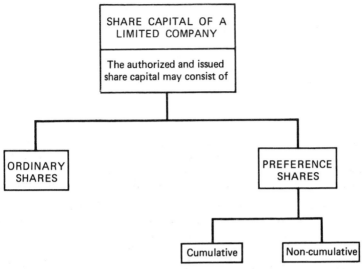

Fig. 41.1 Types of share

In the event of the company ceasing to trade, or 'winding up', ordinary shareholders will be the last to receive any repayment of their investment: other creditors will have to be paid off first.

(b) Preference Shares

These shares usually carry a fixed rate of dividend, for example seven-per-cent preference shares. As their name suggests, this dividend is paid in preference to any dividend paid to the ordinary shareholders. In the event of winding up the company, the preference will also extend to repayment of capital before the ordinary shareholders receive any repayment.

Preference shares take one of two forms:

(a) cumulative preference shares,
(b) non-cumulative preference shares.

Where they are cumulative, this means that, if a preference dividend is not paid in one year, it accumulates and will be paid in the future. In this way, missed dividends will always be paid, provided that the company makes sufficient profits in the future. This contrasts with non-cumulative preference shares, where, if insufficient profits are made during a certain year to pay the preference dividend, there is no provision for 'catching up' this missed dividend in future years. All preference shares are cumulative unless specifically stated otherwise.

The shareholders in a limited company have no right to any say in the day-to-day affairs of the business but, instead, elect a board of directors to run the company for them. Where a partnership has been converted into a private limited company, it is likely that the partners of the former partnership will form the board of directors and will therefore continue to control the business's affairs.

41.3 Loans and Debentures

In addition to money provided by shareholders, who are the owners of the company, further funds can be obtained by borrowing in the forms of loans or debentures—from a bank, for example. The term *debenture* usually refers to a formal certificate issued by a company to acknowledge that a sum of money is owing to a specified person.

Both loans and debentures usually carry a fixed rate of interest that must be paid, just like other business expenses, whether a company makes profits or not. This interest is charged to Profit and Loss Account along with all other expenses.

41.4 Trading and Profit and Loss Accounts

A limited company uses the same form of Trading and Profit and Loss Accounts as a sole trader or partnership. However, there are two items commonly found in the Profit and Loss Account of a limited company that are not found in those of other business entities:

(*a*) *Directors' remuneration*—that is, amounts paid to the directors as salaries etc.—appears among the other expenses of the company and is debited to Profit and Loss Account.

(*b*) *Debenture interest*, as noted above, is debited to Profit and Loss Account.

41.5 Appropriation Account

In a similar way to a partnership, a limited company follows the Profit and Loss Account with an *Appropriation Account*. This account, which does not always have a separate heading, shows how the net profit is to be divided among the shareholders of the company.

The following is an example of a simple Appropriation Account:

Appropriation Account of ABC Ltd for the year ended 31 December 19–1

	£		£
Proposed ordinary dividend	30 000	Balance brought down	25 000
Balance carried down	45 000	Net profit for year	50 000
	75 000		75 000

Points to notice:

(*a*) The company has recorded a net profit for the year of £50 000 in its Profit and Loss Account: this is brought into the Appropriation Account.

(*b*) The company proposes to distribute £30 000 to the ordinary shareholders as a dividend. This will be paid in the early part of the next financial year (and the dividend will be shown as a current liability in the balance sheet at 31 December 19–1).

(c) Added to net profit is a balance brought down of £25 000. This represents profits of the company from previous years that are undistributed, that is, they have not been paid to shareholders in the form of dividends. After this year's transactions there is a balance of undistributed (or retained) profits carried down of £45 000. Such undistributed profits form a *revenue reserve* of the company. It is usual for a company to retain some part of its profits in the form of reserves, to help the company build for the future.

Besides the reserve of undistributed profits—often described as *Profit and Loss Account balance*—companies may use other reserves, for example *general reserve*. Transfers to or from such reserves accounts are made through the Appropriation Account, and hence they are generally known as *revenue reserves* because they are built up from profits (or revenues) of the company. There are two important points to note about reserve accounts:

(a) Reserves are *not* funds of cash but are, in fact, represented by assets on the balance sheet. To explain this more clearly, a houseowner may say that her house is worth more now than when it was bought and, hence, she has a reserve; however, her bank balance is unaffected, because the reserve is represented by assets, *not* in the form of cash.

(b) *Reserves* are undistributed profits retained in the company but which are not intended to meet any liability known to exist at the balance sheet date. This is in contrast to *provisions*, which are amounts set aside from profits to meet specific liabilities existing at the date of the balance sheet, such as provision for depreciation and provision for bad debts, but for which the amount can only be estimated.

A more comprehensive Appropriation Account (which links with the balance sheet shown in Unit 41.6) is as follows:

Appropriation Account of XYZ Ltd for the year ended 31 December 19–4

	£		£
Corporation tax*	15 000	Balance brought down	30 000
Interim dividends paid:		Net profit for year	40 000
Ordinary shares	5 000		
Preference shares	2 000		
Final dividends proposed:			
Ordinary shares	10 000		
Preference shares	2 000		
Transfer to general reserve	6 000		
Balance carried down	30 000		
	70 000		70 000

* Corporation tax is the tax that a company pays on its profits. The amount of tax payable (which will be paid in the following financial year) is debited to the Appropriation Account.

41.6   Balance Sheet

The balance sheet of a limited company follows the same layout as that of a sole trader or a partnership, but the capital section is more complex because of the different classes of shares that may be issued and the various reserves. While a limited-company balance sheet can be presented in horizontal format, it is common to use the vertical format (see Unit 9.8). Fig. 41.2 shows an example of a vertical presentation balance sheet of XYZ Ltd which would follow the Appropriation Account shown in Unit 41.5.

The following points should be noted concerning each section of the balance sheet.

(a) Fixed Assets

As with other balance sheets, this section consists of those items that do not change daily and are likely to be retained for use in the business for some time to come. With the possible exception of freehold land, fixed assets are depreciated over a period of time or with use. The headings used for fixed assets in the balance sheet are 'At cost', 'Depreciation to date', and 'Net'.

Balance sheet of XYZ Ltd as at 31 December 19–4

	£	£	£
Fixed assets:			
	Cost	*Depn to date*	*Net*
Freehold land and buildings	180 000	20 000	160 000
Machinery	280 000	110 000	170 000
Fixtures and fittings	100 000	25 000	75 000
	560 000	155 000	405 000
Current assets:			
Stocks		50 000	
Debtors	40 000		
Less Provision for bad debts	2 000		
		38 000	
Cash at bank		13 000	
Cash in hand		1 000	
		102 000	
Less Current liabilities:			
Creditors	30 000		
Proposed dividends	12 000		
Corporation tax	15 000		
		57 000	
Working capital			45 000
			450 000

Financed by
Authorized share capital:

100 000 10% preference shares of £1 each		100 000
600 000 ordinary shares of £1 each		600 000
		700 000

Issued share capital:

40 000 10% preference shares of £1 each, fully paid		40 000
300 000 ordinary shares of £1 each, fully paid		300 000
		340 000

Capital reserve:

Share premium		20 000

Revenue reserves:
General reserve

(Note: £14 000 + £6 000 transfer)	20 000	
Profit and Loss Account	30 000	
		50 000

Shareholders' funds		410 000

Long-term liabilities:

12% debentures		40 000
		450 000

Fig. 41.2 A vertical presentation balance sheet of a limited company

When preparing the final accounts of a limited company from a trial balance, you should take care to note that a particular fixed asset will usually be shown *at cost* on the debit side of the trial balance, while a provision for depreciation relating to the same asset will be recorded on the credit side. This *provision for depreciation* relates to depreciation charged to past years' Profit and Loss Accounts, but before charging this year's depreciation amount. For example:

Trial balance (extract) as at 31 December 19–7

	£	£
Machinery at cost	10 000	
Provision for depreciation on machinery		3 000

Depreciation at 10 per cent on cost is to be provided on machinery. In this example, the £3 000 showing on the credit side of the trial balance represents depreciation over previous years and it is now necessary to debit the Profit and Loss Account with this year's amount, that is £1 000. When this has been done, accumulated depreciation on machinery amounts to £4 000, and the extract from the fixed assets section of the balance sheet will show:

Balance sheet (extract) of ... as at ...

	£	£	£
Fixed assets:			
	Cost	*Depn to date*	*Net*
Machinery	10 000	4 000	6 000

(b) Current Assets

The usual current assets will be included—that is, stocks, debtors, balance at bank and cash in hand.

(c) Current Liabilities

As with the balance sheets of a sole trader and a partnership, this section contains those liabilities that exist at the balance sheet date and are due to be paid within twelve months, for example creditors and (technically) bank overdraft. For limited companies, this section also contains the amount of proposed dividends and the amount of corporation tax to be paid within the next twelve months: both of these amounts will be shown on the debit side of the Appropriation Account.

(d) Working Capital

One of the advantages of a vertical presentation balance sheet is that it is easy to show the amount of working capital within the balance sheet (see also Unit 40.4(a)). Current liabilities are deducted from current assets, and the amount of working capital is entered in the money column.

(e) Authorized Share Capital

As already explained in Unit 41.2, this is the share capital of the company and its division into shares of a fixed amount, as authorized by the company's Memorandum of Association. It is included on the balance sheet 'for information', but is not added into the balance sheet total unless the issued share capital is of the same amount.

(f) Issued Share Capital

Here are detailed the classes and numbers of shares that have been issued. The amount of issued share capital cannot exceed the authorized share capital. In the balance sheet of XYZ Ltd shown in Fig. 41.2, the shares are described as being *fully paid*, meaning that the company has received the full amount of the nominal value of each share from the shareholders.

Sometimes shares are *partly paid*, for example, ordinary shares with a nominal value of £1 may be 75p paid. This means that the company can make a *call* on the shareholders to pay the additional 25p to make the shares fully paid. Companies often issue partly paid shares and then make calls at certain times; for example, a company that is issuing shares to raise the finance to build and equip a new factory may wish to receive the proceeds as payments for the different stages in construction have to be made.

For the purpose of entering the amount of issued share capital in the balance sheet, multiply the number of shares issued, by the amount called on them; for example, 100 000 ordinary shares of £1 each, 75p paid = £75 000.

(g) **Capital Reserve**

An established company may issue additional shares at a price that is above the nominal value, for example £1 shares may be sold for £2.50. This is done when the company has an established record of profits and it is believed that buyers of the new shares will be prepared to pay the higher price. The extra £1.50 per share (in this example) is credited to a special reserve account known as a *Share Premium Account*. This is an example of a *capital reserve*—that is, it has come about as a result of capital (or non-trading) activities. A capital reserve cannot be drawn on for the payment of dividends.

(h) **Revenue Reserves**

The reserves from profits are the amounts which the directors of the company have retained in the business. There is no reason why revenue reserves should not be drawn on in the future to pay a dividend, provided that the company has sufficient cash in its bank account to pay the dividend.

(i) **Shareholders' Funds**

The total of issued share capital and the reserves (both capital and revenue reserves) form the shareholders' funds in the company.

(j) **Long-term Liabilities**

These are the liabilities that exist at the balance sheet date and that are due to be repaid in *more than* twelve months from the date of the balance sheet. Examples of long-term liabilities are debentures and bank loans.

41.7 Questions

*1. Johnson Ltd has an authorized share capital of £500 000, divided into 400 000 ordinary shares of £1 each and 100 000 eight-per-cent preference shares of £1 each. The following balances remained in the books of the company after preparation of the Trading and Profit and Loss Accounts for the year ended 30 June 19–5.

	£	£
Ordinary shares, fully paid		150 000
8% preference shares, fully paid		50 000
Land and buildings at cost	150 000	
Plant and machinery at cost	80 000	
Provision for depreciation on plant and machinery (including this year's depreciation already charged to Profit and Loss Account)		20 000
Balance of Profit and Loss Account (1 July 19–4)		15 500
Net profit for year ended 30 June 19–5		40 500
Stock	20 850	
Debtors and creditors	16 710	11 840
Expenses prepaid	1 550	
Expenses owing		890
Bank	19 620	
	288 730	288 730

The directors have recommended:

(i) to transfer £5 000 to general reserve,
(ii) a dividend of 10% on the ordinary shares,
(iii) payment of the year's preference dividend.

Required:
    (*a*) The Profit and Loss Appropriation Account for the year ended 30 June 19–5.
    (*b*) The balance sheet at 30 June 19–5, presented in vertical format and clearly showing the shareholders' funds and the working capital.

*2.   The following trial balance was extracted from the books of Technical Co. Ltd at 31 December 19–8:

	£	£
Share capital		350 000
Freehold land and buildings at cost	156 000	
Motor vans at cost	60 000	
Provision for depreciation of motor vans at 1 January 19–8		22 600
Purchases and sales	201 986	324 299
Rent and rates	5 000	
General expenses	8 626	
Wages and salaries	37 437	
Bad debts written off	789	
Provision for doubtful debts at 1 January 19–8		1 249
Directors' salaries	20 000	
Debtors and creditors	28 107	15 060
Retained profit at 1 January 19–8		21 902
Stock in trade at 1 January 19–8	43 008	
Bank	174 157	
	735 110	735 110

You are given the following additional information:
    (i) The authorized share capital is 400 000 ordinary shares of £1 each. All the shares which have been issued are fully paid.
    (ii) Wages outstanding at 31 December 19–8 amounted to £433.
    (iii) The provision for doubtful debts is to be increased by £175.
    (iv) Stock in trade at 31 December 19–8 was £50 305.
    (v) Rent and rates amounting to £300 were paid in advance at 31 December 19–8.
    (vi) It is proposed to pay a dividend of £10 000 for the year 19–8.
    (vii) Depreciation on motor vans is to be charged at the rate of 20 per cent per annum on cost.

Required:
    Trading and Profit and Loss Accounts for the year ended 31 December 19–8 and a balance sheet (presented in vertical format) at 31 December 19–8.

*3.   The following trial balance was extracted from the books of Midland Ltd, a retail concern, at 31 December 19–4.

	£	£
Share capital (ordinary shares of £1 each)		200 000
Share premium		50 000
Retained profit at 1 January 19–4		194 500
10% debentures		120 000
Freehold land and buildings at cost	460 000	
Motor vans at cost	40 000	
Provision for depreciation on motor vans at		
1 January 19–4		22 600
Purchases and sales	1 350 800	1 720 500
Stock at 1 January 19–4	227 100	
Rent and rates	10 350	
General expenses	75 150	
Wages	93 250	
Bad debts written off	1 600	
Provision for doubtful debts at 1 January 19–4		2 100
Trade debtors and trade creditors	246 300	175 900
Bank overdraft		24 950
Debenture interest paid to 30 June 19–4	6 000	
	2 510 550	2 510 550

The following additional information is provided:

  (i) The company depreciates its motor vans at 20% on cost of vehicles owned at the year end.
 (ii) Rates paid in advance at 31 December 19–4 amounted to £1 350.
(iii) Wages outstanding at 31 December 19–4 amounted to £900.
(iv) The provision for doubtful debts is to be increased to £2 450.
 (v) The directors propose to pay a dividend of £60 000 for 19–4.
(vi) Stock at 31 December amounted to £235 350.

Required:
   Trading and Profit and Loss and Appropriation Accounts for Midland Ltd for 19–4, and balance sheet at 31 December 19–4. Ignore depreciation of freehold land and buildings.

[*Royal Society of Arts, Stage II*]

4. The following trial balance was extracted from the books of Printer Ltd at 31 December 19–5:

	£	£
Share capital		300 000
Share premium		70 000
10% debentures		150 000
Freehold buildings at cost	350 000	
Plant at cost	300 000	
Vans at cost	24 000	
Provisions at 1 January:		
Depreciation of plant		130 000
Depreciation of vans		12 500
Doubtful debts		1 300
Sales		767 804
Purchases	490 084	
Debtors and creditors	55 750	32 196
Bad debts	2 532	
Wages	67 924	
Rates	7 812	
Debenture interest paid	7 500	
Profit and Loss Account at 1 January		33 184
Directors' salaries	50 000	
Motor expenses	7 101	
General expenses	12 841	
Stock at 1 January	102 150	
Balance at bank	19 290	
	1 496 984	1 496 984

The following additional information is provided:

(i) Share capital is divided into 300 000 shares of £1 each which are all issued and fully paid.
(ii) Stock at 31 December 19–5 £103 520.
(iii) The provision for doubtful debts is to be increased to £1 500.
(iv) Provisions for depreciation are to be made on plant at 10% per annum of cost and on vans at 20% per annum of cost.
(v) At 31 December 19–5 general expenses of £1 841 are prepaid.
(vi) Unpaid debenture interest for 19–5 is to be provided.
(vii) A dividend of 10p per share is proposed for 19–5.

Required:
Prepare the Trading and Profit and Loss Accounts of Printer Ltd for the year to 31 December 19–5 and the balance sheet at that date.
Note: Ignore taxation.

[*Royal Society of Arts, Stage II*]

Cashflow Statements

42.1 Uses of Cashflow Statements

A cashflow statement uses information from the accounting records (including Profit and Loss Account) and balance sheet. It is produced in order to show an overall view of money flowing in and out of a business during an accounting period.

A cashflow statement concentrates on the liquidity of a business and explains to the owner or shareholders why, after a year of good profits for example, there is a reduced balance at the bank or a larger bank overdraft at the year-end than there was at the beginning of the year.

Cashflow statements are especially important because they deal with flows of money. It is invariably a shortage of money that causes most businesses to fail, rather than a poor quality product or service. The importance of the cashflow statement is such that all but the smallest companies are required to include this statement as a part of their accounts which they publish and send to shareholders. For sole traders and partnerships, the information that the statement contains is of considerable interest to the owner(s) and to a lender, such as a bank.

42.2 Cashflows

Cashflow statements are divided into five sections:

(a) operating activities;
(b) returns on investments and servicing of finance;
(c) taxation;
(d) investing activities;
(e) financing.

(a) Operating Activities

The main source of cashflow for a business is usually that which is generated from the operating (or trading) activities of the business.

The *net cash inflow from operating activities* is calculated as follows:

Net profit (before interest and tax)
add depreciation for the year*
add decrease in debtors, or *deduct* increase in debtors
add increase in creditors, or *deduct* decrease in creditors
add decrease in stock, or *deduct* increase in stock

* Depreciation is added to net profit because depreciation is a *non-cash*

expense, that is, no money is paid out by the business in respect of the depreciation charged to Profit and Loss Account.

Note that changes in the main working capital items of stock, debtors and creditors have an effect on cash balances. For example, an increase in stock reduces cash, while a decrease in debtors increases cash.

(b) Returns on Investments and Servicing of Finance
This section of the cashflow statement shows the cashflows relating to receipts and payments of interest and dividends, e.g.

  (i) interest received;
 (ii) interest paid;
(iii) dividends received;
(iv) dividends paid (drawings—for a sole trader or partnership business).

(c) Taxation
The tax paid during the year is shown.

(d) Investing Activities
This section of the cashflow statement shows the cashflows relating to the purchase or sale of fixed assets, e.g.

 (i) purchase or sale of plant and machinery;
(ii) purchase or sale of investments.

(e) Financing
The financing section of the statement shows the cashflows in respect of shares and loans, e.g.

cash inflows:
 (i) increase in capital/share capital;
(ii) raising/increase of medium/long-term loans.

cash outflows:
 (i) repayment of capital/share capital;
(ii) repayment of medium/long-term loans.

Note that the change in cash/bank balances is not included in this section.

Increase or Decrease in Cash
The subtotals from the five main areas of business activity are totalled to give the *increase/(decrease) in cash* for the year. There then follows a reconciliation of the cash at the start of the year, plus the increase or minus the decrease for the year (as above), which then equals the balance of cash at the end of the year. Note that 'cash' includes cash itself and the balance at the bank.

42.3   Layout of a Cashflow Statement

A cashflow statement uses a common layout which can be amended to suit the particular needs of the business for which it is being prepared. The following layout is commonly used:

Cashflow statement of . . . for the year-ended . . .

	£	£
Operating activities:		
Net profit (before tax and interest)	x	
Depreciation	x	
(Increase)/decrease in stocks	(x) or x	
(Increase)/decrease in debtors	(x) or x	
Increase/(decrease) in creditors	x or (x)	
Net cash inflow from operating activities		x
Returns on investments and servicing of finance:		
Interest received	x	
Interest paid	(x)	
Drawings/dividends paid (note: amount *paid* during year)	(x)	
Net cash inflow/(outflow) from returns on investments and servicing of finance		x or (x)
Taxation:		
Corporation tax paid (note: amount *paid* during year)	(x)	
Tax paid		(x)
Investing activities:		
Payments to acquire fixed assets	(x)	
Receipts from sales of fixed assets	x	
Net cash inflow/(outflow) from investing activities		x or (x)
Net cash inflow/(outflow) before financing		x or (x)
Financing:		
Issue of capital/share capital	x	
Repayment of capital/share capital	(x)	
Increase in loans	x	
Repayment of loans	(x)	
Net cash inflow/(outflow) from financing		x or (x)
Increase/(decrease) in cash		x or (x)*
Analysis of changes in cash during the year:		
Balance at start of year		x or (x)
Net cash inflow/(outflow)		x or (x)*
Balance at end of year		x or (x)

* These two figures will be the same: the change in cash for the year.

Important note: Money amounts given in brackets are deducted or, where a sub-total, are a minus figure.

42.4   A Worked Example

The following balance sheets show the position of John Smith's business at the end of 19–1 and 19–2:

Balance sheets as at 31 December

	19–1 £	19–1 £	19–1 £	19–2 £	19–2 £	19–2 £
Fixed assets:						
Land and buildings at cost			45 000			60 000
Machinery at cost		25 000			35 000	
Less Depreciation to date		7 000			13 000	
			18 000			22 000
			63 000			82 000
Current assets:						
Stock		11 000			14 000	
Debtors		13 000			18 000	
Bank		9 500			—	
		33 500			32 000	
Less Current liabilities:						
Creditors	14 000			15 000		
Bank overdraft	—			12 500		
		14 000			27 500	
Working capital			19 500			4 500
			82 500			86 500
Financed by						
Capital:						
At start of year			50 000			52 500
Add Net profit for year			10 000			15 000
			60 000			67 500
Less Drawings for year			7 500			6 000
			52 500			61 500
Long-term liabilities:						
Loan			30 000			25 000
			82 500			86 500

John Smith says to you: 'I cannot understand why I am overdrawn at the bank on 31 December 19–2 when I made more profit than in the previous year and took less in drawings from the business.' He asks for your assistance in seeking an explanation.

Note: Loan and overdraft interest paid in 19–2 was £3 250.

Answer

A cashflow statement will give John Smith the answer.

Cashflow statement of John Smith for the year-ended 31 December 19–2

	£	£
Operating activities:		
Net profit (before interest)	18 250	
Depreciation for year	6 000	
Increase in stock	(3 000)	
Increase in debtors	(5 000)	
Increase in creditors	1 000	
Net cash inflow from operating activities		17 250
Returns on investments and servicing of finance:		
Interest paid	(3 250)	
Drawings paid	(6 000)	
Net cash inflow/(outflow) from returns on investments and servicing of finance		(9 250)
Taxation:		
Tax paid		—
Investing activities:		
Purchase of land and buildings	(15 000)	
Purchase of machinery	(10 000)	
Net cash inflow/(outflow) from investing activities		(25 000)
Net cash inflow/outflow) before financing		
		(17 000)
Financing:		
Repayment of loan	(5 000)	
Net cash inflow/(outflow) from financing		(5 000)
Increase/(decrease) in cash		(22 000)
Analysis of changes in cash during the year:		
Bank balance at start of year		9 500
Net cash inflow/(outflow)		(22 000)
Bank balance at the end of year		(12 500)

Points to note:

    (*a*) Net profit for the year (before interest) is calculated as:

net profit for 19–2	£15 000
interest for 19–2	£ 3 250
	£18 250

(b) Depreciation for the year of £6 000 is the amount of increase in depreciation to date shown on the balance sheets, that is, £13 000 minus £7 000.

(c) In this example there is no tax paid (because John Smith is a sole trader who will be taxed as an individual, unlike a company which pays tax on its profits); however, the place where tax would appear is indicated on the cashflow statement.

(d) An increase in stock and debtors reduces the cash available to the business (because stock is being bought, and debtors are being allowed more time to pay). In contrast, an increase in creditors gives an increase in cash (because creditors are allowing John Smith more time to pay).

(e) The change in the bank balance is summarized at the end of the cashflow statement: from £9 500 in the bank to an overdraft of £12 500 is a 'swing' in the bank of minus £22 000, which is the amount of the decrease in cash shown by the cashflow statement.

Explanation to John Smith
During 19–2, the operating activities (or trading activities) of the business have generated cash of £17 250. However, there has been a major outflow of £25 000 on investing activities in the form of the purchase of fixed assets. At the same time, during the year, £5 000 of the loan has been repaid, and interest and drawings paid total £9 250. As a result, the bank balance has changed during the year from £9 500 in the bank to an overdraft of £12 500, a swing of minus £22 000.

42.5 Questions

*1. Prepare a cashflow statement for Janet Jones for the year ended 30 June 19–4.

Balance sheets as at 30 June

	19–3 £	19–4 £		19–3 £	19–4 £
Fixed assets:			Capital	25 000	25 200
At cost	30 000	35 000	Net profit/(loss)	5 400	(750)
Less Depreciation					
to date	6 000	11 800		30 400	24 450
	24 000	23 200	Less Drawings	5 200	4 100
Current assets:				25 200	20 350
Stock	4 900	6 800			
Debtors	5 400	7 500	Long-term liabilities:		
			Bank loan	5 000	7 500
			Current liabilities:		
			Creditors	3 600	7 300
			Bank overdraft	500	2 350
	34 300	37 500		34 300	37 500

Note: Loan and overdraft interest paid in 19–4 was £1 250.

Using the cashflow statement, reply to Janet Jones who says: 'I don't know what has gone wrong this last year—I have worked very hard to build the business up so that I could earn profits to repay the bank.'

*2. John Simms runs a book shop in rented premises in a small market town. His balance sheets for the last two years are as follows:

Balance sheets as at 31 December

	19–1			19–2		
	£	£	£	£	£	£
Fixed assets:						
Shop fittings at cost			3 000			4 000
Less Depreciation						
to date			1 000			1 500
			2 000			2 500
Current assets:						
Stock		7 500			9 700	
Debtors		1 250			2 080	
Bank		440				
		9 190			11 780	
Less Current liabilities:						
Creditors	4 040			8 720		
Bank	—			1 450		
		4 040			10 170	
Working capital			5 150			1 610
			7 150			4 110
Financed by						
Capital			6 600			7 150
Add Net profit for year			10 900			8 160
			17 500			15 310
Less Drawings			10 350			13 200
			7 150			2 110
Loan from wife			—			2 000
			7 150			4 110

Note: Loan and overdraft interest paid in 19–2 was £450.

Prepare the cashflow statement for the year to 31 December 19–2, and explain to John Simms what the statement reveals.

3. The balance sheets of Jane Bridge's engineering business at 31 December 19–5 and 19–6 were as follows:

Balance sheets as at 31 December

	19–5			19–6		
	£	£	£	£	£	£
Fixed assets:						
At cost		35 000			45 000	
Less Depreciation						
to date		15 000			25 000	
			20 000			20 000
Current assets:						
Stock		25 000			40 000	
Debtors		65 000			60 000	
Bank/cash		10 000			—	
		100 000			100 000	
Less Current liabilities:						
Creditors	30 000			20 000		
Bank overdraft	—			15 000		
		30 000			35 000	
			70 000			65 000
			90 000			85 000
Financed by						
Capital			40 000			50 000
Add Net profit for						
the year		15 000			25 000	
Less Drawings		5 000			10 000	
			10 000			15 000
			50 000			65 000
Long-term liabilities:						
Loan from bank			40 000			20 000
			90 000			85 000

Note: Loan and overdraft interest paid in 19–6 was £3 000.

Required:
    (a) Prepare a cashflow statement for the year to 31 December 19–6.
    (b) Explain to Jane Bridges what the statement reveals.

*4. The following are the balance sheets of Deansway Trading Co. Ltd as at 31 December 19–5 and 19–6.

Balance sheets as at 31 December

	19–5 £000	19–5 £000	19–5 £000	19–6 £000	19–6 £000	19–6 £000
Fixed assets:						
Land and buildings at cost			180			250
Machinery: see note below			106			130
			286			380
Current assets:						
Stock	44			86		
Debtors	42			56		
Bank	2			—		
		88			142	
Less Current liabilities:						
Creditors	34			52		
Bank	—			38		
Proposed dividend	16			14		
Corporation tax	6			8		
		56			112	
			32			30
			318			410
Financed by:						
£1 ordinary shares			200			300
Profit and loss account			58			60
			258			360
10% debentures			60			50
			318			410

Notes:

(*i*) During 19–6, movements on machinery account were:

Balance at 1 January 19–6	£106 000
Additions during year	£ 40 000
	£146 000
Less Depreciation for year	£ 16 000
	£130 000

(*ii*) Debenture and overdraft interest paid in 19–6 was £7 000.

Required:

Prepare a cashflow statement for the year to 31 December 19–6.

Multiple-choice Questions—11

Read each question carefully. Choose the *one* answer you think is correct. Amswers are given on page 411.

1. In the final accounts of a limited company, directors' remuneration is:

   A debited in the Trading Account
   B debited in the Profit and Loss Account
   C · debited in the Appropriation Account
   D deducted from share capital on the balance sheet

2. Which is the odd one out?

   A Debentures   **C** Equity capital
   B Ordinary shares   **D** Preference shares

3. In the final accounts of a limited company, debenture interest paid is:

   A debited in the Trading Account
   B debited in the Profit and Loss Account
   C debited in the Appropriation Account
   D shown as a long-term liability on the balance sheet

4. Retained profits of a limited company belong to the:

   A directors   **C** debenture-holders
   B shareholders   **D** company

5. Which one of the following is *not* included in shareholders' funds?

   A Debentures   **C** Revenue reserves
   B Ordinary shares   **D** Capital reserves

6. When shares are sold at a premium, the amount of the premium is credited to:

   A Profit and Loss Account   **C** revenue reserves
   B Bank Account   **D** Share Premium Account

7. The authorized share capital of a limited company is the total value of the:

   A shares it has issued
   B issued share capital, plus reserves
   C issued share capital, plus reserves, plus debentures
   D shares it is allowed, by law, to issue

8. Proposed dividends are:

   A shown as a current liability on the balance sheet
   B debited, with other business expenses, to the Profit and Loss Account
   C paid from capital reserves
   D credited to the Appropriation Account

9. A company has a net profit of £12 000. It has 10 000 ten-per-cent preference shares of £1 each in issue, together with 100 000 ordinary shares of £1 each. The directors decide to transfer £3 000 to general reserve and to pay the remaining amount of profit as ordinary dividends. Ignoring taxation, what percentage dividend will be paid to the ordinary shareholders?

A   10%

C   9%

B   8%

D   12%

10. The trial balance of a limited company shows motor vehicles at cost £20 000, and depreciation to date amounting to £7 200. Depreciation is at 20 per cent per annum, using the reducing-balance method. What will be the net book value of motor vehicles showing in the balance sheet, after allowing for this year's depreciation?

A   £11 520

C   £10 240

B   £12 800

D   £ 8 800

11. Which one of the following does *not* appear in the Appropriation Account?

A   corporation tax

C   net profit for year

B   dividends paid

D   debenture interest

12. Which one of the following items in a cashflow statement would *not* be shown in the operating activities section?

A   net profit for the year

B   repayment of loans

C   depreciation for the year

D   increase/decrease in creditors

Questions with Source Documents

Some examination boards include questions with source documents which require candidates to process the documents through the book-keeping system. A selection of such questions follows.

1. John Boyd commenced business on 1 March 19–0 selling electrical goods from rented premises.

    Below is a copy of John's Cash Book for his first week's trading:

	Cash £	Bank £		Cash £	Bank £
Cash Book					
19–0			19–0		
Mar. 1 Capital		20 000	Mar. 2 Shop fittings		15 000
2 Sales		700	3 Purchases		550
3 Transfer	50		3 Transfer		50
6 Sales		810	5 Rent		1 000
6 T. Green		800	6 G. Hobbs		1 200
			6 Cleaning	30	
			6 Balance c/d	20	4 510
	50	22 310		50	22 310
Mar. 6 Balance b/d	20	4 510			

The following invoice was received by John in respect of purchases:

Invoice

G. Hobbs and Son
Church Place
Swinford

2 March 19–0

Invoice no 786

Dr to:

John Boyd
Castle Street
Beckford

To supply of:

300 electric irons @ £4 each   £1 200.00

During the first week John sent out the following sales invoice:

INVOICE

John Boyd
Electrical Wholesaler
Castle Street
Beckford

Invoice no 001

3 March 19–0

Dr to:

T. Green
Water Road
Bosforth

To supply of:

100 electric irons @ £8 each   £800 00

You are required to:
(a) Post John's cash book to his ledger.
   Post the purchase invoice to his ledger.
   Post the sales invoice to his ledger.
(b) Extract a trial balance as at 6 March 19–0.
N.B. Day book entries are not required in this question.
   [Pitman Examinations Institute, Level 1]

2. As a junior book-keeper, one of your duties is to assist the firm's cashier by looking after the petty cash.
   You are required to:

   (a) Enter the following vouchers into the petty cash book having analysis columns for:

   Cleaning
   Motor expenses
   Stationery
   Postage

   The petty cash book is to be kept on the imprest system, the amount spent to be reimbursed at the end of each week.
   (b) Balance the petty cash book at the end of the week, showing the reimbursement.

   The opening petty cash float is £100.

PETTY CASH VOUCHER		
		No 001

Date __1 June__ 19 0

Required for: £ p

Petrol   3·50

Signed by ...E. Brown....

PETTY CASH VOUCHER		
		No 002

Date __1 June__ 19 0

Required for: £ p

Petrol   12·00

Signed by ...J. (J.) Davies.....

PETTY CASH VOUCHER		
		No 003

Date __2 June__ 19 0

Required for: £ p

Envelopes 9·00

Signed by ...R. Clark......

PETTY CASH VOUCHER		
		No 004

Date __2 June__ 19 0

Required for: £ p

Stamps 7·00

Signed by ...A. Johns......

PETTY CASH VOUCHER		
		No 005

Date __2 June__ 19 0

Required for: £ p

Sellotape 3·50

Signed by ...R. Owen.......

PETTY CASH VOUCHER		
		No 006

Date __3 June__ 19 0

Required for: £ p

Dusters 3·00

Signed by ...Brian Amos..

PETTY CASH VOUCHER		
		No 007

Date __3 June__ 19 0

Required for: £ p

Pencils 2·50

Signed by ...R. Clark.....

PETTY CASH VOUCHER		
		No 008

Date __4 June__ 19 0

Required for: £ p

Petrol 10·50

Signed by ...J. (J.) Davies..

PETTY CASH VOUCHER		
		No 009

Date __4 June__ 19 0

Required for: £ p

Dustpan 2·50

Signed by ...E. Brown......

PETTY CASH VOUCHER		
		No 010

Date __5 June__ 19 0

Required for: £ p

OIL 3·20

Signed by ...J. Davies..

PETTY CASH VOUCHER		
		No 011

Date __6 June__ 19 0

Required for: £ p

Stamps 5·00

Signed by ...A. Johns...

PETTY CASH VOUCHER		
		No 012

Date __6 June__ 19 0

Required for: £ p

PENS 4·50

Signed by ...R. Owen.....

[Pitman Examinations Institute, Level 1]

Summary Answers to Questions

Unit 2.3

1.

	Gain	Loss
1 Nov.	Cash	Capital
2 Nov.	Bank	Cash
6 Nov.	Photocopier	Bank
10 Nov.	Office fittings	Cash
15 Nov.	Typewriter	Bank
17 Nov.	Cash	Photocopier

2. Capital *Cr.* £500, Cash *Dr.* £500 and £200, *Cr.* £400 and £75, Bank *Dr.* £400, *Cr.* £200 and £200, Photocopier *Dr.* £200, *Cr.* £200, Office fittings *Dr.* £75, Typewriter *Dr.* £200.

3.

	Gain	Loss
1 Jan.	Cash	Capital
2 Jan.	Bank	Cash
4 Jan.	Van	Bank
6 Jan.	Shop fittings	Cash
10 Jan.	Cash register	Bank
11 Jan.	Shop fittings	Bank
14 Jan.	Bank	Shop fittings
20 Jan.	Bank	Capital
22 Jan.	Cash	Bank

Unit 3.5

1.

	Gain	Loss
1 Apr.	Cash	Capital
2 Apr.	Bank	Cash
4 Apr.	Van	Bank
6 Apr.	Typewriter	Business Equipment Ltd
11 Apr.	Photocopier	Johnson Brothers Ltd
12 Apr.	Business Equipment Ltd	Bank
17 Apr.	Johnson Brothers Ltd	Bank
24 Apr.	Cash	Bank

2. Capital *Cr.* £2 000, Cash *Dr.* £2 000 and £50, *Cr.* £1 750, Bank *Dr.* £1 750, *Cr.* £1 000, £250, £350 and £50, Van *Dr.* £1 000, Typewriter *Dr.* £250, Business Equipment Ltd *Dr.* £250, *Cr.* £250, Photocopier *Dr.* £350, Johnson Brothers Ltd *Dr.* £350, *Cr.* £350.

3. Capital *Cr.* £1 000, Cash *Dr.* £1 000, *Cr.* £750, £100 and £100, Bank *Dr.* £750 and £400, *Cr.* £400 and £250, Machinery *Dr.* £250 and £100, Machinery (Rowcester) Ltd *Dr.* £250, *Cr.* £250, Typewriter *Dr.* £100, Office Supplies Ltd *Dr.* £100, *Cr.* £100, Van *Dr.* £400, *Cr.* £400.

Unit 4.12
1.

	Gain	Loss
1 Jun.	Bank	Capital
3 Jun.	Purchases	Bank
5 Jun.	Purchases	D. Smith
6 Jun.	Bank	Sales
7 Jun.	D. Smith	Returns out
10 Jun.	I. Wain	Sales
12 Jun.	Machinery	Rowcester Machinery Co
14 Jun.	D. Smith	Bank
17 Jun.	Returns in	I. Wain
20 Jun.	Bank	Sales
22 Jun.	Bank	I. Wain
24 Jun.	Returns in	Bank
27 Jun.	Rowcester Machinery Co	Bank

2. Capital *Cr.* £2 000, Bank *Dr.* £2 000, £95, £55 and £80, *Cr.* £200, £100, £55 and £500, Purchases *Dr.* £200 and £150, D. Smith *Dr.* £50 and £100, *Cr.* £150, Sales *Cr.* £95, £105 and £55, Returns out *Cr.* £50, I. Wain *Dr.* £105, *Cr.* £25 and £80, Machinery *Dr.* £500, Rowcester Machinery Co *Dr.* £500, *Cr.* £500, Returns in *Dr.* £25 and £55.

3. Capital *Cr.* £1 750, Bank *Dr.* £1 000 and £110, *Cr.* £100, £200, £175 and £200, Machinery *Dr.* £750 and £200, Purchases *Dr.* £250, £100 and £85, Trade Suppliers Ltd *Dr.* £75 and £175, *Cr.* £250, Sales *Cr.* £110, £55 and £95, T. Smith *Dr.* £110, *Cr.* £110, Returns out *Cr.* £75, Cash *Dr.* £200 and £55, *Cr.* £85, M. Jones *Dr.* £95, *Cr.* £25, Returns in *Dr.* £25.

Unit 5.5
1. Capital *Cr.* £42 500, Bank *Dr.* £5 250, Premises *Dr.* £30 000, Shop fittings *Dr.* £3 300, Purchases *Dr.* £4 560, Shopfitters Ltd nil, Sales *Cr.* £1 140, N. Johnson nil, A. Paul *Dr.* £495, Returns out *Cr.* £125, Cash *Dr.* £125, Returns in *Dr.* £35.

Unit 6.5
1. Capital *Cr.* £2 100, Bank *Dr.* £208, Cash *Dr.* £325, Purchases *Dr.* £1 125, A. Hands nil, Machinery *Dr.* £750, Southern Machines Ltd nil, Sales *Cr.* £457, B. Brittan *Dr.* £82, P. Newbury *Dr.* £74, M. Keegan nil, H. Lewis nil, Returns out *Cr.* £75, Returns in *Dr.* £68. Trial balance totals £2 632.

2. *Dr.:* Cash £65, Bank £98, Van £1 250, Machinery £750, Purchases £610, H. Jones £46, Office equipment £312, Returns in £65.
   Cr.: Sales £485, Capital £2 500, Returns out £84, T. Cook £127. Trial balance totals £3 196.

Unit 7.5
1. (a) *Dr.* Harris   (b) *Dr.* Purchases
       Cr. Sales   *Cr.* Cash

   (c) *Dr.* Cash   (d) *Dr.* Rent
       Cr. Sales   *Cr.* Bank

   (e) *Dr.* Electricity (or heating)   (f) *Dr.* Drawings
       Cr. Bank   *Cr.* Purchases

2. *Dr.:* Bank £1 065, Premises £40 000, Purchases £975, Van £2 500, Cash £50, Wages and salaries £325, Drawings £175, Motor expenses £90, P. Hughes £100, Postages £75, Returns in £12.
   Cr.: Capital £44 000, G. Harrison £175, Returns out £75, Sales £617, Rent received £500.
   Trial balance totals £45 367.

3. *Dr.:* Bank £4 106, Shop fixtures £400, Purchases £1 640, Rent paid £420, Cash £260, Insurance £74, Wages £90, Drawings £60.
   Cr.: Capital £6 000, Sales £1 050.
   Trial balance totals £7 050.

Unit 8.4

1. *Trading Account: Dr.* Purchases £10 850, Gross profit c/d £13 110. *Cr.* Sales £23 960.
   Profit and Loss Account: Dr. Salaries £6 210, Heating and lighting £870, Motor expenses £540, Postages £310, Rent paid £1 250, Net profit £3 930. *Cr.* Gross profit b/d £13 110.
   Capital Account: Cr. Balance b/d £20 000, Net profit £3 930.

2. *Trial balance: Dr.* Bank £723, Purchases £477, Cash £163, Salaries £303, D. Jinks £205, A. Winter £76, Rent paid £100, Sundry expenses £25. *Cr.* Capital £1 000, P. Martin £102, Sales £970.
   Totals £2 072.
   Trading Account: Dr. Purchases £477, Gross profit c/d £493. *Cr.* Sales £970.
   Profit and Loss Account: Dr. Salaries £303, Rent paid £100, Sundry expenses £25, Net profit £65. *Cr.* Gross profit b/d £493.

Unit 9.9

1. *Assets:*
   Fixed assets: Premises £20 750, Fixtures and fittings £1 250, Motor vehicles £5 000, Total £27 000.
   Current assets: Stock £2 350, Debtors £4 110, Cash £85, Total £6 545.

   Capital and liabilities:
   Capital: £20 000, *add* Net profit £3 127, *less* Drawings £2 540, Total £20 587.
   Long-term liabilities: Loan £6 000.
   Current liabilities: Creditors £3 020, Bank overdraft £3 938, Total £6 958.
   Balance sheet totals: £33 545.

2. *Assets:*
   Fixed assets: Goodwill £3 000, Premises £20 000, Fixtures and fittings £4 000, Motor vehicles £8 000, Investments £10 000, Total £45 000.
   Current assets: Stock £6 000, Debtors £5 000, Total £11 000.

   Capital and liabilities:
   Capital £40 000, *add* Net profit £5 000, Total £45 000.
   Current liabilities: Creditors £8 000, Bank overdraft £3 000, Total £11 000.
   Balance sheet totals: £56 000.

Unit 10.7

1. *Trading Account: Dr.* Opening stock £5 000, Purchases £25 000, Carriage inwards £750. *less* Closing stock £4 500, Wages £9 500, Gross profit c/d £1 000. *Cr.* Sales £37 000, *less* Returns inwards £250.

   Profit and Loss Account: Dr. Carriage outwards £1 050, Expenses £750. *Cr.* Gross profit b/d £1 000, Net loss £800.

4. *Assets:*
   Fixed assets: Machinery £3 000, Vans £2 000, Total £5 000.
   Current assets: Stock £1 100, Debtors £1 300, Bank £225, Cash £625, Total £3 250.

   Capital and liabilities:
   Capital £3 000, *add* Net profit £1 200, *less* Drawings £450, Total £3 750.
   Long-term liability: Bank loan £2 000.
   Current liability: Creditors £2 500.
   Balance sheet totals: £8 250.

5. (*a*) £1 600, (*b*) £3 600, (*c*) £6 840, (*d*) £360, (*e*) Gross profit c/d £2 000.

Unit 11.11

1. *Dr.* £300, £300, £100, £200, £250, Balance c/d £50. *Cr.* Profit and Loss Account £1 200.

3. *Rates Account: Dr.* Balance b/d £600, £900, £1 200. *Cr.* Profit and Loss Account £1 900, Balance c/d £800.
   Packing Materials Account: Dr. Balance b/d £621, Bank/cash £1 890. *Cr.* Profit and Loss Account £2 031, Balance c/d £480.

6. (*a*) Capital, (*b*) revenue, (*c*) revenue, (*d*) revenue, (*e*) capital.

8. *Trading Account: Dr.* Opening stock £7 000, Purchases £30 000, *less* Closing stock £9 500, Gross profit c/d £12 500. *Cr.* Sales £40 000.
   Profit and Loss Account: Dr. Rates £1 200, Heating and lighting £1 500, Cleaning £1 700, Packing materials £1 100, Net profit £7 000. *Cr.* Gross profit b/d £12 500.

   Balance sheet:
   Fixed assets: Premises £65 000, Fixtures and fittings £7 500, Total £72 500.
   Current assets: Stocks £9 500, Bank £8 000, Stock of packing material £300, Rates prepaid £400, Total £18 200.
   Capital £85 000, *add* Net profit £7 000, *less* Drawings £5 000, Total £87 000.
   Current liability: Creditors £3 700.
   Balance sheet totals: £90 700.

Unit 12.5

1. Purchases *Dr.* £330, S. Hythe nil, VAT *Dr.* £9, L. Layton *Cr.* £253, Bank *Dr.* £154, Sales *Cr.* £440, T. Lancaster nil, Machinery *Dr.* £200, Machinery Ltd nil. Trial balance totals £693.

2. VAT Account: *Dr.* £600, £800, £900, Bank £1 100. *Cr.* £900, £1 000, £1 500.

Unit 13.10

6. (*a*) Opening balance per statement £21 150, *less* purchases invoice received on 8 May from Smithfield (entered on previous statement) £5 650, *less* cheque sent to Smithfield in April, entered on statement on 4 May £7 000, opening balance per our books £8 500.

(b) Closing balance per our books £960, *add* cheque sent to Smithfield on 29 April not yet entered on statement (amount includes cash discount received) £12 000, closing balance per statement £12 960.

(c) Purchases in our books; sales in Smithfield's accounts.

7. (b) (i) Super 50%, Standard 33.3%.
    (ii) Super 33.3%, Standard 25%.
(c) Credit note.
(d) 18 Super at £4 = £72, 16 Standard at £2.50 = £40, Total £112.

Unit 15.9

1. Totals: Discount allowed £15, Cash £75, Bank £765, Discount received £20.
Balances: Cash £75, Bank £135.

3. Totals: Discount allowed £12, Cash £72, Bank £398, Discount received £9.
Balances: Cash £11, Bank overdraft £234.

Unit 16.6

1. Purchases journal total £792.

2. Sales journal total £547.

Unit 17.7

1. Purchases journal: B. Moran £102, J. James £1 050, Total £1 152.
Returns out journal: J. James £300.
James: *Dr.* £300, £375, Balance c/d £375, *Cr.* £1 050.
Moran: *Dr.* £102, *Cr.* £102.

5. Ajax Services £192.00, VAT £19.20, Total £211.20.
Markups £200.00, VAT £20.00, Total £220.00.
Jones Machines £459.00, VAT £45.90, Total £504.90.
Wye Products £240.00, VAT £24.00, Total £264.00.
General ledger: Sales *Cr.* £1 091.00, VAT *Cr.* £109.10.

Unit 21.7

1. *Dr.* Cash received £50. *Paid:* Total £43, Cleaning £4, Postages £11, Carriage £8, Office expenses £20. 6 June Cash received £43.

2. *Dr.* Balance b/d £7.37, Cash received £42.63. *Paid:* Total £42.36. Stationery £9.58, Wages £16.43, Postages £7.63, Ledger £8.72.
1 March Cash received £42.36.

6. Cash book totals: Discount allowed £1.50, Bank £1 715.30, Discount received £5.00. Balance: Bank £1 374.88.
Petty cash book: *Dr.* Balance b/d £50. *Paid:* Total £29.50, Cleaning £11.00, Postages £2.90, Travelling £3.00, Stationery £12.60.
25 April Cash received £29.50.

Unit 22.7

3. (a) Paid in   (b) £575 *Cr.*   (c) Last three digits of cheque number
(d) Withdrawn   (e) £145 *Dr.* (overdrawn)   (f) Standing Order
(g) £165 *Dr.* (overdrawn)   (h) Current liability

Unit 23.7

2. (a) *Dr.* Balance b/d £164, D. May credit transfer £65. *Cr.* Ace Insurance standing order £26, Bank charges £18, Balance c/d £185.

(b) Cash book balance £185, *add* unpresented cheques: G. Dow 337 £110, K. Peel 339 £401, *less* bank lodgement L. Day £85. Bank statement balance £611.

3. (a) *Dr.* Balance b/d £332, Cash £518, Investment dividends £600. *Cr.* S. Line £235, N. Farden £102, K. O'Connor £136, A. Brown £340, Direct debit insurance £78, Balance c/d £559.

(b) Cash book balance £559, *add* unpresented cheques: S. Line 118 £235, K. O'Connor 120 £136. Bank statement balance £930.

Unit 24.7

1. *Dr.* Petty cash £86, Shop premises £15 000, Equipment £9 640, Stock £7 860, Rates prepaid £134, C. Box £20, D. Dawes £190.

Cr. Bank overdraft £1 220, B. Ihle £860, Electricity accrued £120, Capital £30 730.

Unit 25.10

1. Machine Account: 1 Jan. 19–1 *Dr.* £2 000 (account kept at cost).

Provision for Depreciation Account: 19–1 £600, *plus* 19–2 £600 = £1 200 balance, *plus* 19–3 £600 = £1 800 balance.

Balance sheet as at 31 Dec. 19–3: Machine at cost £2 000, *less* depreciation to date £1 800 = £200 balance.

2. Machine Account (no Provision for Depreciation Account used): £3 000 *less* £150 = £2 850 balance; £2 850 *less* £300 = £2 550 balance; £2 550 *less* £300 = £2 250 balance.

5. *Trading Account: Dr.* Opening stock £900, Purchases £8 000, *less* Returns out £100, Carriage in £200, *less* Closing stock £1 100, Gross profit c/d £4 950. *Cr.* Sales £12 900, *less* Returns in £50.

Profit and Loss Account: Dr. Rates £350, Heating £500, Discount allowed £100, Salaries £1 200, Depreciation, Buildings £500, Fixtures £400, Net profit £2 100. *Cr.* Gross profit b/d £4 950, Commission received £200.

Balance sheet:

Fixed assets: Goodwill £1 000, Buildings £5 000 *less* £1 000, Fixtures £1 200 *less* £400, Total £5 800.

Current assets: Stock £1 100, Debtors £1 500, Bank £600, Rates prepaid £150, Total £3 350.

Capital £6 650, Net profit £2 100, *less* Drawings £300, Total £8 450.

Current liability: Creditors £700.

Balance sheet totals £9 150.

Unit 26.3

1. (a) 1 Jan. 19–1 *Dr.* £85 (account kept at cost), 31 Dec. 19–3 *Cr.* £85 (to Disposals Account).

(b) 31 Dec. 19–1 *Cr.* £20; 31 Dec. 19–2 *Cr.* £20; 31 Dec. 19–3 *Cr.* £20, *Dr.* £60 (to Disposals Account).

(c) *Dr.* £85 (cost of machine), *Cr.* £20 (sale proceeds), £60 (depreciation to date), £5 (loss on sale).

Machine at cost £85, *less* Depreciation to date £40 = £45 net book value.

3. (a) 1 Jan. 19–1 *Dr.* £500, 1 Apr. 19–2 *Dr.* £800, 1 Jul. 19–3 *Dr.* £600, 1 Jul. 19–4 *Cr.* £500 (to Disposals Account).
   (b) 31 Dec. 19–1 *Cr.* £50, 31 Dec. 19–2 *Cr.* £110, 31 Dec. 19–3 *Cr.* £160, 31 Dec. 19–4 *Cr.* £165, 1 Jul. 19–4 *Dr.* £175 (to Disposals Account).
   (c) *Dr.* £500 (cost of machine), *Cr.* £290 (sale proceeds), £175 (depreciation to date), £35 (loss on sale).

Unit 27.7
1. *T. Pitt: Dr.* Balance b/d £59.00, *Cr.* Bank £29.00, Bank £7.50 (from trustee in bankruptcy), Bad debts written off £22.50.
   Bad Debts Written Off: Dr. T. Pitt £22.50.

2. (a) *Dr.* Balance b/d £400, Sales £250, *Cr.* Bank £390, Discount allowed £10, Returns in £50, Cash £100, Bad debts written off £100.
   (b) *Dr.* £100.

5. *Trading Account: Dr.* Opening stock £1 980, Purchases £9 450, *less* Returns out £410, *less* Closing stock £2 050, Gross profit c/d £6 600. *Cr.* Sales £16 330, *less* Returns in £760.
   Profit and Loss Account: Dr. Discount allowed £680, Wages and salaries £3 010, Bad debts written off £190, Rates and insurance £270, Carriage out £520, Sundry expenses £120, Depreciation, Office furniture £70, Fixtures and fittings £20, Net profit £2 000. *Cr.* Gross profit b/d £6 600, Discount received £280.

   Balance sheet:
   Fixed assets: Premises £6 000, Office furniture £700 *less* £70, Fixtures and fittings £600 *less* £20, Total £7 210.
   Current assets: Stock £2 050, Debtors £3 460, Bank £750, Cash £70, Total £6 330.
   Capital £11 100, Net profit £2 000, *less* Drawings £1 700, Total £11 400.
   Current liabilities: Creditors £2 090, Wages accrued £50, Total £2 140.
   Balance sheet totals £13 540.

6. *Trading Account: Dr.* Opening stock £3 940, Purchases £11 468, *less* Returns out £100, Carriage in £160, *less* Closing stock £2 064, Gross profit c/d £7 912. *Cr.* Sales £22 440, *less* Returns in £1 124.
   Profit and Loss Account: Dr. Carriage out £80, Rates £240, Discount allowed £48, Salaries and wages £1 800, Printing and stationery £286, Bad debts £148, Telephone and postage £360, Insurance £84, Depreciation, Premises £480, Fixtures and fittings £280, Net profit £4 178. *Cr.* Gross profit b/d £7 912, Discount received £72.

   Balance sheet:
   Fixed assets: Premises £9 600 *less* £480, Fixtures and fittings £1 400 *less* £280, Total £10 240.
   Current assets: Stock £2 064, Debtors £480, Bank £1 112, Rates prepaid £80, Total £3 736.
   Capital £10 040, Net profit £4 178, *less* Drawings £2 600, Total £11 618.
   Current liabilities: Creditors £2 340, Printing and stationery accrued £18, Total £2 358.
   Balance sheet totals £13 976.

Unit 28.3

3. (*a*) (i) A. Salmon *Dr.* £72, K. Haddock *Cr.* £72.
      (ii) Bad debts written off *Dr.* £48, K. Haddock *Cr.* £48.
      (iii) Repairs *Dr.* £30, Office furniture *Cr.* £30.
   (*b*) K. Haddock: *Dr.* £48, £72. *Cr.* £72, £48.
      A. Salmon: *Dr.* £72, *Cr.* £72.
      Office furniture: *Dr.* £530, £30. *Cr.* £30, £530 (balance c/d).
      Bad debts: *Dr.* £186, £48. *Cr.* £234 (balance c/d).
      Repairs: *Dr.* £30, *Cr.* £30 (balance c/d).

5. *Dr.* Fixtures and fittings £22 000, Delivery vans £20 000, Stocks £8 720, Trade debtors £5 050, Bank £4 650, Cash £626, Purchases £11 086, Drawings £3 500, Delivery van expenses £2 518, Bad debts written off £50, Bank charges £100. *Cr.* Capital £50 000, Trade creditors £3 986, Sales £24 314.
   Trial balance totals £78 300.

Unit 29.4

1. *Dr.* R. Belgrave £36, Returns in £20, H. Singh £4. *Cr.* Error from trial balance £6, T. Lewsey £40, D. Nash £14.

2. (*a*) (i) increase net profit by £2 000, (ii) increase net profit by £360, (iii) increase net profit by £352, (iv) decrease net profit by £1 480, (v) decrease net profit by £112.
   (*b*) Incorrect net profit £4 000, *less* loan credited to Profit and Loss Account £2 000, *less* omission of credit purchases £360, *less* opening stock undervalued £352, *add* discounts received (£740) *debited* to Profit and Loss Account £1 480, *add* deposit account interest (£56) debited in error to Profit and Loss Account £112, corrected net profit £2 880.

4. (*a*) Shop fittings *Dr.* £320, Purchases *Cr.* £320   (*b*) Trade debtors *Dr.* £150
   (*c*) Returns in *Dr.* £30, Trade debtors *Cr.* £30   (*d*) Sundry trade creditors *Cr.* £16 (*e*) Sales *Cr.* £100.
   Trial balance: Dr. Drawings £3 000, Stock £2 500, Trade debtors £3 070, Shop fittings £1 850, Purchases £4 820, General expenses £860, Bank £1 660, Returns in £30.
   Cr. Capital £7 450, Trade creditors £2 700, Sales £7 560, Discount received £40, Returns out £40.
   Trial balance totals £17 790.

6. (*a*) (i) Sales Account overstated by £450, therefore credit side of trial balance overstated by £450. (ii) Discounts received should be credited to Discount Account, therefore debit side of trial balance overstated by £168. (iii) Wages Account understated, Office Furniture Account overstated, trial balance unaffected. (iv) Creditors overstated by £27, therefore credit side of trial balance overstated by £27.
   (*b*) Incorrect net profit £2 770, *less* sales overstated £450, *add* discounts received (£84) *debited* to Discount Account £168, *less* wages debited to Office Furniture Account £66, corrected net profit £2 422. (Item (iv) has no effect on net profit.)

Unit 30.6

1. *Dr.* Balances b/d £3 953, Sales £45 742. *Cr.* Returns in £350, Cheques received £41 270, Discount allowed £450, Bad debts written off £1 059, Balances c/d £6 566.
   Totals £49 695.

2. *Dr.* Balances b/d £6 840, Sales £46 801. *Cr.* Discount allowed £420, Bad debts written off £494, Receipts £43 780, Returns in £296, Balances c/d £8 651. Totals £53 641.

3. *Dr.* Payments £5 100, Discount £300, Returns out £200, Set-off £100, Balances c/d £5 300, *Cr.* Balances b/d £7 000, Purchases £4 000, Totals £11 000.

Unit 31.7

2. (*a*) 900 units in stock at month-end.
(*b*) *Dr.* Opening stock £3 000, Purchases £4 000, *less* Closing stock £1 800, Cost of sales £5 200, Gross profit c/d £2 550. *Cr.* Sales £7 750.

Unit 32.12

1. (*a*) M. Groom: (i) £57.00, (ii) nil, (iii) £57.00.
L. Tarrant: (i) £60.00, (ii) £13.50, (iii) £73.50.
R. Blake: (i) £60.00, (ii) £18.00, (iii) £78.00.
C. Ford: (i) £60.00, (ii) £14.25, (iii) £74.25.
(*b*) M. Groom £64: time basis.
L. Tarrant £80: time basis.
R. Blake £76: piecework.
C. Ford £72: piecework.

2. (*a*) Basic wage £87.50, Overtime £22.50, Bonus £5, Gross pay £115.
(*b*) Deductions: Social and welfare £1, National Insurance £4.25, Income tax £21, Take-home pay £88.75.

Unit 33.5

1. (*a*) Debtors at 30 Sep. 19–0 £1 460, Sales for year £5 950, *less* Cash received £6 390, Debtors at 30 Sep. 19–1 £1 020.
Creditors at 30 Sep. 19–0 £1 040, Purchases for year £3 890, *less* Cash paid £4 130, Creditors at 30 Sep. 19–1 £800.
(*b*) Capital at 30 Sep. 19–0: Fixtures and fittings £400, Stock £1 280, Debtors £1 460, Bank £720, Cash £30, *less* Creditors £1 040, Total £2 850.
Capital at 30 Sep. 19–1: Fixtures and fittings £360, Stock £1 490, Debtors £1 020, Bank £940, Cash £40, *less* Creditors £800, Total £3 050.
(*c*) Net profit for year to 30 Sep. 19–1: £3 050 *less* £2 850, *add* Drawings £1 250 = £1 450.

2. (*a*) Capital at 30 Apr. 19–1: Stock £2 280, Debtors £3 170, Bank £1 160, Office furniture £250, *less* Creditors £1 980, Total £4 880.
Capital at 30 Apr. 19–2: Stock £2 760, Debtors £4 040, Bank £930, Office furniture £600, *less* Creditors £2 020, Total £6 310.
(*b*) Net profit for year to 30 Apr. 19–2: £6 310 *less* £4 880, *less* increase in capital £350, *add* Drawings £1 380 = £2 460.
(*c*) *Dr.* Drawings £1 380, Balance c/d £6 310. *Cr.* Balance b/d £4 880. Office furniture £350, Profit and loss £2 460.

3. (*a*) Bank/cash £541, Debtors £194, Stock £989, Furniture and shop fittings £250, Van £600, *less* Creditors £1 240, *less* Rent accrued £25, Total £1 309.
(*b*) *Trading Account: Dr.* Opening stock £989, Purchases £6 318 (£5 988, *less* £1 240, *add* £1 570), *less* Closing stock £910, Gross profit c/d £1 724. *Cr.* Cash sales £6 943, Credit sales £1 178 (£1 236, *less* £194, *add* £136).

Profit and Loss Account: Dr. Rent, rates and insurance £485 (£540, *less* £25, *less* £30), Lighting and heating £53, Motor van expenses £226, Repairs £17, General expenses £84, Depreciation, Furniture and shop fittings £30, Van £120, Net profit £709. *Cr.* Gross profit b/d £1 724.

(*c*) *Balance sheet:*

Fixed assets: Furniture and shop fittings £250, *add* £50, *less* £30, Van £600, *less* £120, Total £750.

Current assets: Stock £910, Debtors £136, Bank/cash £1 073 (£541, *add* total receipts £8 179, *less* total payments £7 647), Rates and insurance prepaid £30, Total £2 149.

Capital £1 309, Net profit £709, *less* Drawings £700, Total £1 318.

Current liabilities: Creditors £1 570, Lighting and heating accrued £11, Total £1 581.

Balance sheet totals £2 899.

Unit 34.9

1. *Income and Expenditure Account: Dr.* Printing and stationery £10, Rent £20, Sundry expenses £15, Surplus £320. *Cr.* Subscriptions £320, Sale of dance tickets £80, *less* Dance expenses £45, Profit £35, Sale of refreshments £30, *less* Cost of refreshments £20, Profit £10.

   Balance sheet:

   Assets: Furniture £150, Stock of stationery £5, Bank £175.

   Capital and liabilities: Surplus for year £320, Rent accrued £10.

   Balance sheet totals: £330.

2. *Income and Expenditure Account: Dr.* Travelling expenses £112, Printing and stationery £53, Repairs £85, Prizes £150, Surplus £2 280. *Cr.* Subscriptions £2 200, Refreshments £430, Rent received £50.

   Balance sheet:

   Assets: Land £2 000, Clubhouse £7 000, Equipment £700, Bank £1 350.

   Capital and liabilities: Accumulated fund £8 700, Surplus £2 280, Subscriptions in advance £70.

   Balance sheet totals £11 050.

6. *Income and Expenditure Account: Dr.* Travelling expenses £96, Printing £48, Stationery and postage £34, Rent £200, Cricket league fees £69, Rates and insurance £150, Interest on loans from members £36, Club treasurer £80, Surplus £32. *Cr.* Bar takings £246, *less* Bar refreshments purchased £203, *less* Closing bar stocks £48, Profit on bar £91, Subscriptions £540, Match receipts £114.

   Balance sheet:

   Assets: Lockers £180, Sporting equipment £152, Bar stocks £48, Bank £199, Rent prepaid £25.

   Capital and liabilities: Surplus for year £32, Loans from members £450, Stationery accrued £6, Interest accrued on members' loans £36, Accrued to club treasurer £80. Balance sheet totals £604.

7. *Bar Trading Account: Dr.* Opening stock £1 070, Purchases £4 280, *less* Closing stock £1 150, Wages £770, Gross profit c/d £1 400. *Cr.* Bar takings £6 370.

   Income and Expenditure Account: Dr. Wages £1 540, Salary £750, Rent and rates £580, Postages and stationery £220, Depreciation of fixtures and fittings £90, Insurance £140, Sundry expenses £210, Surplus £1 100. *Cr.* Gross profit on bar b/d £1 400, Subscriptions £2 970, Discount received £260.

Balance sheet:
Assets: Fixtures and fittings £900, *less* £270, Bar stock £1 150, Bank £1 820, Cash £70, Rent and rates prepaid £60, Subscriptions due £50.
Capital and liabilities: Accumulated fund £2 120, Surplus £1 100, Creditors £440, Wages accrued £120.
Balance sheet totals £3 780.

Unit 35.4

1. *Dr.* Opening stock of raw materials £1 000, Purchases £12 000, Carriage in £200, *less* Closing stock £2 000, Cost of raw materials used £11 200, Direct wages £4 000, Direct expenses £200, Prime cost £15 400, Supervision wages £2 000, Fuel and power £1 000, Rent and rates £400, Depreciation of plant £300, Factory insurance £100, Total factory overheads £3 800, Opening stock of work in progress £400, *less* Closing stock £600. *Cr.* Cost of goods manufactured c/d £19 000.

2. *Manufacturing Account: Dr.* Opening stock of raw materials £3 186, Purchases £23 766, *less* Closing stock £4 479, Manufacturing wages £23 463. Prime cost £45 936, Rent and rates £2 469, Power £765, Heat and light £237, Expenses and maintenance £819, Wages and salaries £6 935, Depreciation of plant and machinery £745, Total factory overheads £11 970. *Cr.* Factory cost of goods completed c/d £57 906.
Trading Account: Dr. Opening stock of finished goods £4 264, Factory cost of goods completed b/d £57 906, *less* Closing stock of finished goods £9 651, Cost of goods sold £52 519, Gross profit c/d £27 176. *Cr.* Sales £79 695.
Profit and Loss Account: Dr. Rent and rates £823, Wages and salaries £6 935, Advertising £2 217, Office expenses £786, Net profit £16 415. *Cr.* Gross profit b/d £27 176.

Unit 36.5

1. *Trading Account: Dr.* Opening stock A £600, B £800, Total £1 400, Purchases A £1 008, B £145, Total £1 153, *less* Closing stock A £810, B £465, Total £1 275, Wages A £50, B £100, Total £150, Gross profit c/d A £288, B £683, Total £971. *Cr.* Sales A £1 136, B £1 263, Total £2 399.
Profit and Loss Account: Dr. Telephone A £38, B £76, Total £114, Lighting A £13, B £26, Total £39, Advertising A £49, B £98, Total £147, Net profit A £188, B £483, Total £671. *Cr.* Gross profit b/d A £288, B £683, Total £971.

2. *Trading Account: Dr.* Opening stock A £8 000, B £12 000, Purchases A £16 000, B £20 000, Carriage in A £400, B £600, *less* Closing stock A £9 000, B £4 000, Wages A £10 000, B £15 000, Gross profit c/d A £12 600, B £8 400. *Cr.* Sales A £38 000, B £52 000.
Profit and Loss Account: Dr. Salaries A £5 000, B £8 000, Heat and light A £1 600, B £2 400, Rent and rates A £480, B £720, Carriage out A £200, B £300, Office expenses A £800, B £1 200, Net profit A £4 520. *Cr.* Gross profit b/d A £12 600, B £8 400, Net loss B £4 220.

Balance sheet:
Assets: Stock A £9 000, B £4 000, Debtors £2 000, Bank £15 000.
Capital £21 700, Net profit A £4 520, *less* Net loss B £4 220, Total £22 000.
Current liability: Creditors £8 000.
Balance sheet totals £30 000.

Unit 37.6

1. *F. Ames: Dr.* (1 Sep.) Bills payable £320. *Cr.* Purchases £320.
R. Potter: Dr. Sales £270. *Cr.* (3 Sep.) Bills receivable £270.
P. Jones: Dr. Sales £190, (7 Nov.) Bills receivable (dishonoured bill) £190, (7 Nov.)
Bank charges £5. *Cr.* (7 Sep.) Bills receivable £190.
T. Jeffries: Dr. (11 Sep.) Bills payable £150. *Cr.* Purchases £150.
Bills payable: Dr. (1 Oct.) Bank £320, (11 Oct.) £150. *Cr.* (1 Sep.) F. Ames £320,
(11 Sep.) T. Jeffries £150.
Bills receivable: Dr. (3 Sep.) R. Potter £270, (7 Sep.) P. Jones £190. *Cr.* (3 Oct.)
Bank £270, (7 Nov.) P. Jones (dishonoured bill) £190.
Cash book: Dr. (3 Oct.) Bills receivable £270. *Cr.* (1 Oct.) Bills payable £320, (11
Oct.) Bills payable £150, (7 Nov.) Charges (re Jones) £5.

2. 2 Jan. 19–1. Bills receivable *Dr.* £470, A. Parsons *Cr.* £470.
5 Jan. 19–1. Bank *Dr.* £448, Bank interest *Dr.* £22, Bills receivable *Cr.* £470.
14 Jan. 19–1. N. Martin *Dr.* £274, Bills payable *Cr.* £262, Discount received *Cr.*
£12.
2 Feb. 19–1. A. Parsons *Dr.* £470, Bank *Cr.* £470.
14 Feb. 19–1. Bills payable *Dr.* £262, Bank *Cr.* £262.

Unit 38.10

1. (a) *Dr.* Printing and stationery £500, Salaries and wages £1 544, Rent and rates
£480, Insurance £1 200, Discount allowed £192, Net profit c/d £4 692.
Cr. Gross profit b/d £8 000, Discount received £608.
(b) *Dr.* Interest on capital, Shilton £360, Rough £480, Share of remaining profits,
Shilton £2 140, Rough £1 712. *Cr.* Net profit b/d £4 692.
(c) *Shilton: Dr.* Drawings £1 128, Balance c/d £1 596. *Cr.* Balance b/d £224,
Interest on capital £360, Share of profits £2 140.
Rough: Dr. Balance b/d 240, Drawings £1 016, Balance c/d £936.
Cr. Interest on capital £480, Share of profits £1 712.

4. *Trading Account: Dr.* Opening stock £1 780, Purchases £7 630, *less* Closing stock
£2 120, Gross profit c/d £6 700. *Cr.* Sales £13 990.
Profit and Loss Account: Dr. Wages and salaries £2 930, Discount allowed £390,
Rent and rates £380, Sundry expenses £370, Net profit c/d £2 800. *Cr.* Gross profit
b/d £6 700, Discount received £170.
Appropriation Account: Dr. Interest on Capital Accounts: Gibson £250, Powell
£150, Share of profits: Gibson £1 600, Powell £800. *Cr.* Net profit b/d £2 800.
Balance sheet: Assets: Office furniture £660, Stock £2 120, Debtors £3 830, Bank
£4 560, Cash £80, Prepayment £60.
Capital: Capital Accounts: Gibson £5 000, Powell £3 000; Current Accounts: Gib-
son £890, Powell £440.
Current liabilities: Creditors £1 910, Accrual £70.
Balance sheet totals: £11 310.

Unit 39.4

1. (a) *Taken over from Adams:* Van *Dr.* £400, Office furniture *Dr.* £350, Stock *Dr.*
£760, Debtors *Dr.* £860, Bank *Dr.* £840, Cash *Dr.* £30, Creditors *Cr.* £580, Capital
Cr. £2 660.
Taken over from Brown: Office furniture *Dr.* £500, Stock *Dr.* £910, Debtors *Dr.*
£2 140, Cash *Dr.* £40, Creditors *Cr.* £970, Capital *Cr.* £2 620.

(b) Fixed assets: Delivery van £400, Office furniture £850, Total £1 250.
Current assets: Stock £1 670, Debtors £3 000, Bank £840, Cash £70, Total £5 580.
Capital: Adams £2 660, Brown £2 620, Total £5 280.
Current liabilities: Creditors £1 550.
Balance sheet totals: £6 830.

Unit 40.5

2.
Stock at cost on 26 Dec.	£5 900
Add Purchases on 27 Dec.	£2 000
Add Returns in on 27 Dec. at cost (£90 × $\frac{2}{3}$)	£ 60
	£7 960
Less Sales on 28 Dec. at cost (£2 700 × $\frac{2}{3}$)	£1 800
	£6 160
Less Returns out on 29 Dec.	£ 40
Stock at cost on 31 Dec.	£6 120

4.
Stock at 1 Jan. 19–3		£1 500
Add Purchases 1 Jan.–15 Feb. 19–3		£1 520
		£3 020
Less Goods in transit	£70	
Goods in locked room	£90	£ 160
		£2 860
Less Sales at cost £2 460 × $\frac{5}{6}$[1]		£2 050
Cost price of goods stolen on 15 Feb. 19–3		£ 810

[1] gross profit is one-sixth

6. (a) 25%, (b) 5 times, (c) 10.4 weeks, (d) 6.5 weeks, (e) 13 weeks, (f) 15%.

Unit 41.7

1. *Appropriation Account: Dr.* Transfer to General reserve £5 000, Proposed dividends: Preference £4 000, Ordinary £15 000, Retained profits c/d £32 000. *Cr.* Retained profits b/d £15 500, Net profit for year £40 500.
Balance sheet:
Fixed assets: Land and buildings at cost £150 000, Plant and machinery at cost £80 000, *less* Depreciation to date £20 000, Total £210 000.
Current assets: Stock £20 850, Debtors £16 710, Expenses prepaid £1 550, Bank £19 620, Total £58 730.
Current liabilities: Creditors £11 840, Expenses owing £890, Proposed dividends: Preference £4 000, Ordinary £15 000, Total £31 730.
Working capital: £27 000
Total net assets: £237 000
Financed by:
Issued share capital: Ordinary shares, fully paid £150 000; 8% preference shares, fully paid £50 000, Total £200 000.
Revenue reserves: General reserve £5 000, Retained profits £32 000, Total £37 000.
Total of shareholders' funds: £237 000.

2. *Trading Account: Dr.* Opening stock £43 008, Purchases £201 986, *less* Closing stock £50 305, Gross profit c/d £129 610. *Cr.* Sales £324 299.

Profit and Loss Account: Dr. Rent and rates £4 700, General expenses £8 626, Wages and salaries £37 870, Bad debts written off £789, Increase in provision for bad debts £175, Directors' salaries £20 000, Depreciation, motor vans £12 000, Net profit £45 450. *Cr.* Gross profit b/d £129 610.

Appropriation Account: Dr. Proposed ordinary dividend £10 000, Retained profits c/d £57 352. *Cr.* Retained profits b/d £21 902, Net profit for year £45 450.

Balance sheet:

Fixed assets: Freehold land and buildings at cost £156 000, Motor vans at cost £60 000, *less* Depreciation to date £34 600, Total £181 400.

Current assets: Stock £50 305, Debtors £28 107, *less* Provision for bad debts £1 424, Expenses prepaid £300, Bank £174 157, Total £251 445.

Current liabilities: Creditors £15 060, Proposed ordinary dividend £10 000, Wages owing £433, Total £25 493.

Working capital: £225 952.

Total net assets: £407 352.

Financed by:

Issued share capital: Ordinary shares, fully paid £350 000.

Revenue reserve: Retained profits £57 352.

Total of shareholders' funds: £407 352.

3. *Trading Account: Dr.* Opening stock £227 100, Purchases £1 350 800, *less* Closing stock £235 350, Gross profit c/d £377 950.
Cr. Sales £1 720 500.

Profit and Loss Account: Dr. Rent and rates £9 000, General expenses £75 150, Wages £94 150, Bad debts written off £1 600, Increase in provision for bad debts £350, Debenture interest £12 000, Depreciation, motor vans £8 000, Net profit £177 700. *Cr.* Gross profit b/d £377 950.

Appropriation Account: Dr. Proposed ordinary dividend £60 000, Retained profits c/d £312 200. *Cr.* Retained profits b/d £194 500, Net profit for year £177 700.

Balance sheet:

Fixed assets: Freehold land and buildings at cost £460 000, Motor vans at cost £40 000, *less* Depreciation to date £30 600, Total £469 400.

Current assets: Stock £235 350, Debtors £246 300, *less* Provision for bad debts £2 450, Rates prepaid £1 350, Total £480 550.

Current liabilities: Creditors £175 900, Bank overdraft £24 950, Proposed ordinary dividend £60 000, Debenture interest due £6 000, Wages owing £900, Total £267 750.

Working capital: £212 800.

Total net assets: £682 200.

Financed by:

Issued share capital: Ordinary shares, fully paid £200 000.

Capital reserve: Share premium £50 000.

Revenue reserve: Retained profits £312 200.

Total of shareholders' funds: £562 200.

Long-term liabilities: 10% debentures £120 000.

Total £682 200.

Unit 42.5

1. *Operating activities:* Net profit (before interest) £500, Depreciation £5 800, increase in Stock (£1 900), increase in Debtors (£2 100), increase in Creditors £3 700, Total £6 000.

Returns on investments and servicing of finance: Interest paid (£1 250), Drawings paid (£4 100), Total (£5 350).
Taxation: nil
Investing activities: Purchase of fixed assets (£5 000).
Net cash inflow/(outflow) before financing: (£4 350).
Financing: Bank loan £2 500.
Increase/(decrease) in cash: (£1 850).
Analysis of changes in cash during the year: Bank balance at start of year (£500), Net cash inflow/(outflow) (£1 850), Bank balance at end of year (£2 350).

2. *Operating activities:* Net profit (before interest) £8 610, Depreciation £500, increase in Stock (£2 200), increase in Debtors (£830), increase in Creditors £4 680, Total £10 760.
Returns on investments and servicing of finance: Interest paid (£450), Drawings paid (£13 200), Total (£13 650).
Taxation: nil.
Investing activities: Purchase of shop fittings (£1 000).
Net cash inflow/(outflow) before financing: (£3 890).
Financing: Loan from wife £2 000.
Increase/(decrease) in cash: (£1 890).
Analysis of changes in cash during the year: Bank balance at start of year £440, Net cash inflow/(outflow) (£1 890), Bank balance at end of year (£1 450).

4. *All figures in 000s.*
Net profit (before interest): Increase in Profit and Loss Account £2, *add* Dividend for year £14, *add* Corporation Tax for year £8, *add* Interest for year £7, Total £31.
Operating activities: Net profit (before interest) £31, Depreciation £16, increase in Stock (£42), increase in Debtors (£14), increase in Creditors £18, Total £9.
Returns on investments and servicing of finance: Interest paid (£7), Dividends paid (£16), Total (£23).
Taxation: Corporation tax paid (£6).
Investing activities: Purchase of land and buildings (£70), Purchase of machinery (£40), Total (£110).
Net cash inflow/(outflow) before financing: (£130).
Financing: Issue of shares £100, Repayment of debentures (£10), Total £90.
Increase/(decrease) in cash: £40.
Analysis of changes in cash during the year: Bank balance at start of year £2, Net cash inflow/(outflow) (£40), Bank balance at end of year (£38).

Answers to Multiple-choice Questions

Question number:	1	2	3	4	5	6	7	8	9	10	11	12
Set number 1:	C	D	D	A	C	D	A	B	C	B	D	A
2:	A	A	C	D	B	A	B	D	D	B	B	B
3:	A	B	C	A	A	C	D	D	A	A	B	B
4:	A	D	A	A	B	C	B	D	D	C	C	B
5:	C	A	A	C	A	B	D	B	B	C	A	B
6:	D	C	A	A	B	C	D	A	A	C	B	D
7:	B	C	C	D	D	B	B	A	A	C	B	C
8:	B	C	C	A	D	B	A	A	D	B	A	D
9:	C	D	A	B	B	C	A	B	D	B	C	B
10:	D	A	C	B	C	B	C	C	C	C	B	C
11:	B	A	B	B	A	D	D	A	B	C	D	B

Index